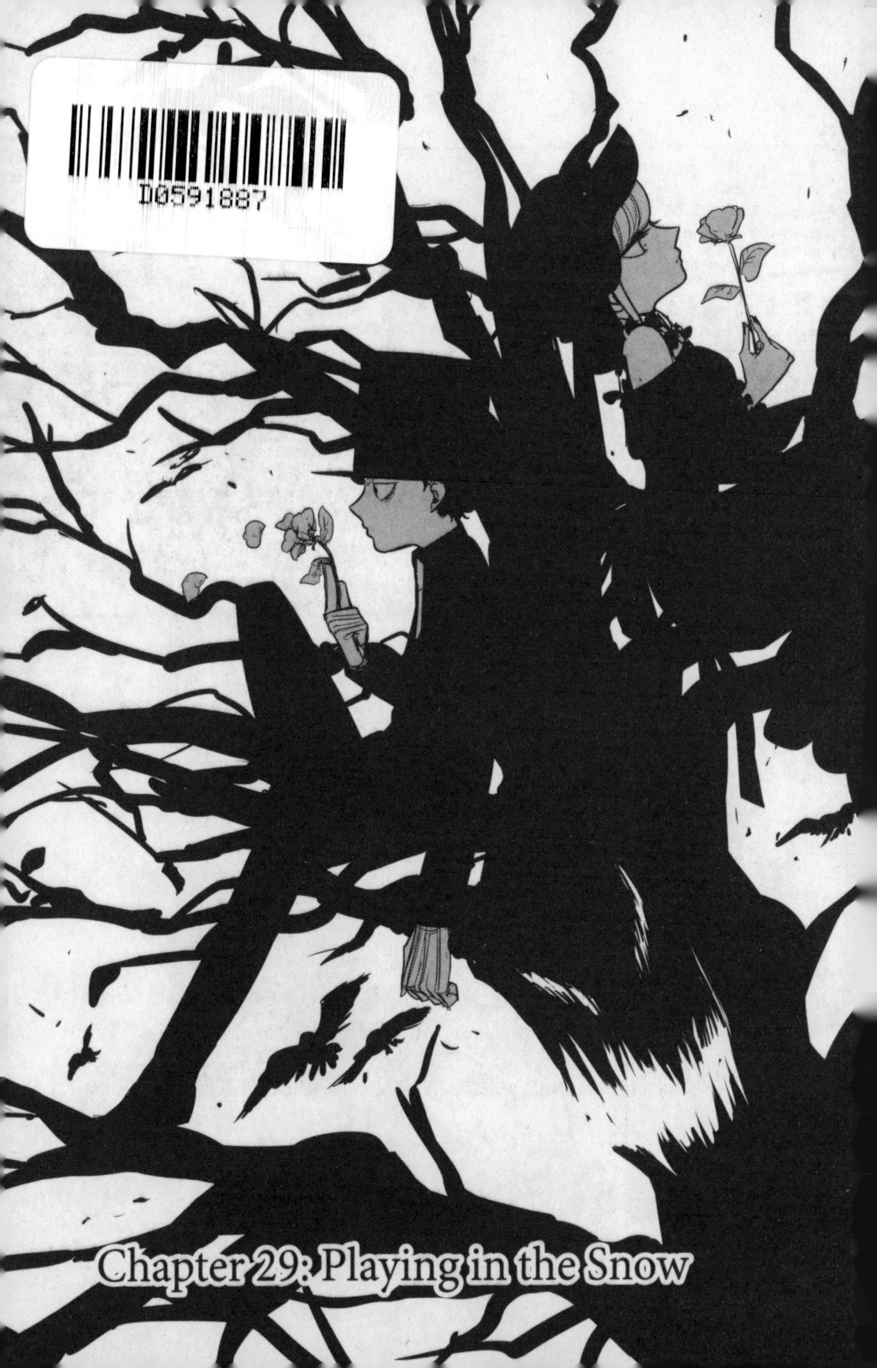

Chapter 29: Playing in the Snow

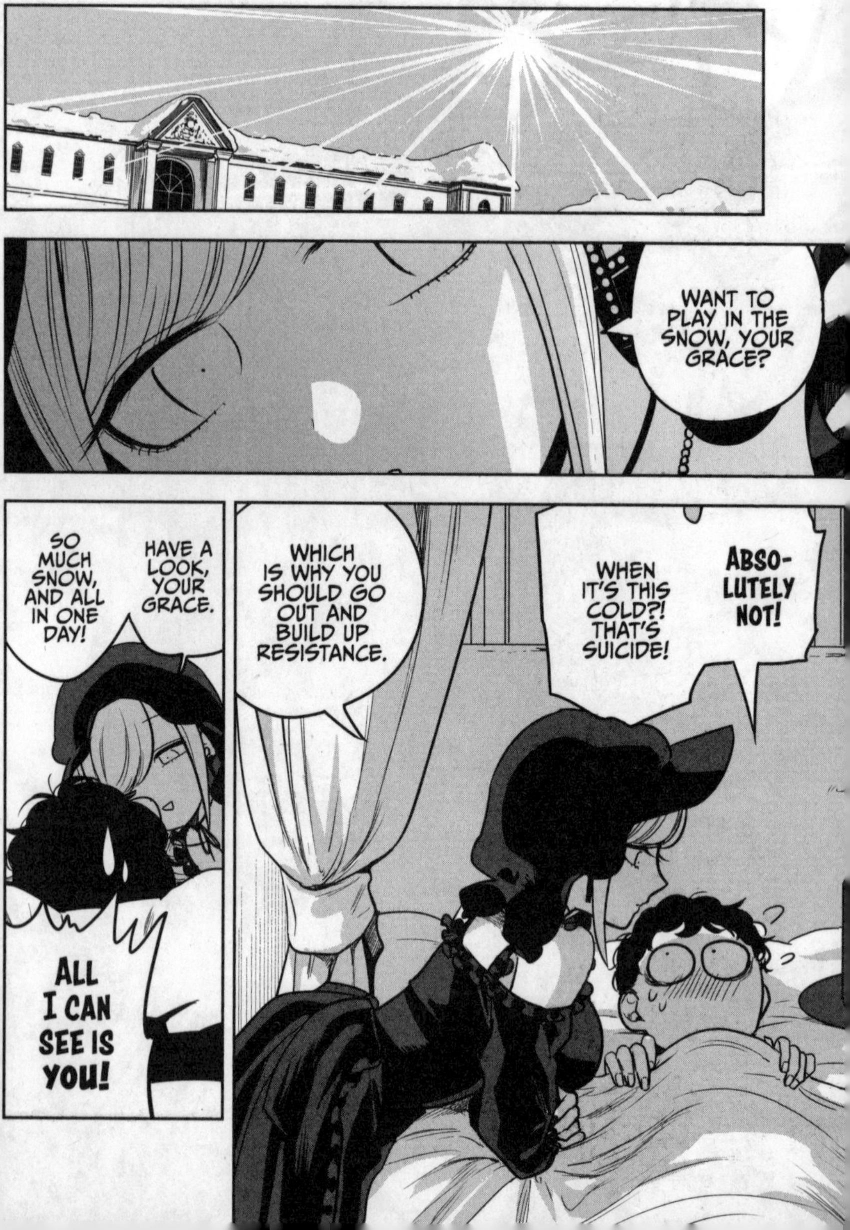
WANT TO PLAY IN THE SNOW, YOUR GRACE?
ABSO-LUTELY NOT!
WHEN IT'S THIS COLD?! THAT'S SUICIDE!
WHICH IS WHY YOU SHOULD GO OUT AND BUILD UP RESISTANCE.
HAVE A LOOK, YOUR GRACE.
SO MUCH SNOW, AND ALL IN ONE DAY!
ALL I CAN SEE IS YOU!

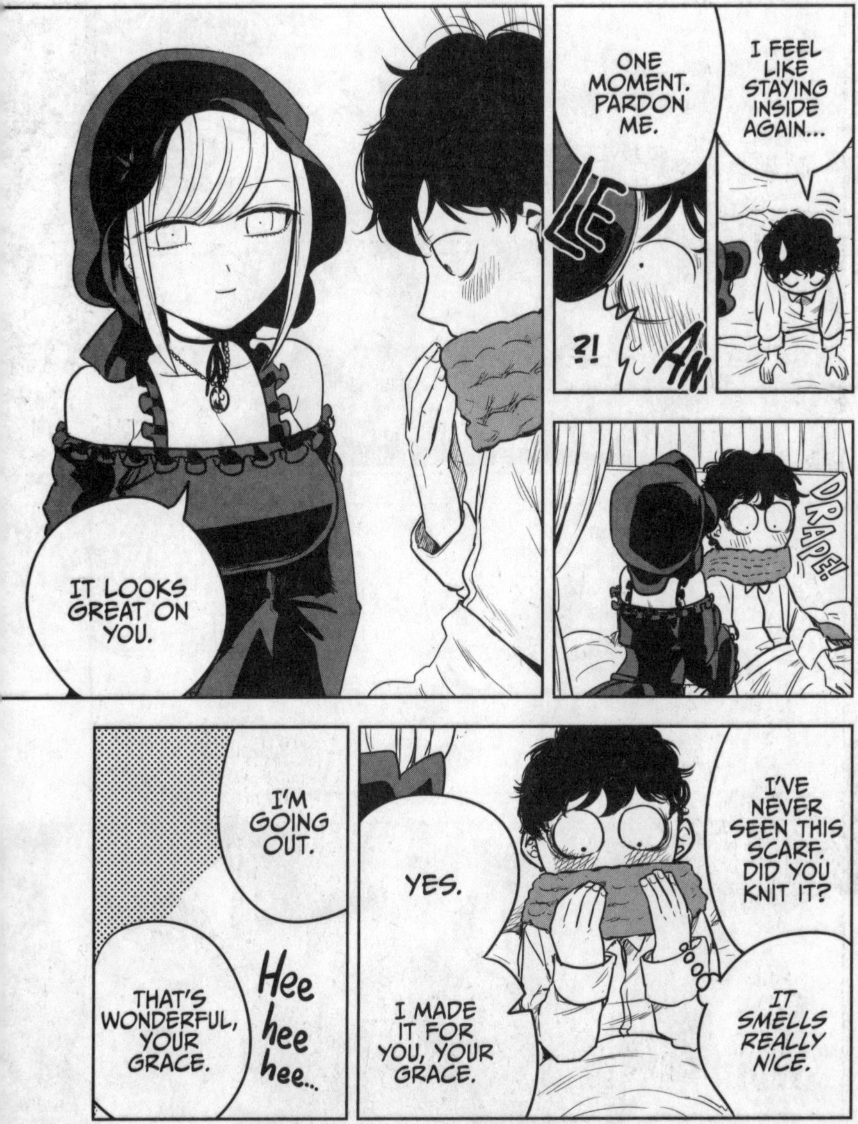
I FEEL LIKE STAYING INSIDE AGAIN...
ONE MOMENT. PARDON ME.
LEAN
?!
DRAPE!
IT LOOKS GREAT ON YOU.
I'VE NEVER SEEN THIS SCARF. DID YOU KNIT IT?
YES.
IT SMELLS REALLY NICE.
I MADE IT FOR YOU, YOUR GRACE.
I'M GOING OUT.
Hee hee hee...
THAT'S WONDERFUL, YOUR GRACE.

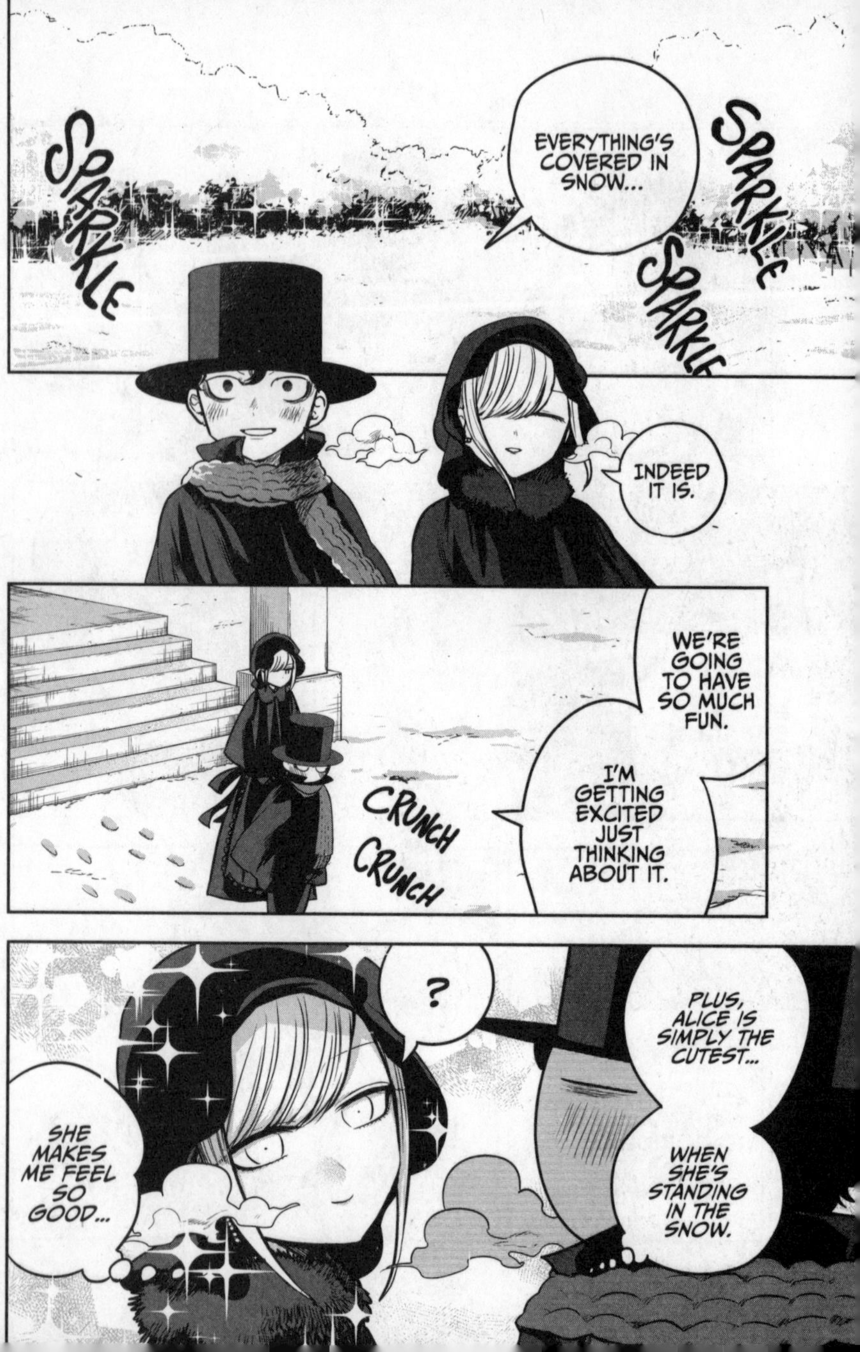
SPARKLE
SPARKLE
EVERYTHING'S COVERED IN SNOW...
SPARKLE
INDEED IT IS.
WE'RE GOING TO HAVE SO MUCH FUN.
I'M GETTING EXCITED JUST THINKING ABOUT IT.
CRUNCH CRUNCH
PLUS, ALICE IS SIMPLY THE CUTEST...
WHEN SHE'S STANDING IN THE SNOW.
?
SHE MAKES ME FEEL SO GOOD...

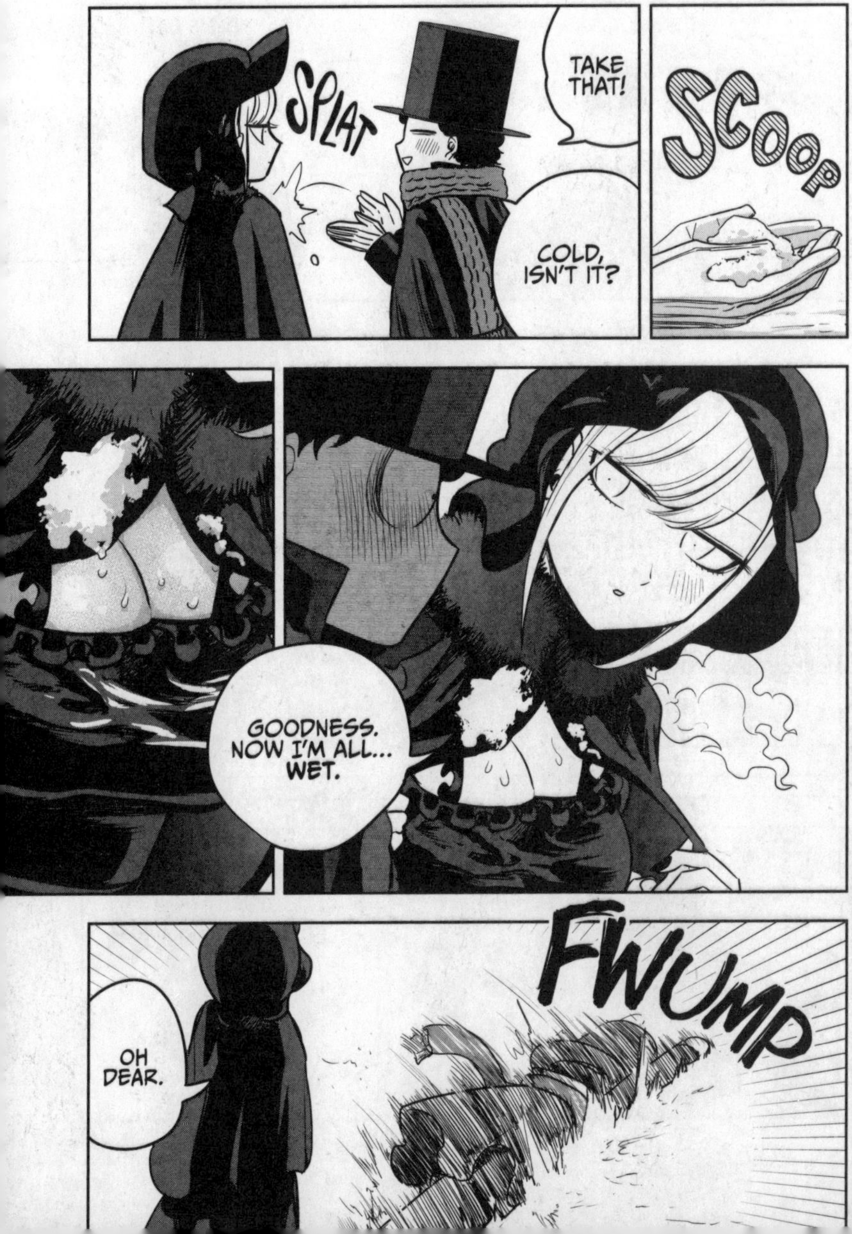
SCOOP
TAKE THAT!
SPLAT
COLD, ISN'T IT?
GOODNESS. NOW I'M ALL... WET.
FWUMP
OH DEAR.

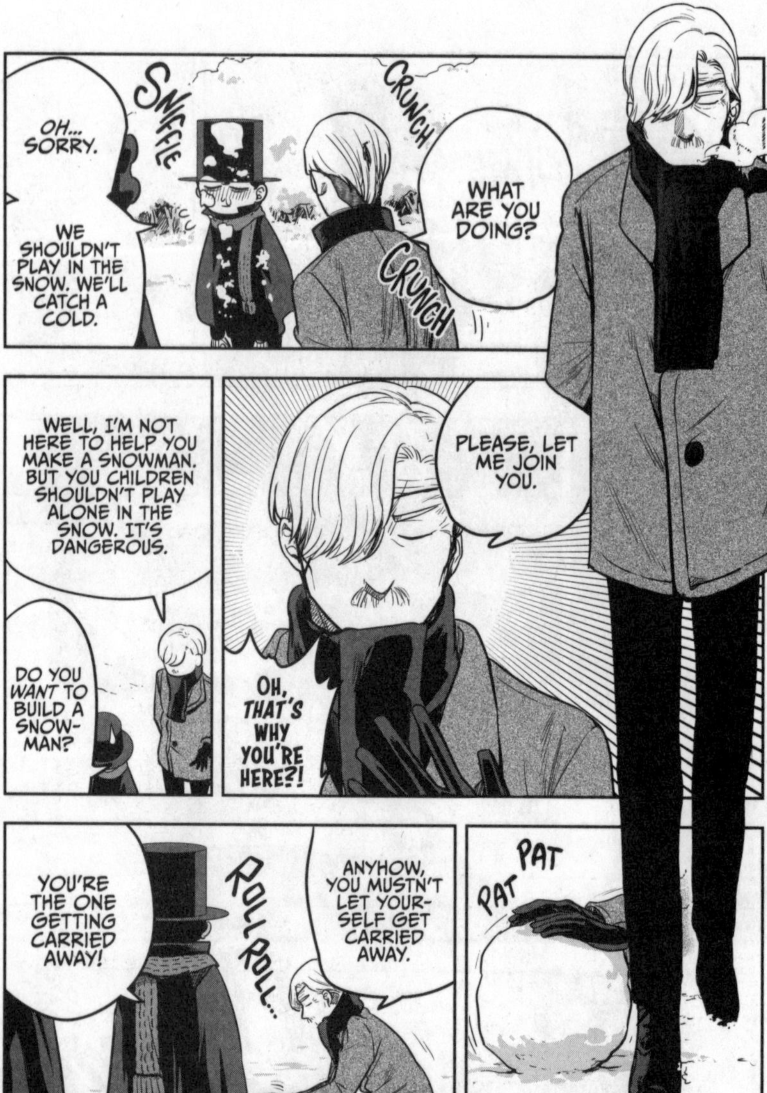
CRUNCH
WHAT ARE YOU DOING?
CRUNCH
SNIFFLE
OH... SORRY.
WE SHOULDN'T PLAY IN THE SNOW. WE'LL CATCH A COLD.
PLEASE, LET ME JOIN YOU.
OH, THAT'S WHY YOU'RE HERE?!
WELL, I'M NOT HERE TO HELP YOU MAKE A SNOWMAN. BUT YOU CHILDREN SHOULDN'T PLAY ALONE IN THE SNOW. IT'S DANGEROUS.
DO YOU WANT TO BUILD A SNOW-MAN?
PAT PAT
ANYHOW, YOU MUSTN'T LET YOUR-SELF GET CARRIED AWAY.
ROLL ROLL...
YOU'RE THE ONE GETTING CARRIED AWAY!

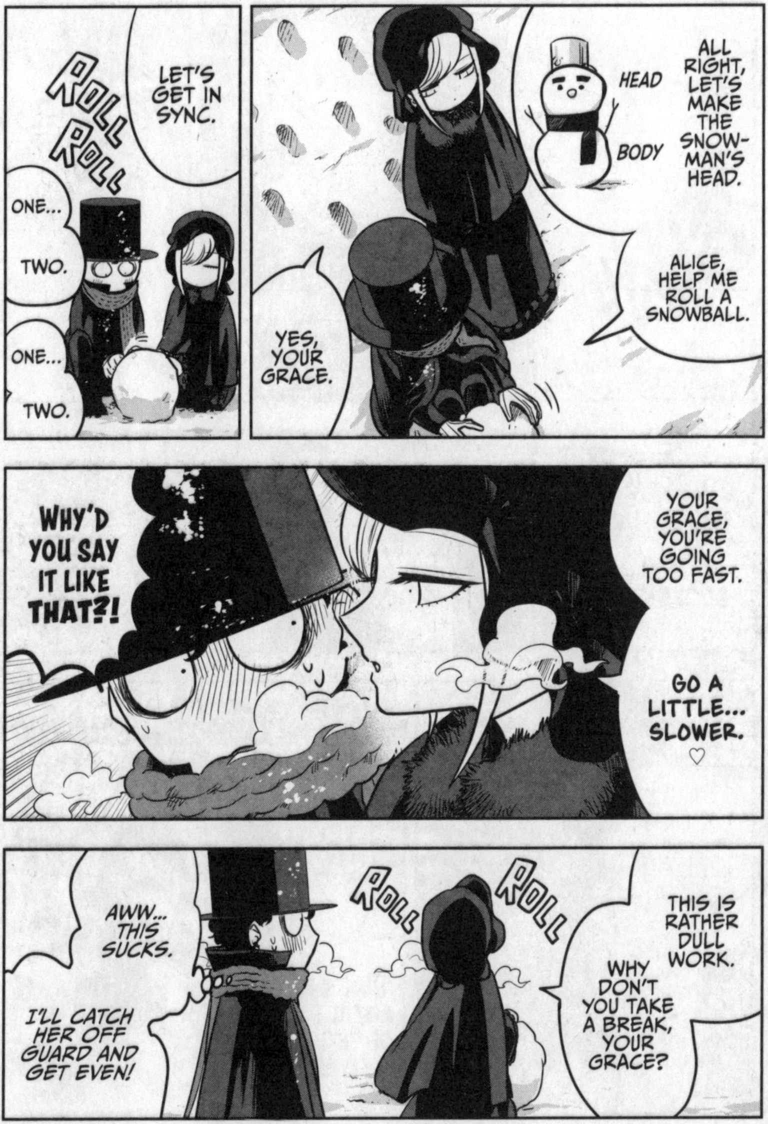
ALL RIGHT, LET'S MAKE THE SNOW-MAN'S HEAD.
HEAD
BODY
ALICE, HELP ME ROLL A SNOWBALL.
YES, YOUR GRACE.
LET'S GET IN SYNC.
ROLL ROLL
ONE... TWO.
ONE... TWO.
YOUR GRACE, YOU'RE GOING TOO FAST.
GO A LITTLE... SLOWER. ♡
WHY'D YOU SAY IT LIKE THAT?!
ROLL ROLL
THIS IS RATHER DULL WORK.
WHY DON'T YOU TAKE A BREAK, YOUR GRACE?
AWW... THIS SUCKS.
I'LL CATCH HER OFF GUARD AND GET EVEN!

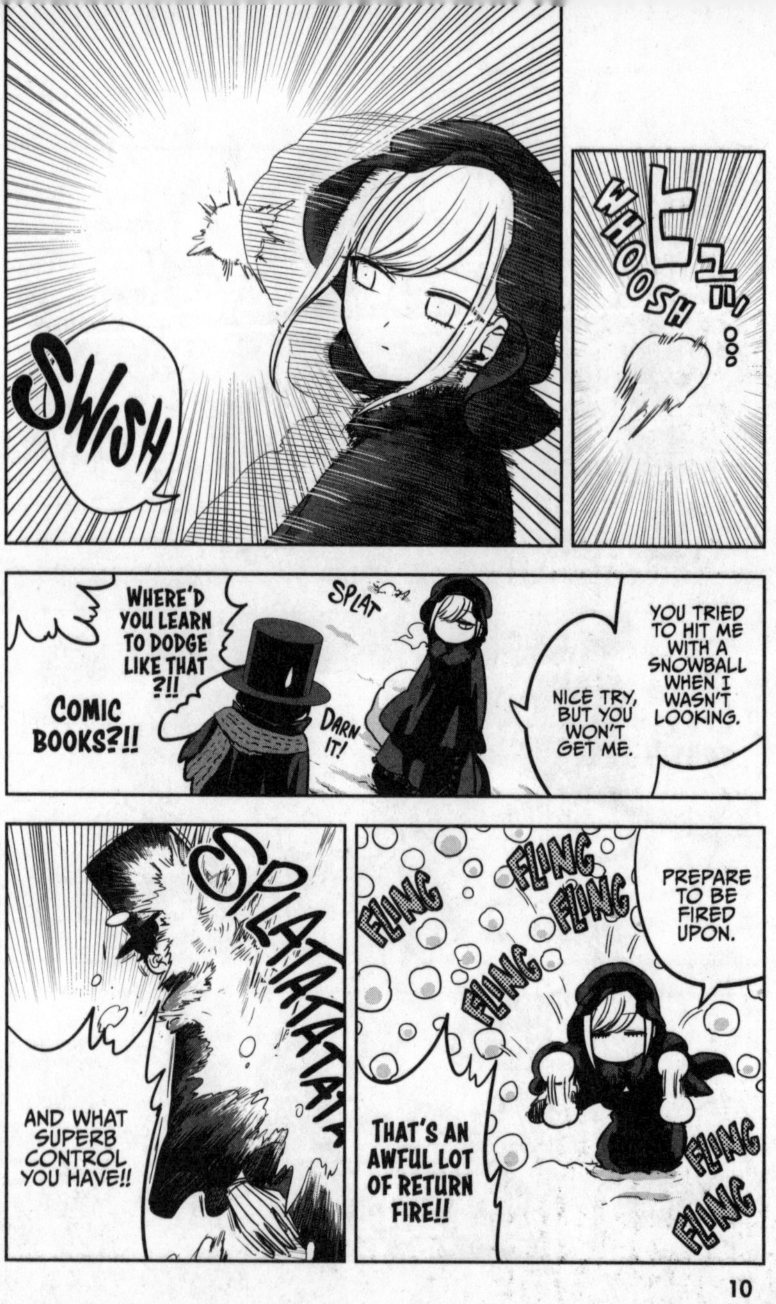

ヒュ
WHOOSH
SWISH
YOU TRIED TO HIT ME WITH A SNOWBALL WHEN I WASN'T LOOKING.
NICE TRY, BUT YOU WON'T GET ME.
SPLAT
DARN IT!
WHERE'D YOU LEARN TO DODGE LIKE THAT?!!
COMIC BOOKS?!!
PREPARE TO BE FIRED UPON.
FLING FLING FLING FLING FLING
FLING FLING
THAT'S AN AWFUL LOT OF RETURN FIRE!!
SPLATATATATA
AND WHAT SUPERB CONTROL YOU HAVE!!

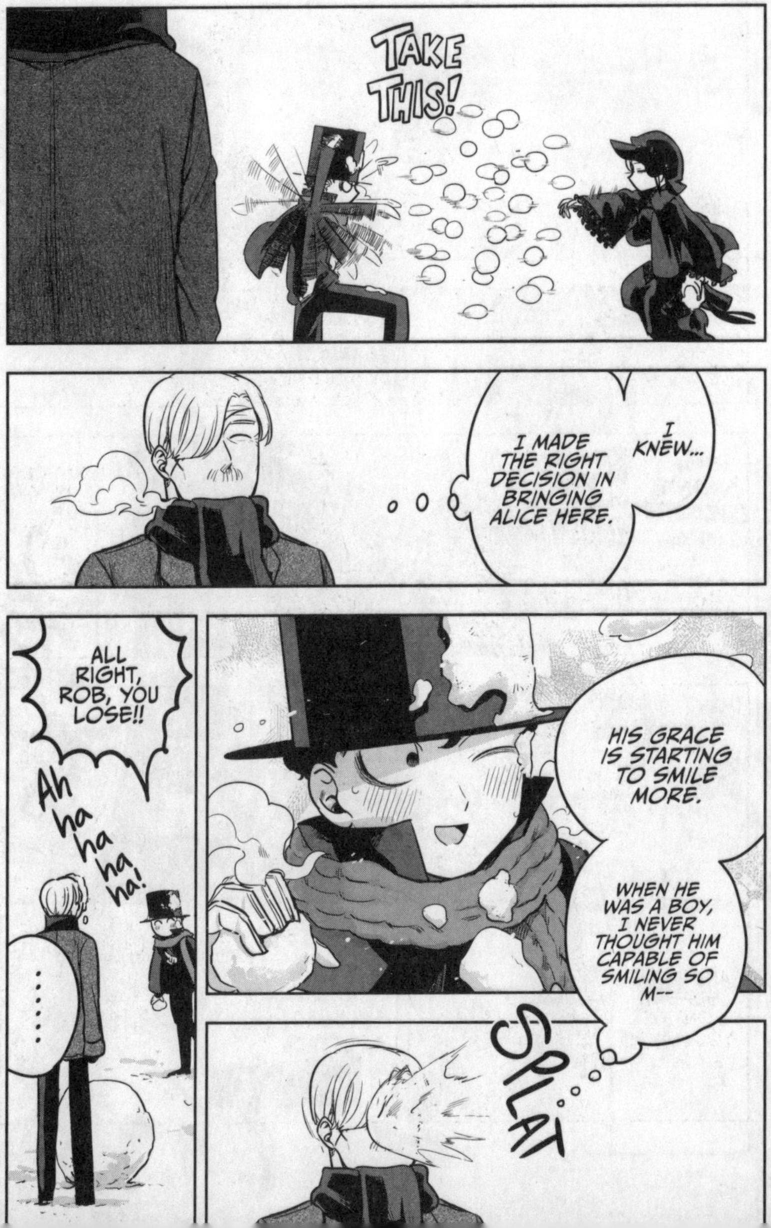
TAKE THIS!
I KNEW...
I MADE THE RIGHT DECISION IN BRINGING ALICE HERE.
HIS GRACE IS STARTING TO SMILE MORE.
WHEN HE WAS A BOY, I NEVER THOUGHT HIM CAPABLE OF SMILING SO M--
SPLAT
ALL RIGHT, ROB, YOU LOSE!!
Ah ha ha ha ha!
......

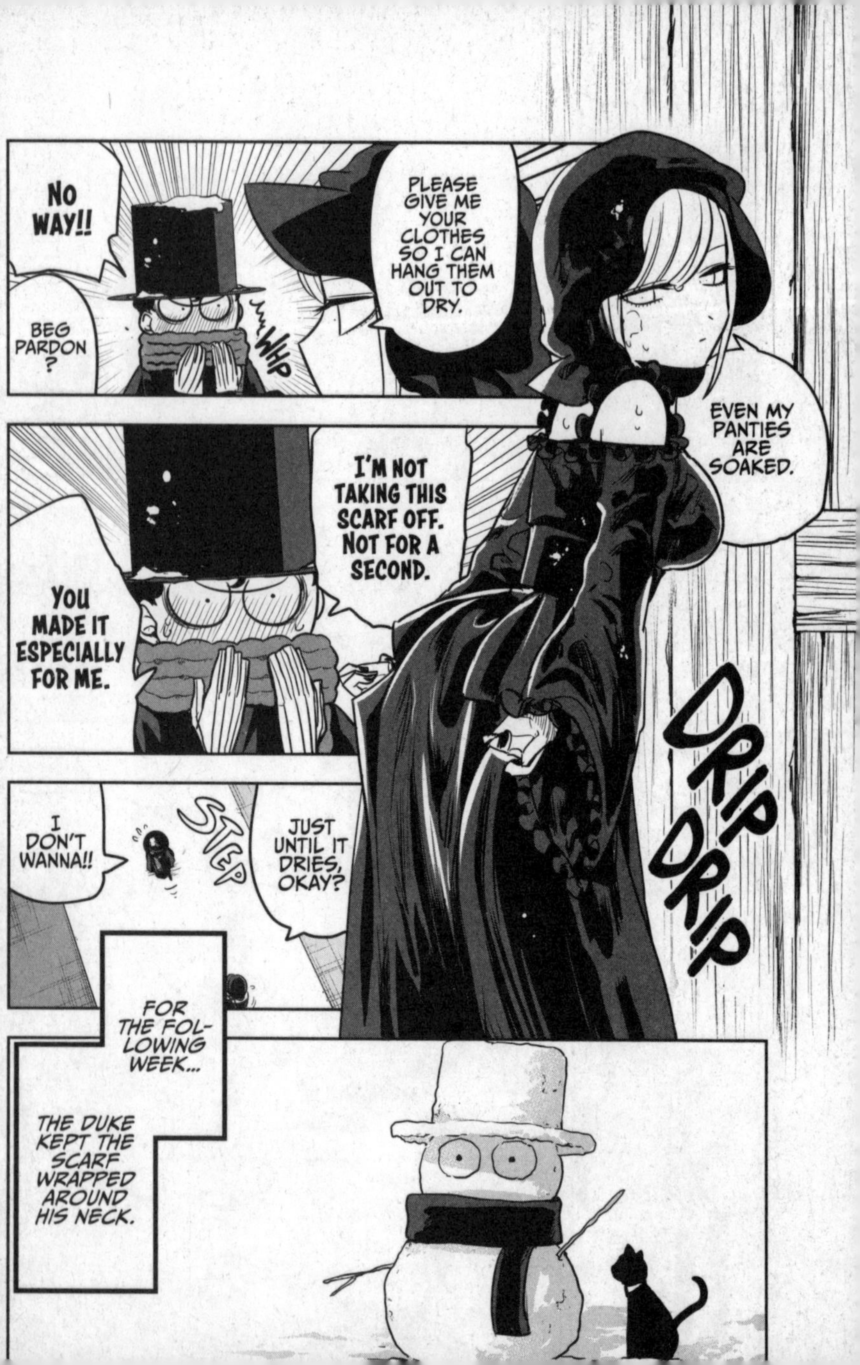
PLEASE GIVE ME YOUR CLOTHES SO I CAN HANG THEM OUT TO DRY.
BEG PARDON?
EVEN MY PANTIES ARE SOAKED.
WHIP
NO WAY!!
I'M NOT TAKING THIS SCARF OFF. NOT FOR A SECOND.
YOU MADE IT ESPECIALLY FOR ME.
DRIP DRIP
JUST UNTIL IT DRIES, OKAY?
STEP
I DON'T WANNA!!
FOR THE FOL-LOWING WEEK...
THE DUKE KEPT THE SCARF WRAPPED AROUND HIS NECK.

THE DUKE OF DEATH AND HIS MAID

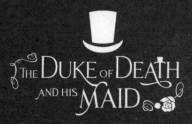

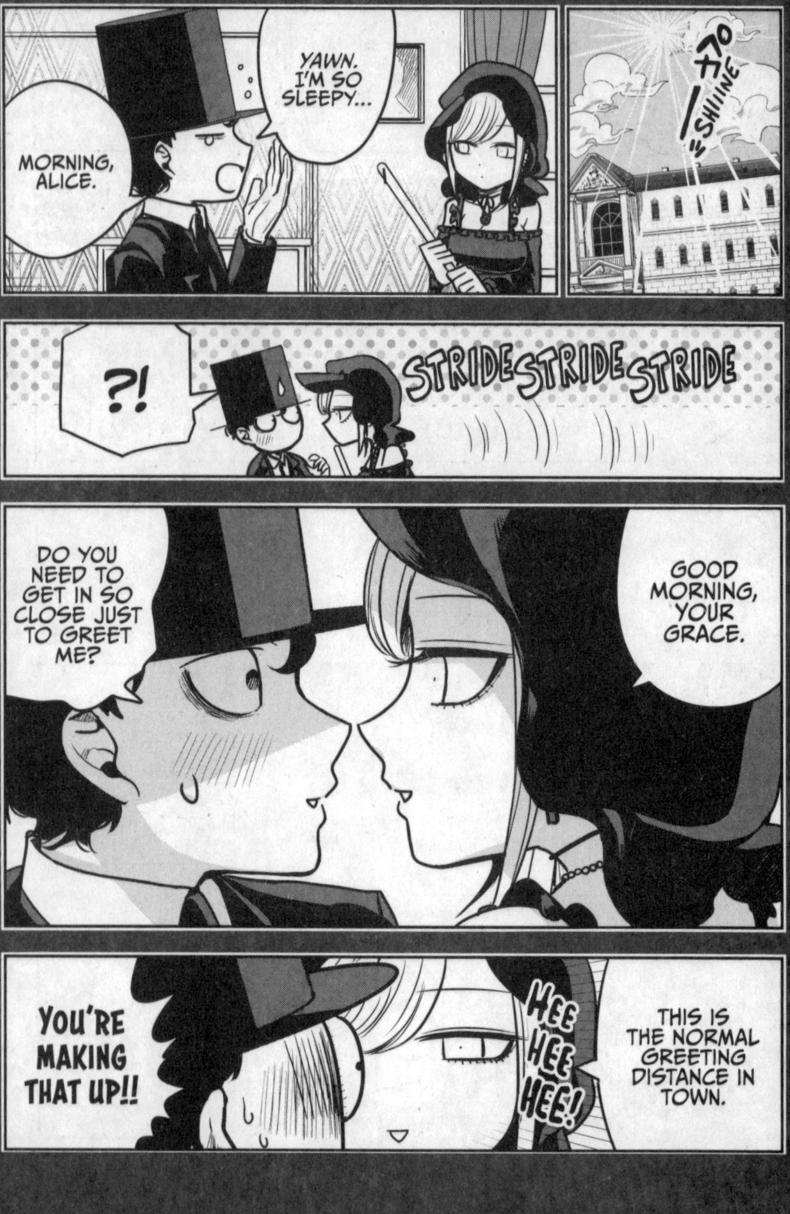
SHIIINE
YAWN. I'M SO SLEEPY...
MORNING, ALICE.
STRIDE STRIDE STRIDE
?!
GOOD MORNING, YOUR GRACE.
DO YOU NEED TO GET IN SO CLOSE JUST TO GREET ME?
THIS IS THE NORMAL GREETING DISTANCE IN TOWN.
HEE HEE HEE!
YOU'RE MAKING THAT UP!!

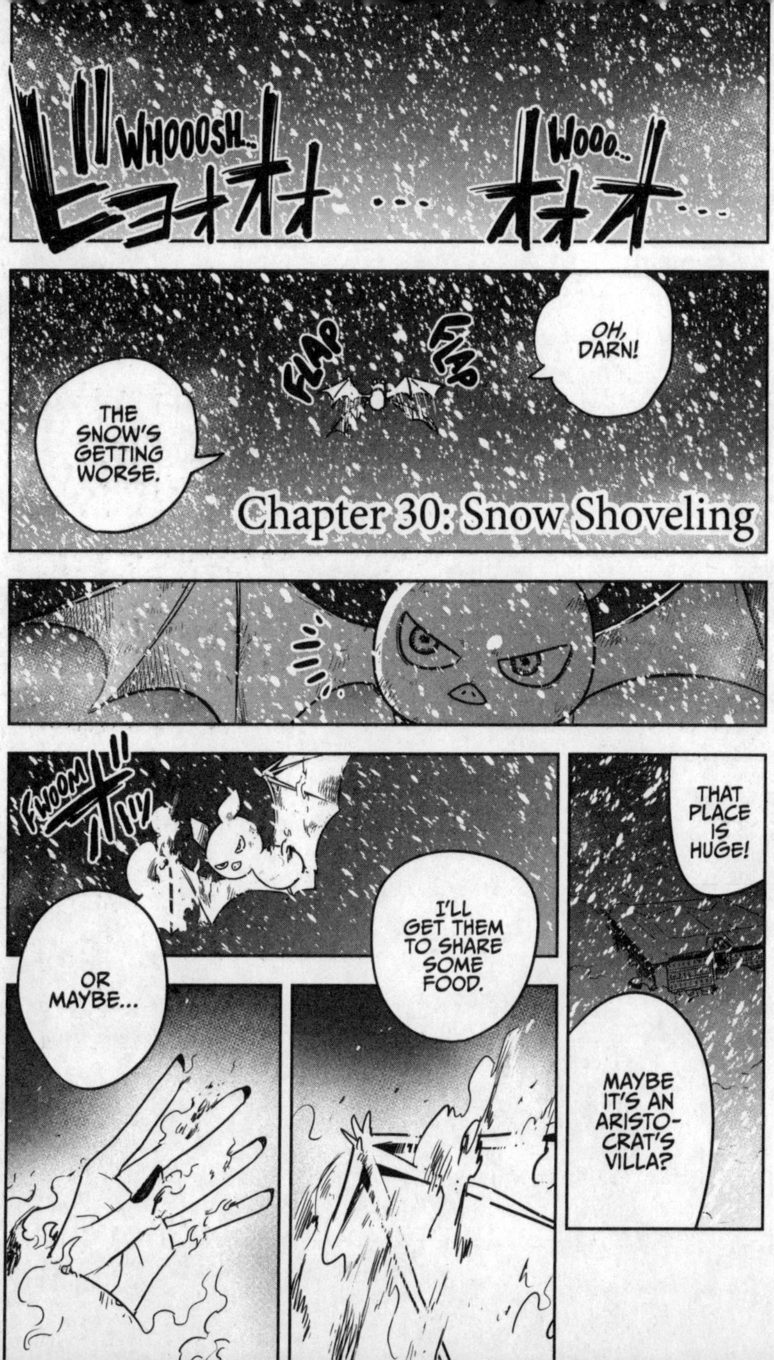
WHOOOSH... WOOO...
ヒョォオオ… オオオ…
OH, DARN!
FLAP FLAP
THE SNOW'S GETTING WORSE.
Chapter 30: Snow Shoveling
THAT PLACE IS HUGE!
MAYBE IT'S AN ARISTOCRAT'S VILLA?
FWOOM
I'LL GET THEM TO SHARE SOME FOOD.
OR MAYBE...

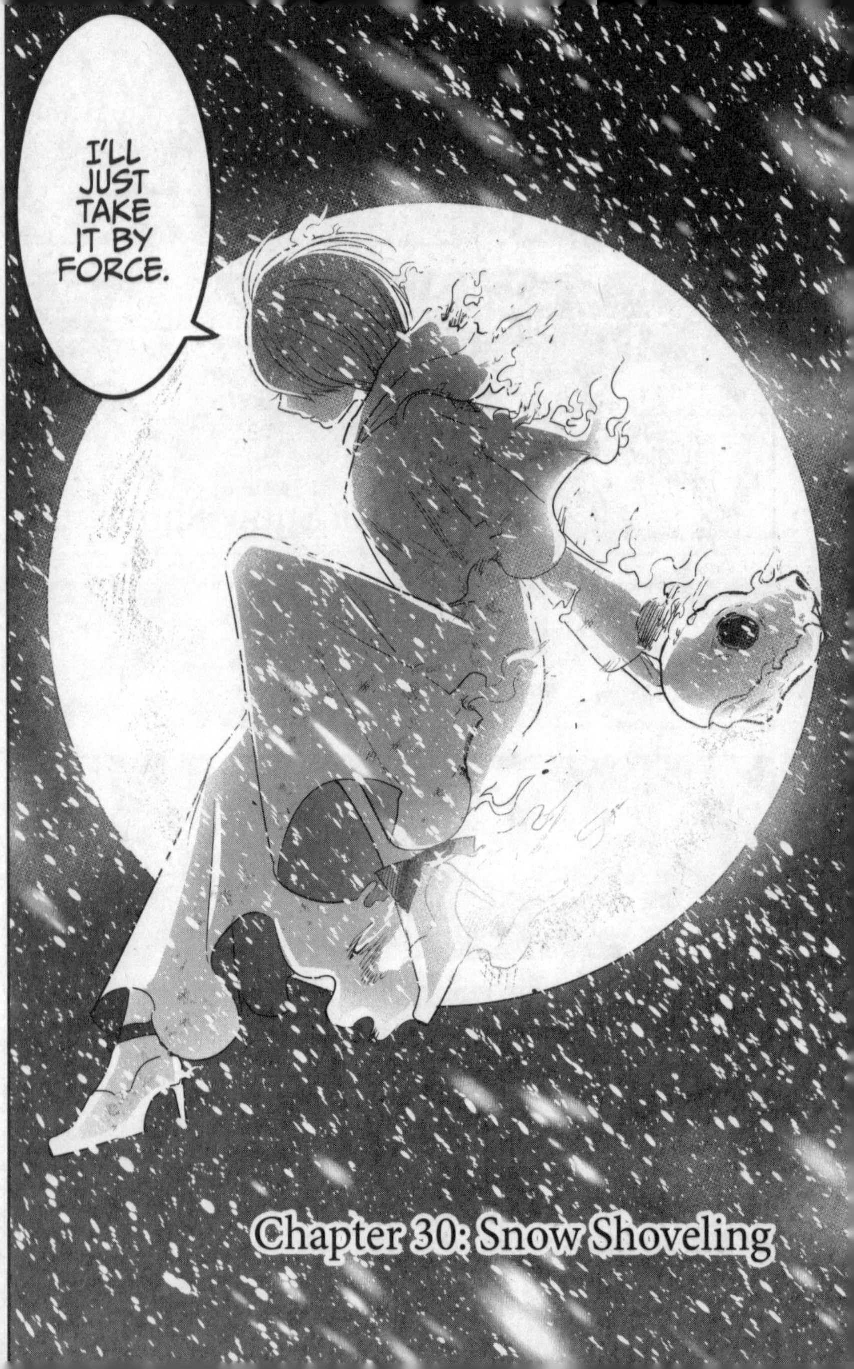
I'LL JUST TAKE IT BY FORCE.
Chapter 30: Snow Shoveling

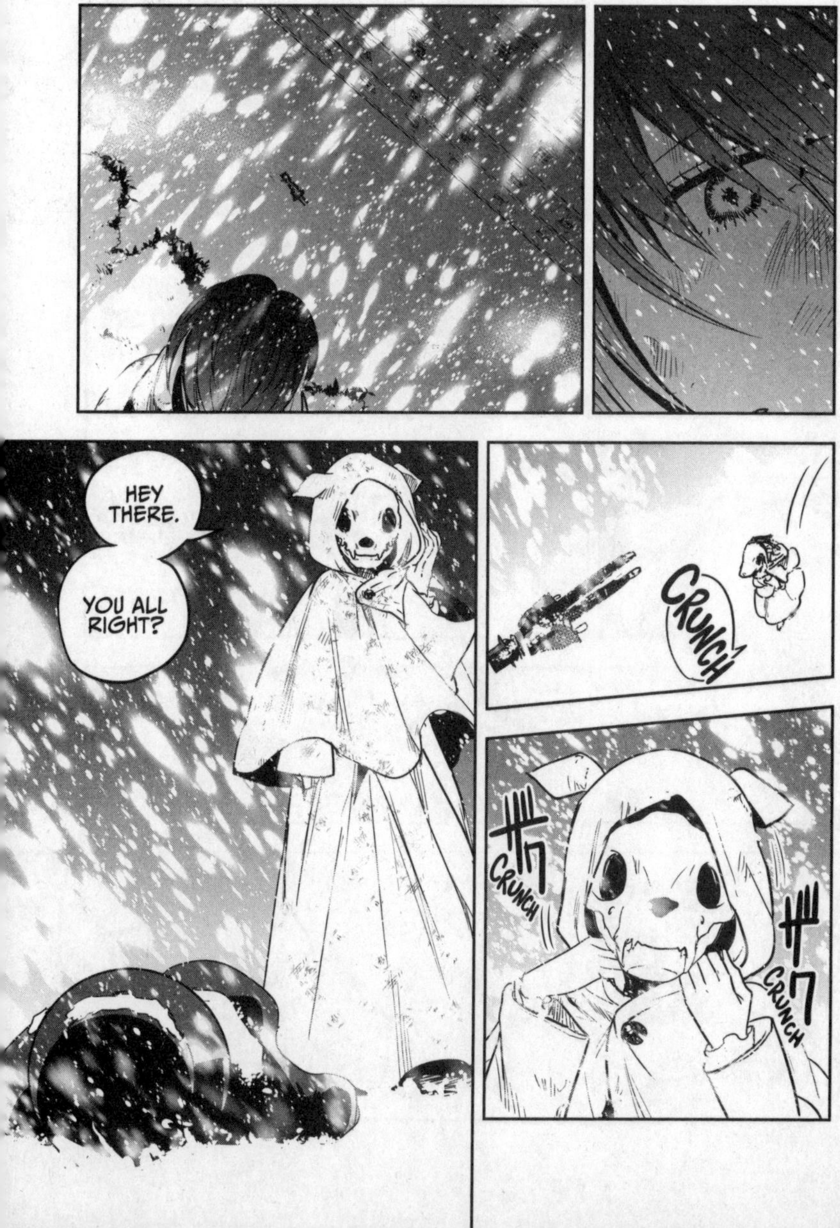
CRUNCH
CRUNCH
CRUNCH
HEY THERE.
YOU ALL RIGHT?

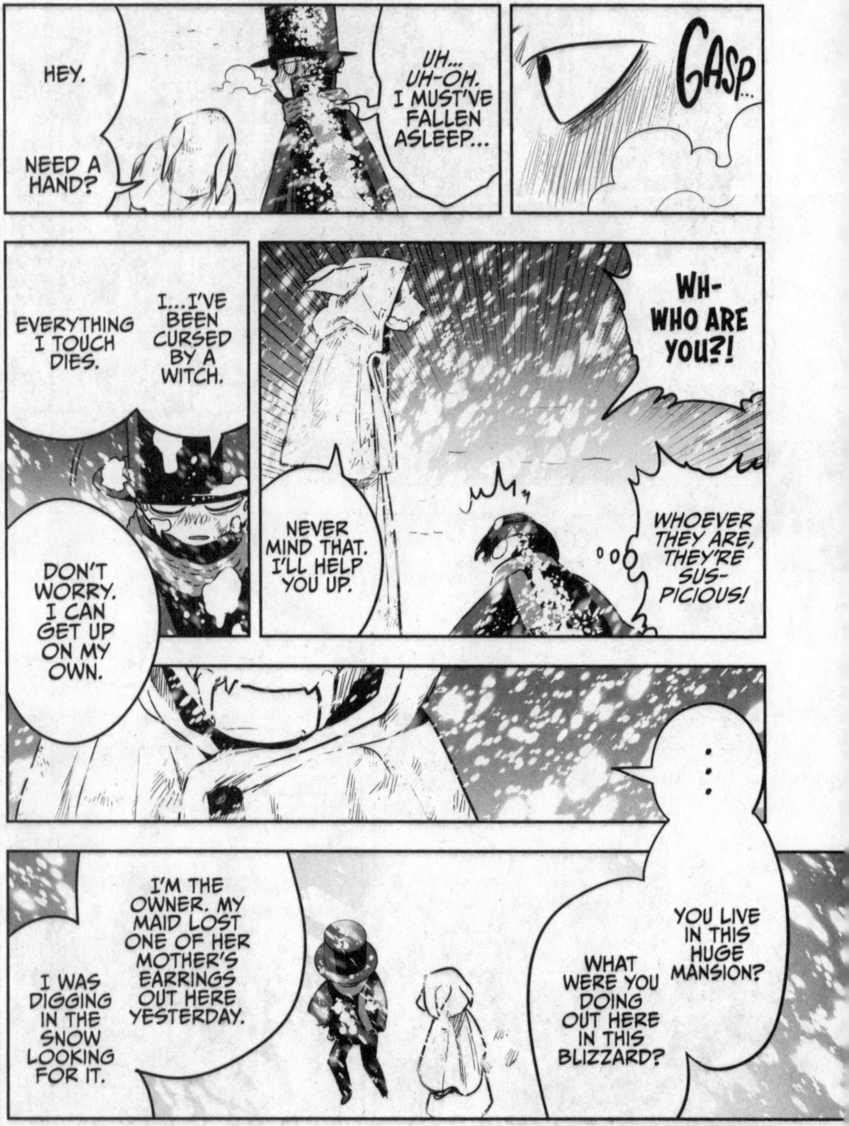
GASP...
UH... UH-OH. I MUST'VE FALLEN ASLEEP...
HEY.
NEED A HAND?
WH- WHO ARE YOU?!
WHOEVER THEY ARE, THEY'RE SUS-PICIOUS!
NEVER MIND THAT. I'LL HELP YOU UP.
I...I'VE BEEN CURSED BY A WITCH.
EVERYTHING I TOUCH DIES.
DON'T WORRY. I CAN GET UP ON MY OWN.
...
YOU LIVE IN THIS HUGE MANSION?
WHAT WERE YOU DOING OUT HERE IN THIS BLIZZARD?
I'M THE OWNER. MY MAID LOST ONE OF HER MOTHER'S EARRINGS OUT HERE YESTERDAY.
I WAS DIGGING IN THE SNOW LOOKING FOR IT.

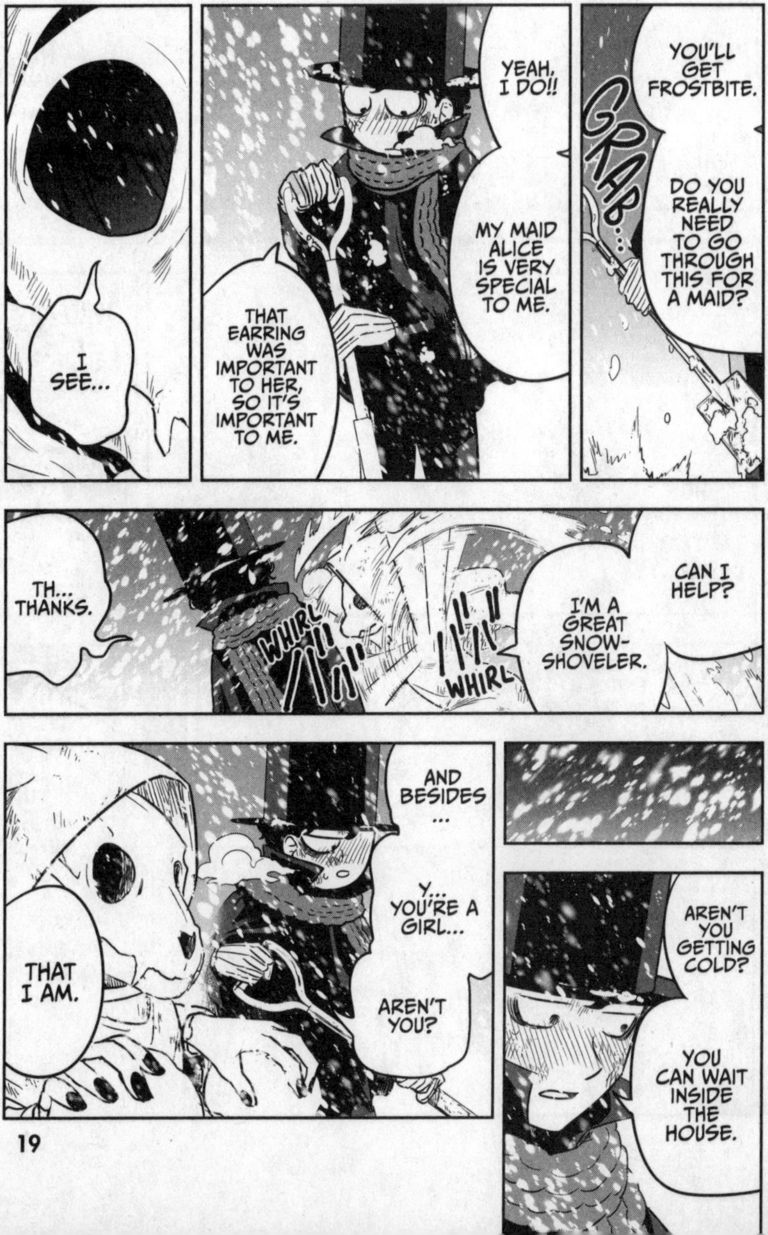
YOU'LL GET FROSTBITE.
GRAB...
DO YOU REALLY NEED TO GO THROUGH THIS FOR A MAID?
YEAH, I DO!!
MY MAID ALICE IS VERY SPECIAL TO ME.
THAT EARRING WAS IMPORTANT TO HER, SO IT'S IMPORTANT TO ME.
I SEE...
CAN I HELP?
I'M A GREAT SNOW-SHOVELER.
WHIRL
WHIRL
TH... THANKS.
AREN'T YOU GETTING COLD?
YOU CAN WAIT INSIDE THE HOUSE.
AND BESIDES...
Y... YOU'RE A GIRL...
AREN'T YOU?
THAT I AM.

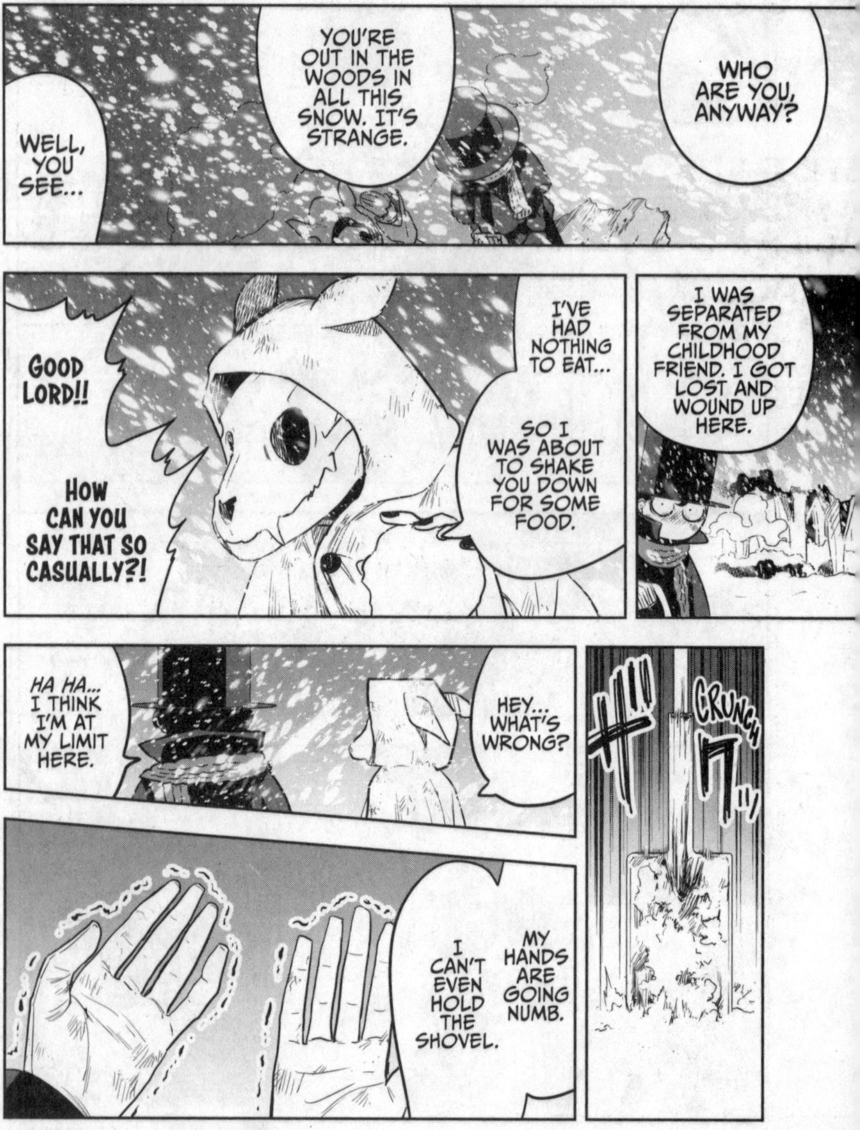
WHO ARE YOU, ANYWAY?
YOU'RE OUT IN THE WOODS IN ALL THIS SNOW. IT'S STRANGE.
WELL, YOU SEE...
I WAS SEPARATED FROM MY CHILDHOOD FRIEND. I GOT LOST AND WOUND UP HERE.
I'VE HAD NOTHING TO EAT...
SO I WAS ABOUT TO SHAKE YOU DOWN FOR SOME FOOD.
GOOD LORD!!
HOW CAN YOU SAY THAT SO CASUALLY?!
CRUNCH
HEY... WHAT'S WRONG?
HA HA... I THINK I'M AT MY LIMIT HERE.
MY HANDS ARE GOING NUMB.
I CAN'T EVEN HOLD THE SHOVEL.

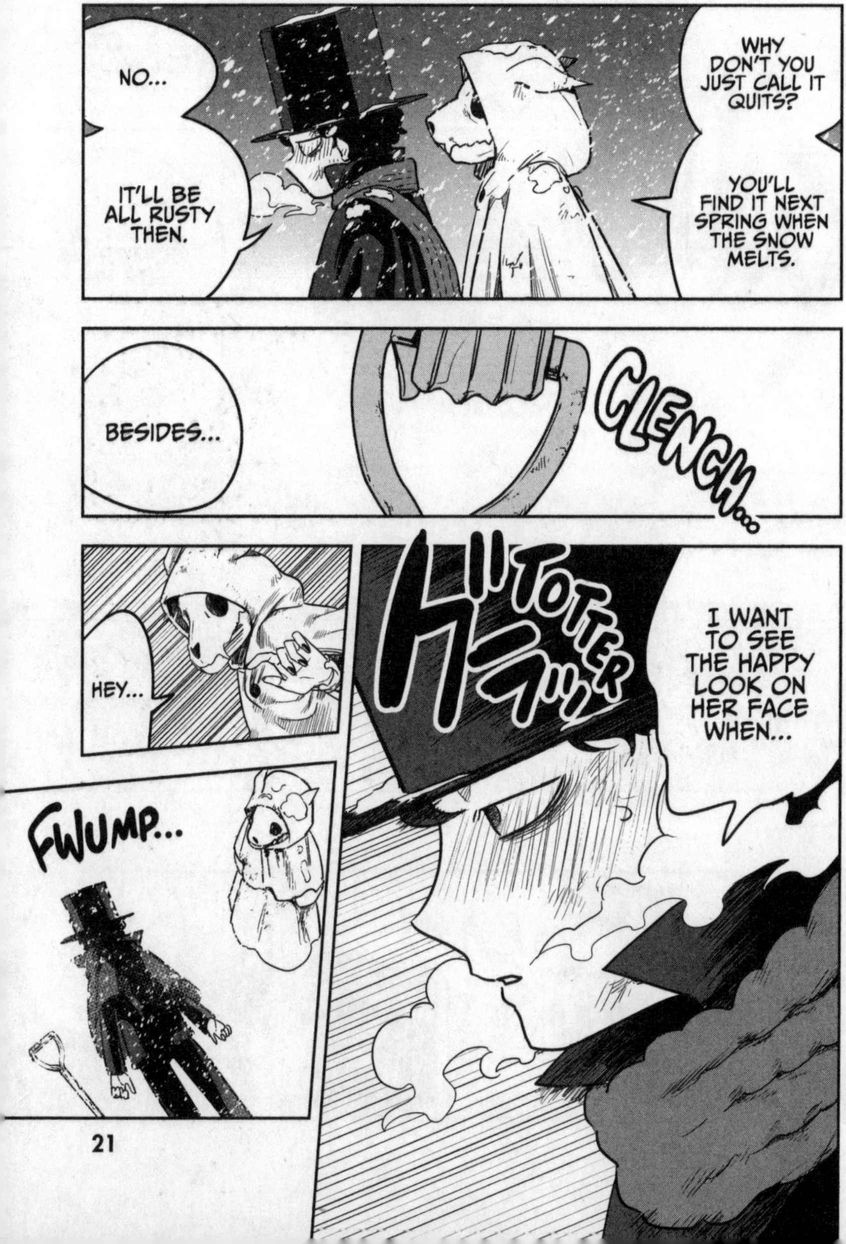
WHY DON'T YOU JUST CALL IT QUITS?
YOU'LL FIND IT NEXT SPRING WHEN THE SNOW MELTS.
NO...
IT'LL BE ALL RUSTY THEN.
CLENCH...
BESIDES...
TOTTER
I WANT TO SEE THE HAPPY LOOK ON HER FACE WHEN...
HEY...
FWUMP...

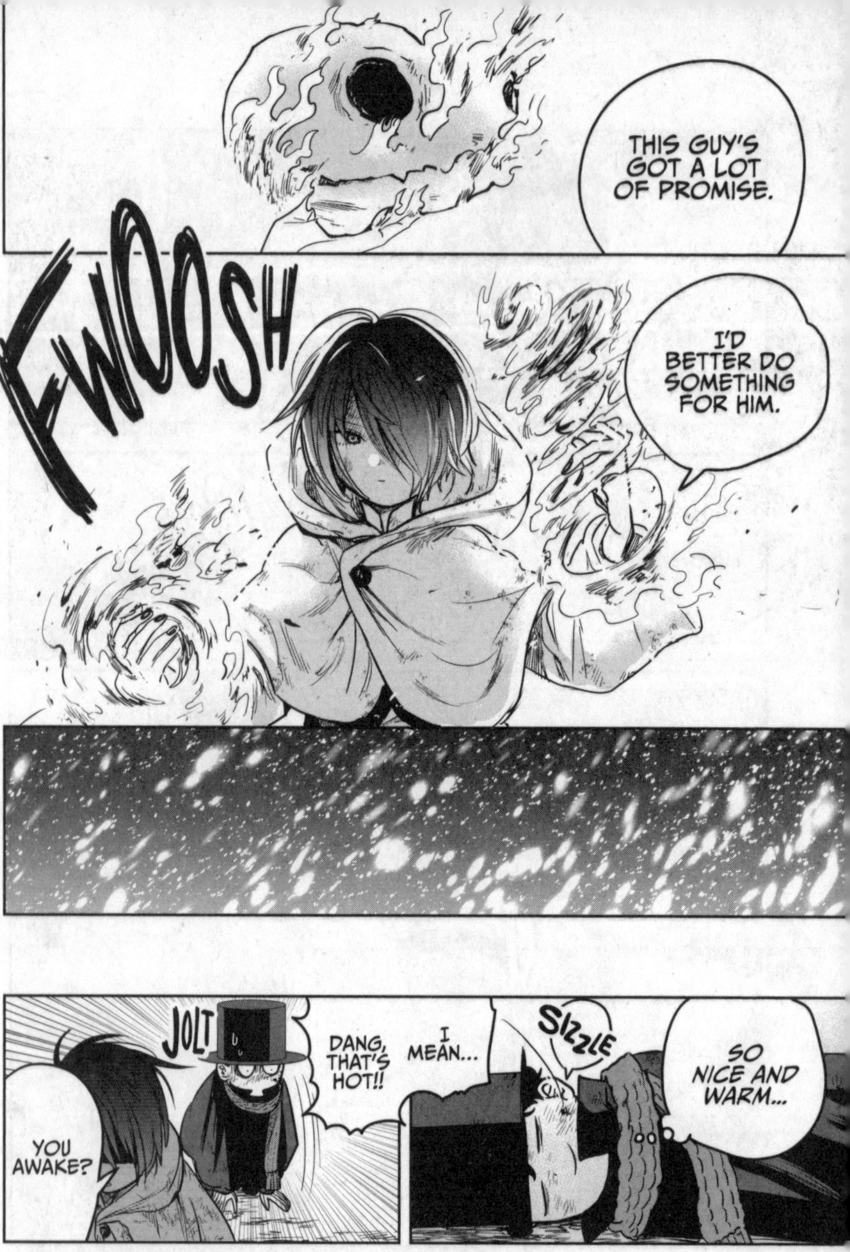
THIS GUY'S GOT A LOT OF PROMISE.
I'D BETTER DO SOMETHING FOR HIM.
FWOOSH
SO NICE AND WARM...
SIZZLE
I MEAN...
DANG, THAT'S HOT!!
JOLT
YOU AWAKE?

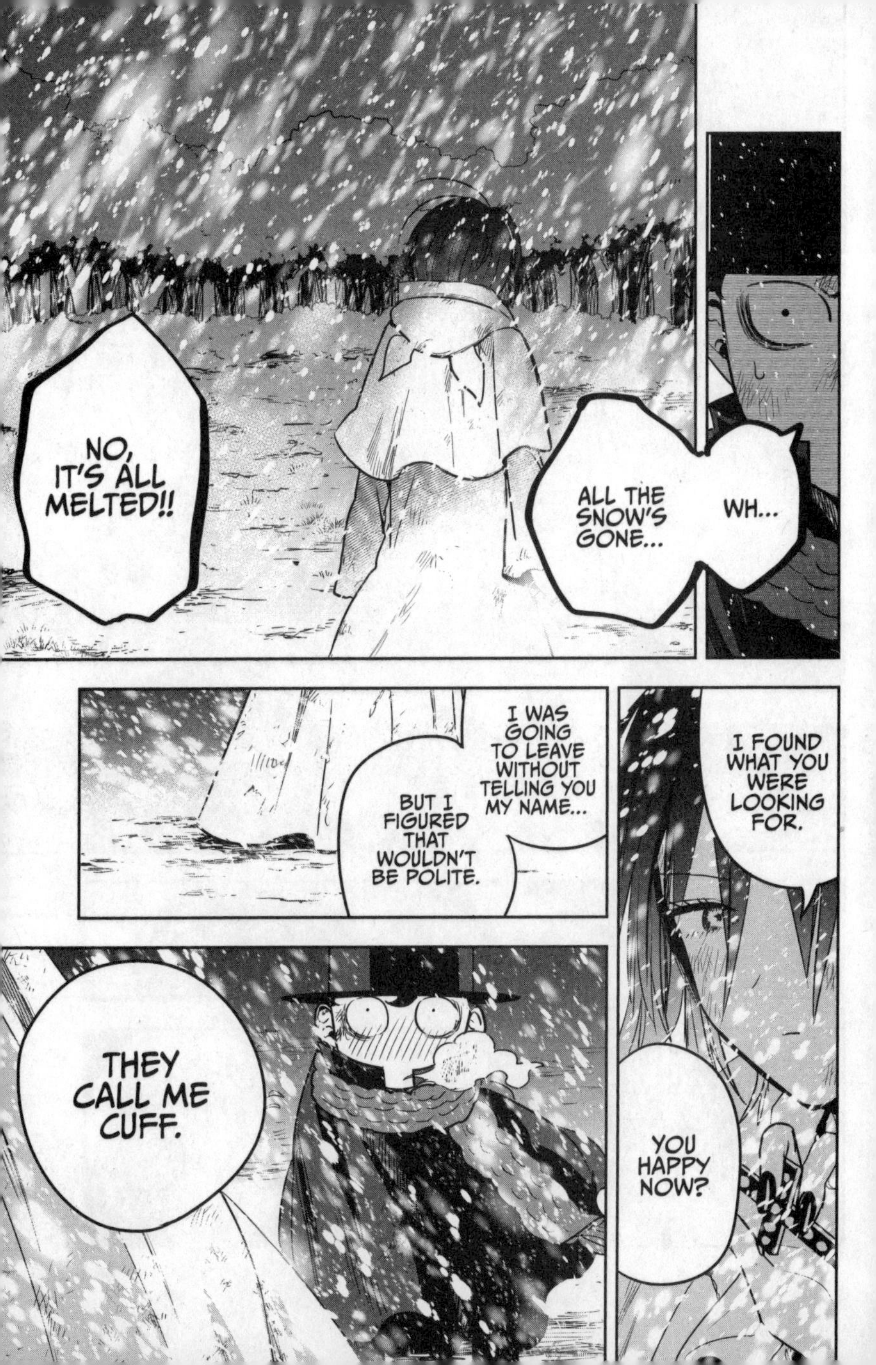
WH...
ALL THE SNOW'S GONE...
NO, IT'S ALL MELTED!!
I FOUND WHAT YOU WERE LOOKING FOR.
YOU HAPPY NOW?
I WAS GOING TO LEAVE WITHOUT TELLING YOU MY NAME...
BUT I FIGURED THAT WOULDN'T BE POLITE.
THEY CALL ME CUFF.

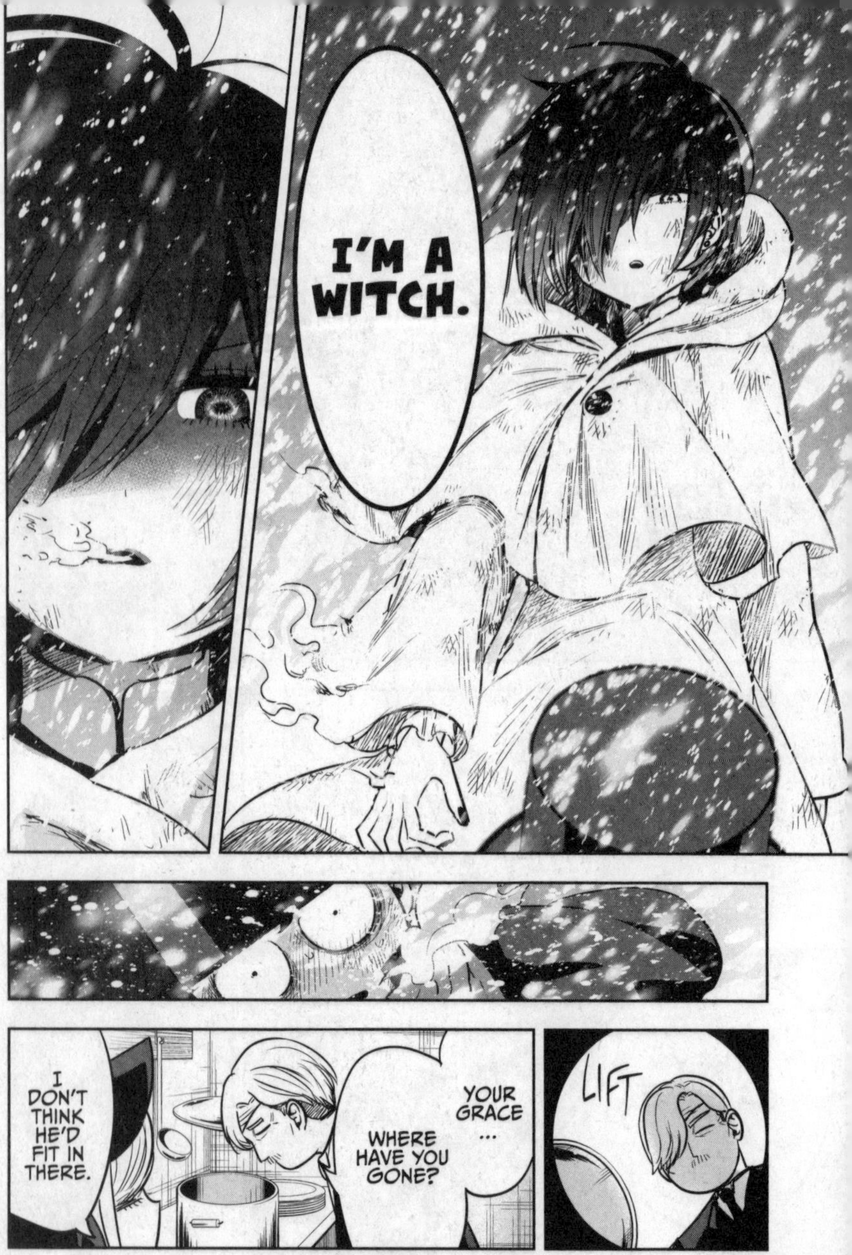
I'M A WITCH.
LIFT
YOUR GRACE ...
WHERE HAVE YOU GONE?
I DON'T THINK HE'D FIT IN THERE.

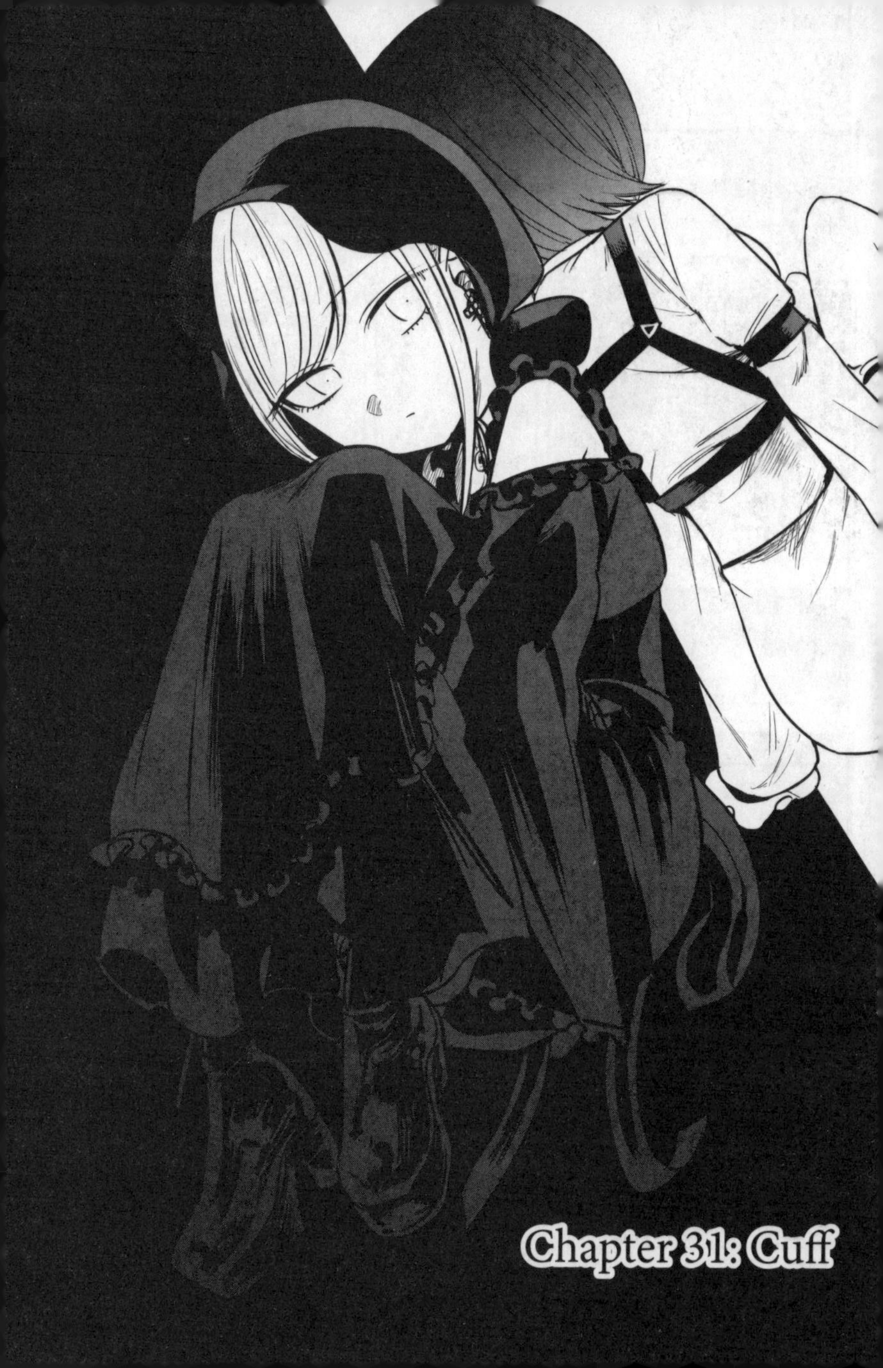
Chapter 31: Cuff

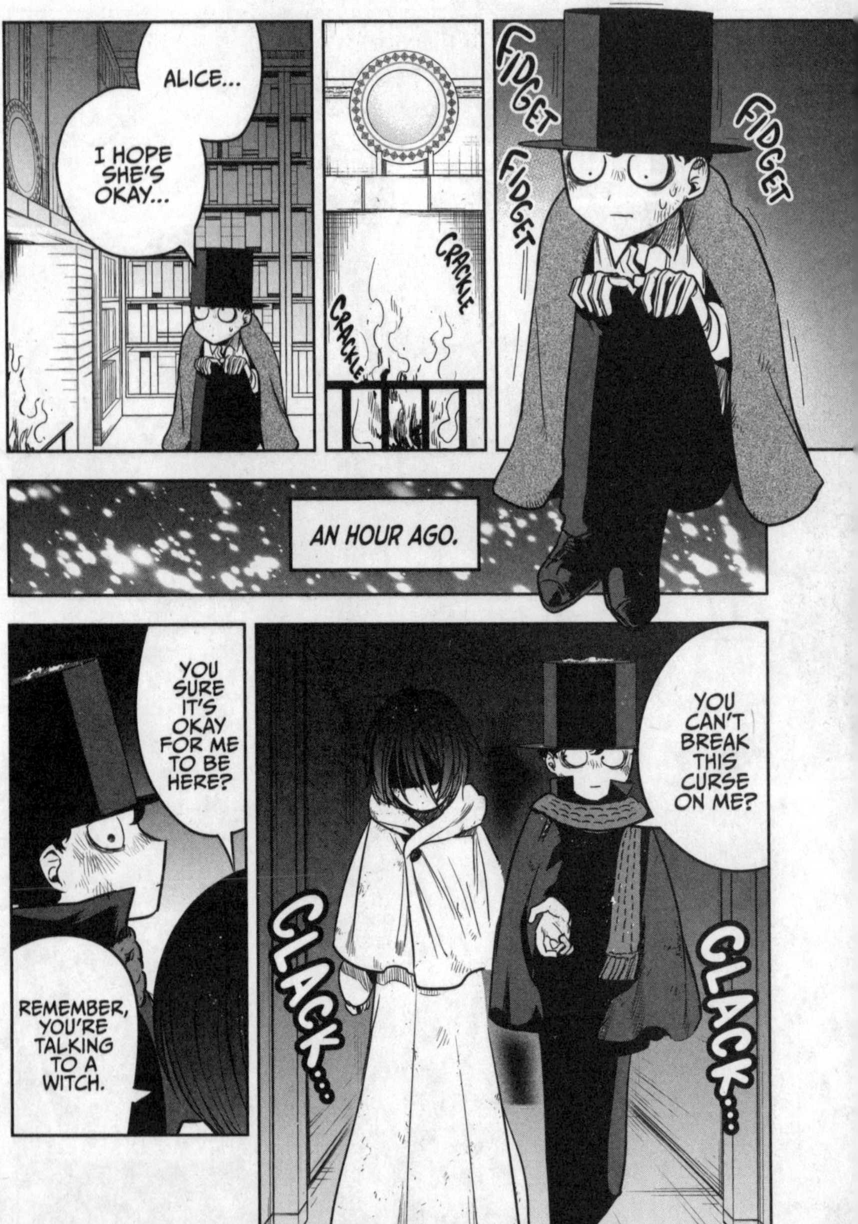
FIDGET
FIDGET
FIDGET
FIDGET
CRACKLE
CRACKLE
ALICE...
I HOPE SHE'S OKAY...
AN HOUR AGO.
YOU CAN'T BREAK THIS CURSE ON ME?
CLACK...
CLACK...
YOU SURE IT'S OKAY FOR ME TO BE HERE?
REMEMBER, YOU'RE TALKING TO A WITCH.

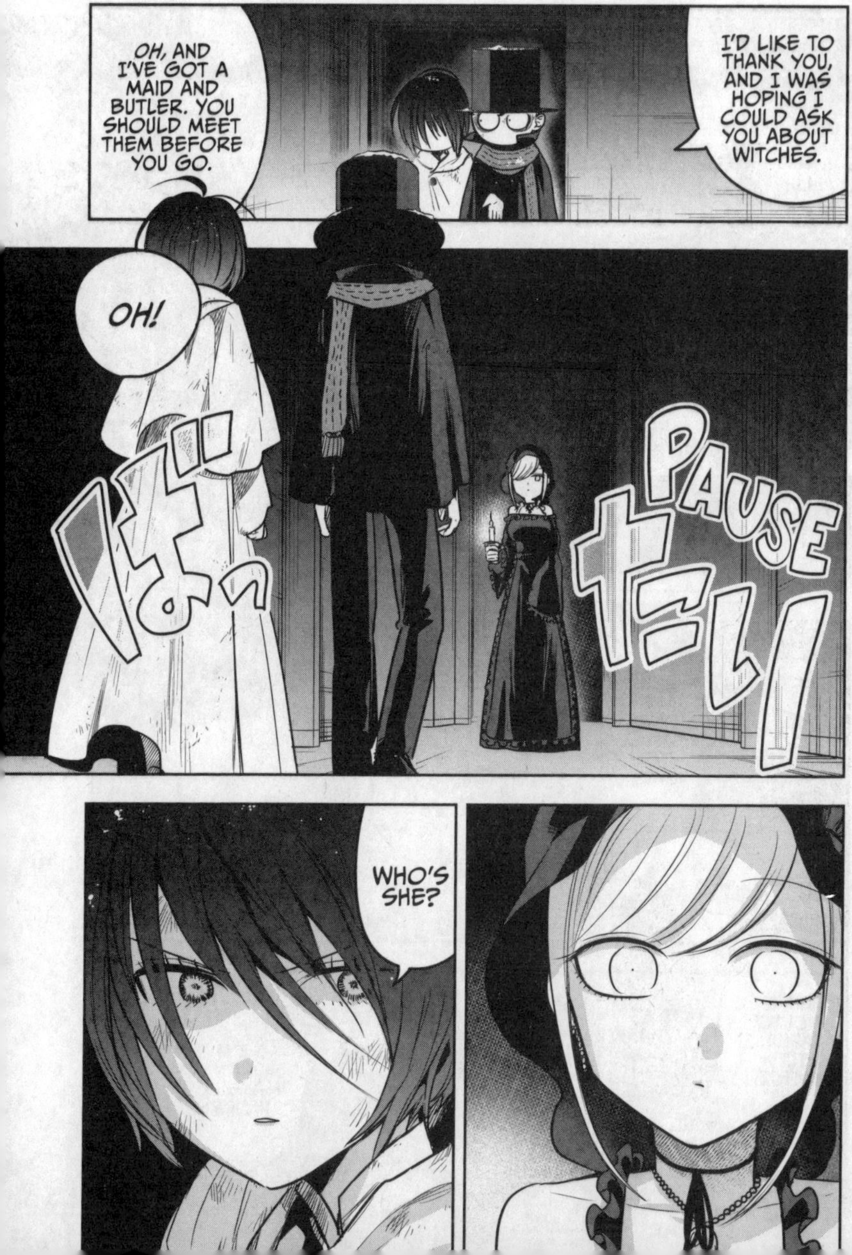
I'D LIKE TO THANK YOU, AND I WAS HOPING I COULD ASK YOU ABOUT WITCHES.
OH, AND I'VE GOT A MAID AND BUTLER. YOU SHOULD MEET THEM BEFORE YOU GO.
PAUSE
OH!
WHO'S SHE?

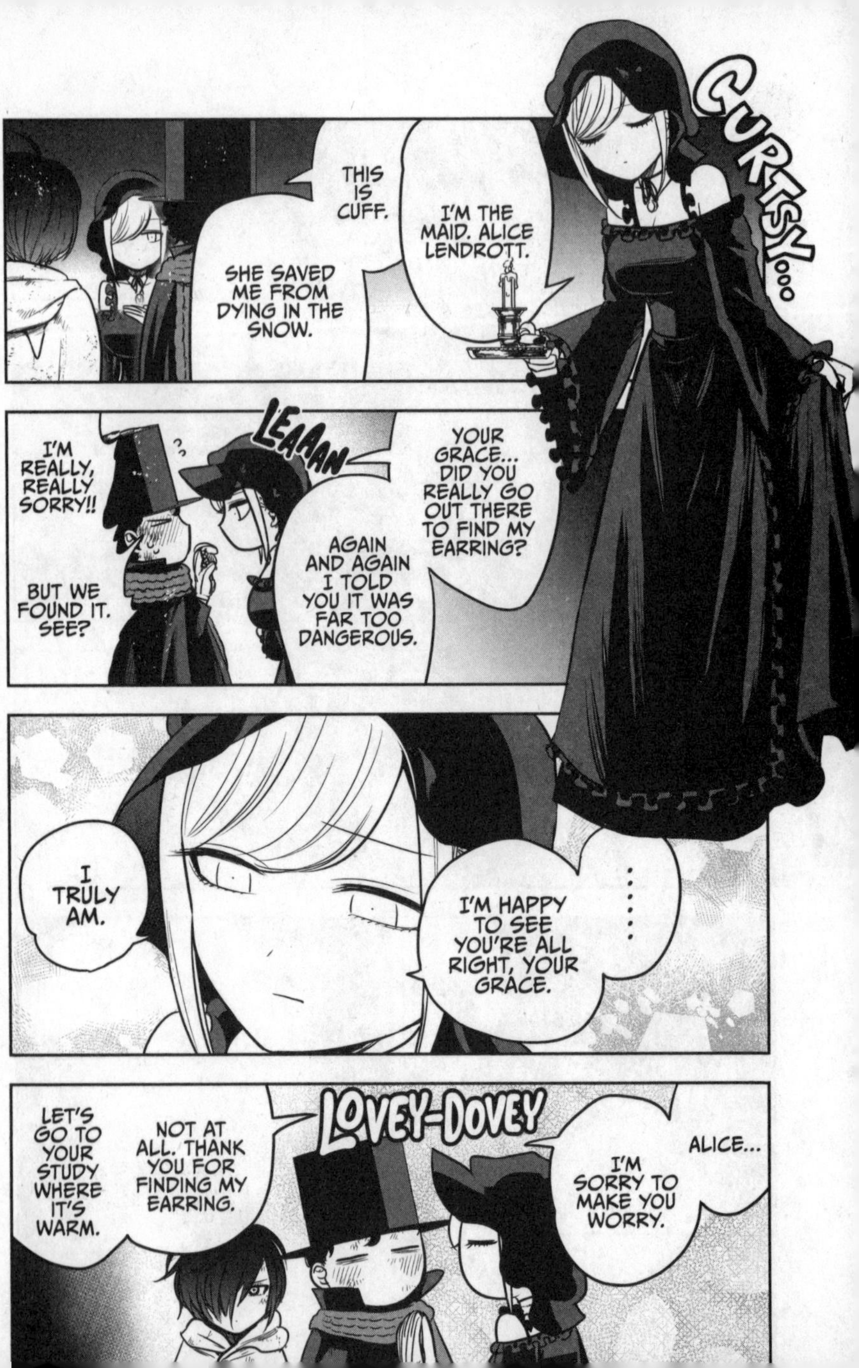
CURTSY...
I'M THE MAID. ALICE LENDROTT.
THIS IS CUFF.
SHE SAVED ME FROM DYING IN THE SNOW.
YOUR GRACE... DID YOU REALLY GO OUT THERE TO FIND MY EARRING?
LEAAAAN
AGAIN AND AGAIN I TOLD YOU IT WAS FAR TOO DANGEROUS.
I'M REALLY, REALLY SORRY!!
BUT WE FOUND IT. SEE?
......
I'M HAPPY TO SEE YOU'RE ALL RIGHT, YOUR GRACE.
I TRULY AM.
ALICE...
I'M SORRY TO MAKE YOU WORRY.
LOVEY-DOVEY
NOT AT ALL. THANK YOU FOR FINDING MY EARRING.
LET'S GO TO YOUR STUDY WHERE IT'S WARM.

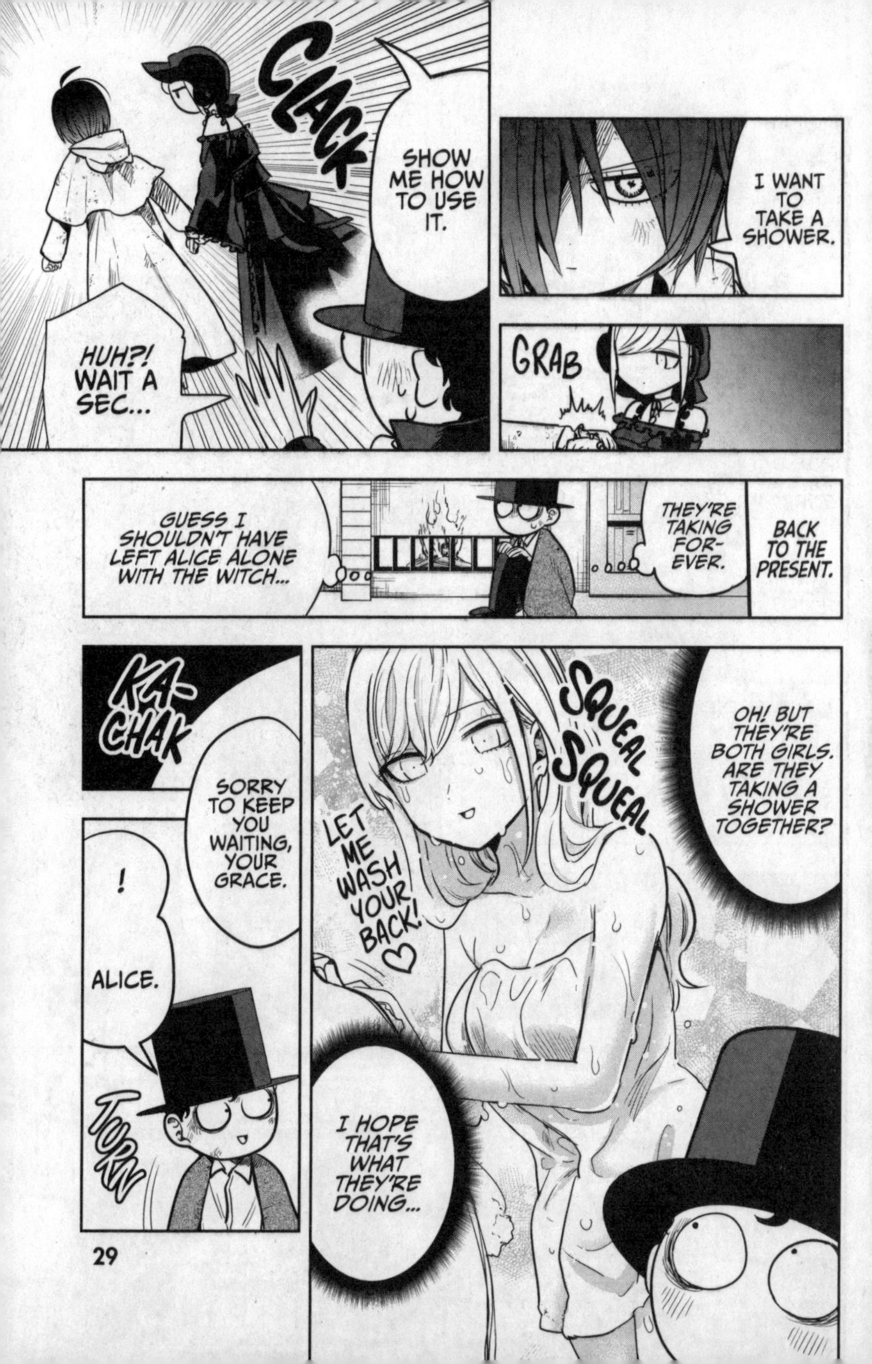
I WANT TO TAKE A SHOWER.
GRAB
CLACK
SHOW ME HOW TO USE IT.
HUH?! WAIT A SEC...
BACK TO THE PRESENT.
THEY'RE TAKING FOR-EVER.
GUESS I SHOULDN'T HAVE LEFT ALICE ALONE WITH THE WITCH...
OH! BUT THEY'RE BOTH GIRLS. ARE THEY TAKING A SHOWER TOGETHER?
SQUEAL SQUEAL
LET ME WASH YOUR BACK! ♡
I HOPE THAT'S WHAT THEY'RE DOING...
KA-CHAK
SORRY TO KEEP YOU WAITING, YOUR GRACE.
!
ALICE.
TURN

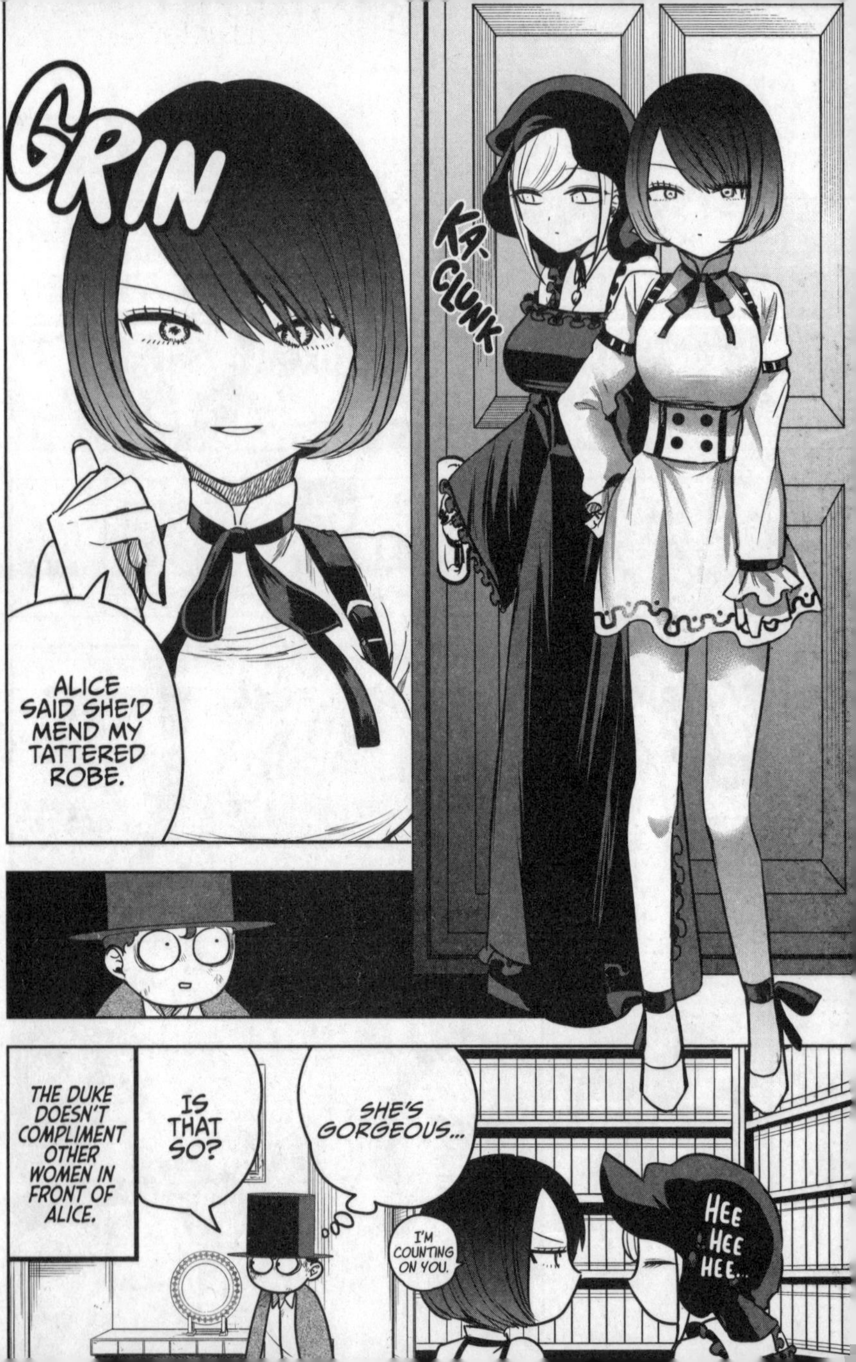
KA-CLUNK
GRIN
ALICE SAID SHE'D MEND MY TATTERED ROBE.
HEE HEE HEE...
I'M COUNTING ON YOU.
SHE'S GORGEOUS...
IS THAT SO?
THE DUKE DOESN'T COMPLIMENT OTHER WOMEN IN FRONT OF ALICE.

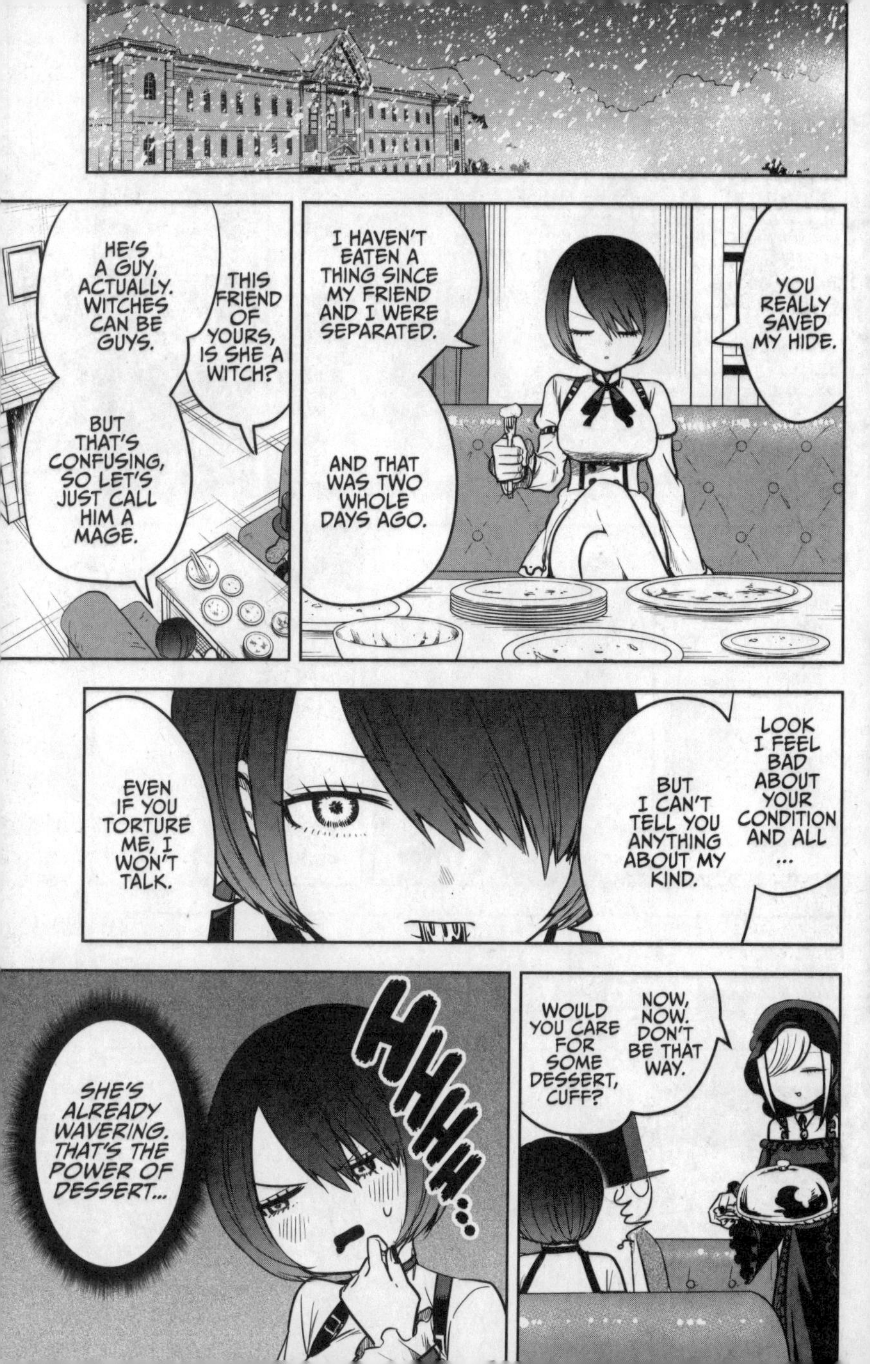
YOU REALLY SAVED MY HIDE.
I HAVEN'T EATEN A THING SINCE MY FRIEND AND I WERE SEPARATED.
AND THAT WAS TWO WHOLE DAYS AGO.
THIS FRIEND OF YOURS, IS SHE A WITCH?
HE'S A GUY, ACTUALLY. WITCHES CAN BE GUYS.
BUT THAT'S CONFUSING, SO LET'S JUST CALL HIM A MAGE.
LOOK I FEEL BAD ABOUT YOUR CONDITION AND ALL ...
BUT I CAN'T TELL YOU ANYTHING ABOUT MY KIND.
EVEN IF YOU TORTURE ME, I WON'T TALK.
NOW, NOW. DON'T BE THAT WAY.
WOULD YOU CARE FOR SOME DESSERT, CUFF?
HHHH...
SHE'S ALREADY WAVERING. THAT'S THE POWER OF DESSERT...

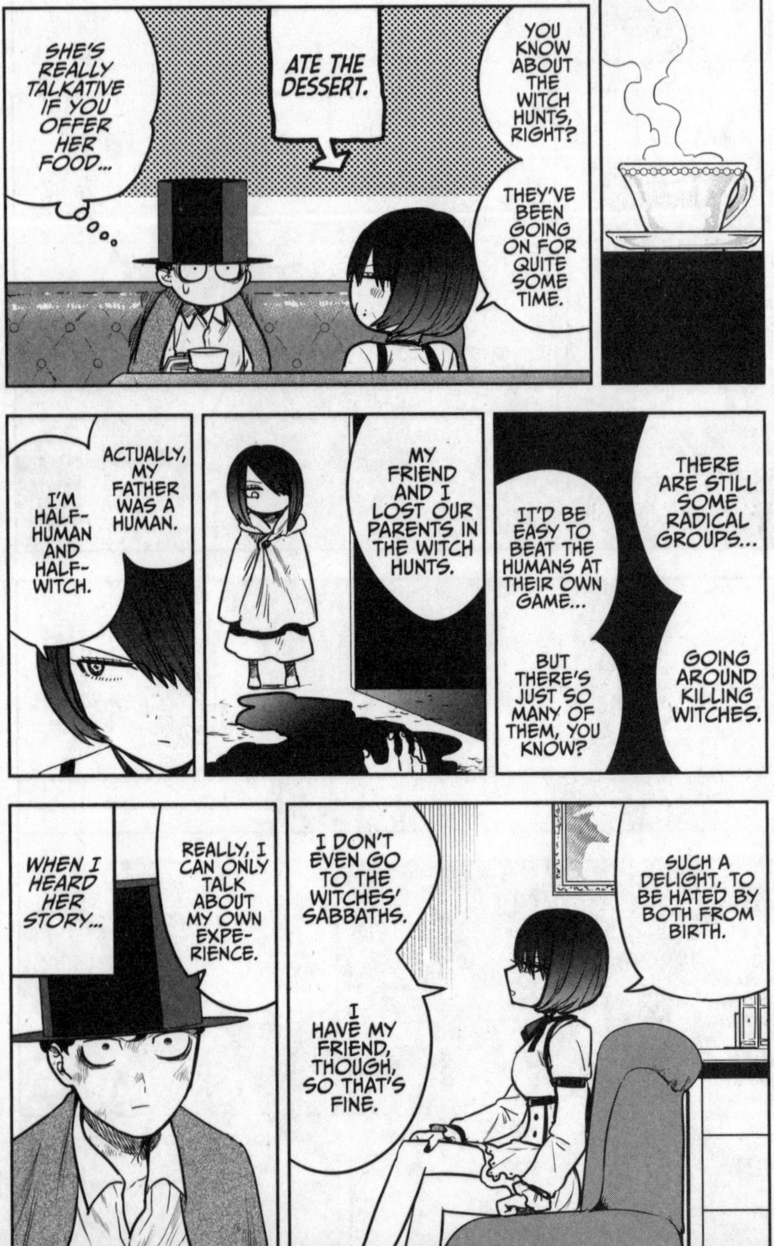
YOU KNOW ABOUT THE WITCH HUNTS, RIGHT?
THEY'VE BEEN GOING ON FOR QUITE SOME TIME.
ATE THE DESSERT.
SHE'S REALLY TALKATIVE IF YOU OFFER HER FOOD...
THERE ARE STILL SOME RADICAL GROUPS...
GOING AROUND KILLING WITCHES.
IT'D BE EASY TO BEAT THE HUMANS AT THEIR OWN GAME...
BUT THERE'S JUST SO MANY OF THEM, YOU KNOW?
MY FRIEND AND I LOST OUR PARENTS IN THE WITCH HUNTS.
ACTUALLY, MY FATHER WAS A HUMAN.
I'M HALF-HUMAN AND HALF-WITCH.
SUCH A DELIGHT, TO BE HATED BY BOTH FROM BIRTH.
I DON'T EVEN GO TO THE WITCHES' SABBATHS.
I HAVE MY FRIEND, THOUGH, SO THAT'S FINE.
REALLY, I CAN ONLY TALK ABOUT MY OWN EXPE-RIENCE.
WHEN I HEARD HER STORY...

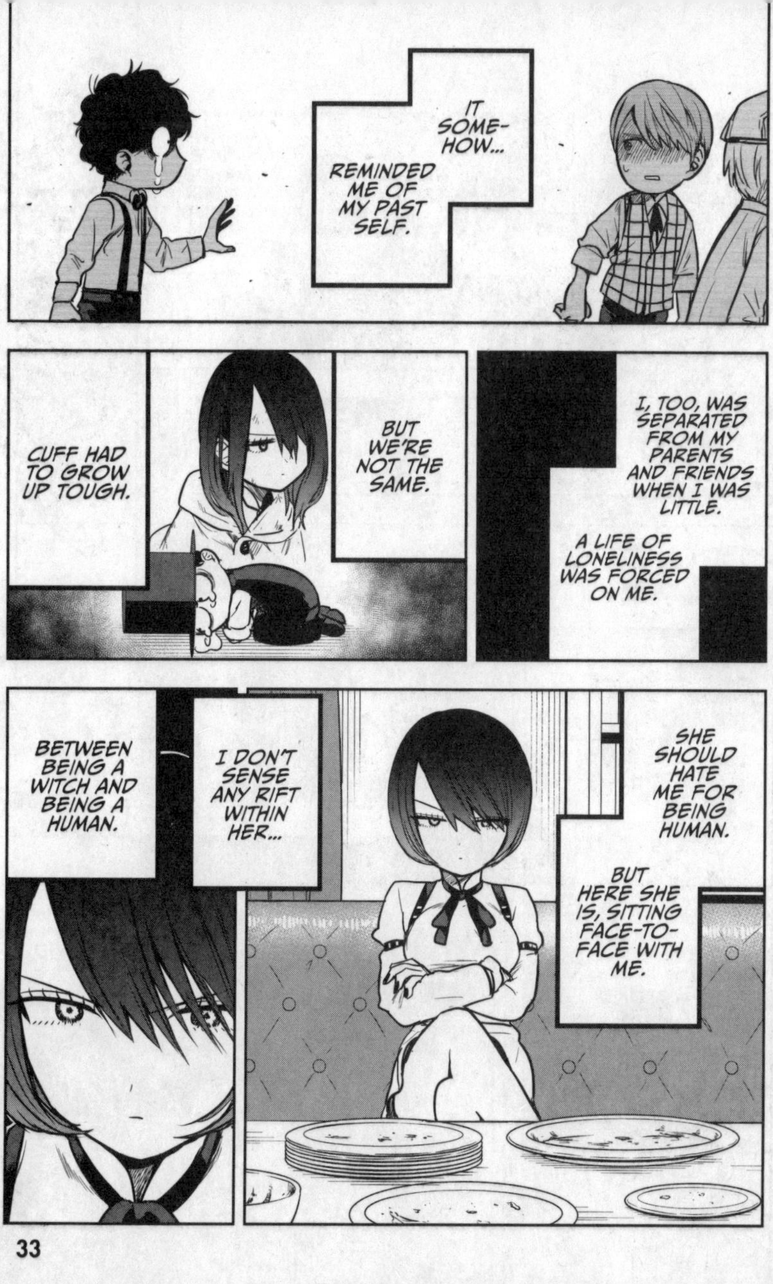
IT SOMEHOW...
REMINDED ME OF MY PAST SELF.
I, TOO, WAS SEPARATED FROM MY PARENTS AND FRIENDS WHEN I WAS LITTLE.
A LIFE OF LONELINESS WAS FORCED ON ME.
BUT WE'RE NOT THE SAME.
CUFF HAD TO GROW UP TOUGH.
SHE SHOULD HATE ME FOR BEING HUMAN.
BUT HERE SHE IS, SITTING FACE-TO-FACE WITH ME.
I DON'T SENSE ANY RIFT WITHIN HER...
BETWEEN BEING A WITCH AND BEING A HUMAN.

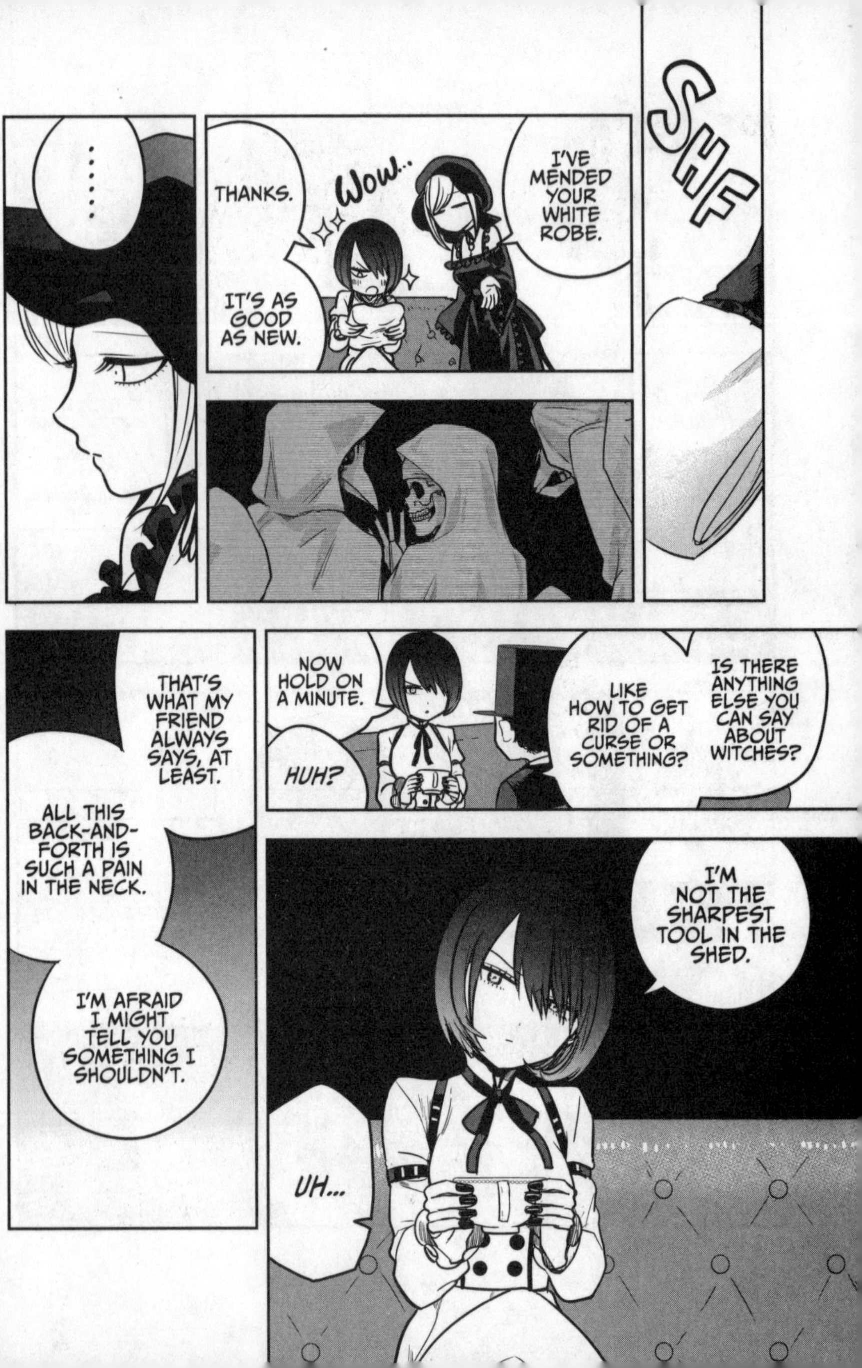
SHF
I'VE MENDED YOUR WHITE ROBE.
WOW...
THANKS.
IT'S AS GOOD AS NEW.
......
IS THERE ANYTHING ELSE YOU CAN SAY ABOUT WITCHES?
LIKE HOW TO GET RID OF A CURSE OR SOMETHING?
NOW HOLD ON A MINUTE.
HUH?
I'M NOT THE SHARPEST TOOL IN THE SHED.
UH...
THAT'S WHAT MY FRIEND ALWAYS SAYS, AT LEAST.
ALL THIS BACK-AND-FORTH IS SUCH A PAIN IN THE NECK.
I'M AFRAID I MIGHT TELL YOU SOMETHING I SHOULDN'T.

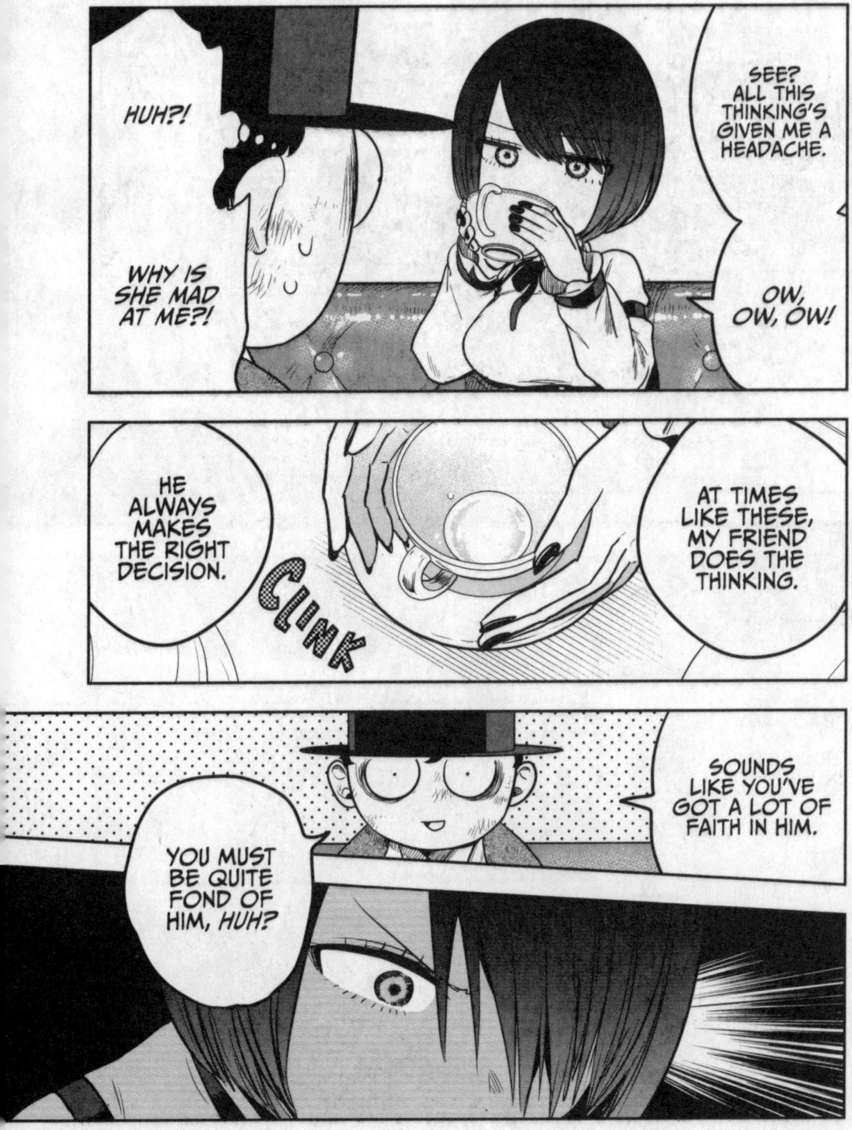
SEE? ALL THIS THINKING'S GIVEN ME A HEADACHE.
OW, OW, OW!
HUH?!
WHY IS SHE MAD AT ME?!
AT TIMES LIKE THESE, MY FRIEND DOES THE THINKING.
CLINK
HE ALWAYS MAKES THE RIGHT DECISION.
SOUNDS LIKE YOU'VE GOT A LOT OF FAITH IN HIM.
YOU MUST BE QUITE FOND OF HIM, *HUH?*

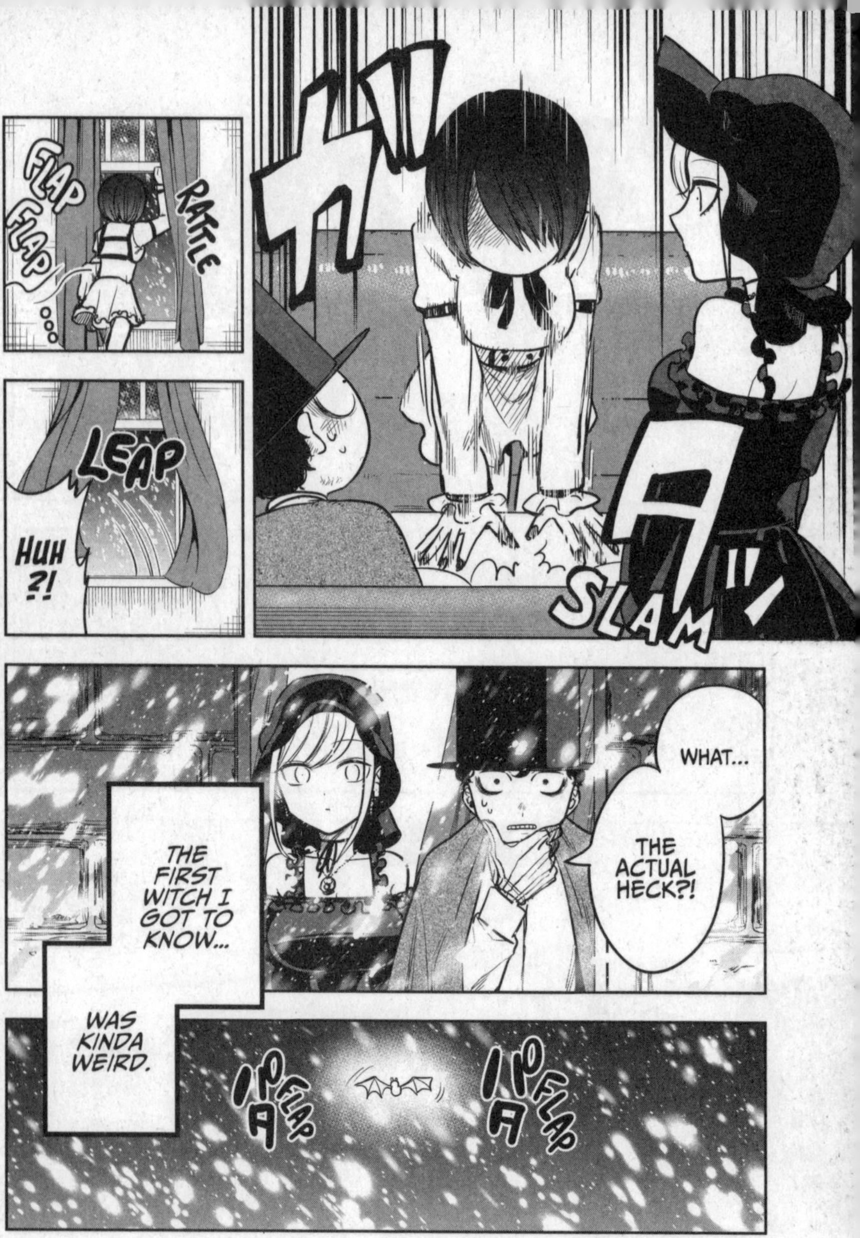
SLAM
RATTLE
FLAP FLAP
LEAP
HUH ?!
WHAT...
THE ACTUAL HECK?!
THE FIRST WITCH I GOT TO KNOW...
WAS KINDA WEIRD.
FLAP
FLAP

THE DUKE OF DEATH AND HIS MAID

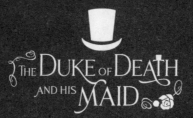

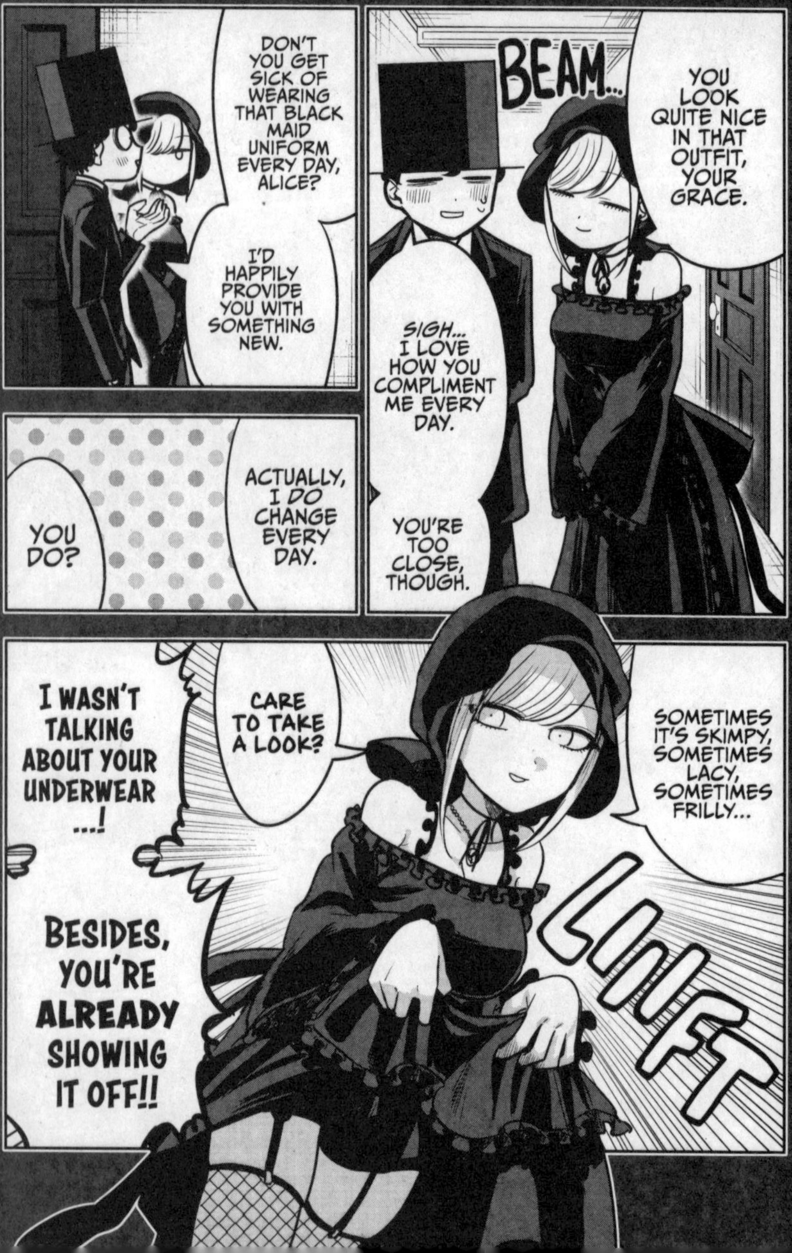
BEAM...
YOU LOOK QUITE NICE IN THAT OUTFIT, YOUR GRACE.
SIGH... I LOVE HOW YOU COMPLIMENT ME EVERY DAY.
YOU'RE TOO CLOSE, THOUGH.
DON'T YOU GET SICK OF WEARING THAT BLACK MAID UNIFORM EVERY DAY, ALICE?
I'D HAPPILY PROVIDE YOU WITH SOMETHING NEW.
ACTUALLY, I *DO* CHANGE EVERY DAY.
YOU DO?
SOMETIMES IT'S SKIMPY, SOMETIMES LACY, SOMETIMES FRILLY...
CARE TO TAKE A LOOK?
LIIFT
I WASN'T TALKING ABOUT YOUR UNDERWEAR ...!
BESIDES, YOU'RE **ALREADY** SHOWING IT OFF!!

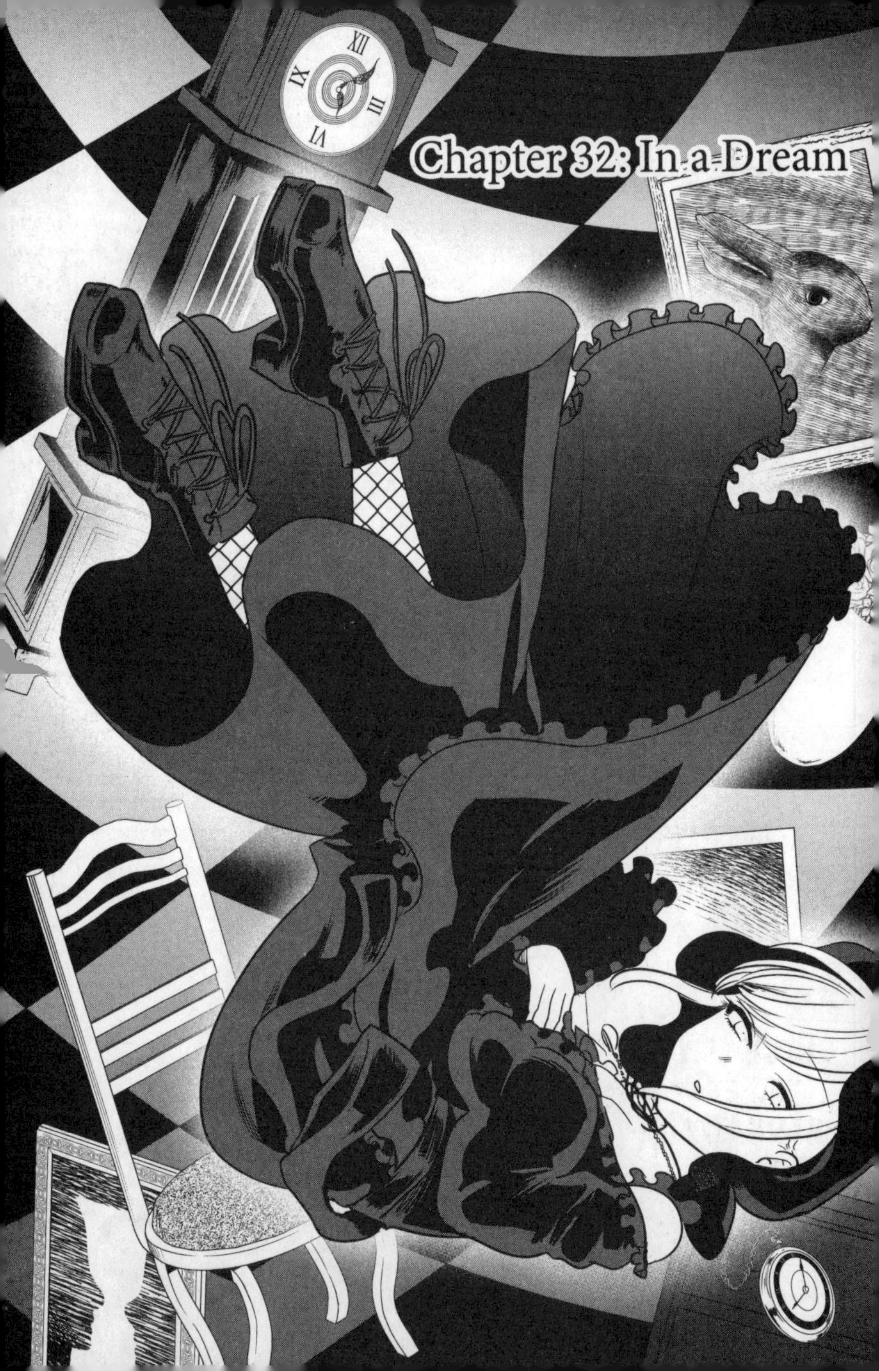
Chapter 32: In a Dream

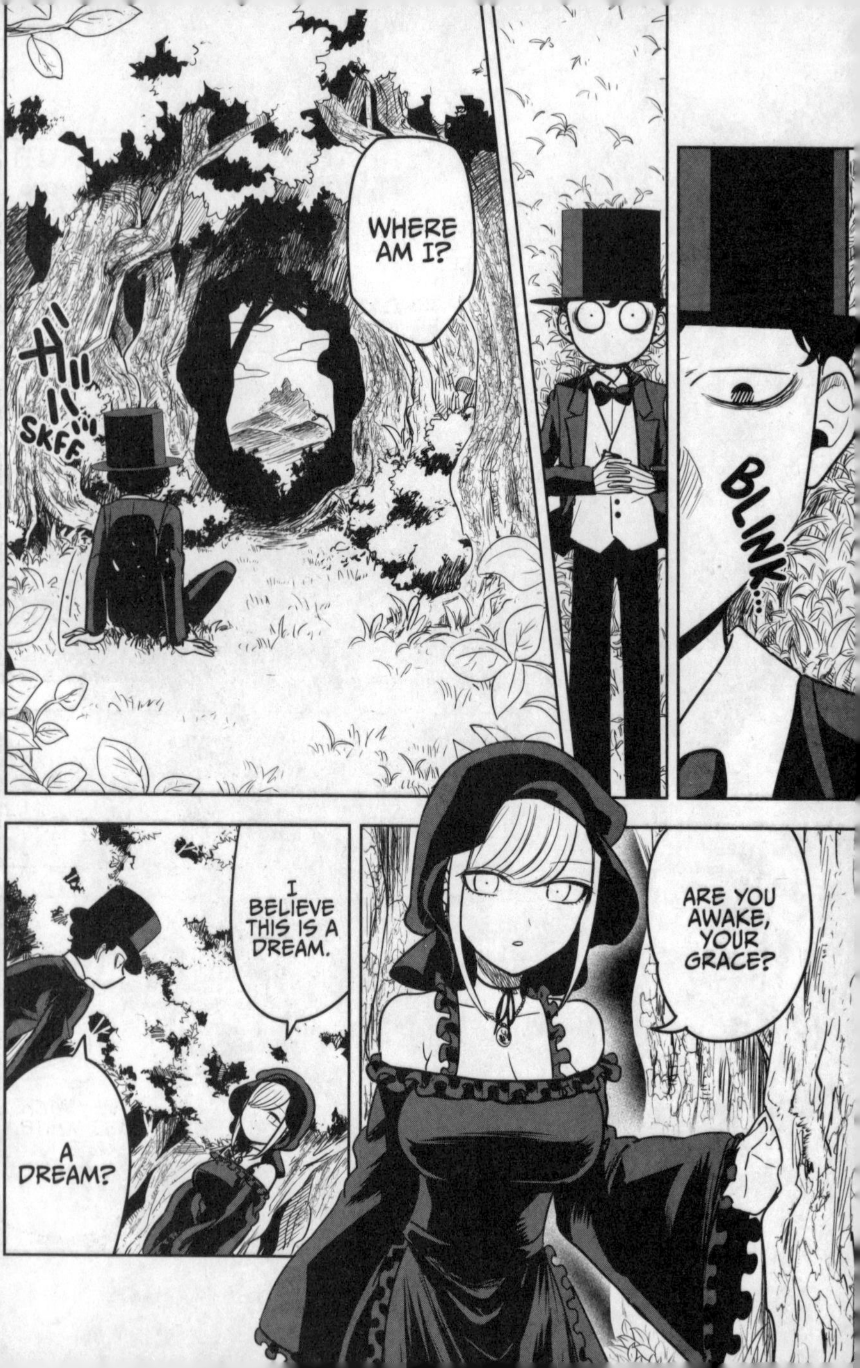
BLINK...
WHERE AM I?
ガバッ
SKFF
ARE YOU AWAKE, YOUR GRACE?
I BELIEVE THIS IS A DREAM.
A DREAM?

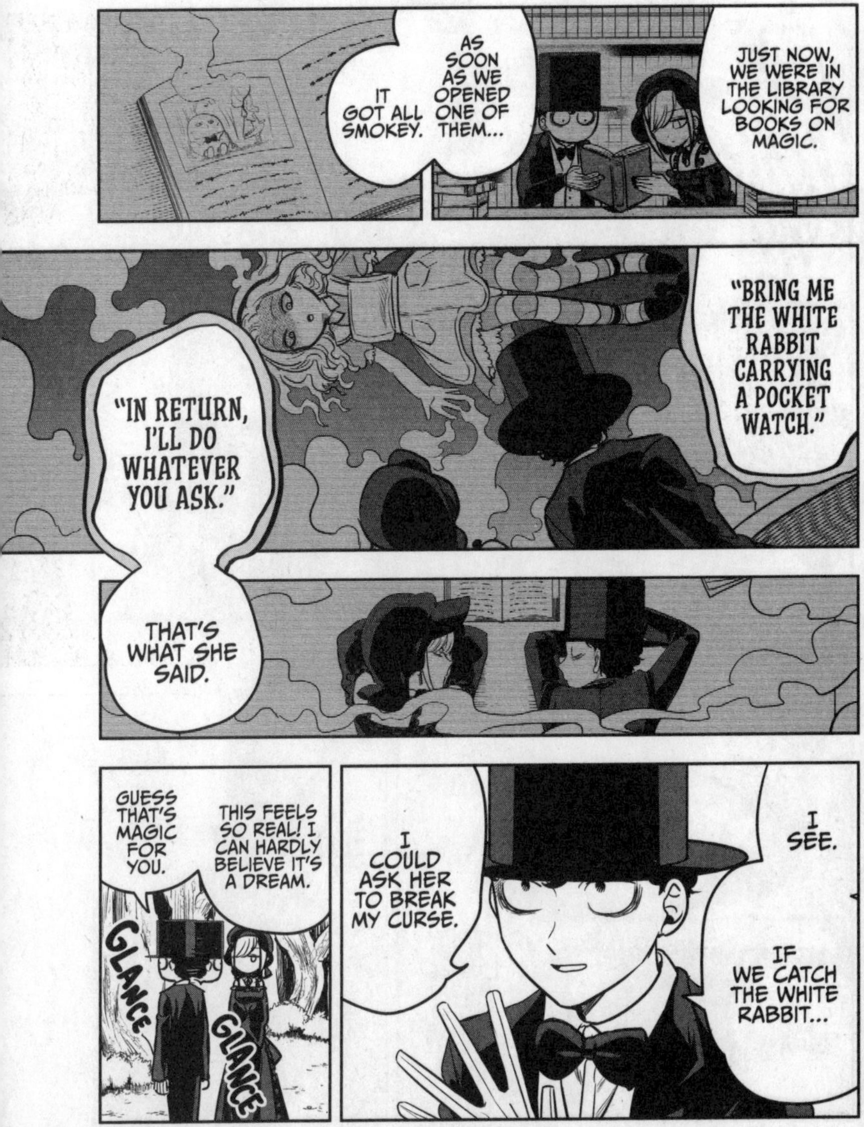
JUST NOW, WE WERE IN THE LIBRARY LOOKING FOR BOOKS ON MAGIC.
AS SOON AS WE OPENED ONE OF THEM...
IT GOT ALL SMOKEY.
"BRING ME THE WHITE RABBIT CARRYING A POCKET WATCH."
"IN RETURN, I'LL DO WHATEVER YOU ASK."
THAT'S WHAT SHE SAID.
I SEE.
IF WE CATCH THE WHITE RABBIT...
I COULD ASK HER TO BREAK MY CURSE.
THIS FEELS SO REAL! I CAN HARDLY BELIEVE IT'S A DREAM.
GUESS THAT'S MAGIC FOR YOU.
GLANCE
GLANCE

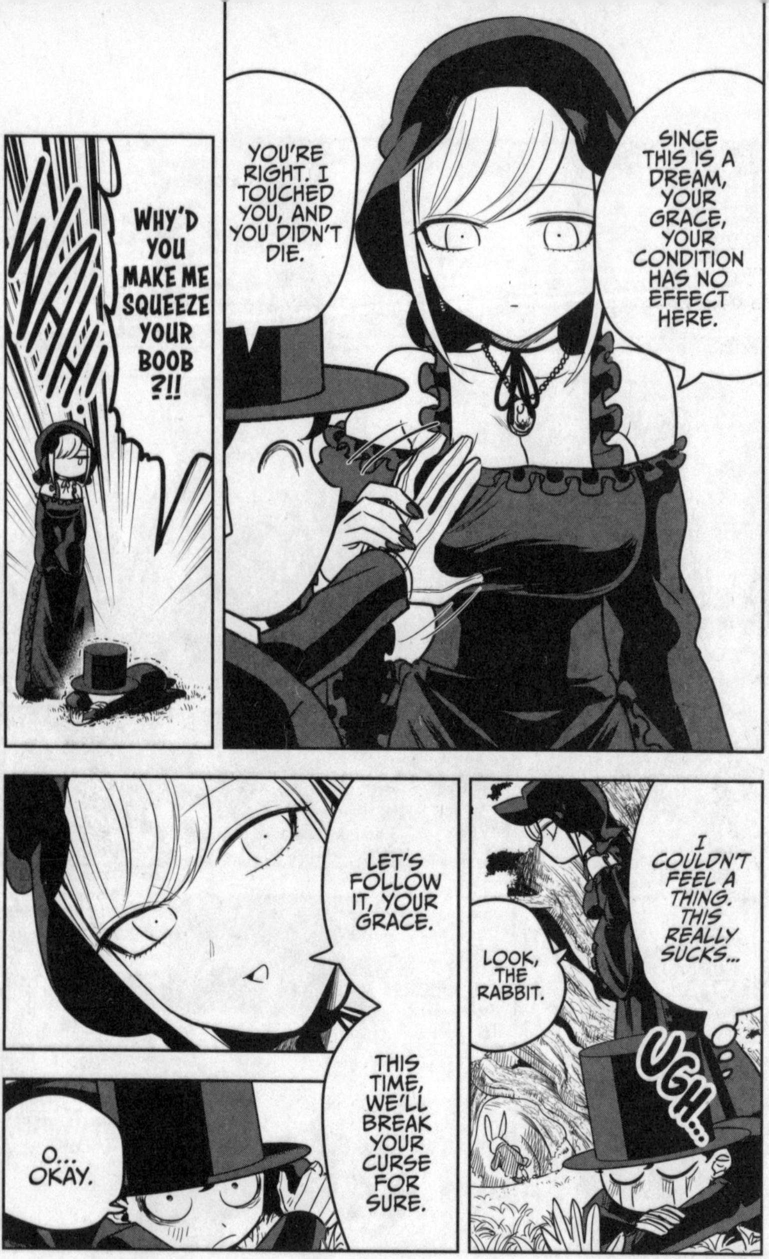
SINCE THIS IS A DREAM, YOUR GRACE, YOUR CONDITION HAS NO EFFECT HERE.
YOU'RE RIGHT. I TOUCHED YOU, AND YOU DIDN'T DIE.
WAH!
WHY'D YOU MAKE ME SQUEEZE YOUR BOOB?!!
I COULDN'T FEEL A THING. THIS REALLY SUCKS...
LOOK, THE RABBIT.
UGH...
LET'S FOLLOW IT, YOUR GRACE.
THIS TIME, WE'LL BREAK YOUR CURSE FOR SURE.
O... OKAY.

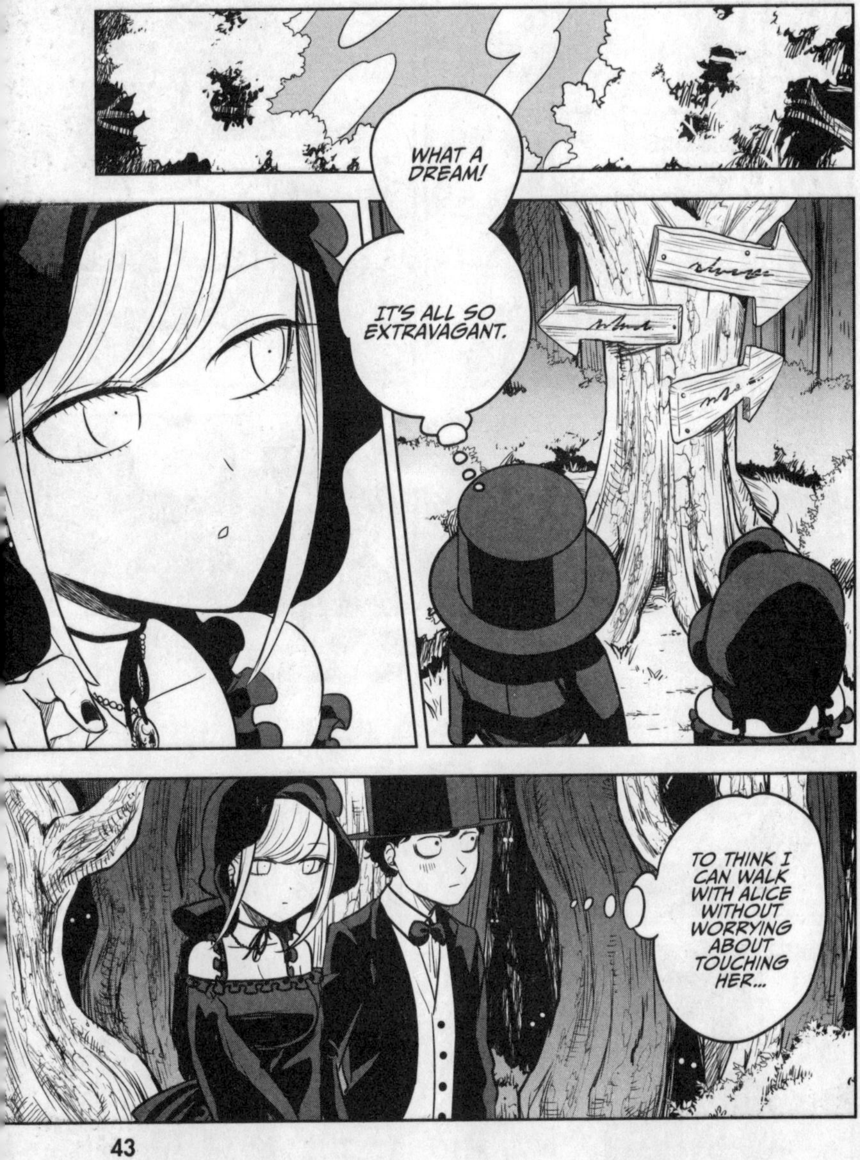
WHAT A DREAM!
IT'S ALL SO EXTRAVAGANT.
TO THINK I CAN WALK WITH ALICE WITHOUT WORRYING ABOUT TOUCHING HER...

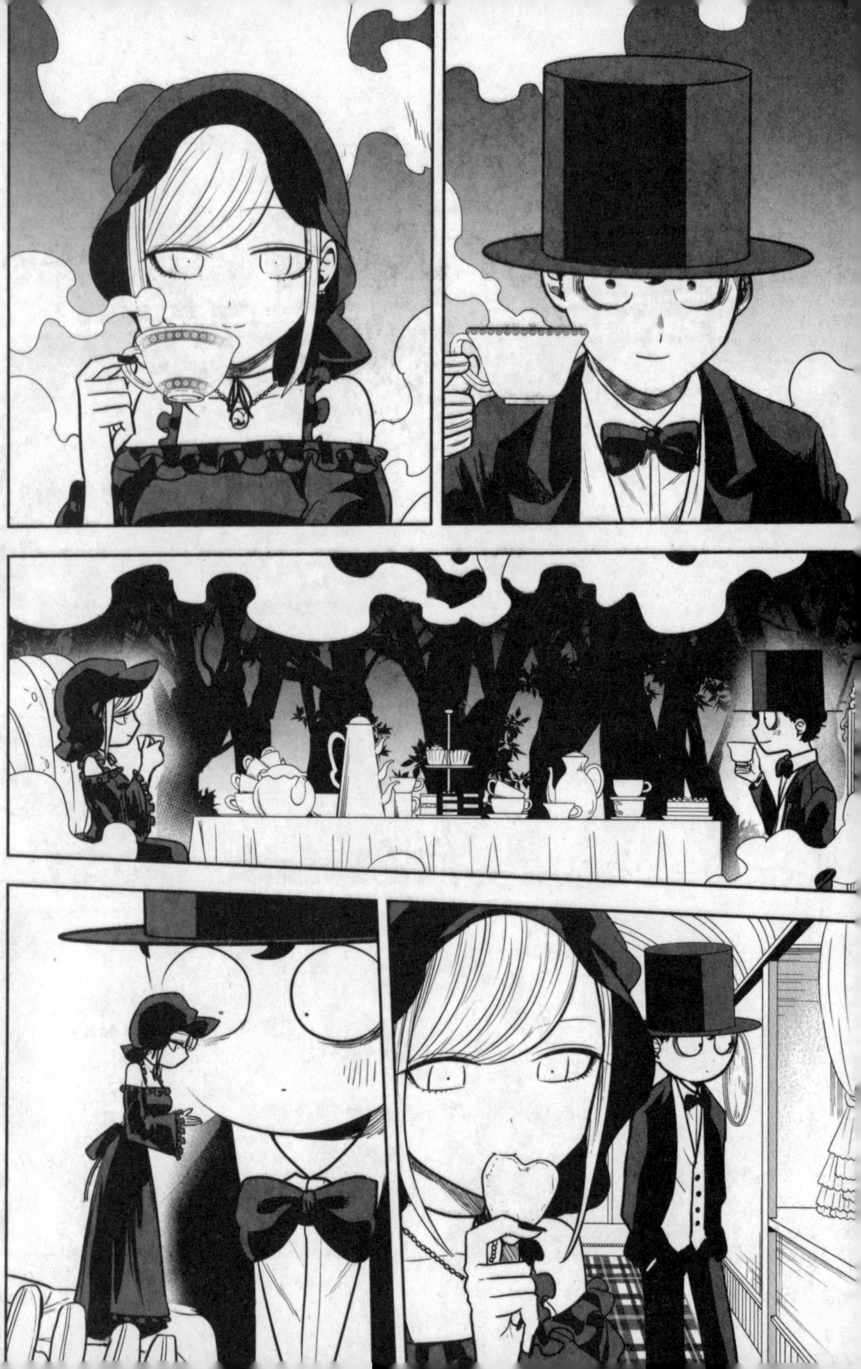

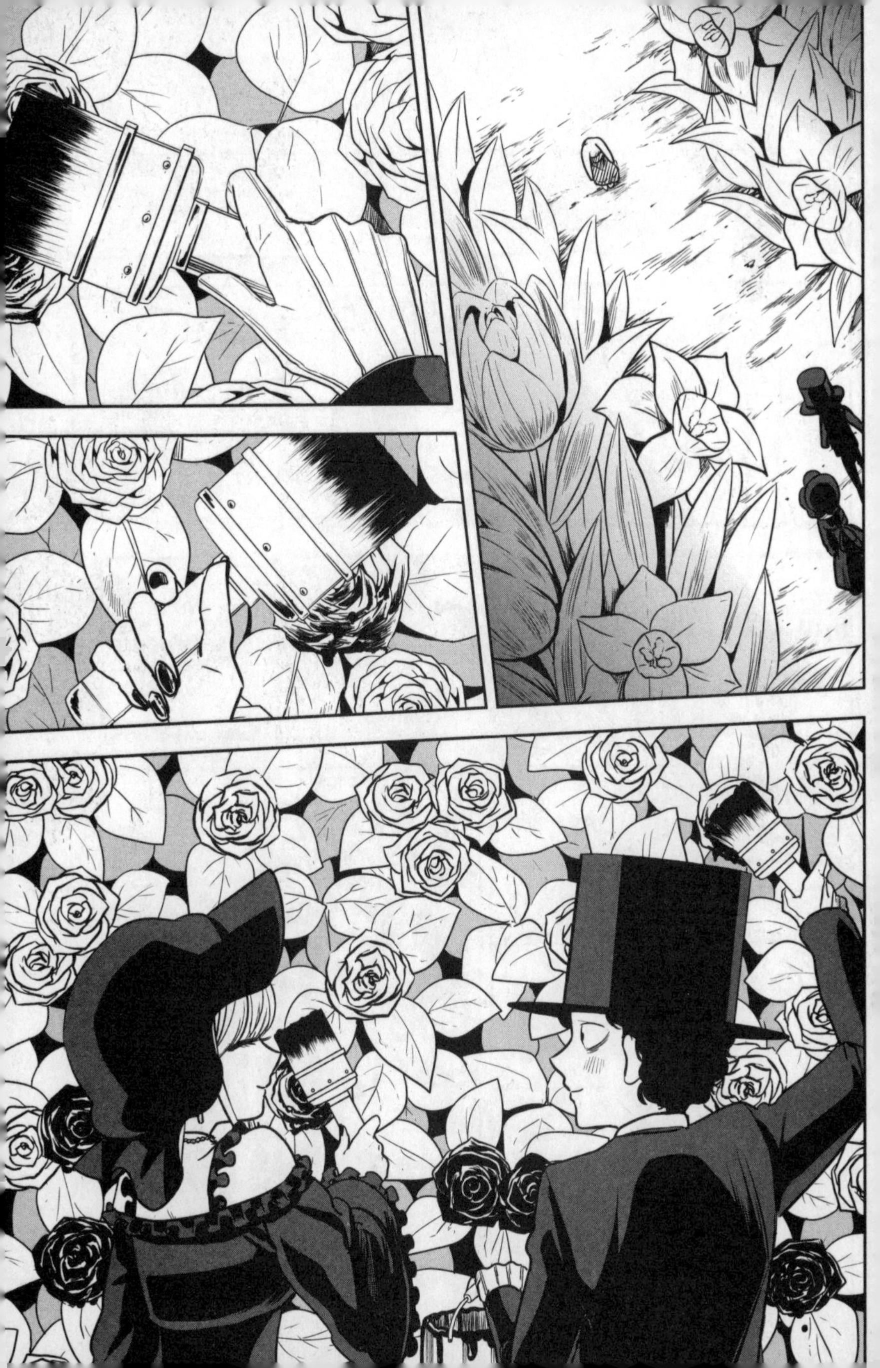

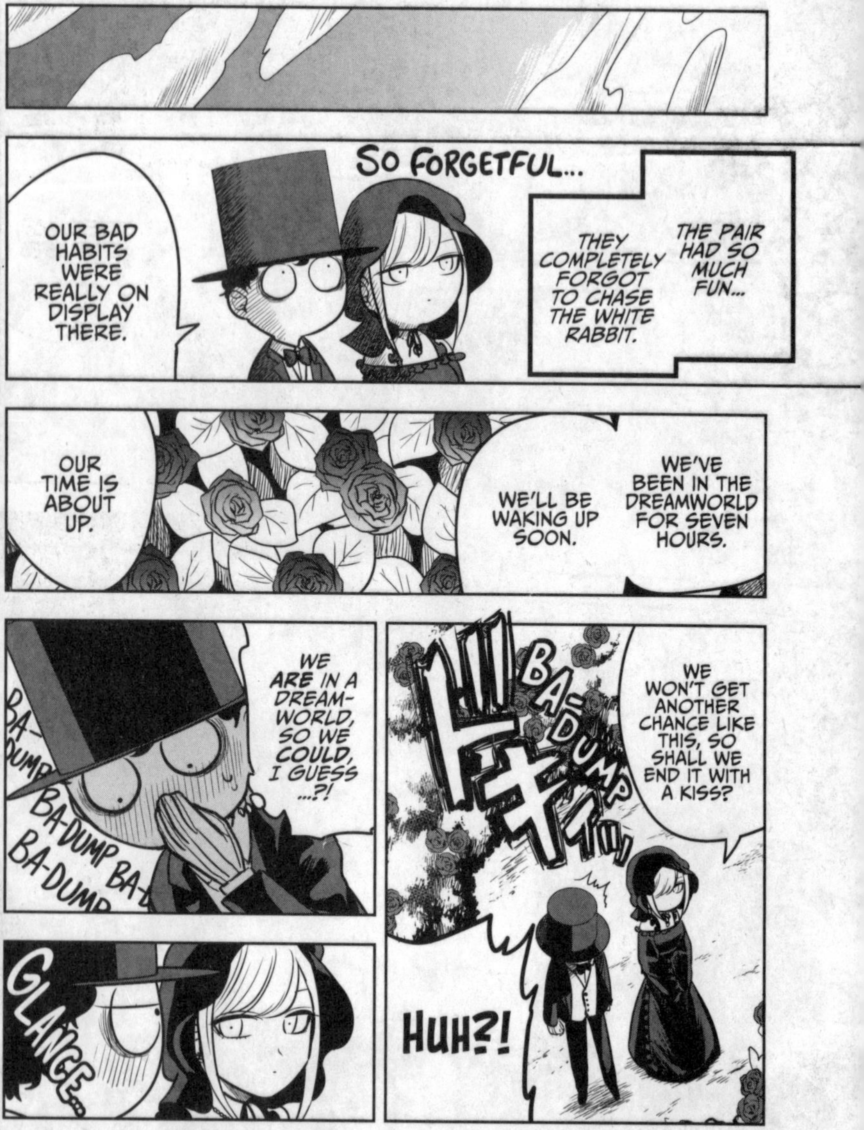
THE PAIR HAD SO MUCH FUN...
THEY COMPLETELY FORGOT TO CHASE THE WHITE RABBIT.
SO FORGETFUL...
OUR BAD HABITS WERE REALLY ON DISPLAY THERE.
WE'VE BEEN IN THE DREAMWORLD FOR SEVEN HOURS.
WE'LL BE WAKING UP SOON.
OUR TIME IS ABOUT UP.
WE WON'T GET ANOTHER CHANCE LIKE THIS, SO SHALL WE END IT WITH A KISS?
BA-DUMP
ドキ
HUH?!
WE ARE IN A DREAM-WORLD, SO WE COULD, I GUESS ...?!
BA-DUMP
BA-DUMP
BA-DUMP
BA-DUMP
GLANCE...

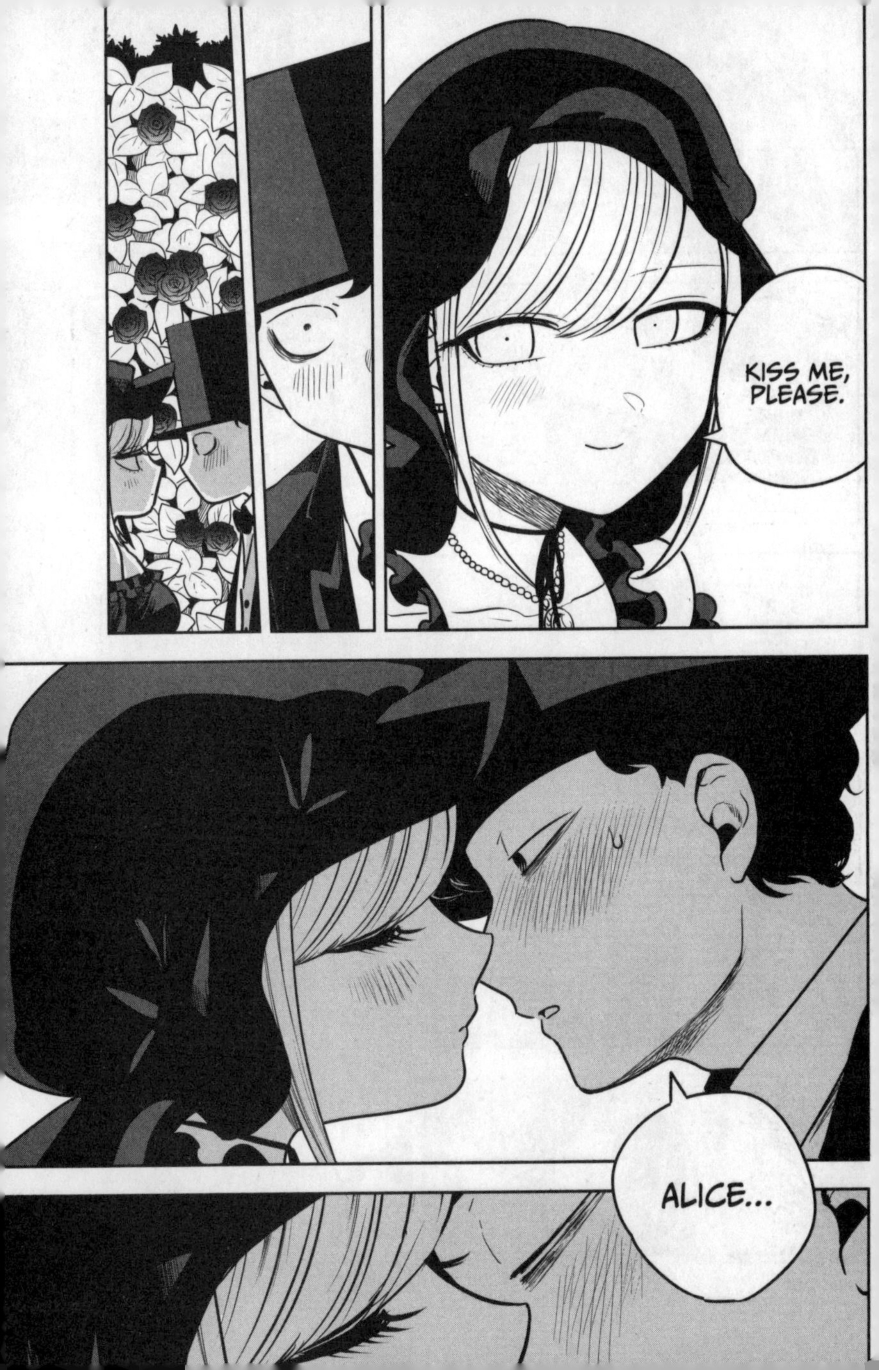
KISS ME, PLEASE.
ALICE...

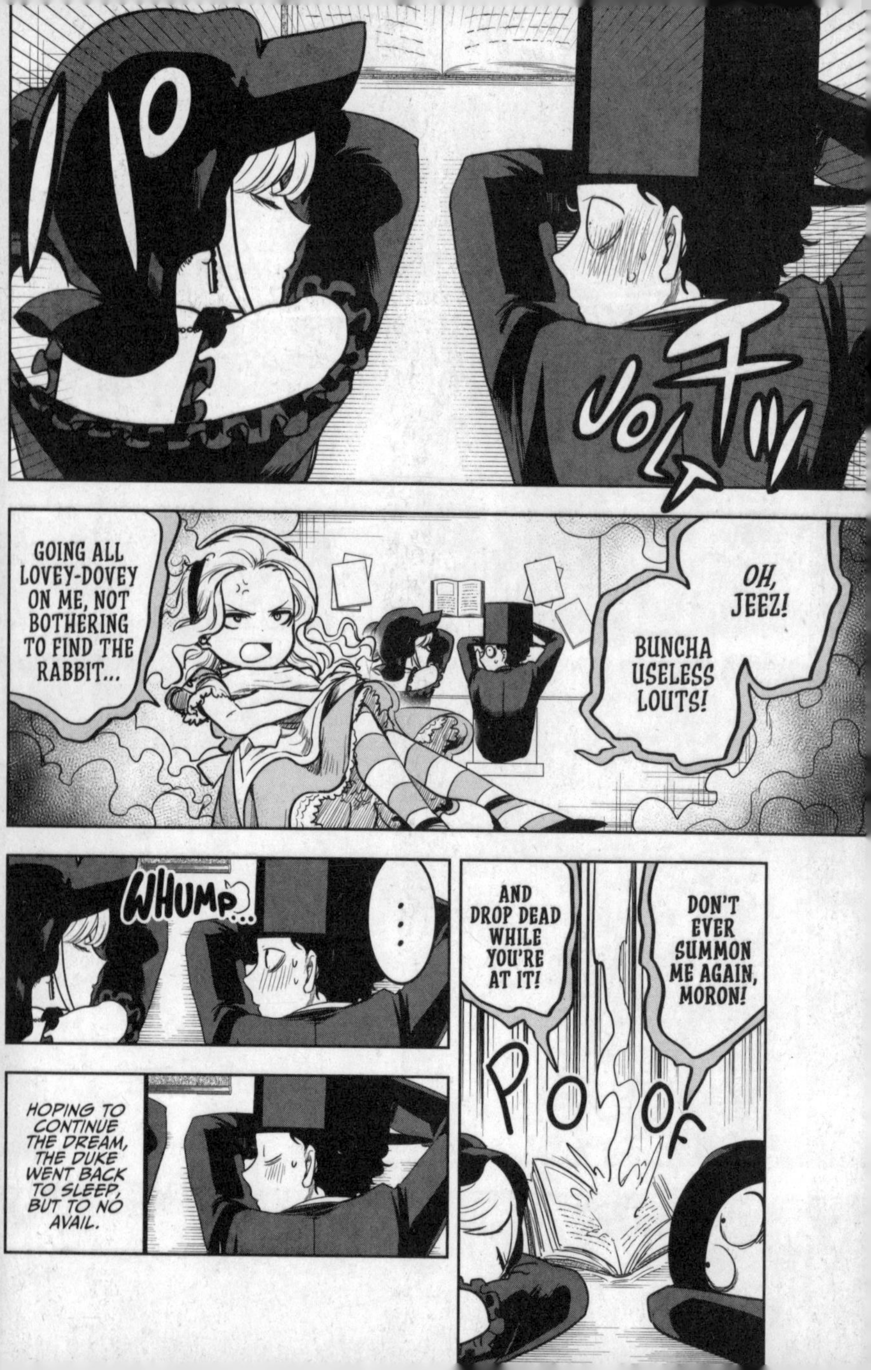
JOLT
OH, JEEZ!
BUNCHA USELESS LOUTS!
GOING ALL LOVEY-DOVEY ON ME, NOT BOTHERING TO FIND THE RABBIT...
DON'T EVER SUMMON ME AGAIN, MORON!
AND DROP DEAD WHILE YOU'RE AT IT!
POOF
...
WHUMP...
HOPING TO CONTINUE THE DREAM, THE DUKE WENT BACK TO SLEEP, BUT TO NO AVAIL.

THE DUKE OF DEATH AND HIS MAID

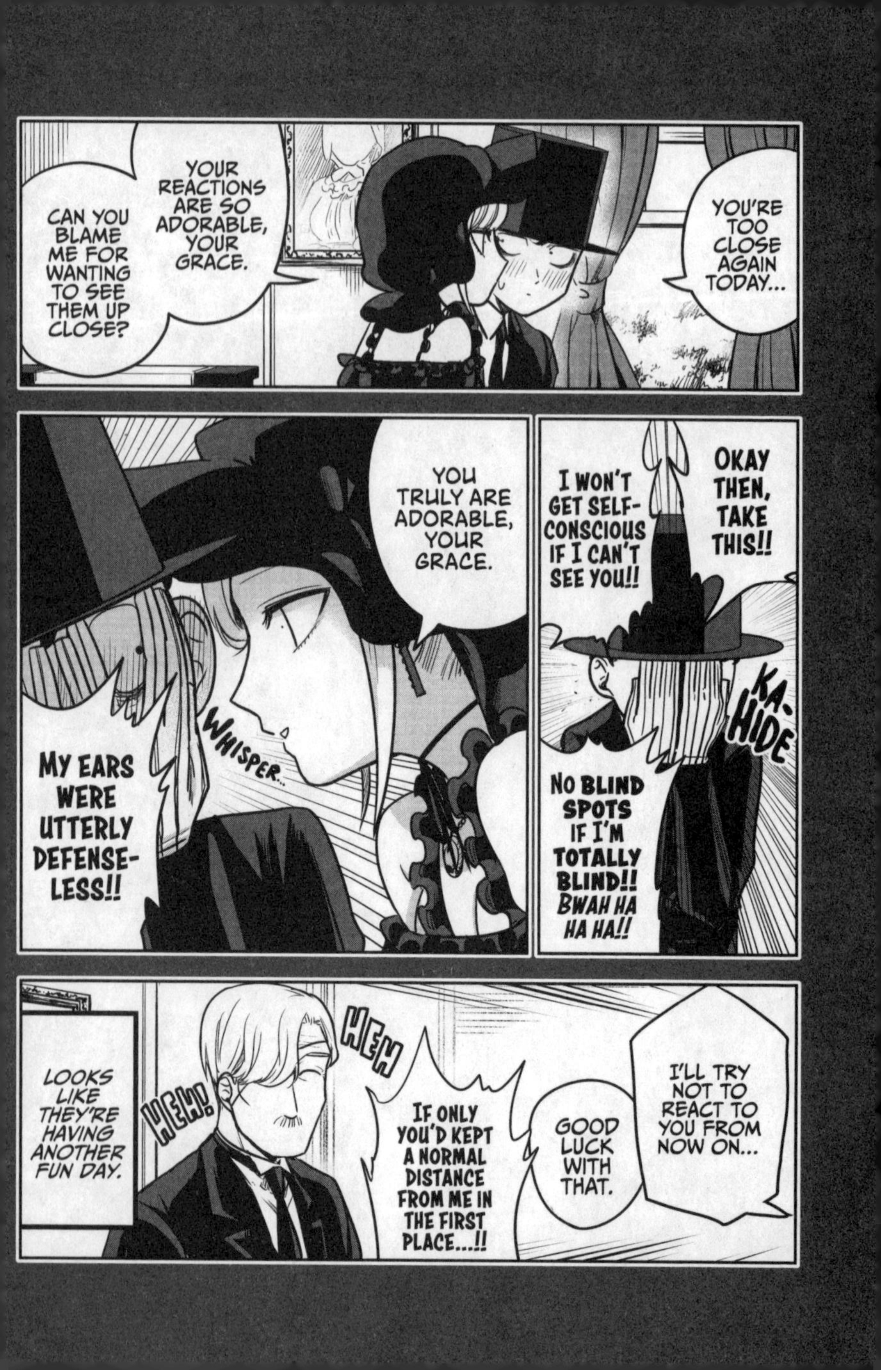
YOU'RE TOO CLOSE AGAIN TODAY...
YOUR REACTIONS ARE SO ADORABLE, YOUR GRACE.
CAN YOU BLAME ME FOR WANTING TO SEE THEM UP CLOSE?
OKAY THEN, TAKE THIS!!
I WON'T GET SELF-CONSCIOUS IF I CAN'T SEE YOU!!
KA-HIDE
NO BLIND SPOTS IF I'M TOTALLY BLIND!! BWAH HA HA HA!!
YOU TRULY ARE ADORABLE, YOUR GRACE.
WHISPER...
MY EARS WERE UTTERLY DEFENSE-LESS!!
I'LL TRY NOT TO REACT TO YOU FROM NOW ON...
GOOD LUCK WITH THAT.
IF ONLY YOU'D KEPT A NORMAL DISTANCE FROM ME IN THE FIRST PLACE...!!
HEH
HEH!
LOOKS LIKE THEY'RE HAVING ANOTHER FUN DAY.

Chapter 33: Bread

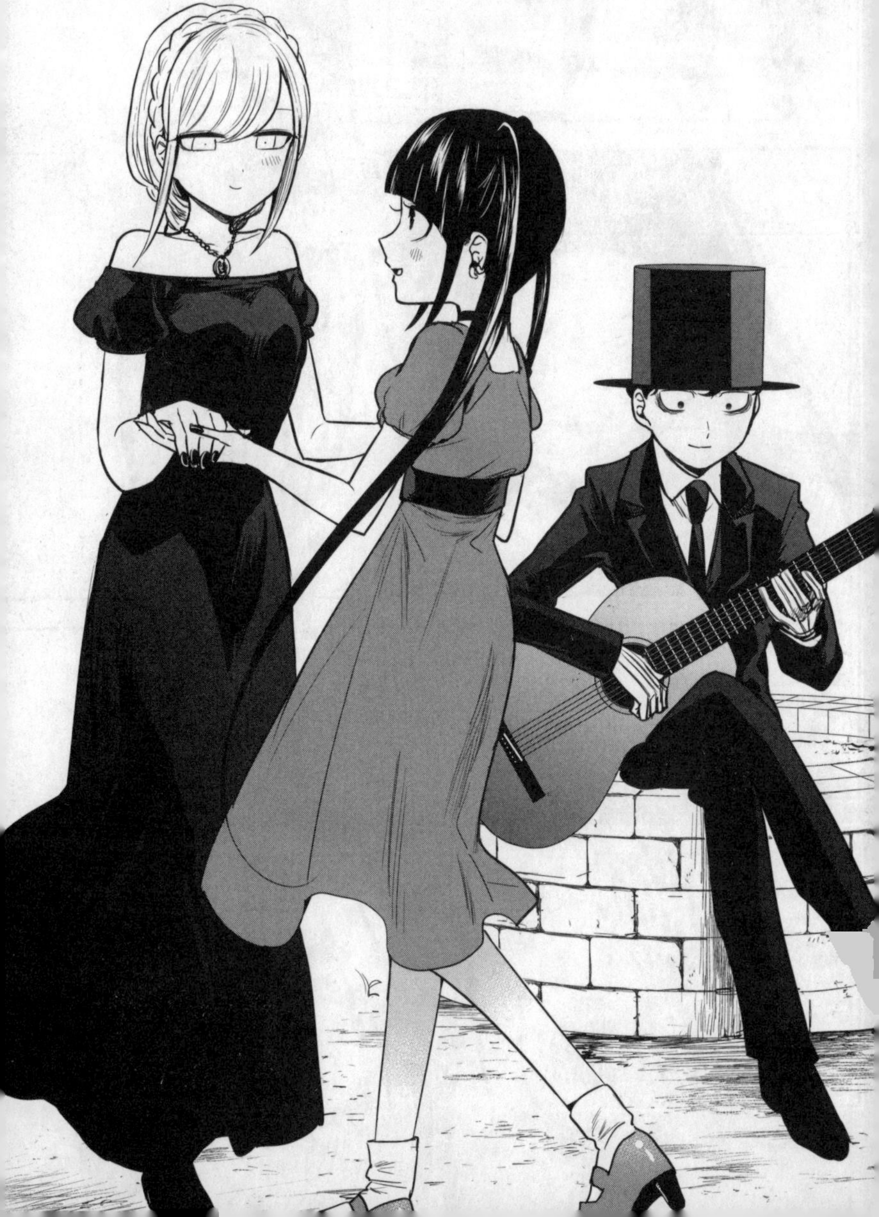

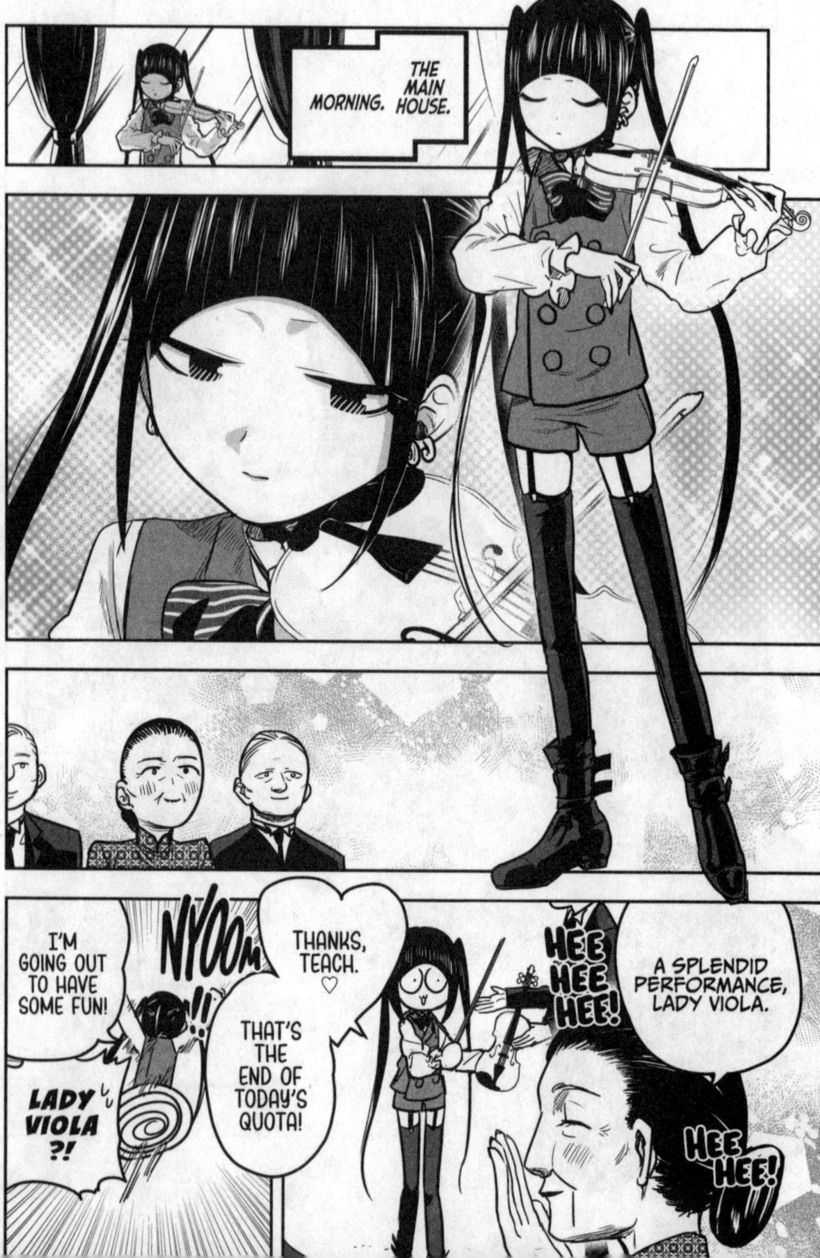
THE MAIN HOUSE.
MORNING.
A SPLENDID PERFORMANCE, LADY VIOLA.
HEE HEE HEE!
HEE HEE!
THANKS, TEACH. ♡
THAT'S THE END OF TODAY'S QUOTA!
NYOOM
!!
I'M GOING OUT TO HAVE SOME FUN!
LADY VIOLA ?!

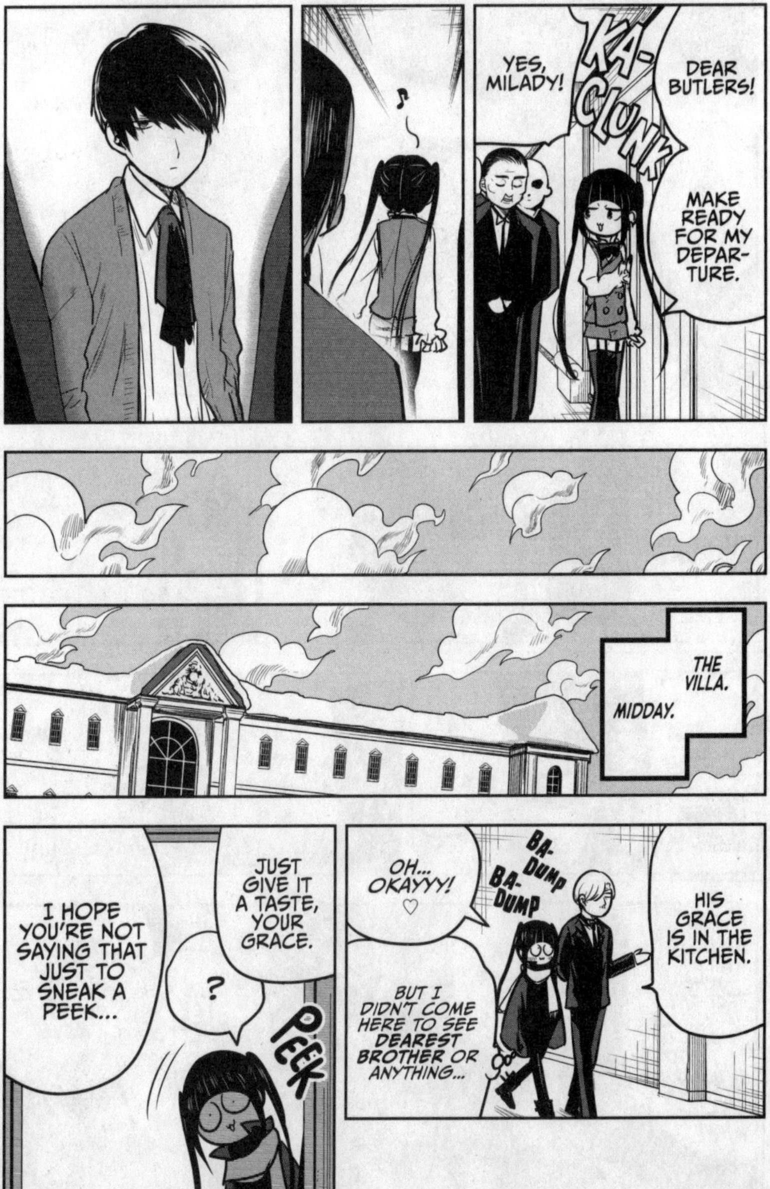
DEAR BUTLERS!
MAKE READY FOR MY DEPARTURE.
KA-CLUNK
YES, MILADY!
THE VILLA.
MIDDAY.
HIS GRACE IS IN THE KITCHEN.
BA-DUMP
BA-DUMP
OH... OKAYYY! ♡
BUT I DIDN'T COME HERE TO SEE DEAREST BROTHER OR ANYTHING...
JUST GIVE IT A TASTE, YOUR GRACE.
?
PEEK
I HOPE YOU'RE NOT SAYING THAT JUST TO SNEAK A PEEK...

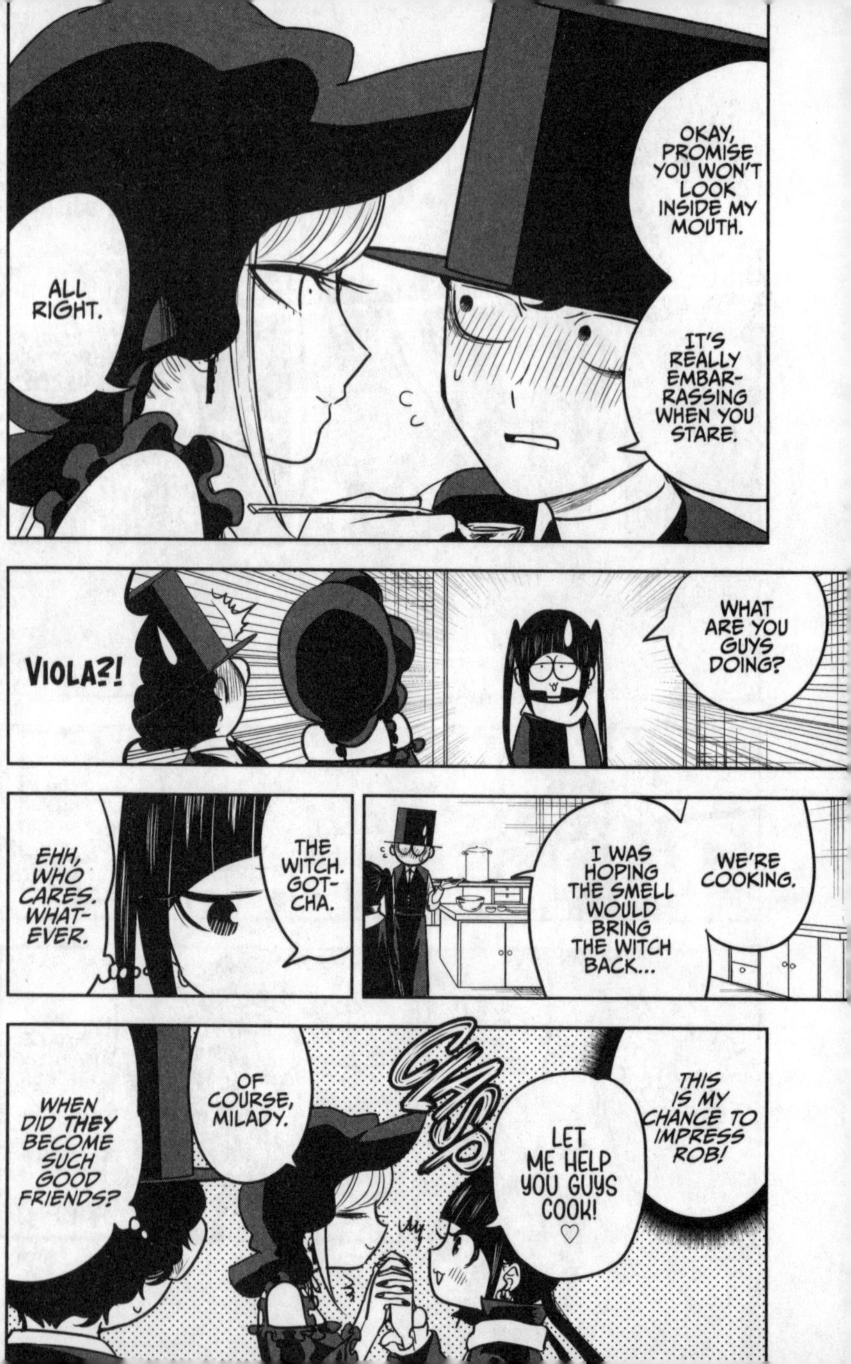
OKAY, PROMISE YOU WON'T LOOK INSIDE MY MOUTH.
IT'S REALLY EMBARRASSING WHEN YOU STARE.
ALL RIGHT.
WHAT ARE YOU GUYS DOING?
VIOLA?!
WE'RE COOKING.
I WAS HOPING THE SMELL WOULD BRING THE WITCH BACK...
THE WITCH. GOTCHA.
EHH, WHO CARES. WHATEVER.
THIS IS MY CHANCE TO IMPRESS ROB!
LET ME HELP YOU GUYS COOK! ♡
GASP
OF COURSE, MILADY.
WHEN DID THEY BECOME SUCH GOOD FRIENDS?

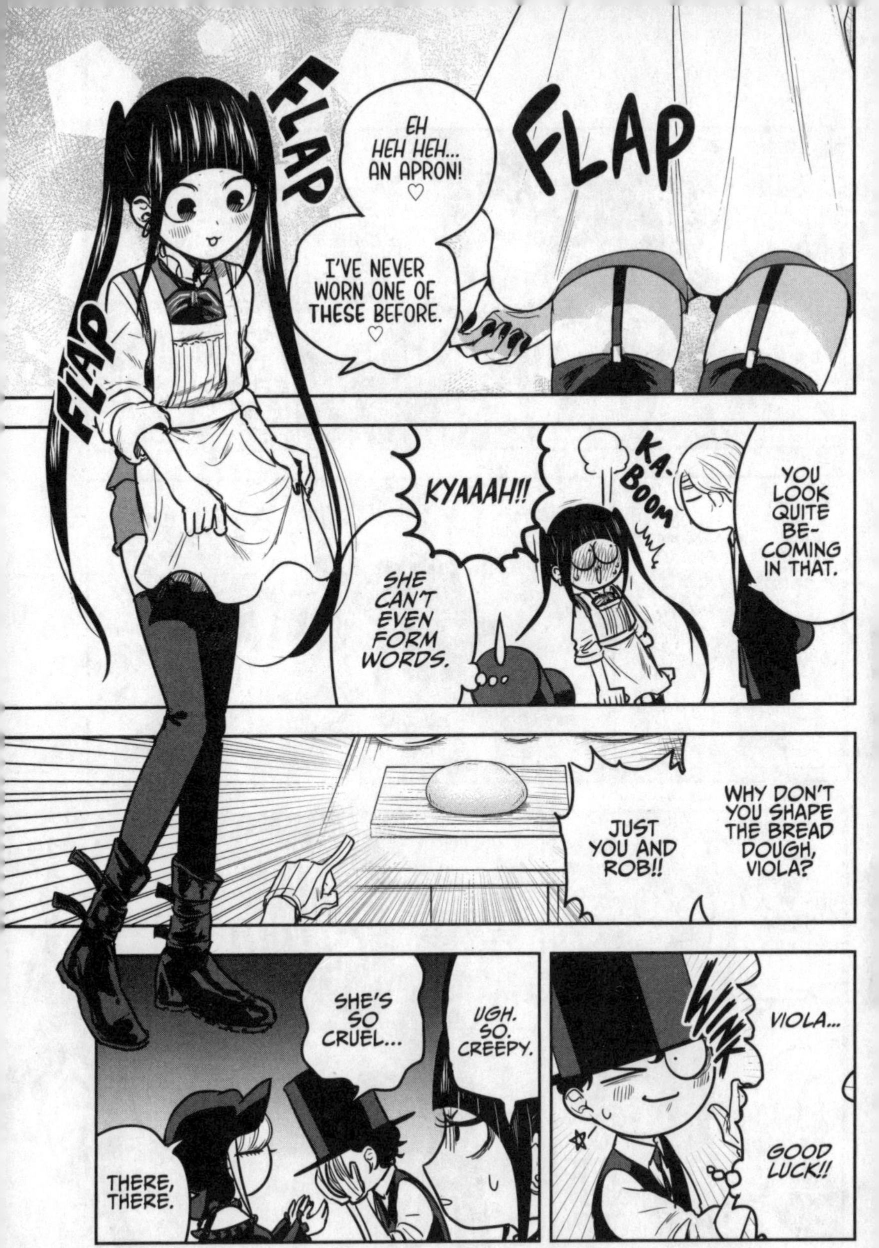
FLAP
EH HEH HEH... AN APRON! ♡
I'VE NEVER WORN ONE OF THESE BEFORE. ♡
FLAP
FLAP
FLAP
YOU LOOK QUITE BE-COMING IN THAT.
KA-BOOM
KYAAAH!!
SHE CAN'T EVEN FORM WORDS.
WHY DON'T YOU SHAPE THE BREAD DOUGH, VIOLA?
JUST YOU AND ROB!!
VIOLA...
WINK
GOOD LUCK!!
SHE'S SO CRUEL...
UGH. SO. CREEPY.
THERE, THERE.

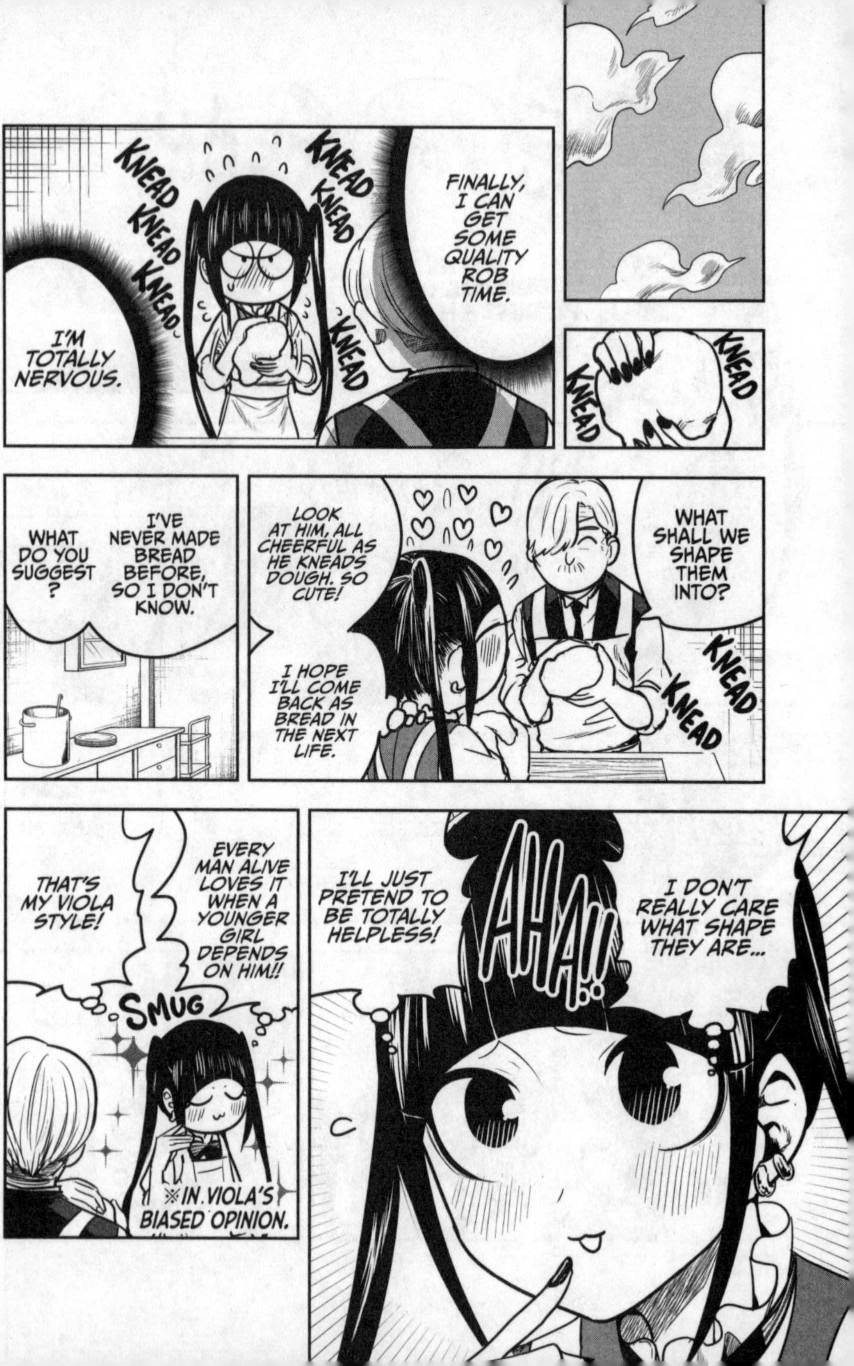
KNEAD
KNEAD
FINALLY, I CAN GET SOME QUALITY ROB TIME.
KNEAD KNEAD
KNEAD
KNEAD KNEAD KNEAD
I'M TOTALLY NERVOUS.
WHAT SHALL WE SHAPE THEM INTO?
KNEAD
KNEAD
LOOK AT HIM, ALL CHEERFUL AS HE KNEADS DOUGH. SO CUTE!
I HOPE I'LL COME BACK AS BREAD IN THE NEXT LIFE.
I'VE NEVER MADE BREAD BEFORE, SO I DON'T KNOW.
WHAT DO YOU SUGGEST?
I DON'T REALLY CARE WHAT SHAPE THEY ARE...
AHA!!
I'LL JUST PRETEND TO BE TOTALLY HELPLESS!
EVERY MAN ALIVE LOVES IT WHEN A YOUNGER GIRL DEPENDS ON HIM!!
THAT'S MY VIOLA STYLE!
SMUG
※IN VIOLA'S BIASED OPINION.

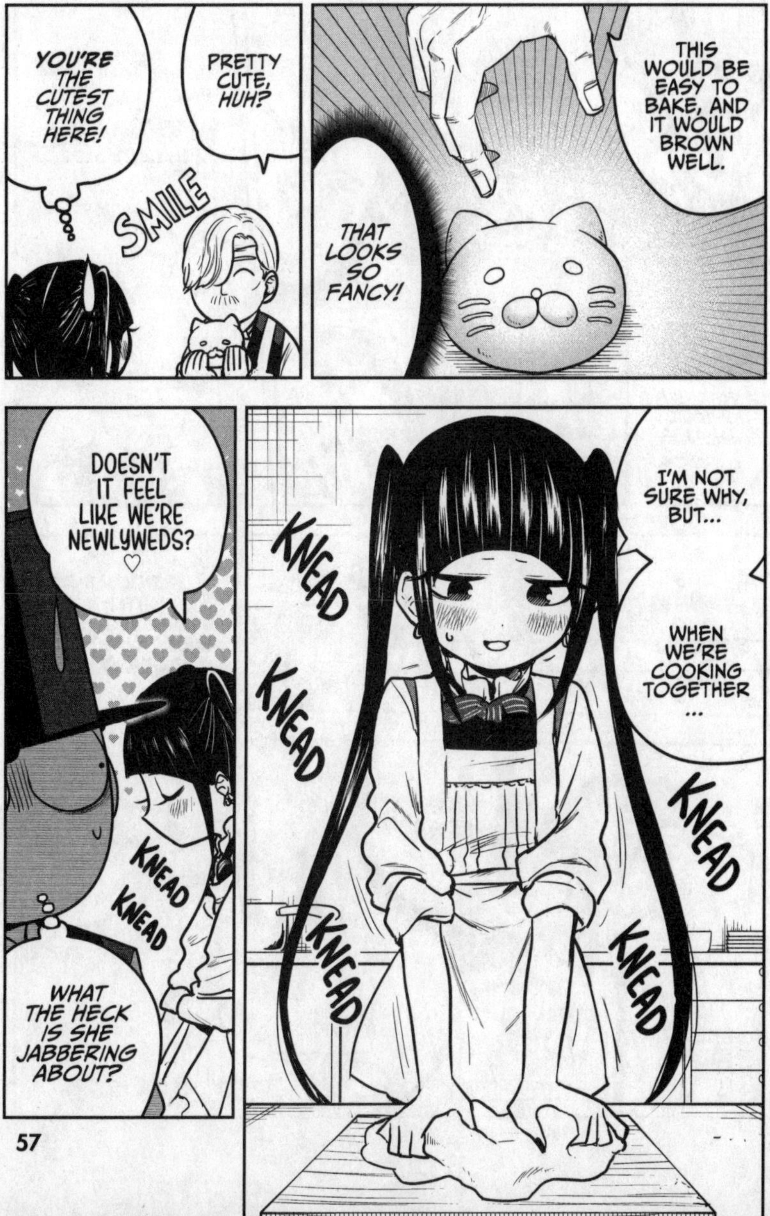
THIS WOULD BE EASY TO BAKE, AND IT WOULD BROWN WELL.
THAT LOOKS SO FANCY!
PRETTY CUTE, HUH?
SMILE
YOU'RE THE CUTEST THING HERE!
I'M NOT SURE WHY, BUT...
WHEN WE'RE COOKING TOGETHER ...
KNEAD
KNEAD
KNEAD
KNEAD
DOESN'T IT FEEL LIKE WE'RE NEWLYWEDS? ♡
KNEAD
KNEAD
WHAT THE HECK IS SHE JABBERING ABOUT?

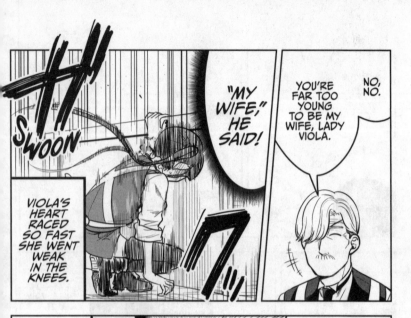

NO, NO.
YOU'RE FAR TOO YOUNG TO BE MY WIFE, LADY VIOLA.
"MY WIFE," HE SAID!
SWOON
VIOLA'S HEART RACED SO FAST SHE WENT WEAK IN THE KNEES.
IF I WEREN'T A BUTLER, I MIGHT HAVE A GRANDDAUGHTER YOUR AGE.
BA-DUMP
"GRAND-DAUGH-TER," HE SAID!
HER HEART'S RACING AT BASICALLY EVERYTHING.
AREN'T YOU GOING TO MAKE THAT BREAD?
"BREAD," HE SAID!
U-UH...
BREAD! RIGHT!

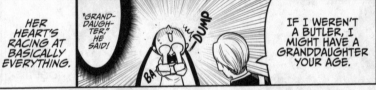

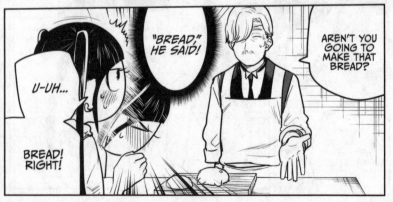

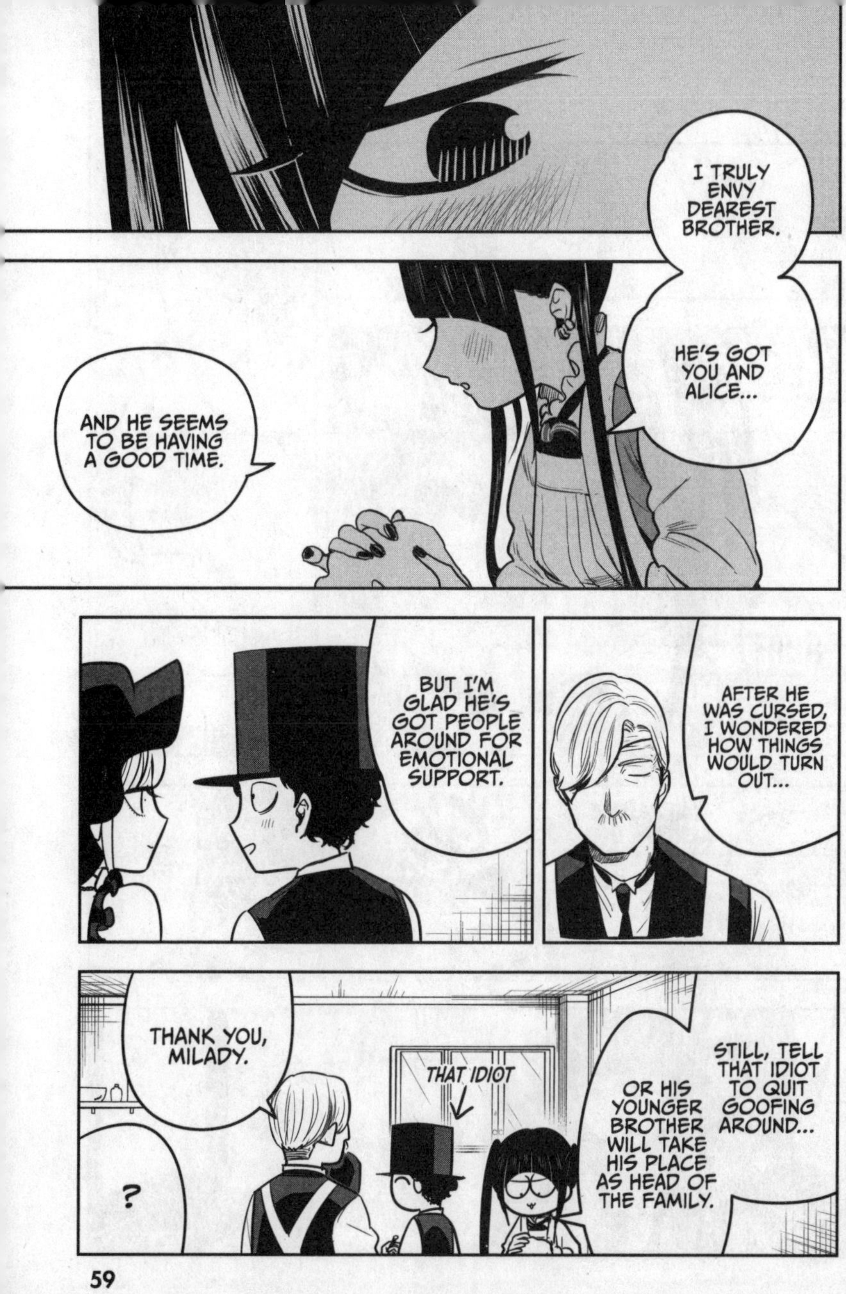
I TRULY ENVY DEAREST BROTHER.
HE'S GOT YOU AND ALICE...
AND HE SEEMS TO BE HAVING A GOOD TIME.
AFTER HE WAS CURSED, I WONDERED HOW THINGS WOULD TURN OUT...
BUT I'M GLAD HE'S GOT PEOPLE AROUND FOR EMOTIONAL SUPPORT.
STILL, TELL THAT IDIOT TO QUIT GOOFING AROUND...
OR HIS YOUNGER BROTHER WILL TAKE HIS PLACE AS HEAD OF THE FAMILY.
THAT IDIOT
THANK YOU, MILADY.
?

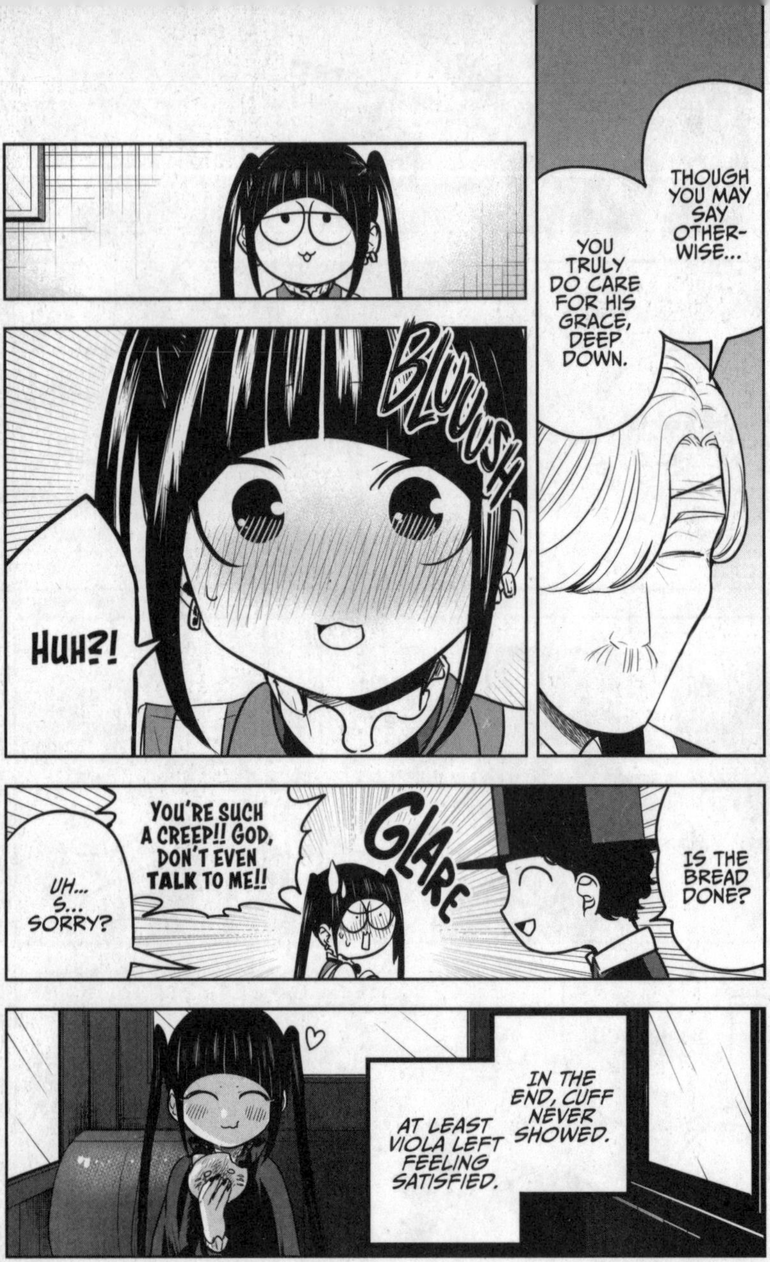
THOUGH YOU MAY SAY OTHER-WISE...
YOU TRULY DO CARE FOR HIS GRACE, DEEP DOWN.
BLUUSH
HUH?!
IS THE BREAD DONE?
GLARE
YOU'RE SUCH A CREEP!! GOD, DON'T EVEN TALK TO ME!!
UH... S... SORRY?
IN THE END, CUFF NEVER SHOWED.
AT LEAST VIOLA LEFT FEELING SATISFIED.

The Duke of Death and His Maid

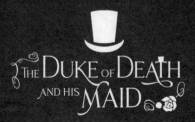

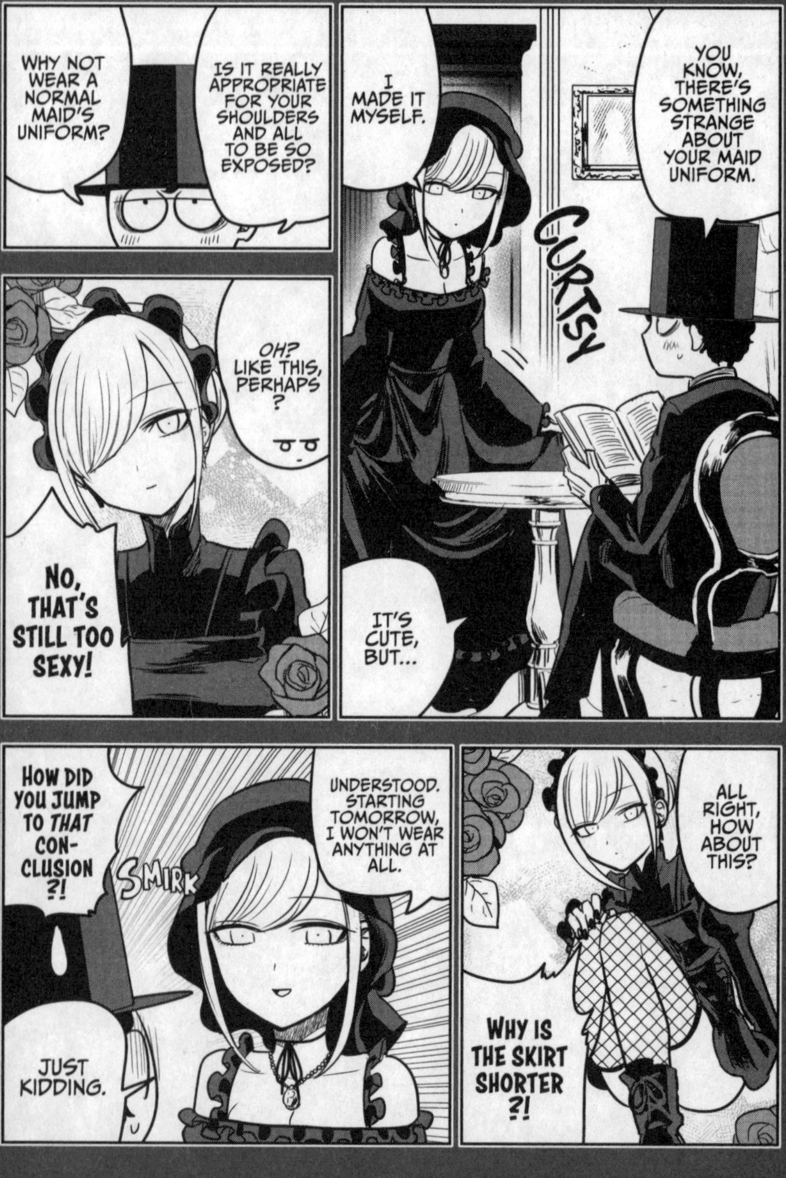
YOU KNOW, THERE'S SOMETHING STRANGE ABOUT YOUR MAID UNIFORM.
CURTSY
I MADE IT MYSELF.
IT'S CUTE, BUT...
IS IT REALLY APPROPRIATE FOR YOUR SHOULDERS AND ALL TO BE SO EXPOSED?
WHY NOT WEAR A NORMAL MAID'S UNIFORM?
OH? LIKE THIS, PERHAPS?
NO, THAT'S STILL TOO SEXY!
ALL RIGHT, HOW ABOUT THIS?
WHY IS THE SKIRT SHORTER?!
UNDERSTOOD. STARTING TOMORROW, I WON'T WEAR ANYTHING AT ALL.
SMIRK
HOW DID YOU JUMP TO *THAT* CON-CLUSION?!
JUST KIDDING.

Chapter 34: Ice Skating

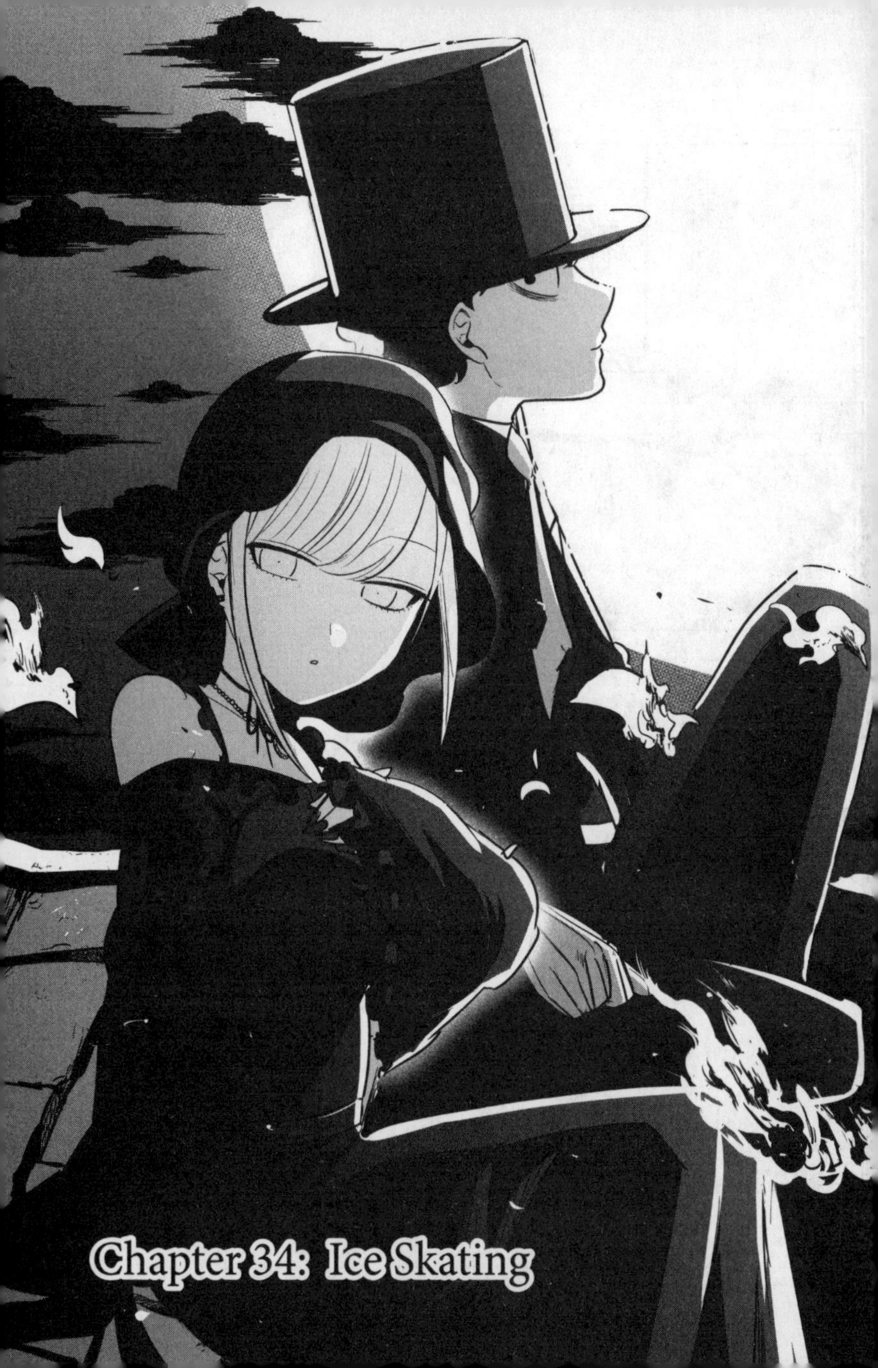

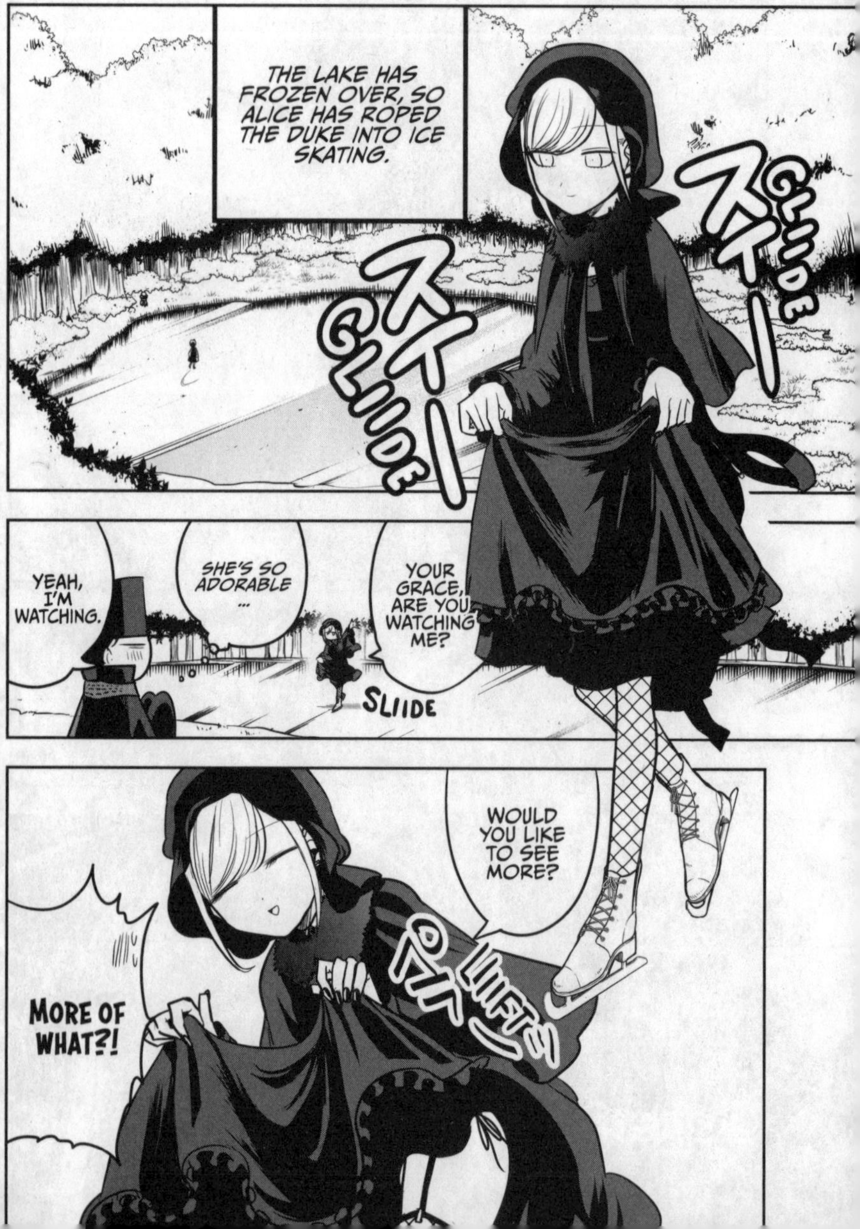
GLIIDE
THE LAKE HAS FROZEN OVER, SO ALICE HAS ROPED THE DUKE INTO ICE SKATING.
GLIIDE
YOUR GRACE, ARE YOU WATCHING ME?
SLIIDE
SHE'S SO ADORABLE ...
YEAH, I'M WATCHING.
WOULD YOU LIKE TO SEE MORE?
LIIFT
MORE OF WHAT?!

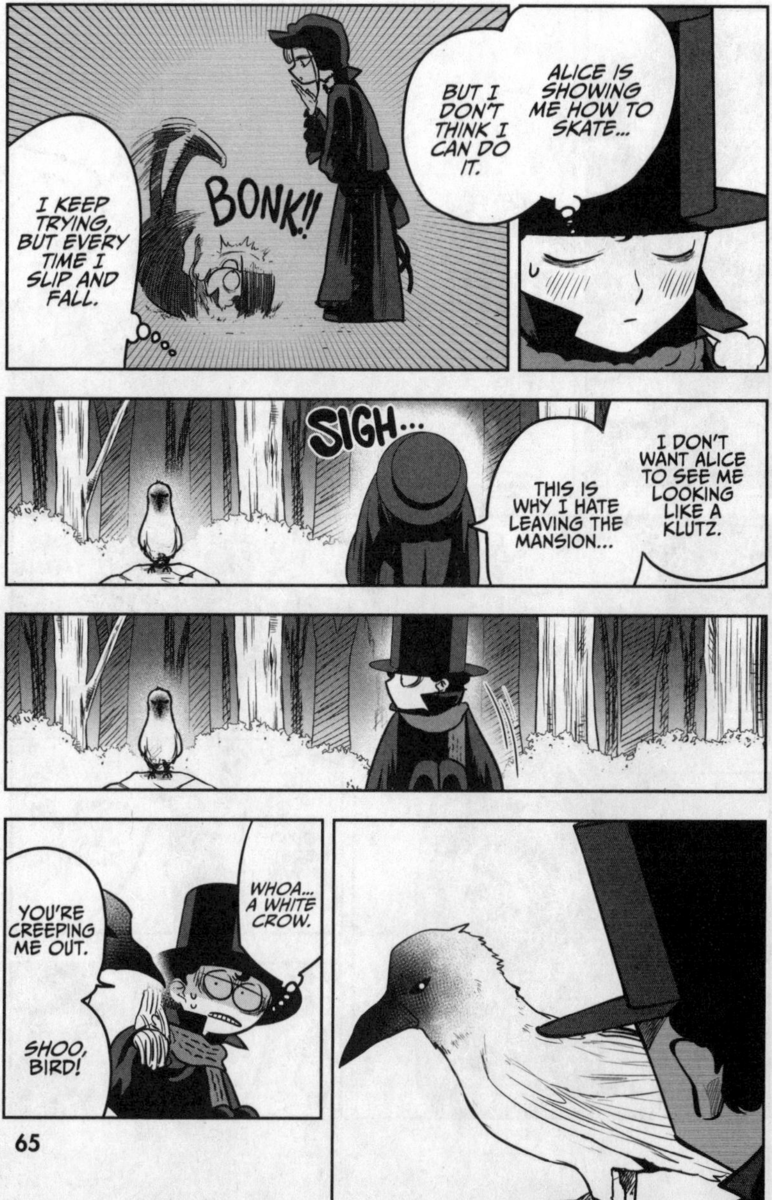
ALICE IS SHOWING ME HOW TO SKATE...
BUT I DON'T THINK I CAN DO IT.
BONK!!
I KEEP TRYING, BUT EVERY TIME I SLIP AND FALL.
I DON'T WANT ALICE TO SEE ME LOOKING LIKE A KLUTZ.
THIS IS WHY I HATE LEAVING THE MANSION...
SIGH...
WHOA... A WHITE CROW.
YOU'RE CREEPING ME OUT.
SHOO, BIRD!

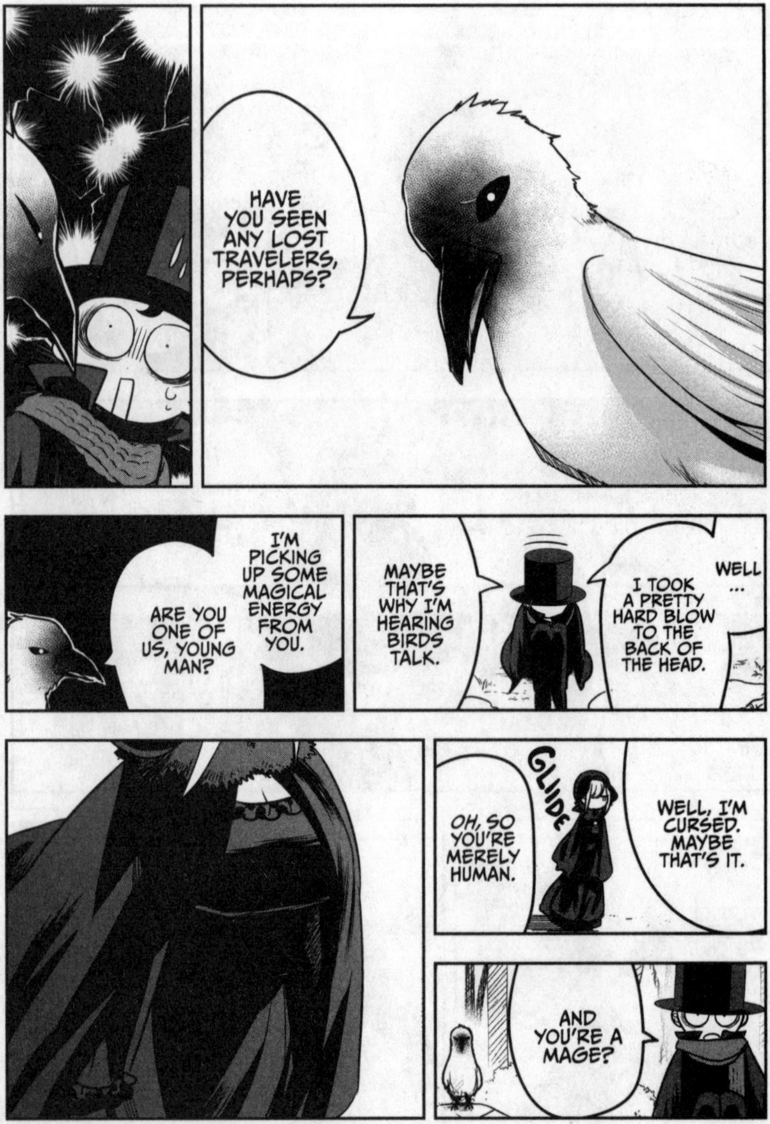
HAVE YOU SEEN ANY LOST TRAVELERS, PERHAPS?
WELL ...
I TOOK A PRETTY HARD BLOW TO THE BACK OF THE HEAD.
MAYBE THAT'S WHY I'M HEARING BIRDS TALK.
I'M PICKING UP SOME MAGICAL ENERGY FROM YOU.
ARE YOU ONE OF US, YOUNG MAN?
WELL, I'M CURSED. MAYBE THAT'S IT.
GLIDE
OH, SO YOU'RE MERELY HUMAN.
AND YOU'RE A MAGE?

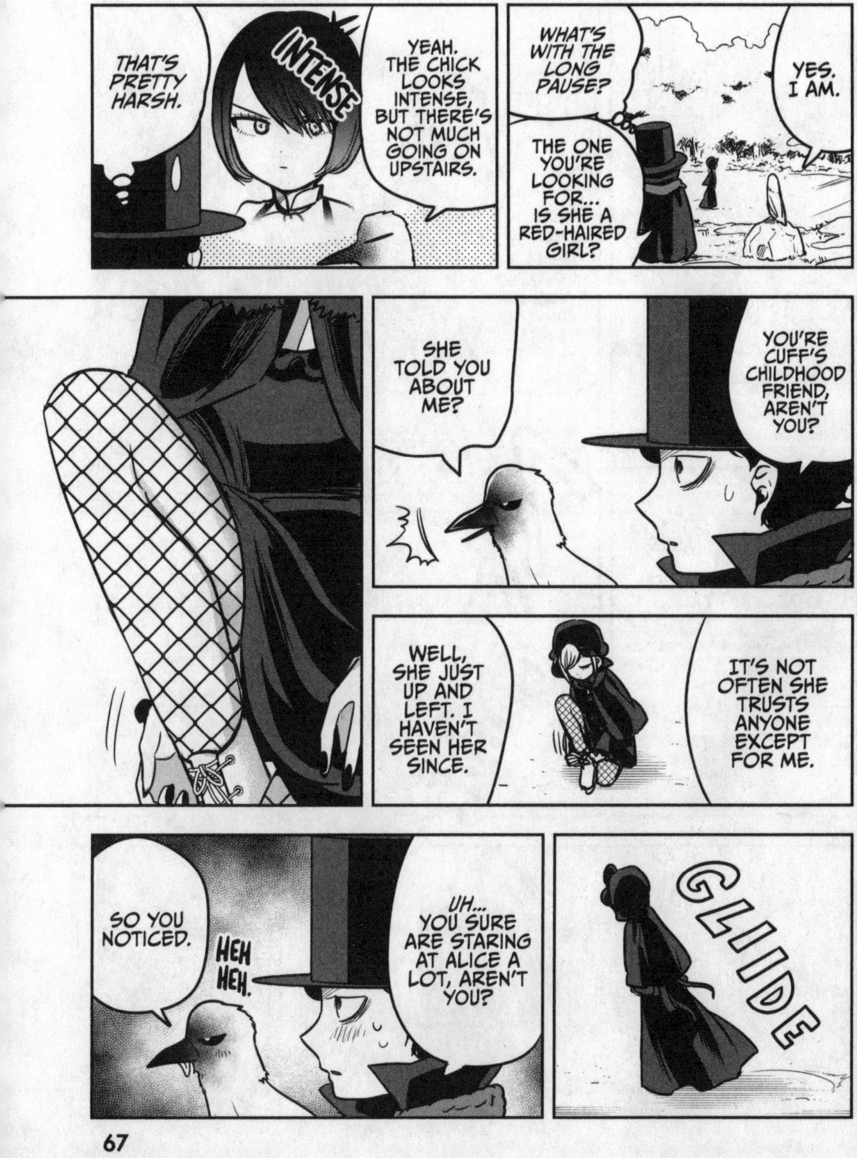
YES. I AM.
WHAT'S WITH THE LONG PAUSE?
THE ONE YOU'RE LOOKING FOR... IS SHE A RED-HAIRED GIRL?
YEAH. THE CHICK LOOKS INTENSE, BUT THERE'S NOT MUCH GOING ON UPSTAIRS.
INTENSE
THAT'S PRETTY HARSH.
YOU'RE CUFF'S CHILDHOOD FRIEND, AREN'T YOU?
SHE TOLD YOU ABOUT ME?
IT'S NOT OFTEN SHE TRUSTS ANYONE EXCEPT FOR ME.
WELL, SHE JUST UP AND LEFT. I HAVEN'T SEEN HER SINCE.
GLIDE
UH... YOU SURE ARE STARING AT ALICE A LOT, AREN'T YOU?
HEH HEH.
SO YOU NOTICED.

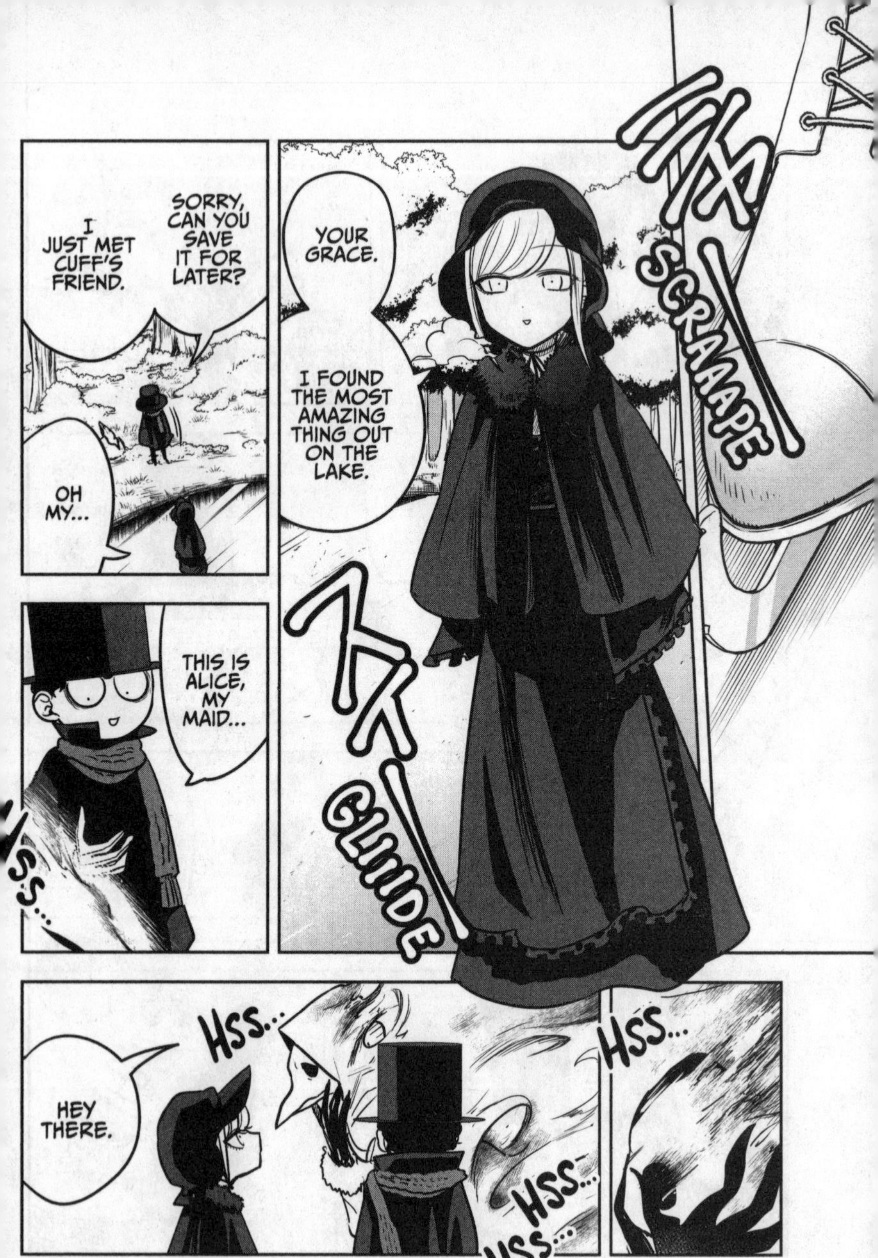
SCRAAAPE
YOUR GRACE.
I FOUND THE MOST AMAZING THING OUT ON THE LAKE.
GLIDE
SORRY, CAN YOU SAVE IT FOR LATER?
I JUST MET CUFF'S FRIEND.
OH MY...
THIS IS ALICE, MY MAID...
HSS...
HSS...
HSS...
HEY THERE.
HSS...
HSS...

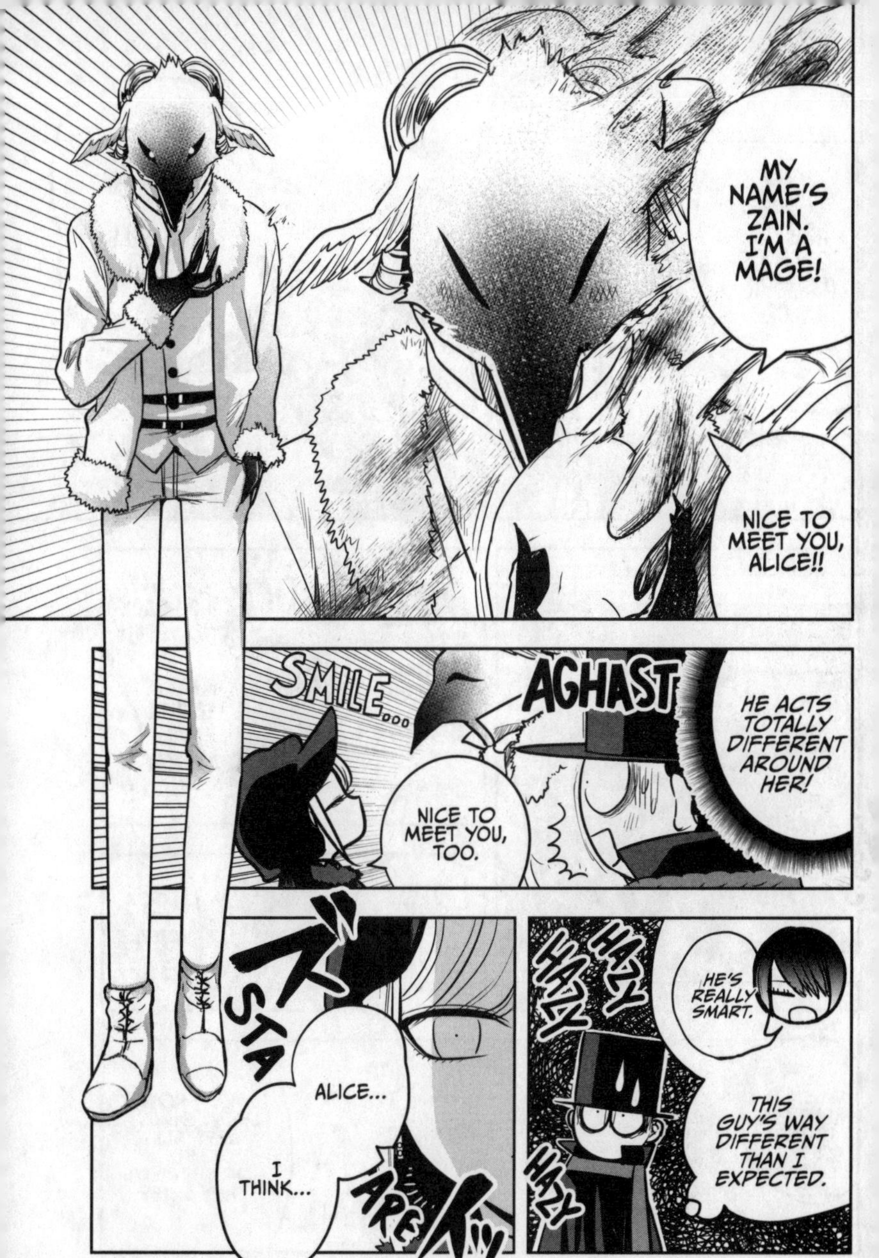
MY NAME'S ZAIN. I'M A MAGE!
NICE TO MEET YOU, ALICE!!
AGHAST
HE ACTS TOTALLY DIFFERENT AROUND HER!
SMILE...
NICE TO MEET YOU, TOO.
HAZY HAZY
HE'S REALLY SMART.
THIS GUY'S WAY DIFFERENT THAN I EXPECTED.
HAZY
STA
ALICE...
I THINK...
ARE

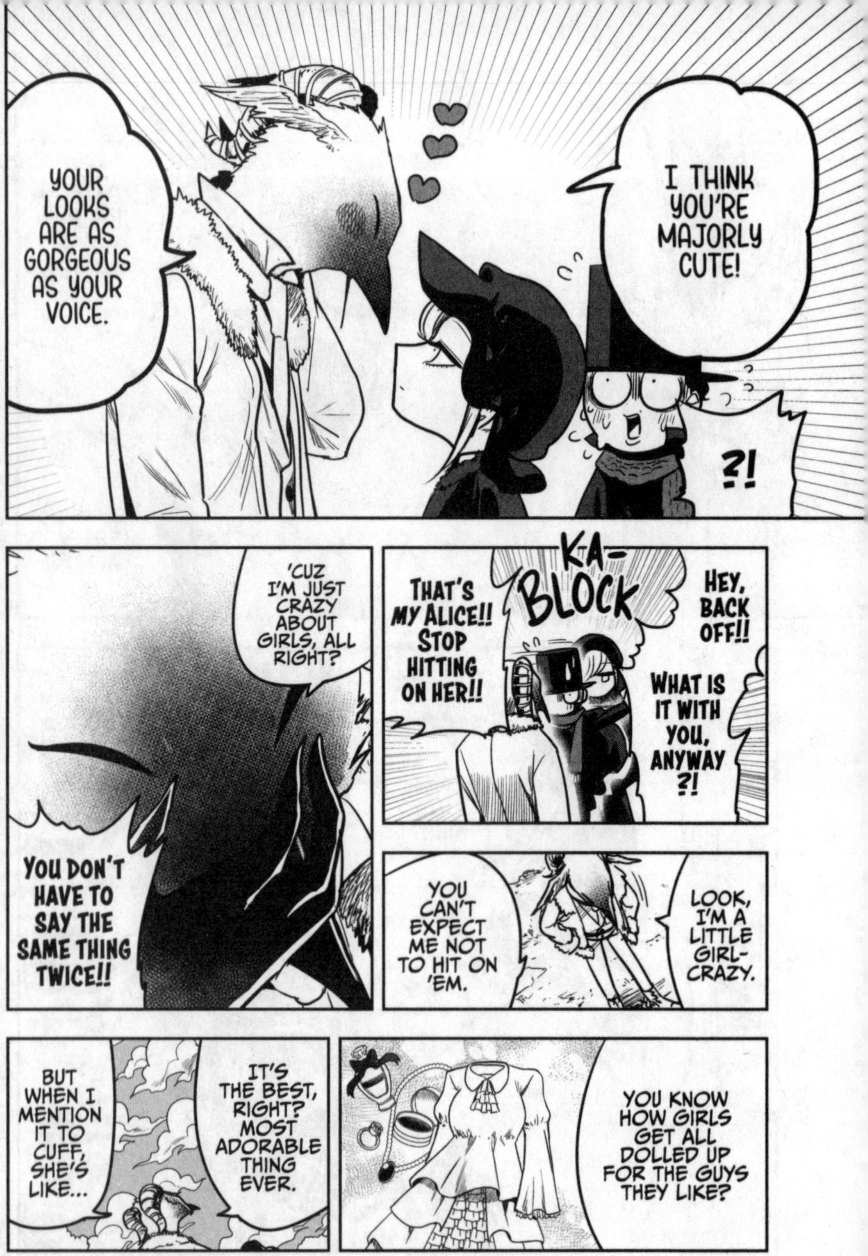
I THINK YOU'RE MAJORLY CUTE!
YOUR LOOKS ARE AS GORGEOUS AS YOUR VOICE.
?!
KA-BLOCK
HEY, BACK OFF!!
WHAT IS IT WITH YOU, ANYWAY?!
THAT'S MY ALICE!! STOP HITTING ON HER!!
LOOK, I'M A LITTLE GIRL-CRAZY.
YOU CAN'T EXPECT ME NOT TO HIT ON 'EM.
'CUZ I'M JUST CRAZY ABOUT GIRLS, ALL RIGHT?
YOU DON'T HAVE TO SAY THE SAME THING TWICE!!
YOU KNOW HOW GIRLS GET ALL DOLLED UP FOR THE GUYS THEY LIKE?
IT'S THE BEST, RIGHT? MOST ADORABLE THING EVER.
BUT WHEN I MENTION IT TO CUFF, SHE'S LIKE...

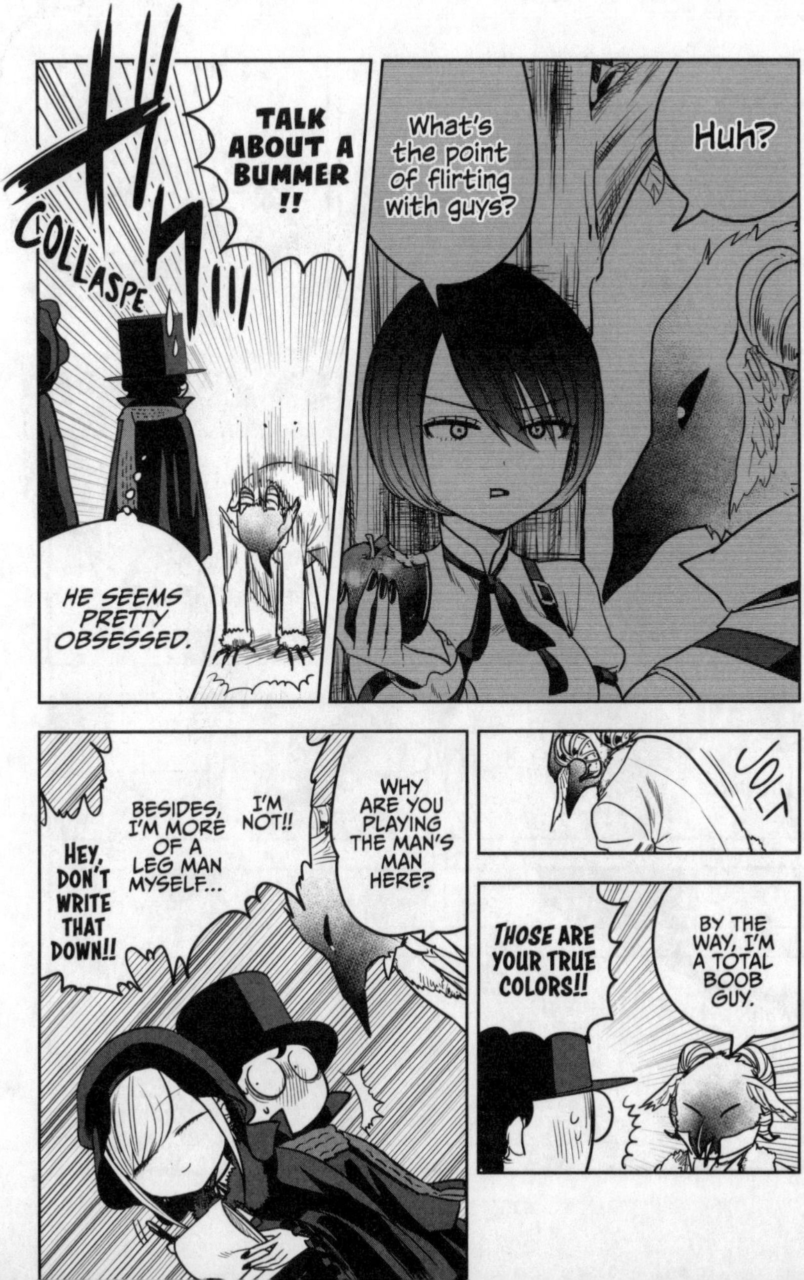
Huh?
What's the point of flirting with guys?
TALK ABOUT A BUMMER !!
COLLASPE
HE SEEMS PRETTY OBSESSED.
JOLT
BY THE WAY, I'M A TOTAL BOOB GUY.
THOSE ARE YOUR TRUE COLORS!!
WHY ARE YOU PLAYING THE MAN'S MAN HERE?
I'M NOT!!
BESIDES, I'M MORE OF A LEG MAN MYSELF...
HEY, DON'T WRITE THAT DOWN!!

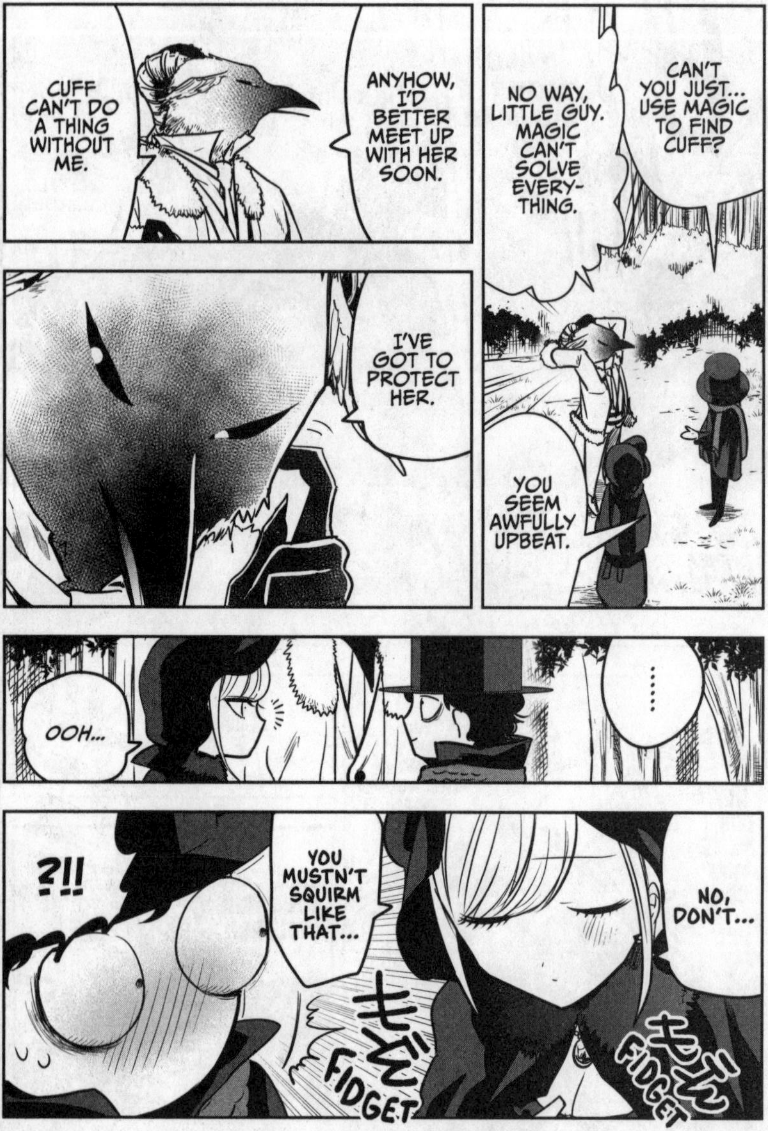
CAN'T YOU JUST... USE MAGIC TO FIND CUFF?
NO WAY, LITTLE GUY. MAGIC CAN'T SOLVE EVERY-THING.
YOU SEEM AWFULLY UPBEAT.
ANYHOW, I'D BETTER MEET UP WITH HER SOON.
CUFF CAN'T DO A THING WITHOUT ME.
I'VE GOT TO PROTECT HER.
......
OOH...
NO, DON'T...
もぞ FIDGET
YOU MUSTN'T SQUIRM LIKE THAT...
もぞ FIDGET
?!!

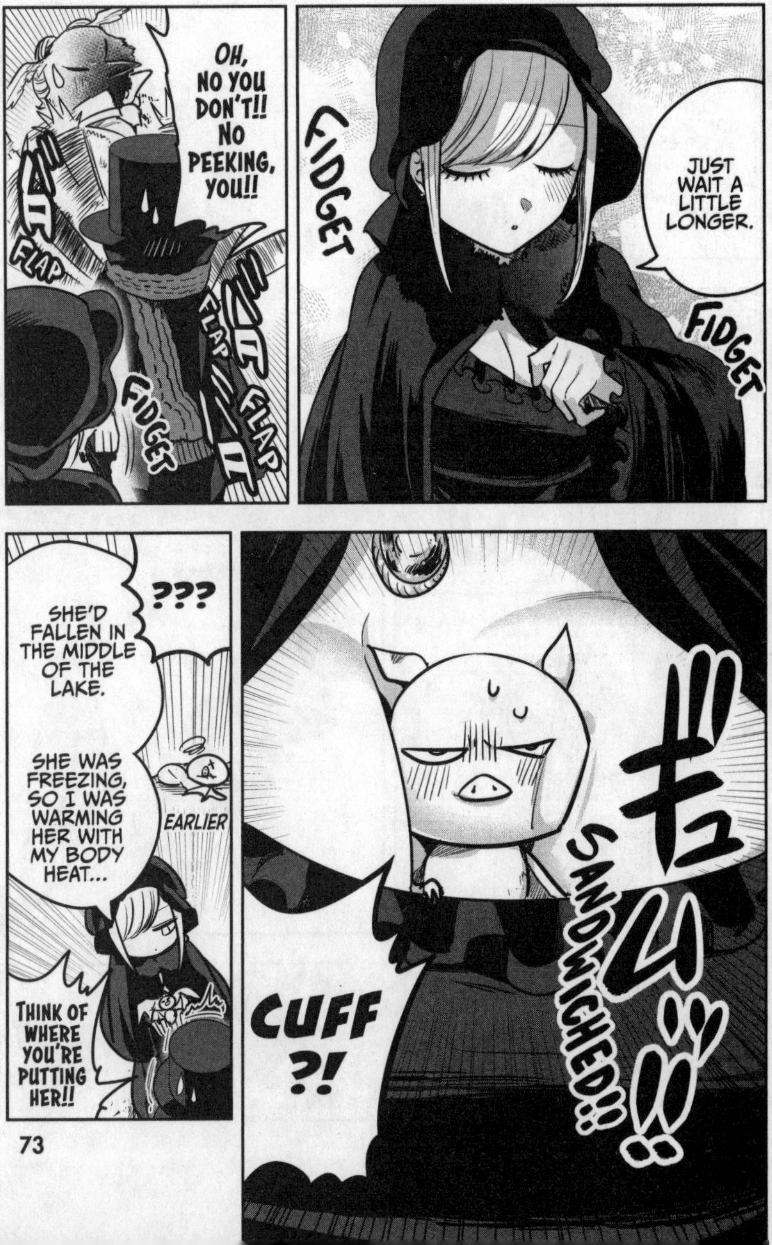
JUST WAIT A LITTLE LONGER.
FIDGET
FIDGET
OH, NO YOU DON'T!! NO PEEKING, YOU!!
FLAP
FLAP
FLAP
FLAP
FIDGET
ギュムッ!!
SANDWICHED!!
CUFF ?!
???
SHE'D FALLEN IN THE MIDDLE OF THE LAKE.
SHE WAS FREEZING, SO I WAS WARMING HER WITH MY BODY HEAT...
EARLIER
THINK OF WHERE YOU'RE PUTTING HER!!

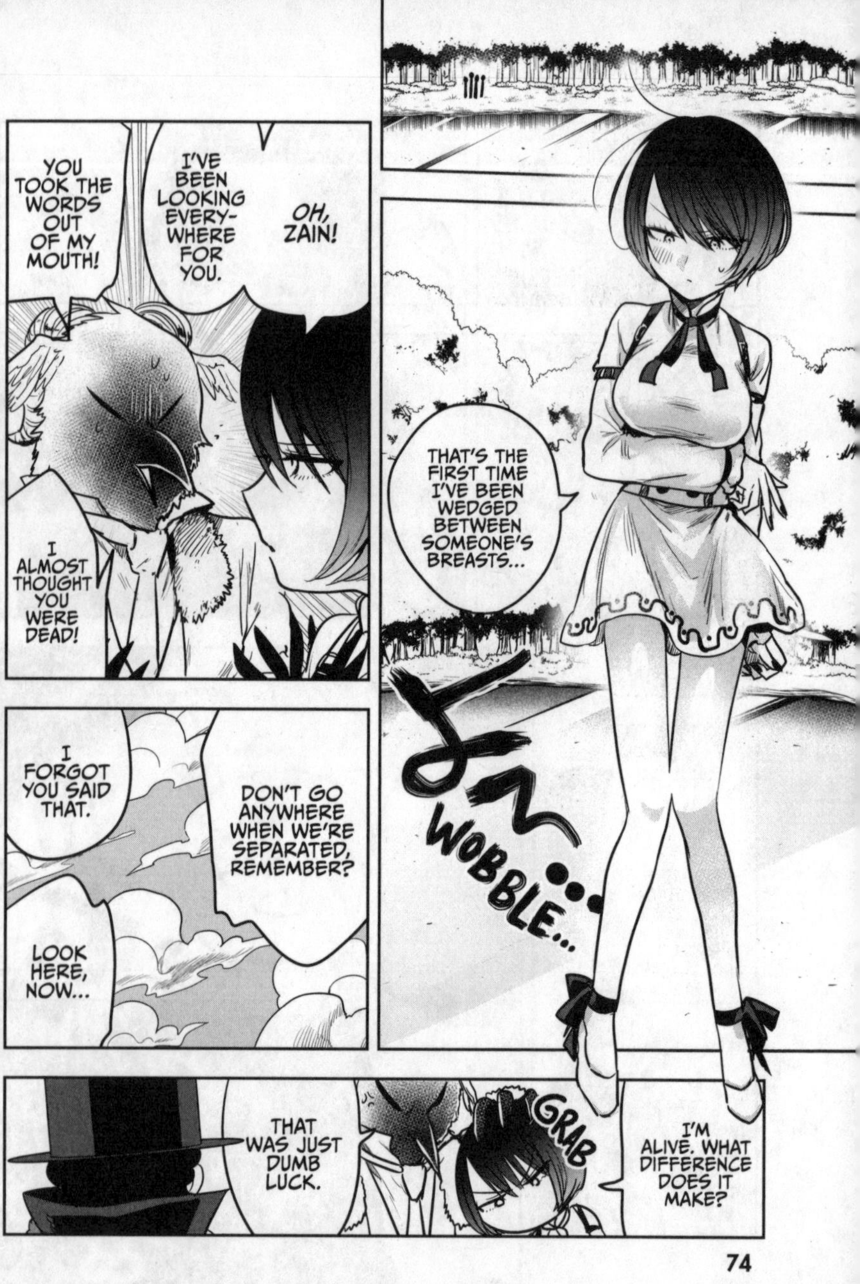
THAT'S THE FIRST TIME I'VE BEEN WEDGED BETWEEN SOMEONE'S BREASTS...
WOBBLE...
OH, ZAIN!
I'VE BEEN LOOKING EVERY-WHERE FOR YOU.
YOU TOOK THE WORDS OUT OF MY MOUTH!
I ALMOST THOUGHT YOU WERE DEAD!
DON'T GO ANYWHERE WHEN WE'RE SEPARATED, REMEMBER?
I FORGOT YOU SAID THAT.
LOOK HERE, NOW...
I'M ALIVE. WHAT DIFFERENCE DOES IT MAKE?
GRAB
THAT WAS JUST DUMB LUCK.

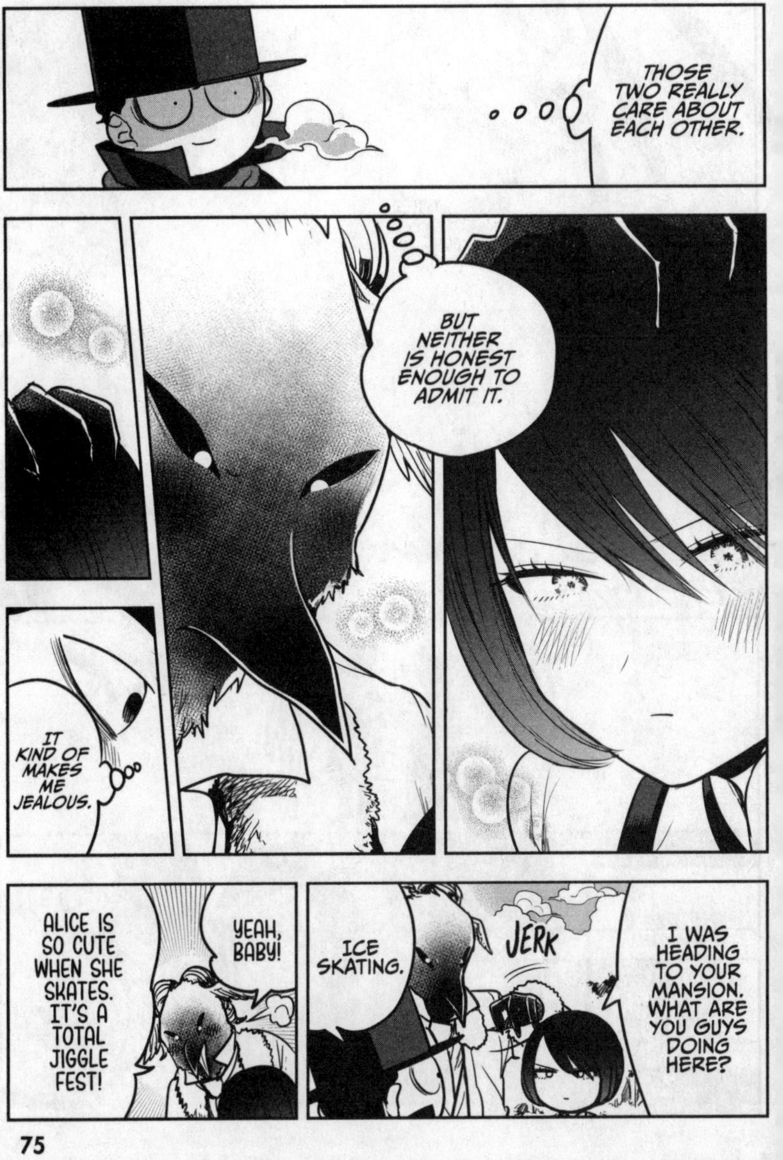
...
THOSE TWO REALLY CARE ABOUT EACH OTHER.
BUT NEITHER IS HONEST ENOUGH TO ADMIT IT.
IT KIND OF MAKES ME JEALOUS.
I WAS HEADING TO YOUR MANSION. WHAT ARE YOU GUYS DOING HERE?
JERK
ICE SKATING.
YEAH, BABY!
ALICE IS SO CUTE WHEN SHE SKATES. IT'S A TOTAL JIGGLE FEST!

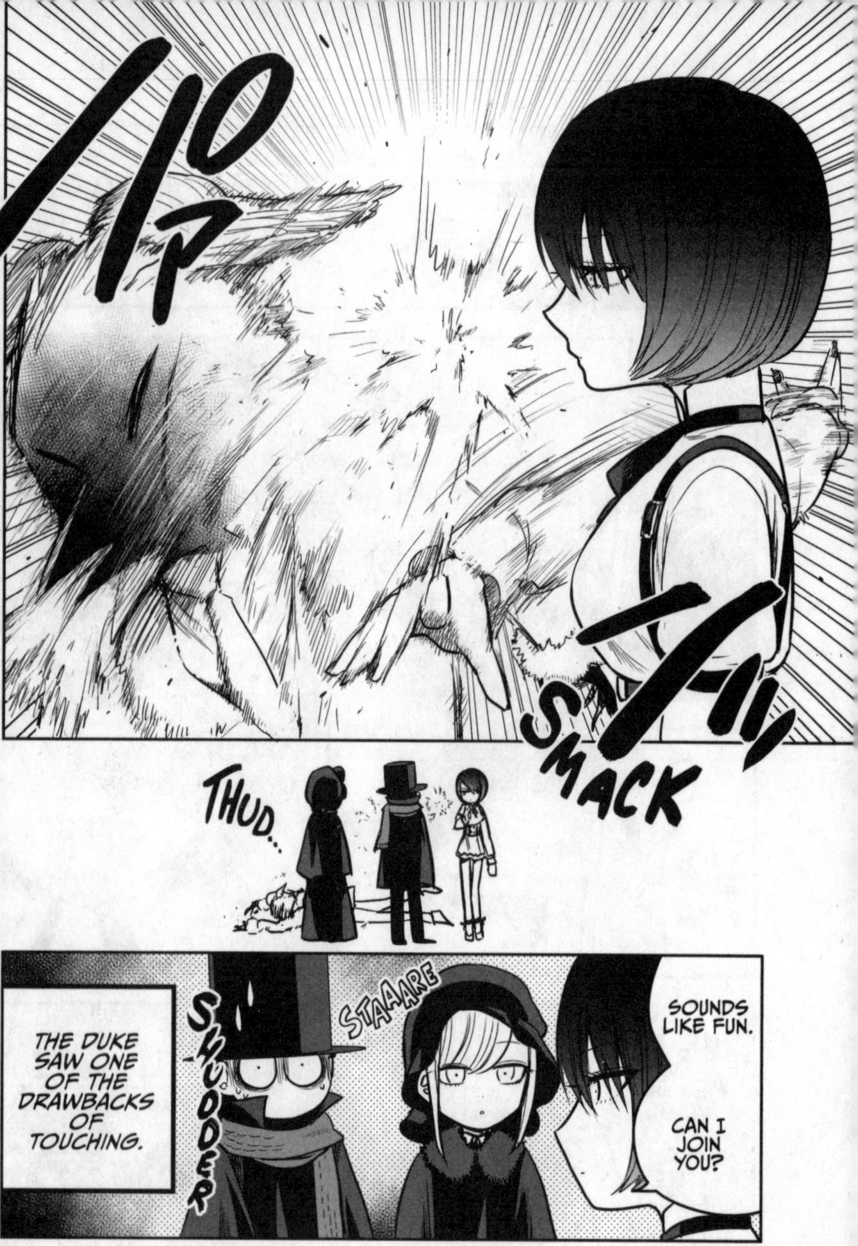
SMACK
THUD...
SOUNDS LIKE FUN.
CAN I JOIN YOU?
STAAARE
SHUDDER
THE DUKE SAW ONE OF THE DRAWBACKS OF TOUCHING.

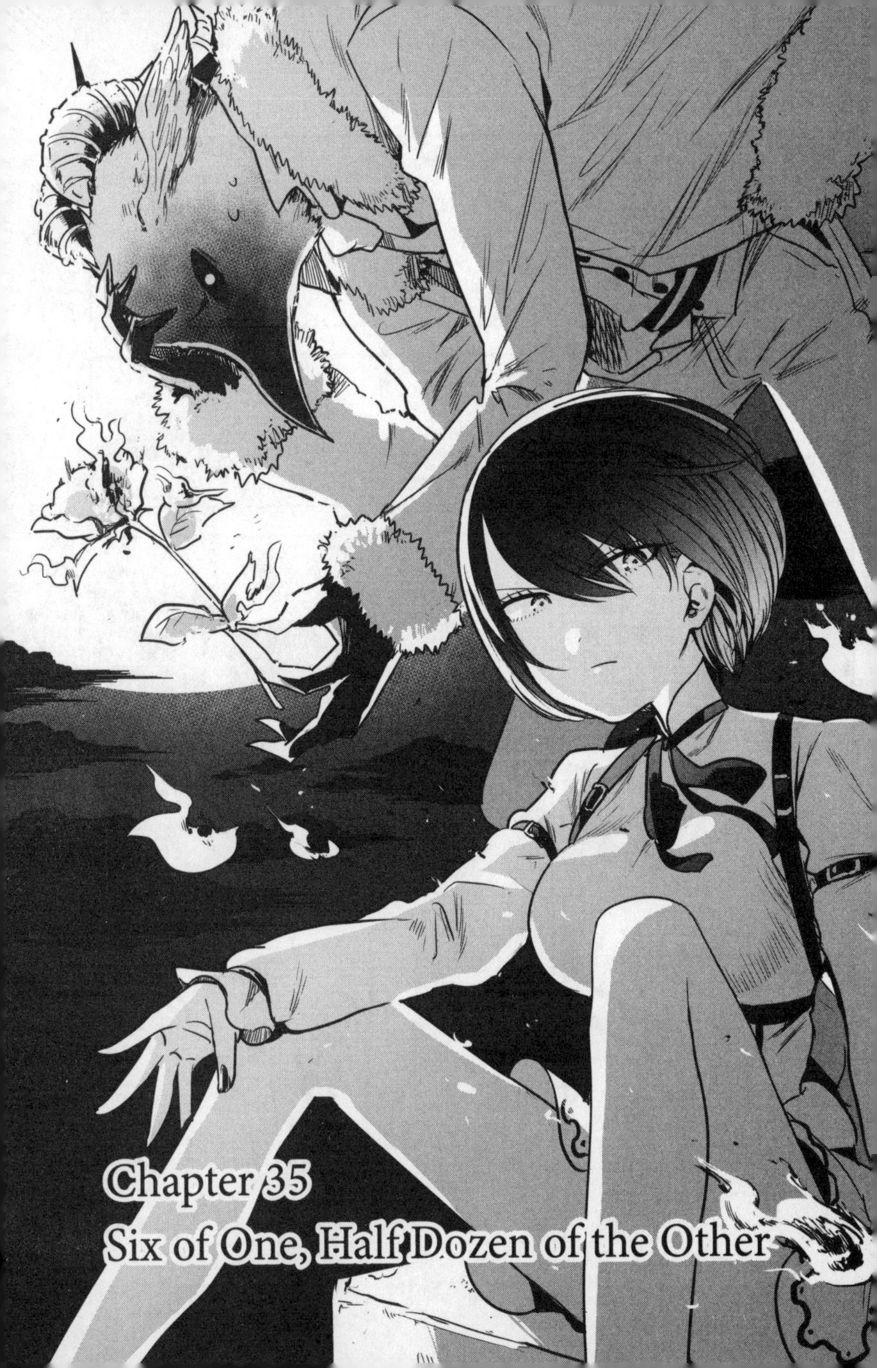
Chapter 35
Six of One, Half Dozen of the Other

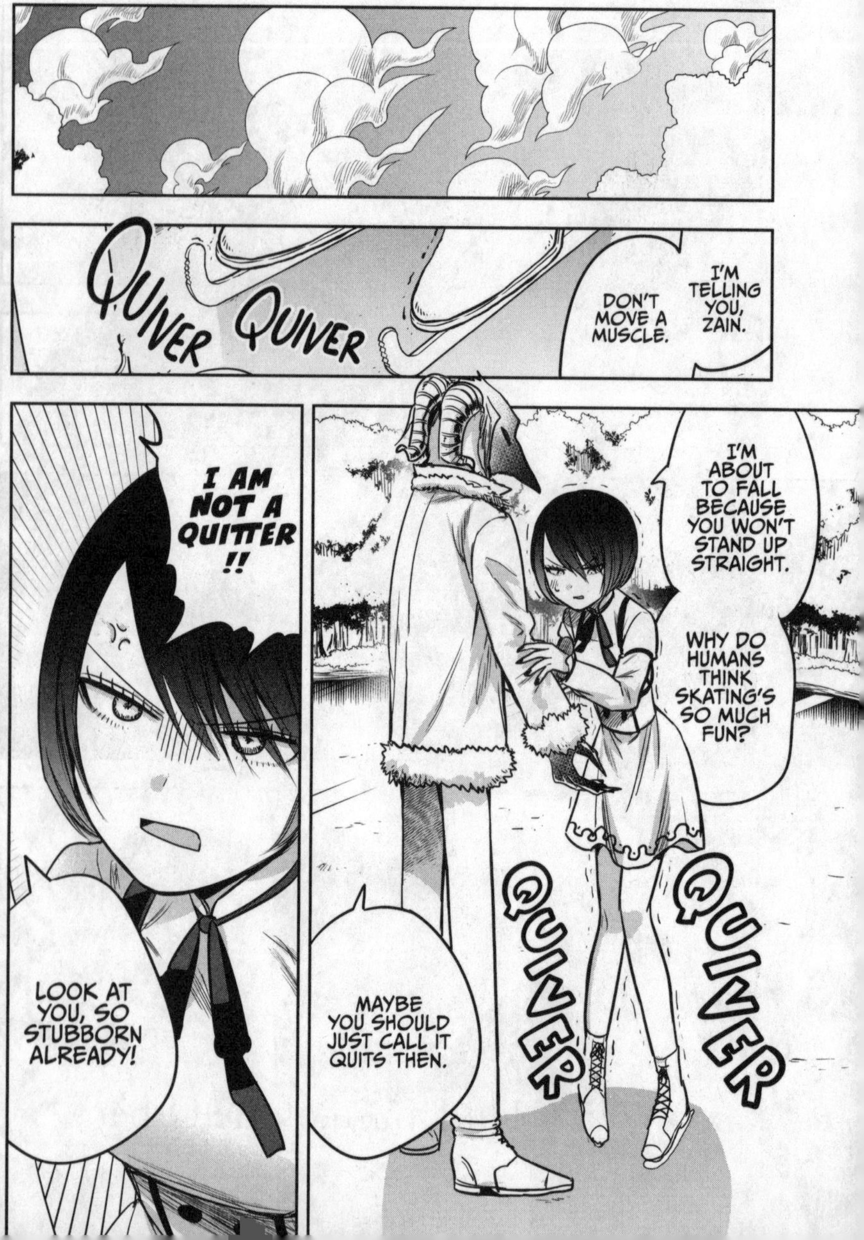
QUIVER
QUIVER
I'M TELLING YOU, ZAIN.
DON'T MOVE A MUSCLE.
I'M ABOUT TO FALL BECAUSE YOU WON'T STAND UP STRAIGHT.
WHY DO HUMANS THINK SKATING'S SO MUCH FUN?
QUIVER
QUIVER
MAYBE YOU SHOULD JUST CALL IT QUITS THEN.
I AM NOT A QUITTER!!
LOOK AT YOU, SO STUBBORN ALREADY!

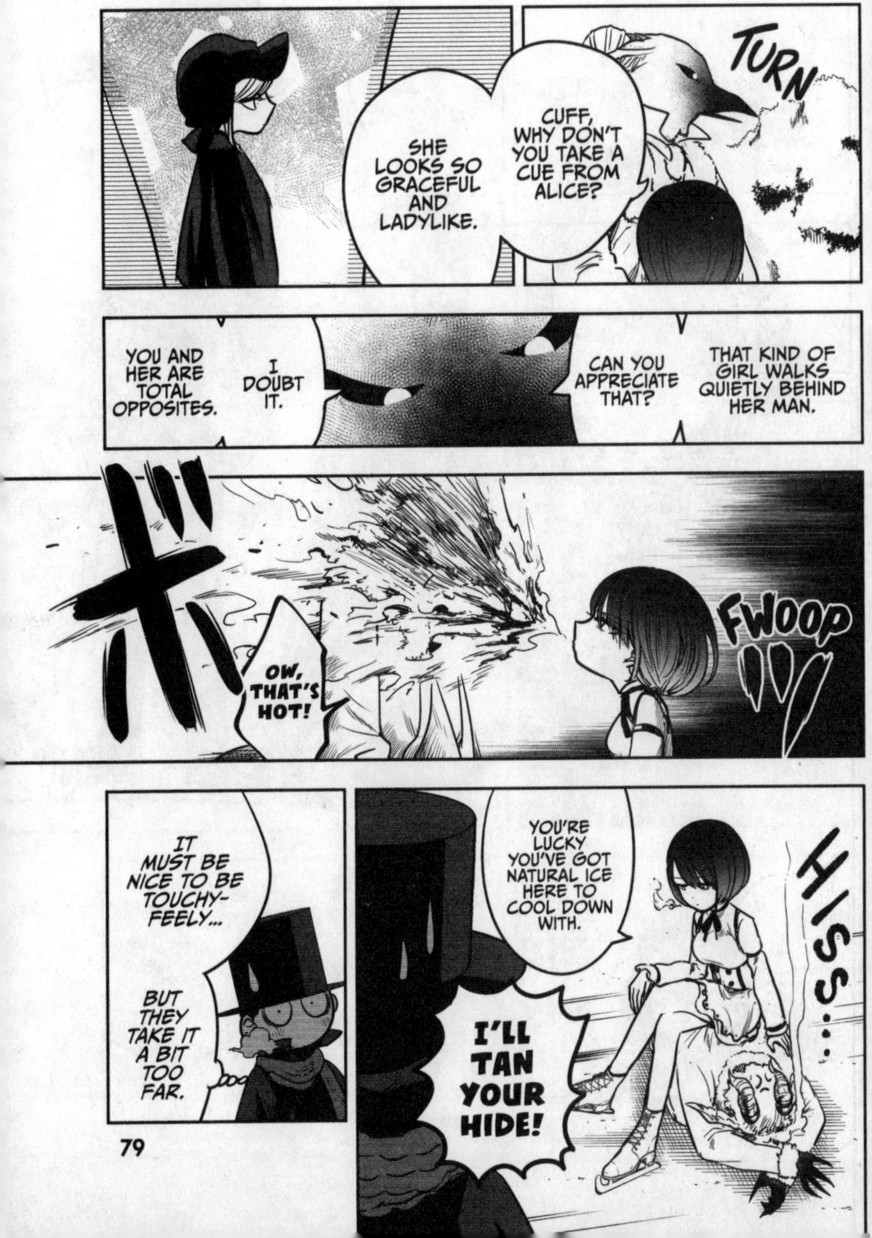
TURN
CUFF, WHY DON'T YOU TAKE A CUE FROM ALICE?
SHE LOOKS SO GRACEFUL AND LADYLIKE.
THAT KIND OF GIRL WALKS QUIETLY BEHIND HER MAN.
CAN YOU APPRECIATE THAT?
I DOUBT IT.
YOU AND HER ARE TOTAL OPPOSITES.
FWOOP
ボ
OW, THAT'S HOT!
HISS...
YOU'RE LUCKY YOU'VE GOT NATURAL ICE HERE TO COOL DOWN WITH.
I'LL TAN YOUR HIDE!
IT MUST BE NICE TO BE TOUCHY-FEELY...
BUT THEY TAKE IT A BIT TOO FAR.

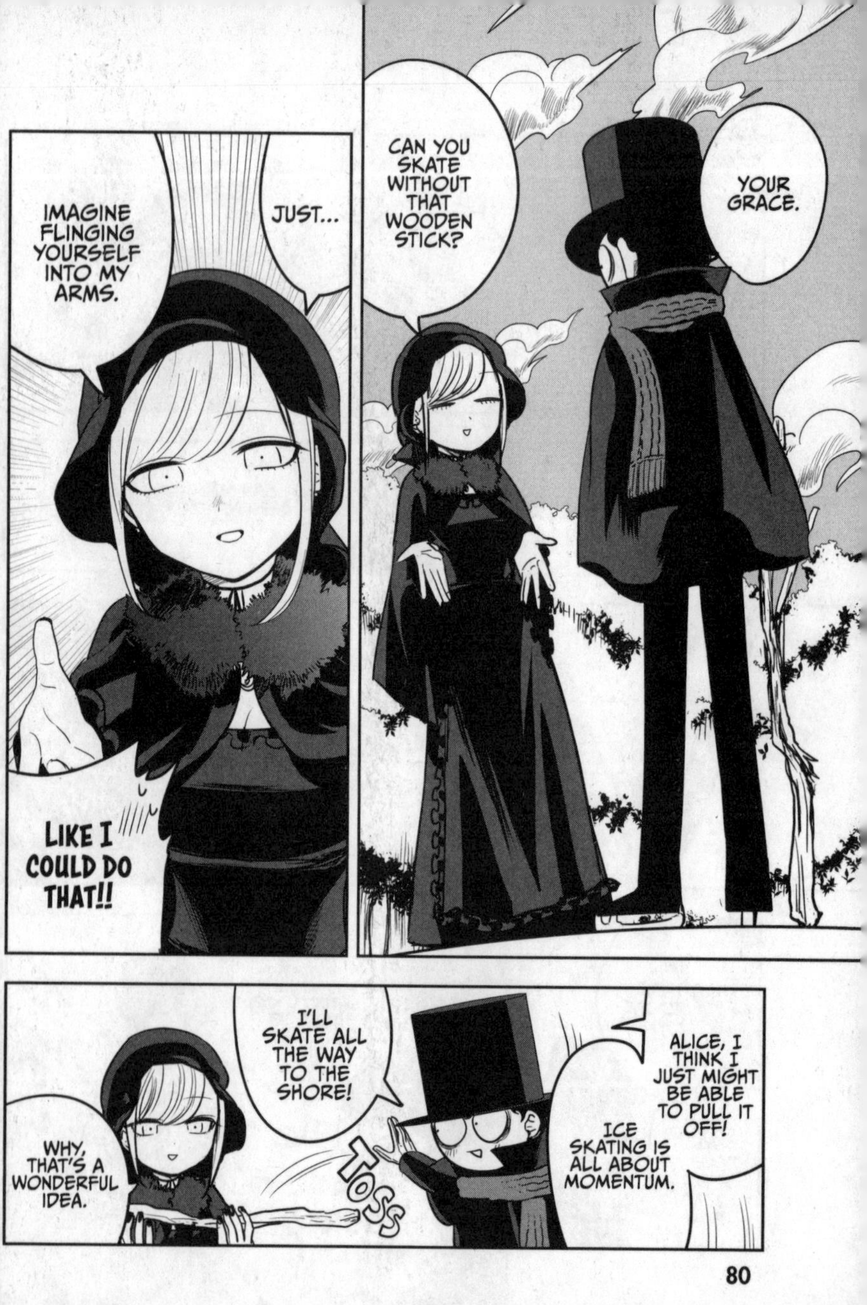
YOUR GRACE.
CAN YOU SKATE WITHOUT THAT WOODEN STICK?
JUST...
IMAGINE FLINGING YOURSELF INTO MY ARMS.
LIKE I COULD DO THAT!!
ALICE, I THINK I JUST MIGHT BE ABLE TO PULL IT OFF!
ICE SKATING IS ALL ABOUT MOMENTUM.
I'LL SKATE ALL THE WAY TO THE SHORE!
TOSS
WHY, THAT'S A WONDERFUL IDEA.

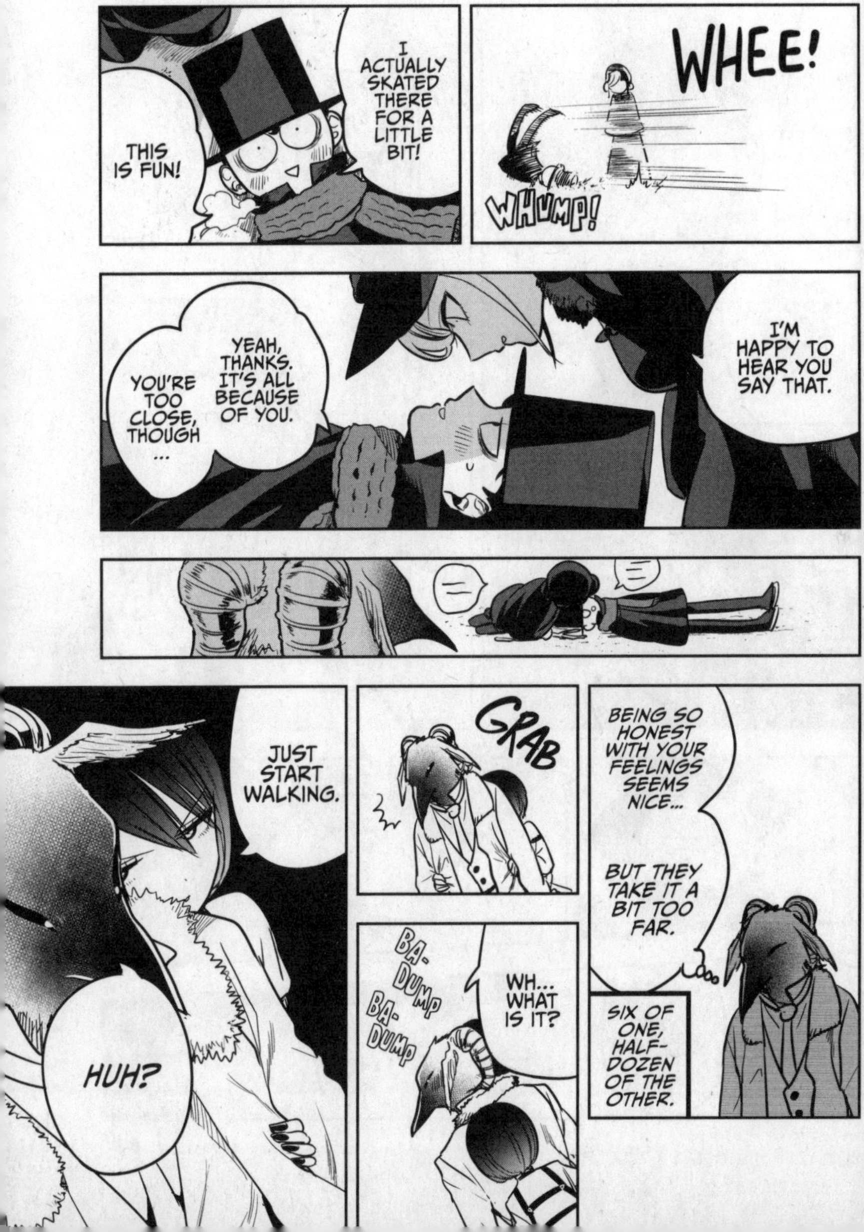
WHEE!
WHUMP!
I ACTUALLY SKATED THERE FOR A LITTLE BIT!
THIS IS FUN!
I'M HAPPY TO HEAR YOU SAY THAT.
YEAH, THANKS. IT'S ALL BECAUSE OF YOU.
YOU'RE TOO CLOSE, THOUGH...
BEING SO HONEST WITH YOUR FEELINGS SEEMS NICE...
BUT THEY TAKE IT A BIT TOO FAR.
SIX OF ONE, HALF-DOZEN OF THE OTHER.
GRAB
BA-DUMP
BA-DUMP
WH... WHAT IS IT?
JUST START WALKING.
HUH?

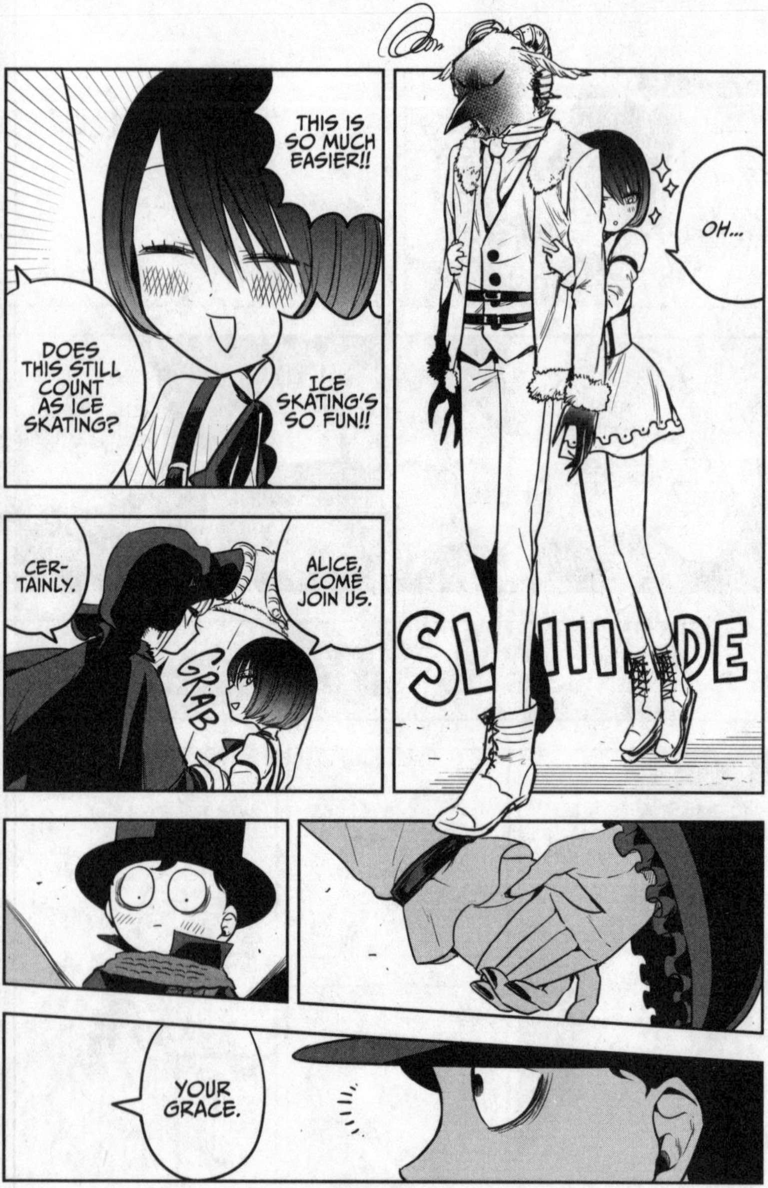
OH...
SLIIIIDE
THIS IS SO MUCH EASIER!!
ICE SKATING'S SO FUN!!
DOES THIS STILL COUNT AS ICE SKATING?
ALICE, COME JOIN US.
CER-TAINLY.
GRAB
YOUR GRACE.

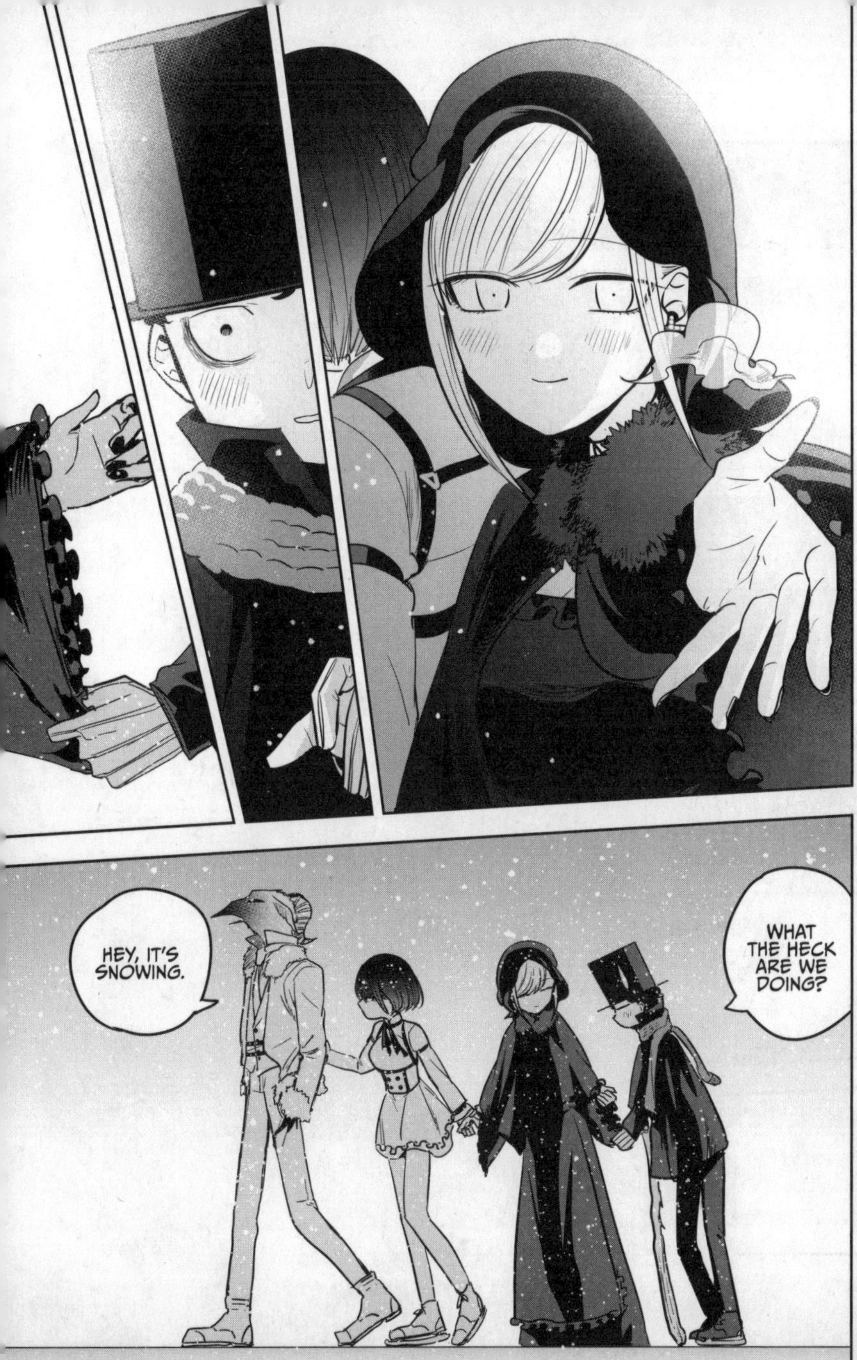
WHAT THE HECK ARE WE DOING?
HEY, IT'S SNOWING.

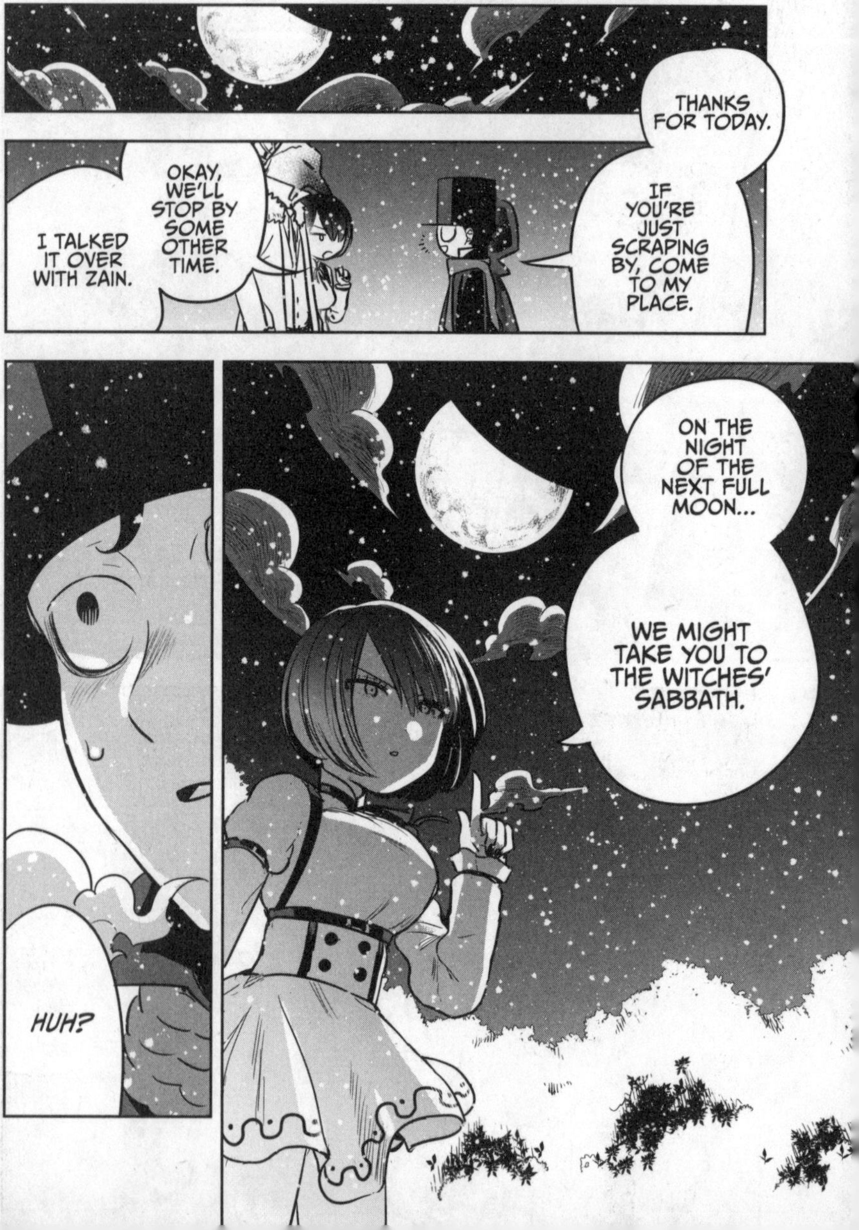
THANKS FOR TODAY.
IF YOU'RE JUST SCRAPING BY, COME TO MY PLACE.
OKAY, WE'LL STOP BY SOME OTHER TIME.
I TALKED IT OVER WITH ZAIN.
ON THE NIGHT OF THE NEXT FULL MOON...
WE MIGHT TAKE YOU TO THE WITCHES' SABBATH.
HUH?

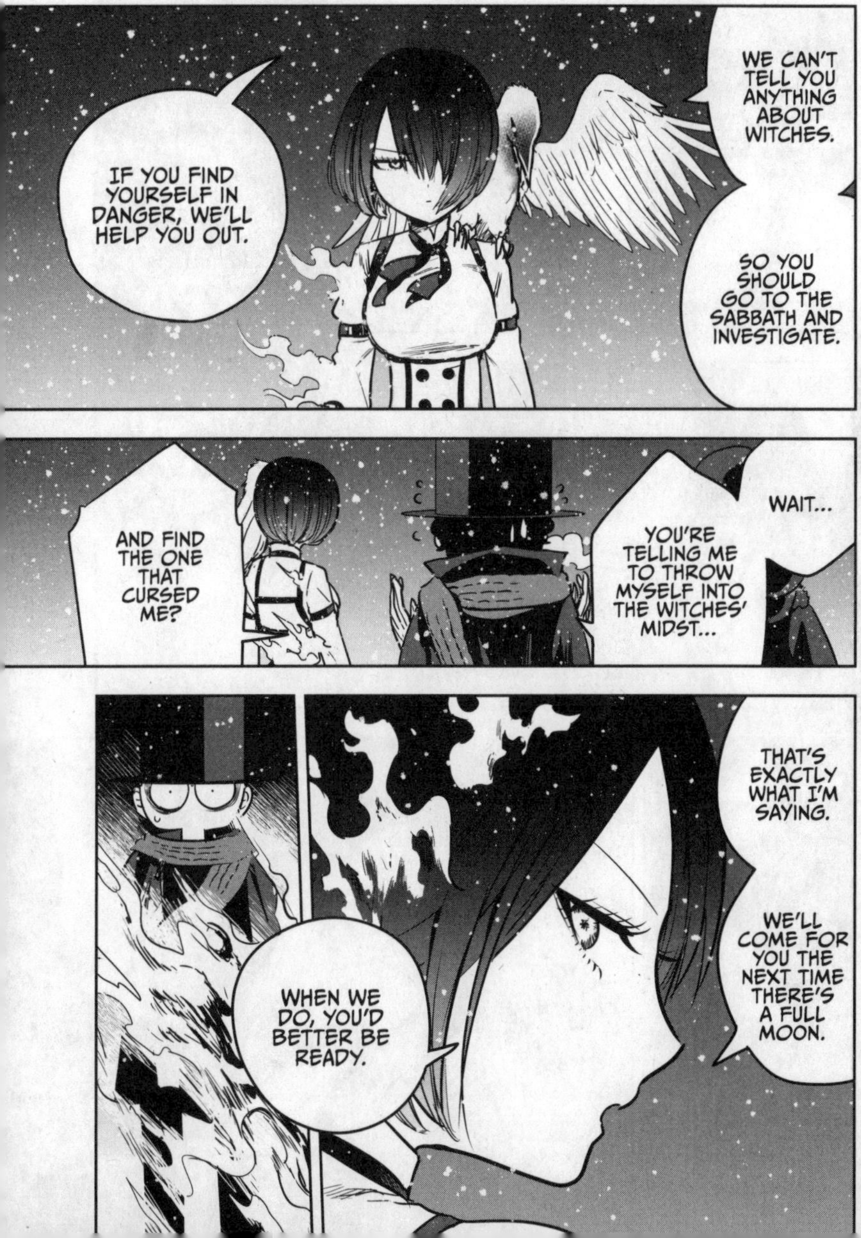
WE CAN'T TELL YOU ANYTHING ABOUT WITCHES.
SO YOU SHOULD GO TO THE SABBATH AND INVESTIGATE.
IF YOU FIND YOURSELF IN DANGER, WE'LL HELP YOU OUT.
WAIT...
YOU'RE TELLING ME TO THROW MYSELF INTO THE WITCHES' MIDST...
AND FIND THE ONE THAT CURSED ME?
THAT'S EXACTLY WHAT I'M SAYING.
WE'LL COME FOR YOU THE NEXT TIME THERE'S A FULL MOON.
WHEN WE DO, YOU'D BETTER BE READY.

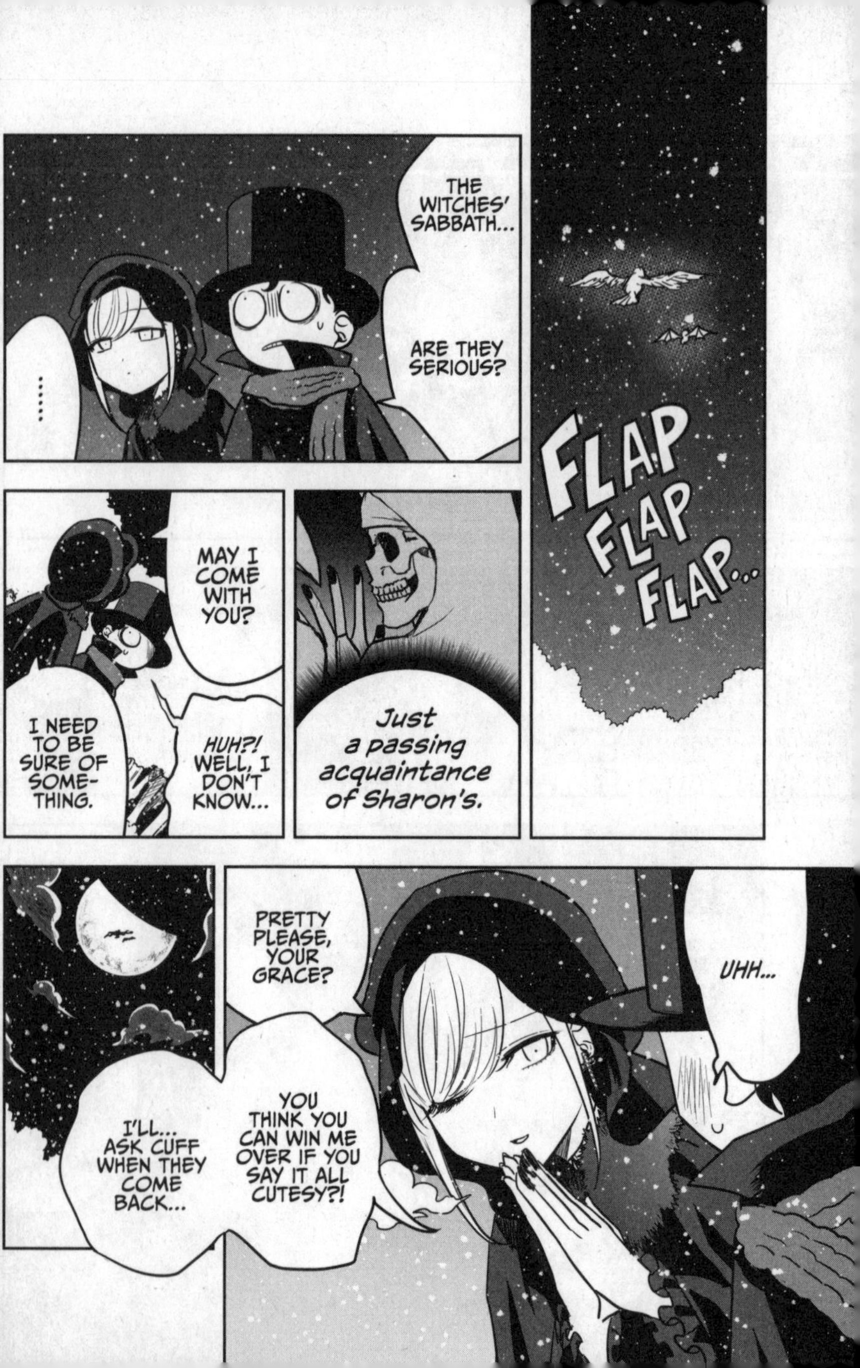
FLAP FLAP FLAP...
THE WITCHES' SABBATH...
ARE THEY SERIOUS?
......
Just a passing acquaintance of Sharon's.
MAY I COME WITH YOU?
HUH?! WELL, I DON'T KNOW...
I NEED TO BE SURE OF SOME-THING.
UHH...
PRETTY PLEASE, YOUR GRACE?
YOU THINK YOU CAN WIN ME OVER IF YOU SAY IT ALL CUTESY?!
I'LL... ASK CUFF WHEN THEY COME BACK...

THE DUKE OF DEATH AND HIS MAID

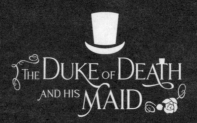

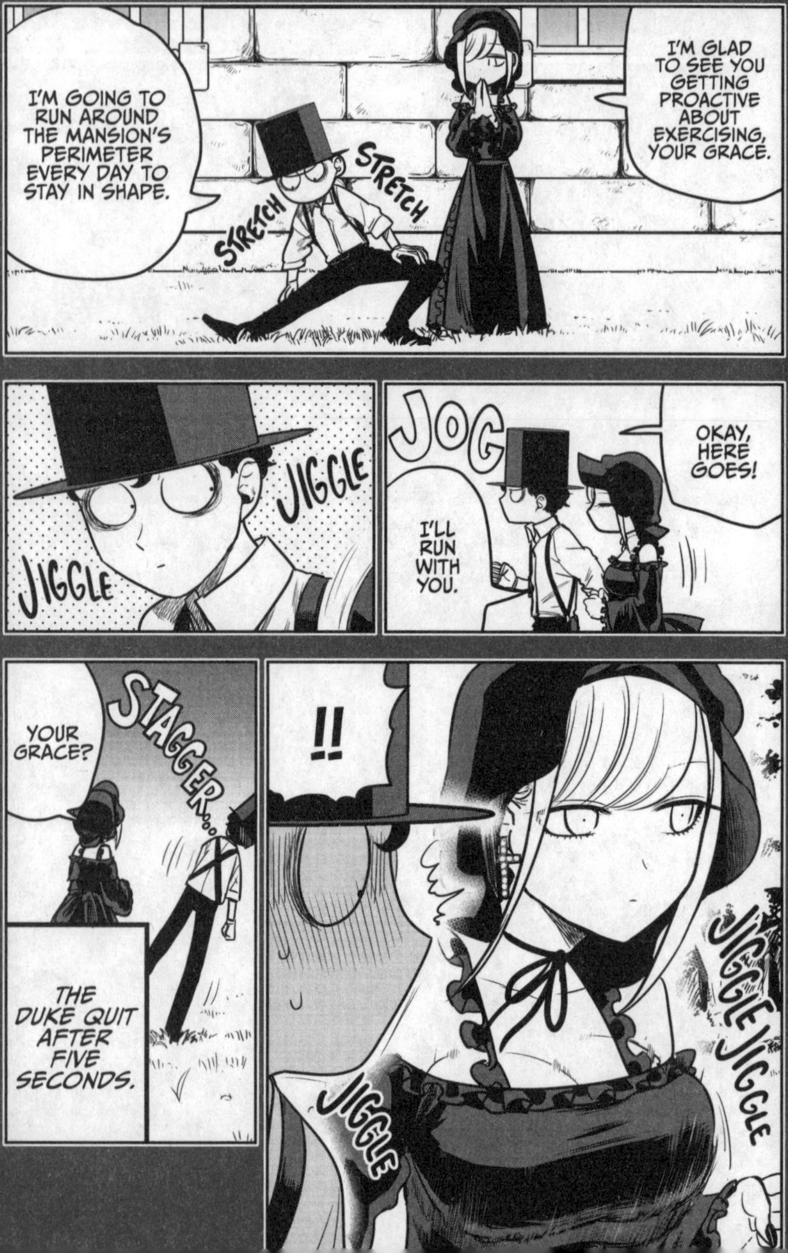
I'M GLAD TO SEE YOU GETTING PROACTIVE ABOUT EXERCISING, YOUR GRACE.
I'M GOING TO RUN AROUND THE MANSION'S PERIMETER EVERY DAY TO STAY IN SHAPE.
STRETCH
STRETCH
OKAY, HERE GOES!
JOG
I'LL RUN WITH YOU.
JIGGLE
JIGGLE
!!
JIGGLE JIGGLE
JIGGLE
STAGGER...
YOUR GRACE?
THE DUKE QUIT AFTER FIVE SECONDS.

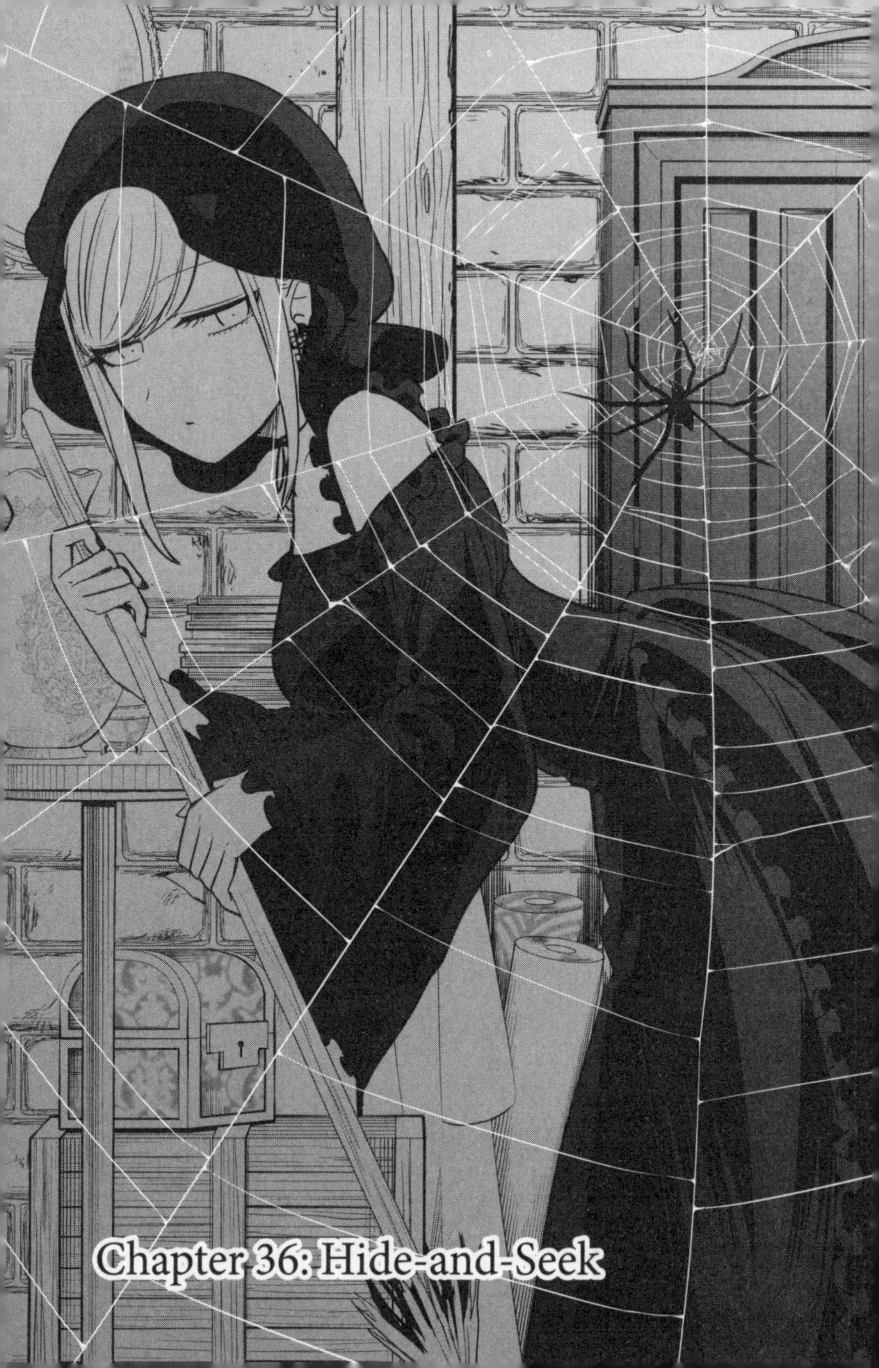
Chapter 36: Hide-and-Seek

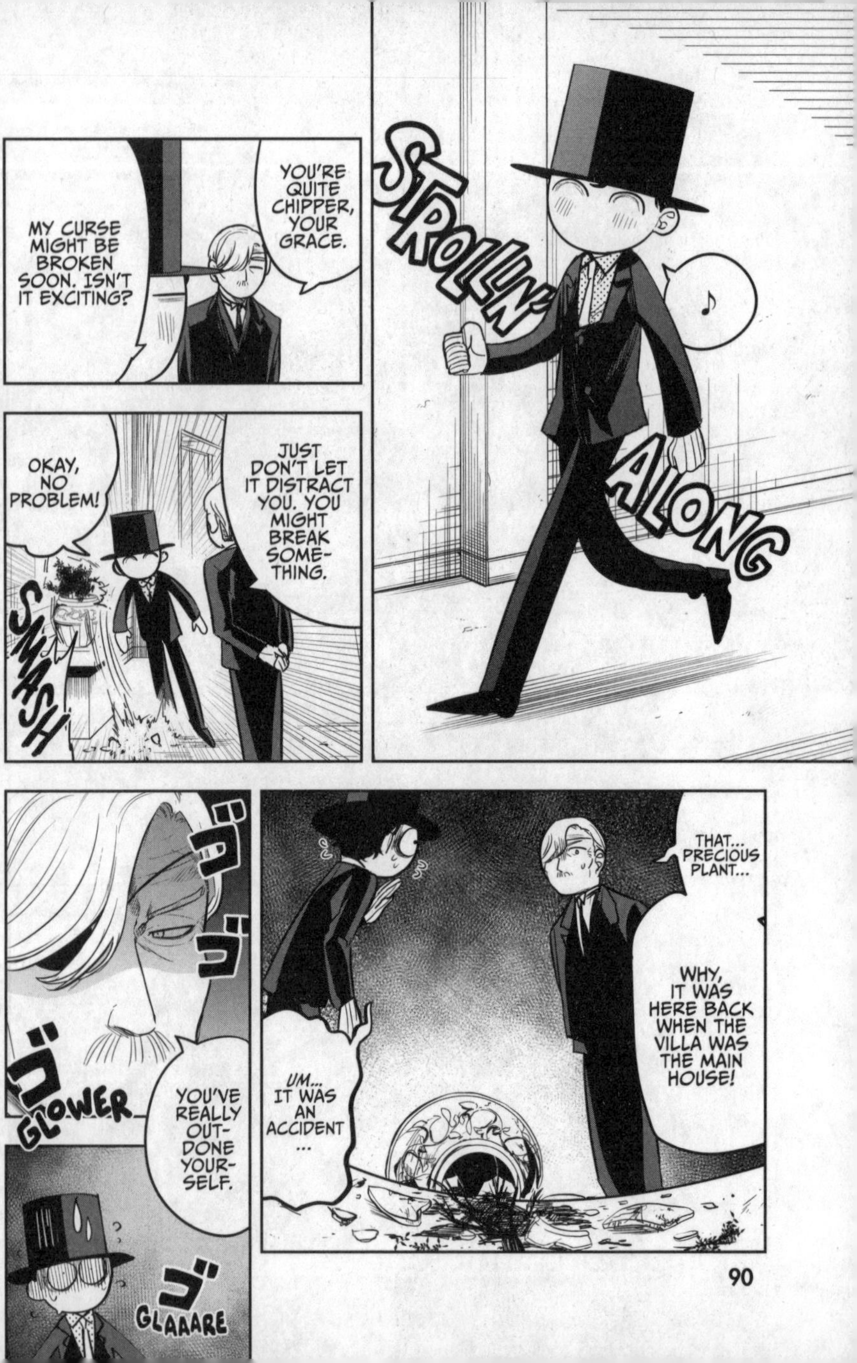
STROLLIN'
ALONG
♪
YOU'RE QUITE CHIPPER, YOUR GRACE.
MY CURSE MIGHT BE BROKEN SOON. ISN'T IT EXCITING?
JUST DON'T LET IT DISTRACT YOU. YOU MIGHT BREAK SOME-THING.
OKAY, NO PROBLEM!
SMASH
THAT... PRECIOUS PLANT...
WHY, IT WAS HERE BACK WHEN THE VILLA WAS THE MAIN HOUSE!
UM... IT WAS AN ACCIDENT...
ゴゴゴ
GLOWER
YOU'VE REALLY OUT-DONE YOUR-SELF.
ゴ
GLAAARE

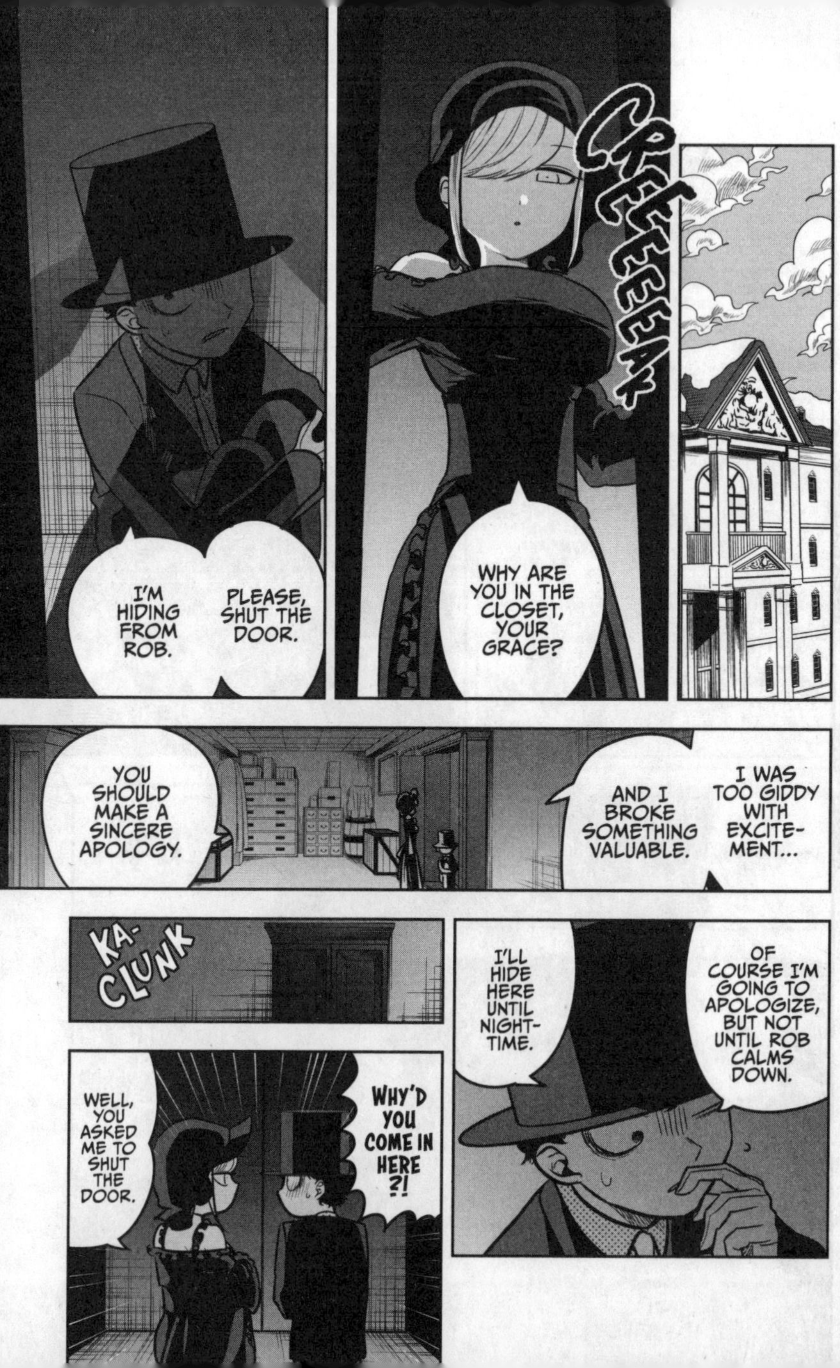
CREEEEEAK
WHY ARE YOU IN THE CLOSET, YOUR GRACE?
PLEASE, SHUT THE DOOR.
I'M HIDING FROM ROB.
I WAS TOO GIDDY WITH EXCITE-MENT...
AND I BROKE SOMETHING VALUABLE.
YOU SHOULD MAKE A SINCERE APOLOGY.
OF COURSE I'M GOING TO APOLOGIZE, BUT NOT UNTIL ROB CALMS DOWN.
I'LL HIDE HERE UNTIL NIGHT-TIME.
KA-CLUNK
WHY'D YOU COME IN HERE?!
WELL, YOU ASKED ME TO SHUT THE DOOR.

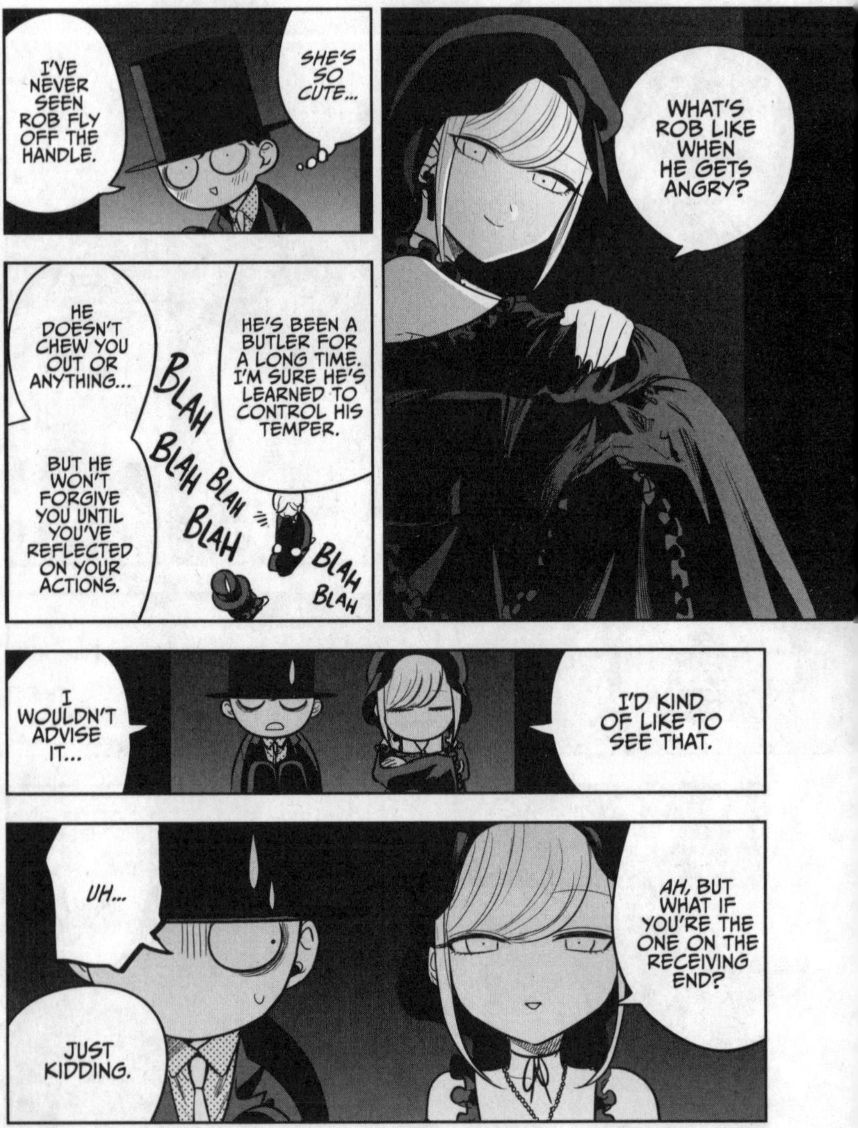
WHAT'S ROB LIKE WHEN HE GETS ANGRY?
SHE'S SO CUTE...
I'VE NEVER SEEN ROB FLY OFF THE HANDLE.
HE'S BEEN A BUTLER FOR A LONG TIME. I'M SURE HE'S LEARNED TO CONTROL HIS TEMPER.
BLAH BLAH BLAH BLAH BLAH BLAH
HE DOESN'T CHEW YOU OUT OR ANYTHING...
BUT HE WON'T FORGIVE YOU UNTIL YOU'VE REFLECTED ON YOUR ACTIONS.
I'D KIND OF LIKE TO SEE THAT.
I WOULDN'T ADVISE IT...
AH, BUT WHAT IF YOU'RE THE ONE ON THE RECEIVING END?
UH...
JUST KIDDING.

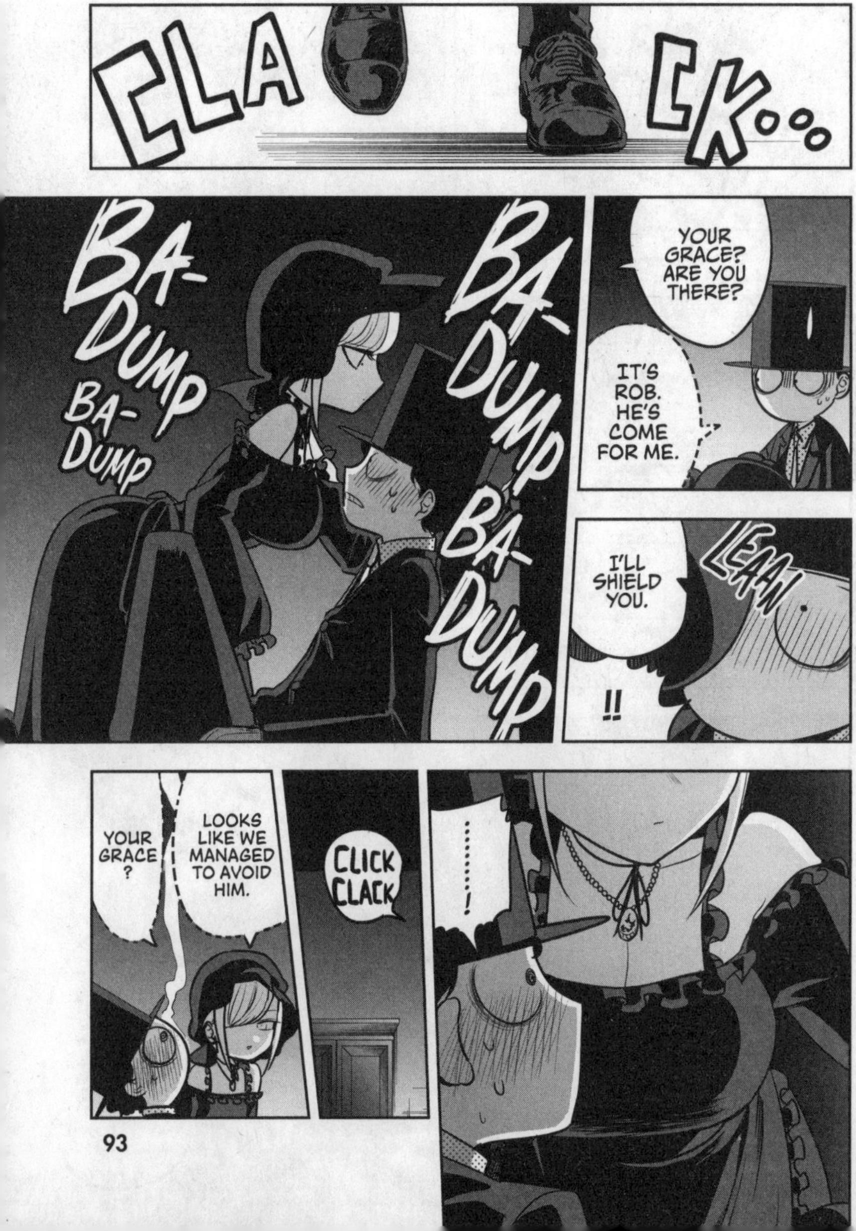
CLA
CK...
YOUR GRACE? ARE YOU THERE?
IT'S ROB. HE'S COME FOR ME.
I'LL SHIELD YOU.
LEAAN
!!
BA-DUMP BA-DUMP
BA-DUMP BA-DUMP
......!
CLICK CLACK
LOOKS LIKE WE MANAGED TO AVOID HIM.
YOUR GRACE?

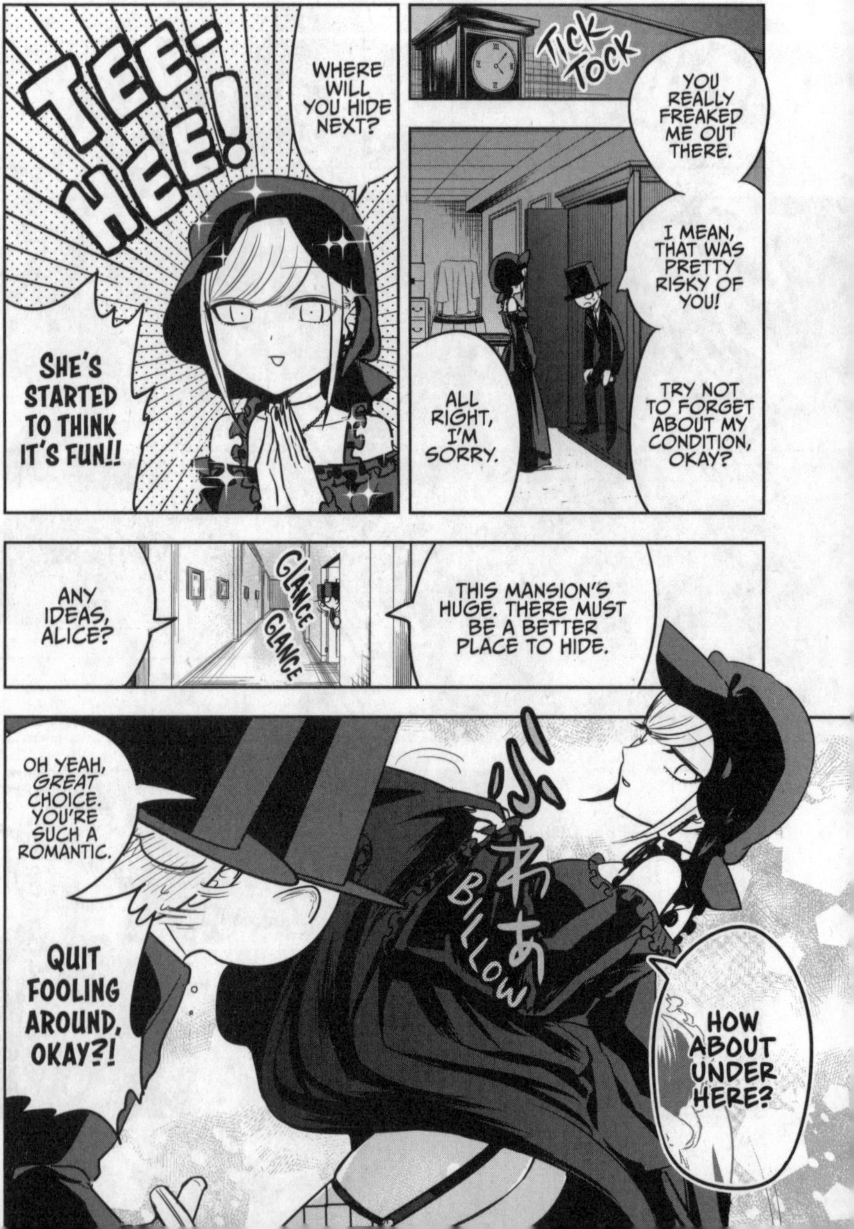
TICK TOCK
YOU REALLY FREAKED ME OUT THERE.
I MEAN, THAT WAS PRETTY RISKY OF YOU!
TRY NOT TO FORGET ABOUT MY CONDITION, OKAY?
ALL RIGHT, I'M SORRY.
WHERE WILL YOU HIDE NEXT?
TEE-HEE!
SHE'S STARTED TO THINK IT'S FUN!!
THIS MANSION'S HUGE. THERE MUST BE A BETTER PLACE TO HIDE.
GLANCE GLANCE GLANCE
ANY IDEAS, ALICE?
HOW ABOUT UNDER HERE?
ふわあ
BILLOW
OH YEAH, *GREAT* CHOICE. YOU'RE SUCH A ROMANTIC.
QUIT FOOLING AROUND, OKAY?!

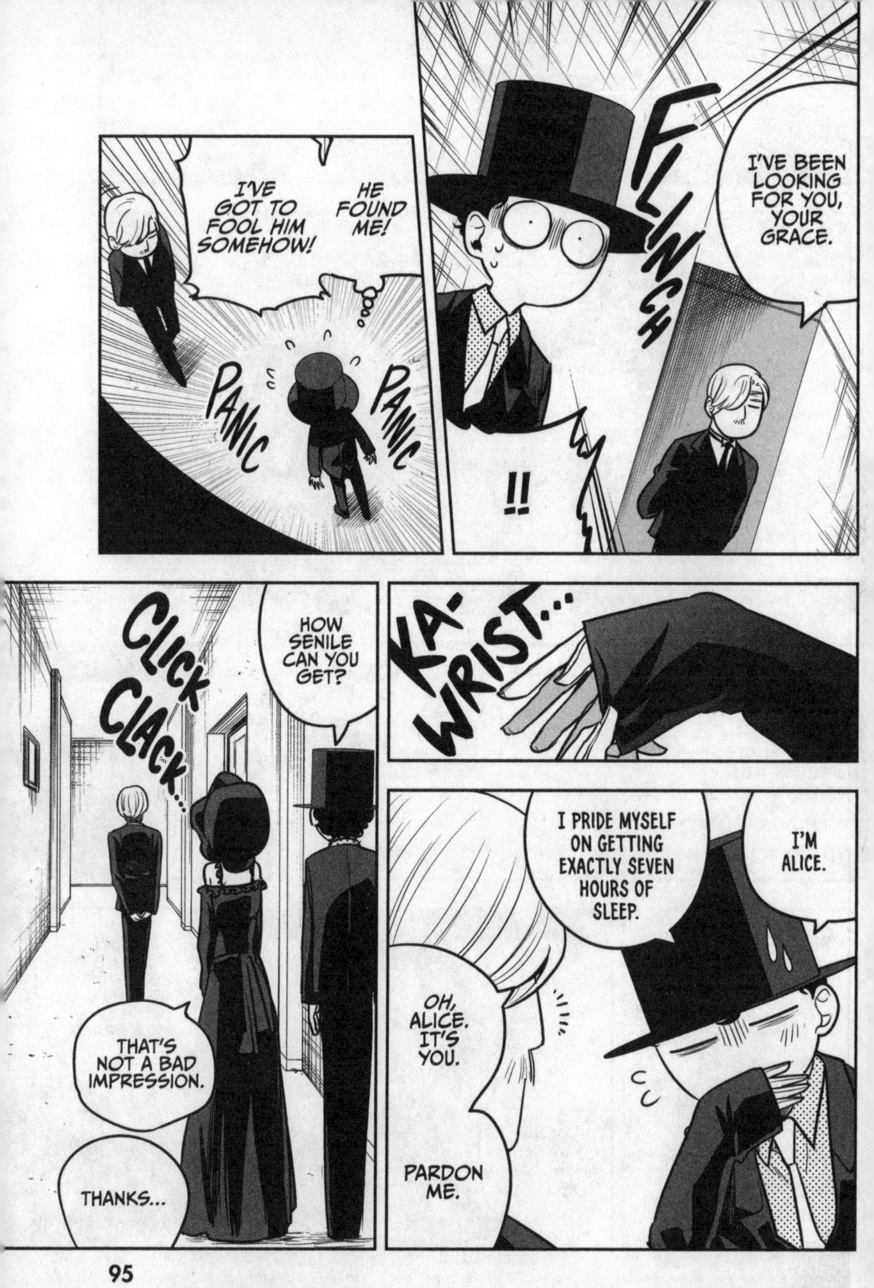
I'VE BEEN LOOKING FOR YOU, YOUR GRACE.
FLINCH
!!
HE FOUND ME!
I'VE GOT TO FOOL HIM SOMEHOW!
PANIC
PANIC
KA-WRIST...
I'M ALICE.
I PRIDE MYSELF ON GETTING EXACTLY SEVEN HOURS OF SLEEP.
OH, ALICE. IT'S YOU.
PARDON ME.
HOW SENILE CAN YOU GET?
CLICK CLACK...
THAT'S NOT A BAD IMPRESSION.
THANKS...

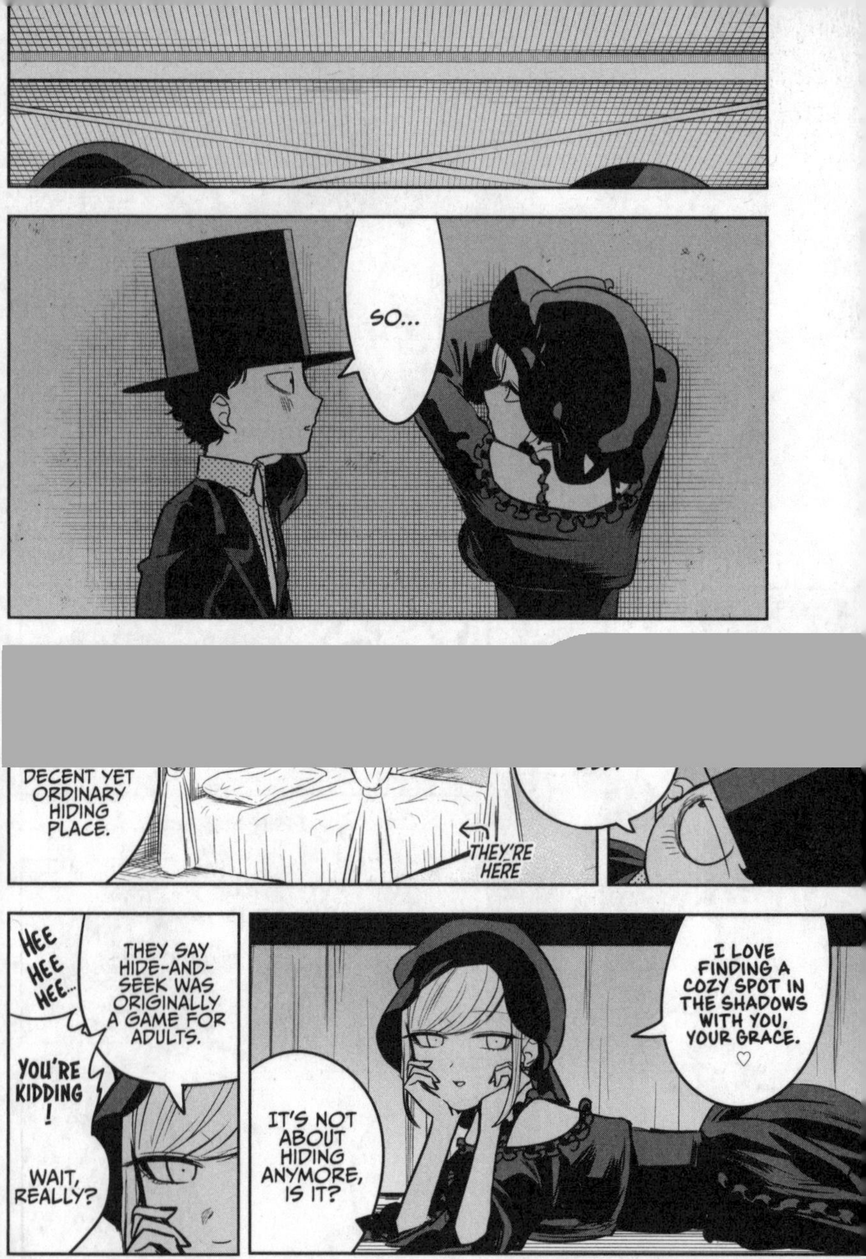
SO...
DECENT YET ORDINARY HIDING PLACE.
THEY'RE HERE
I LOVE FINDING A COZY SPOT IN THE SHADOWS WITH YOU, YOUR GRACE. ♡
IT'S NOT ABOUT HIDING ANYMORE, IS IT?
THEY SAY HIDE-AND-SEEK WAS ORIGINALLY A GAME FOR ADULTS.
HEE HEE HEE...
YOU'RE KIDDING!
WAIT, REALLY?

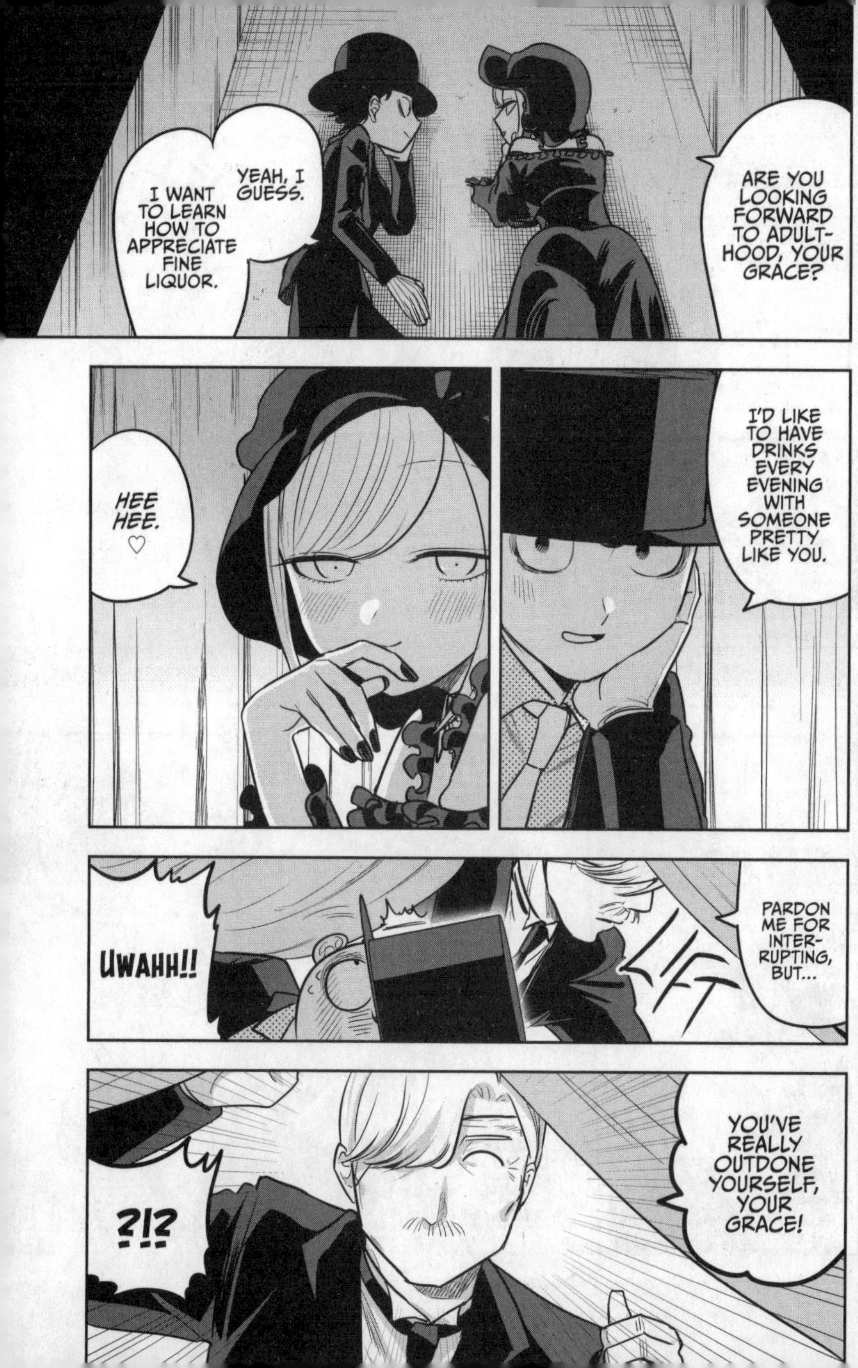
ARE YOU LOOKING FORWARD TO ADULT-HOOD, YOUR GRACE?
YEAH, I GUESS.
I WANT TO LEARN HOW TO APPRECIATE FINE LIQUOR.
I'D LIKE TO HAVE DRINKS EVERY EVENING WITH SOMEONE PRETTY LIKE YOU.
HEE HEE. ♡
PARDON ME FOR INTER-RUPTING, BUT...
UWAHH!!
YOU'VE REALLY OUTDONE YOURSELF, YOUR GRACE!
?!?

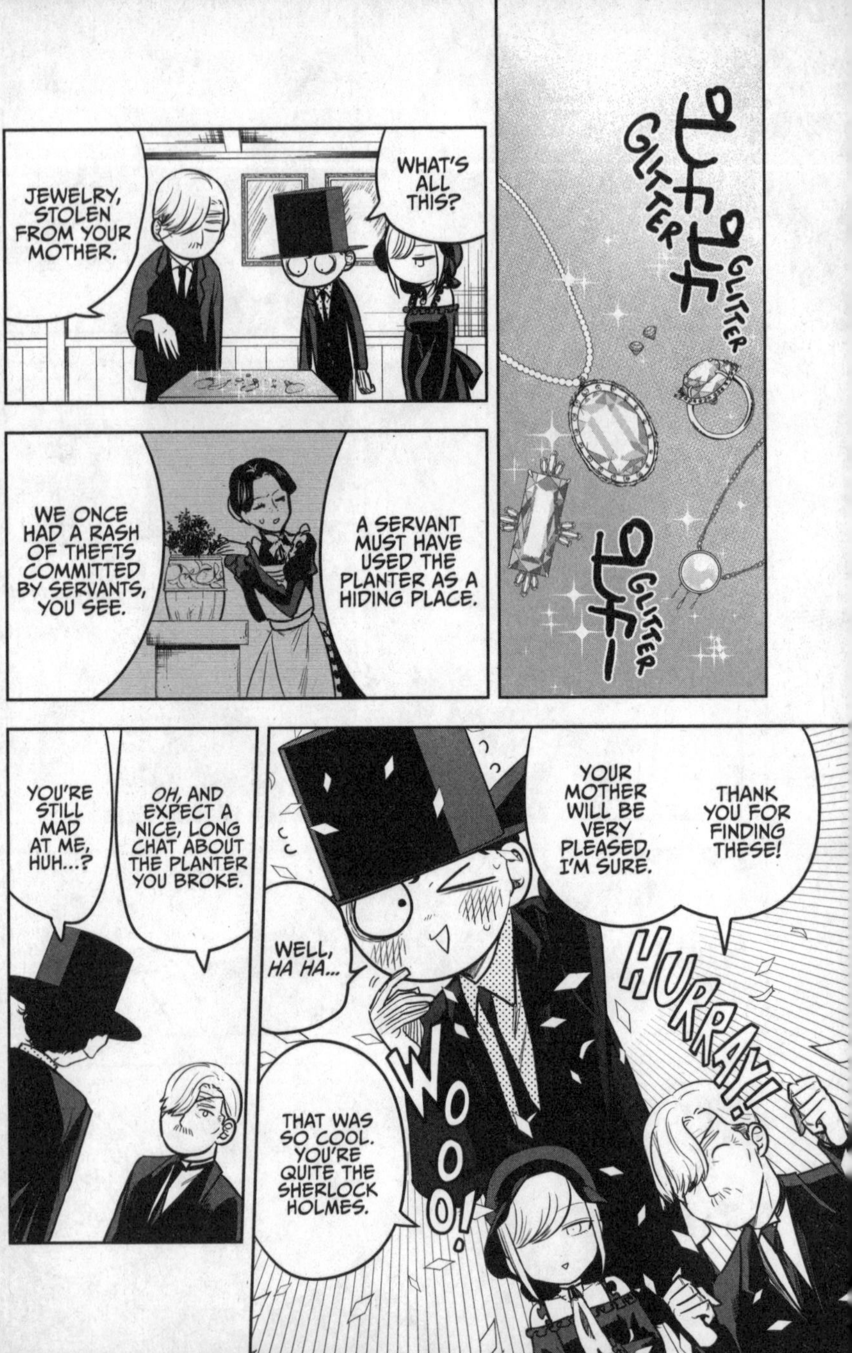
GLITTER GLITTER
GLITTER
WHAT'S ALL THIS?
JEWELRY, STOLEN FROM YOUR MOTHER.
A SERVANT MUST HAVE USED THE PLANTER AS A HIDING PLACE.
WE ONCE HAD A RASH OF THEFTS COMMITTED BY SERVANTS, YOU SEE.
THANK YOU FOR FINDING THESE!
YOUR MOTHER WILL BE VERY PLEASED, I'M SURE.
HURRAY!
WELL, *HA HA*...
WOOOO!
THAT WAS SO COOL. YOU'RE QUITE THE SHERLOCK HOLMES.
OH, AND EXPECT A NICE, LONG CHAT ABOUT THE PLANTER YOU BROKE.
YOU'RE STILL MAD AT ME, HUH...?

THE DUKE OF DEATH AND HIS MAID

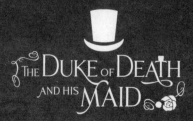

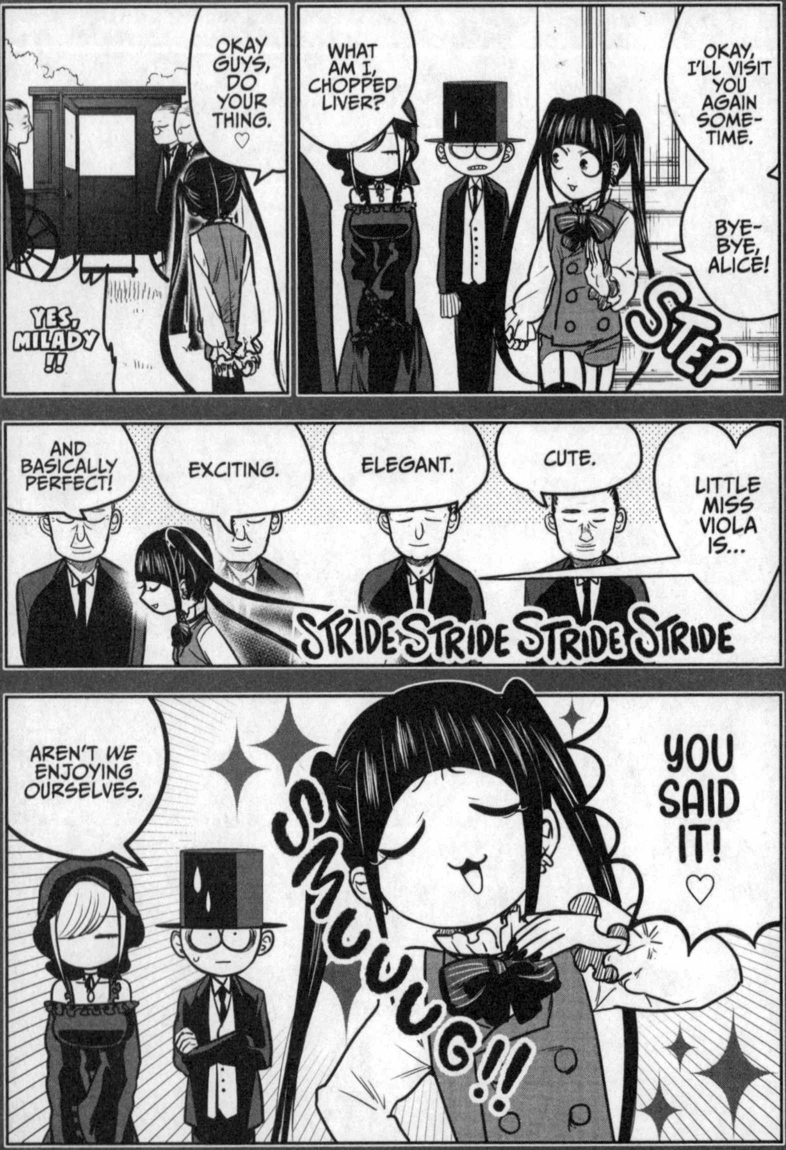
OKAY, I'LL VISIT YOU AGAIN SOME-TIME.
BYE-BYE, ALICE!
STEP
WHAT AM I, CHOPPED LIVER?
OKAY GUYS, DO YOUR THING. ♡
YES, MILADY!!
LITTLE MISS VIOLA IS...
CUTE.
ELEGANT.
EXCITING.
AND BASICALLY PERFECT!
STRIDE STRIDE STRIDE STRIDE
YOU SAID IT! ♡
SMUUUG!!
AREN'T WE ENJOYING OURSELVES.

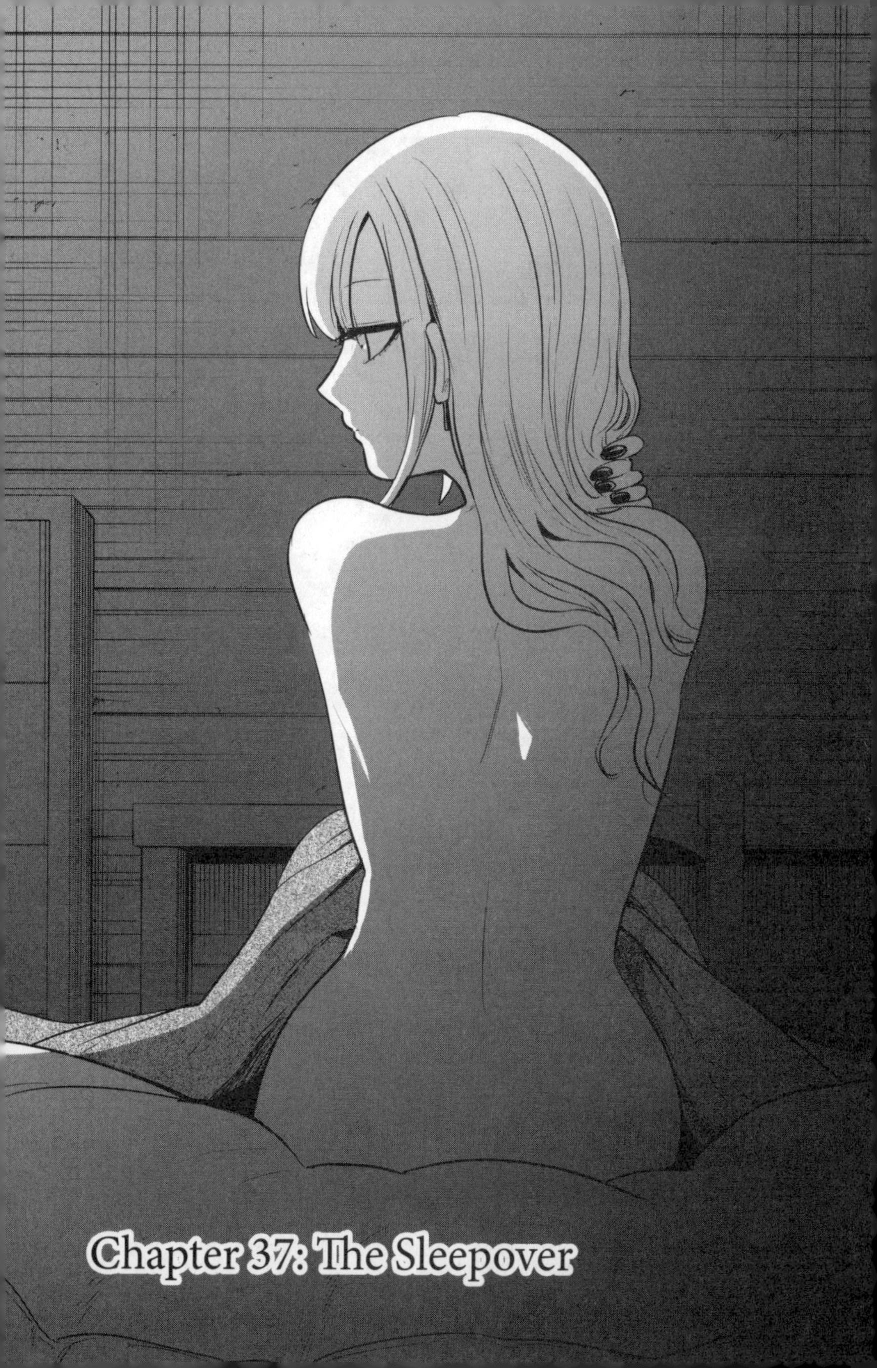

Chapter 37: The Sleepover

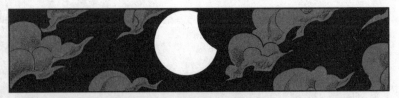

CREAAK.

JUST A MOMENT...

KNOCK KNOCK

OH...

IT'S YOU, LADY VIOLA.

HELLO THERE, ALICE.

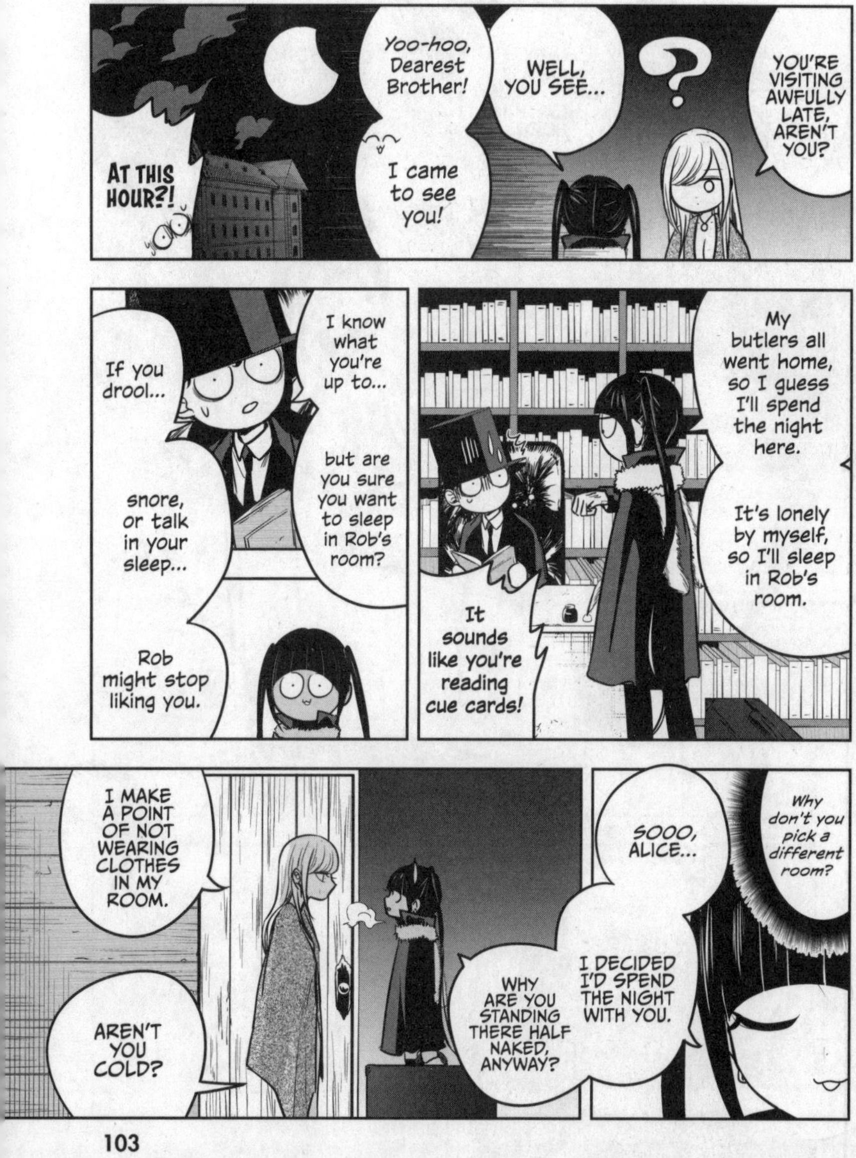
YOU'RE VISITING AWFULLY LATE, AREN'T YOU?
WELL, YOU SEE...
Yoo-hoo, Dearest Brother!
I came to see you!
AT THIS HOUR?!
My butlers all went home, so I guess I'll spend the night here.
It's lonely by myself, so I'll sleep in Rob's room.
It sounds like you're reading cue cards!
I know what you're up to...
but are you sure you want to sleep in Rob's room?
If you drool...
snore, or talk in your sleep...
Rob might stop liking you.
Why don't you pick a different room?
SOOO, ALICE...
I DECIDED I'D SPEND THE NIGHT WITH YOU.
WHY ARE YOU STANDING THERE HALF NAKED, ANYWAY?
I MAKE A POINT OF NOT WEARING CLOTHES IN MY ROOM.
AREN'T YOU COLD?

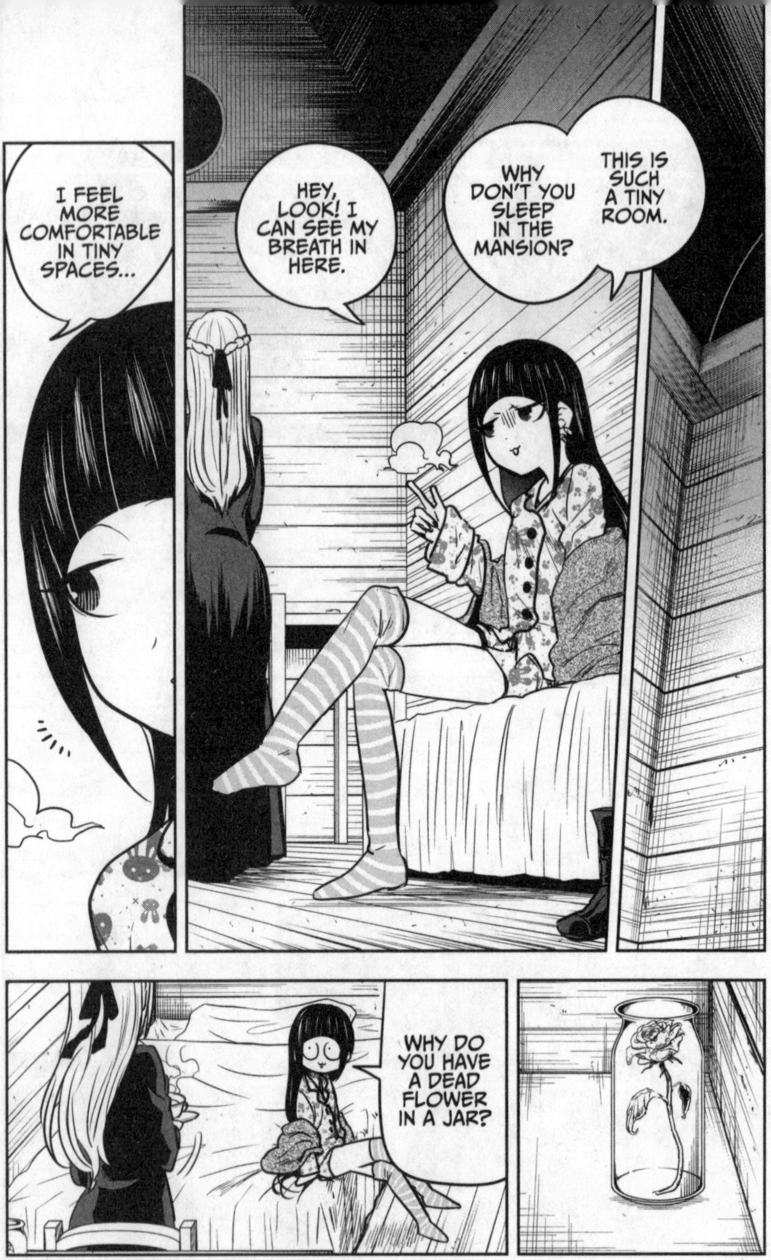
THIS IS SUCH A TINY ROOM.
WHY DON'T YOU SLEEP IN THE MANSION?
HEY, LOOK! I CAN SEE MY BREATH IN HERE.
I FEEL MORE COMFORTABLE IN TINY SPACES...
WHY DO YOU HAVE A DEAD FLOWER IN A JAR?

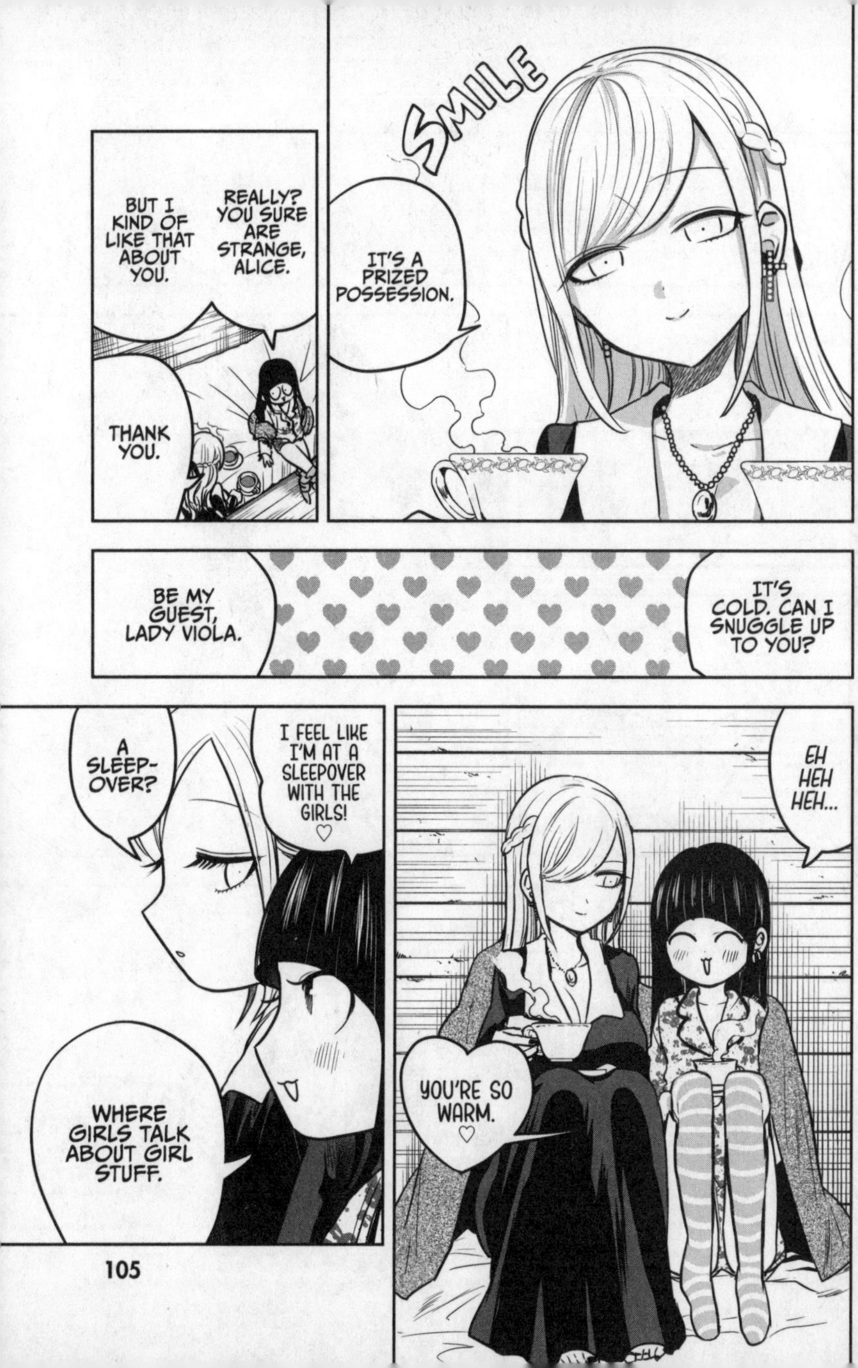
SMILE
IT'S A PRIZED POSSESSION.
REALLY? YOU SURE ARE STRANGE, ALICE.
BUT I KIND OF LIKE THAT ABOUT YOU.
THANK YOU.
IT'S COLD. CAN I SNUGGLE UP TO YOU?
BE MY GUEST, LADY VIOLA.
EH HEH HEH...
YOU'RE SO WARM. ♡
I FEEL LIKE I'M AT A SLEEPOVER WITH THE GIRLS! ♡
A SLEEP-OVER?
WHERE GIRLS TALK ABOUT GIRL STUFF.

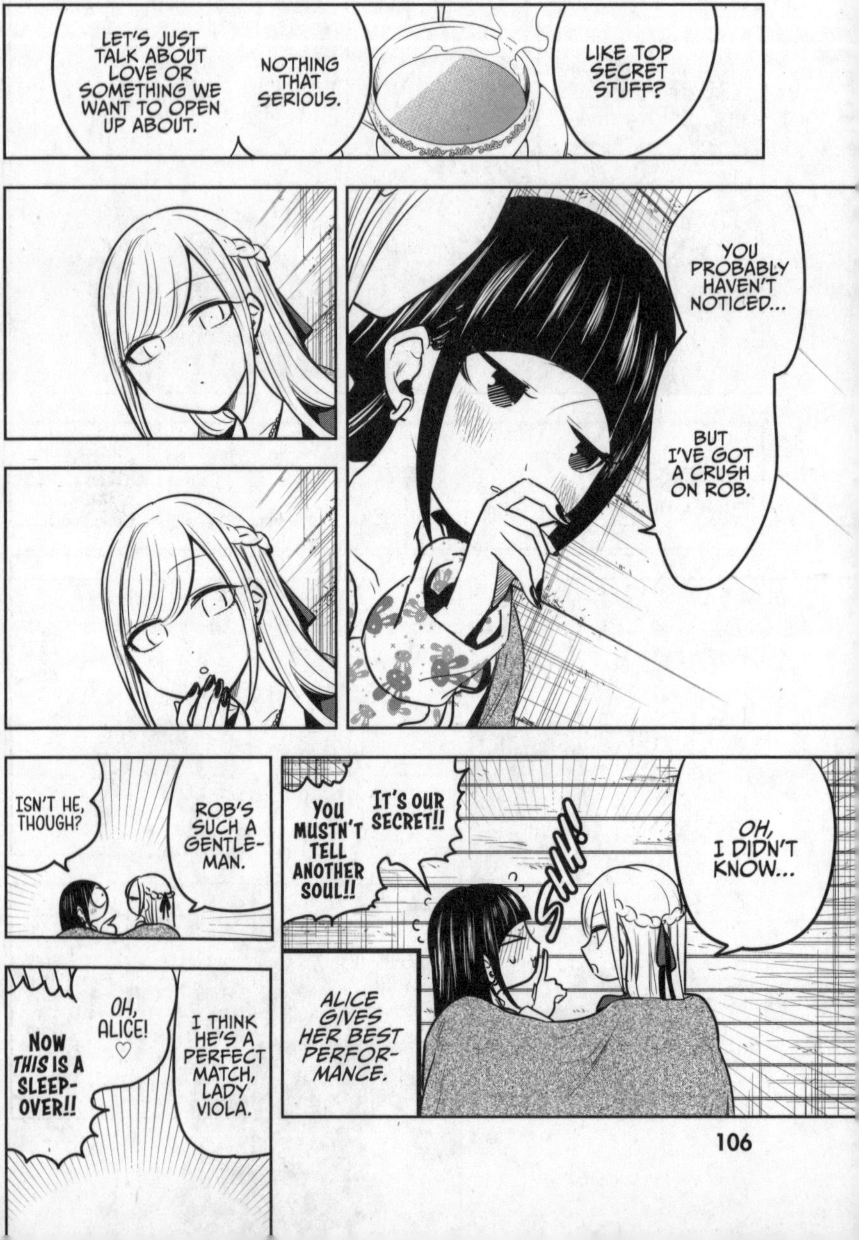
LIKE TOP SECRET STUFF?
NOTHING THAT SERIOUS.
LET'S JUST TALK ABOUT LOVE OR SOMETHING WE WANT TO OPEN UP ABOUT.
YOU PROBABLY HAVEN'T NOTICED...
BUT I'VE GOT A CRUSH ON ROB.
OH, I DIDN'T KNOW...
SHH!
IT'S OUR SECRET!!
YOU MUSTN'T TELL ANOTHER SOUL!!
ROB'S SUCH A GENTLEMAN.
ISN'T HE, THOUGH?
ALICE GIVES HER BEST PERFORMANCE.
I THINK HE'S A PERFECT MATCH, LADY VIOLA.
OH, ALICE! ♡
NOW THIS IS A SLEEPOVER!!

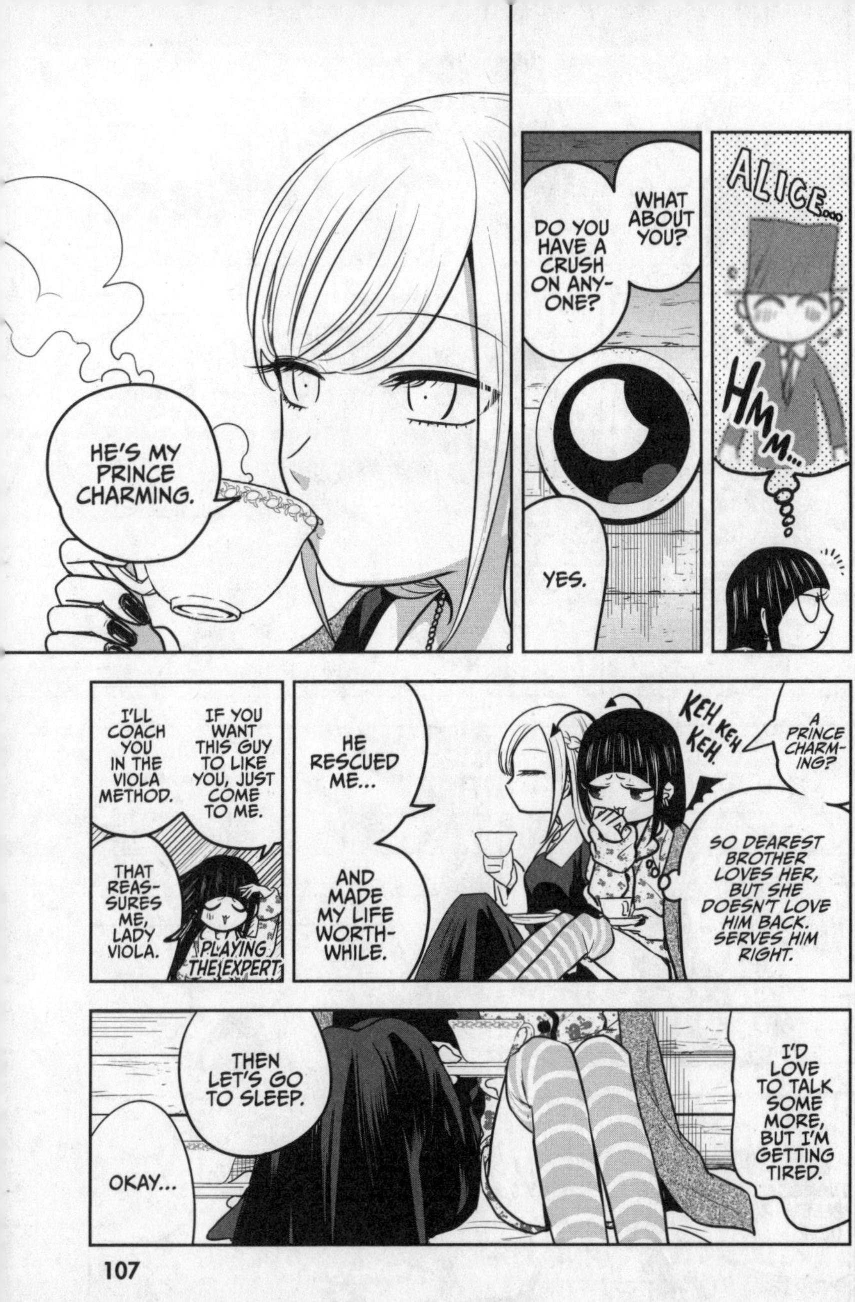
ALICE...
HMM...
WHAT ABOUT YOU?
DO YOU HAVE A CRUSH ON ANY-ONE?
YES.
HE'S MY PRINCE CHARMING.
KEH KEH KEH.
A PRINCE CHARM-ING?
SO DEAREST BROTHER LOVES HER, BUT SHE DOESN'T LOVE HIM BACK. SERVES HIM RIGHT.
HE RESCUED ME...
AND MADE MY LIFE WORTH-WHILE.
IF YOU WANT THIS GUY TO LIKE YOU, JUST COME TO ME.
I'LL COACH YOU IN THE VIOLA METHOD.
THAT REAS-SURES ME, LADY VIOLA.
PLAYING THE EXPERT
I'D LOVE TO TALK SOME MORE, BUT I'M GETTING TIRED.
THEN LET'S GO TO SLEEP.
OKAY...

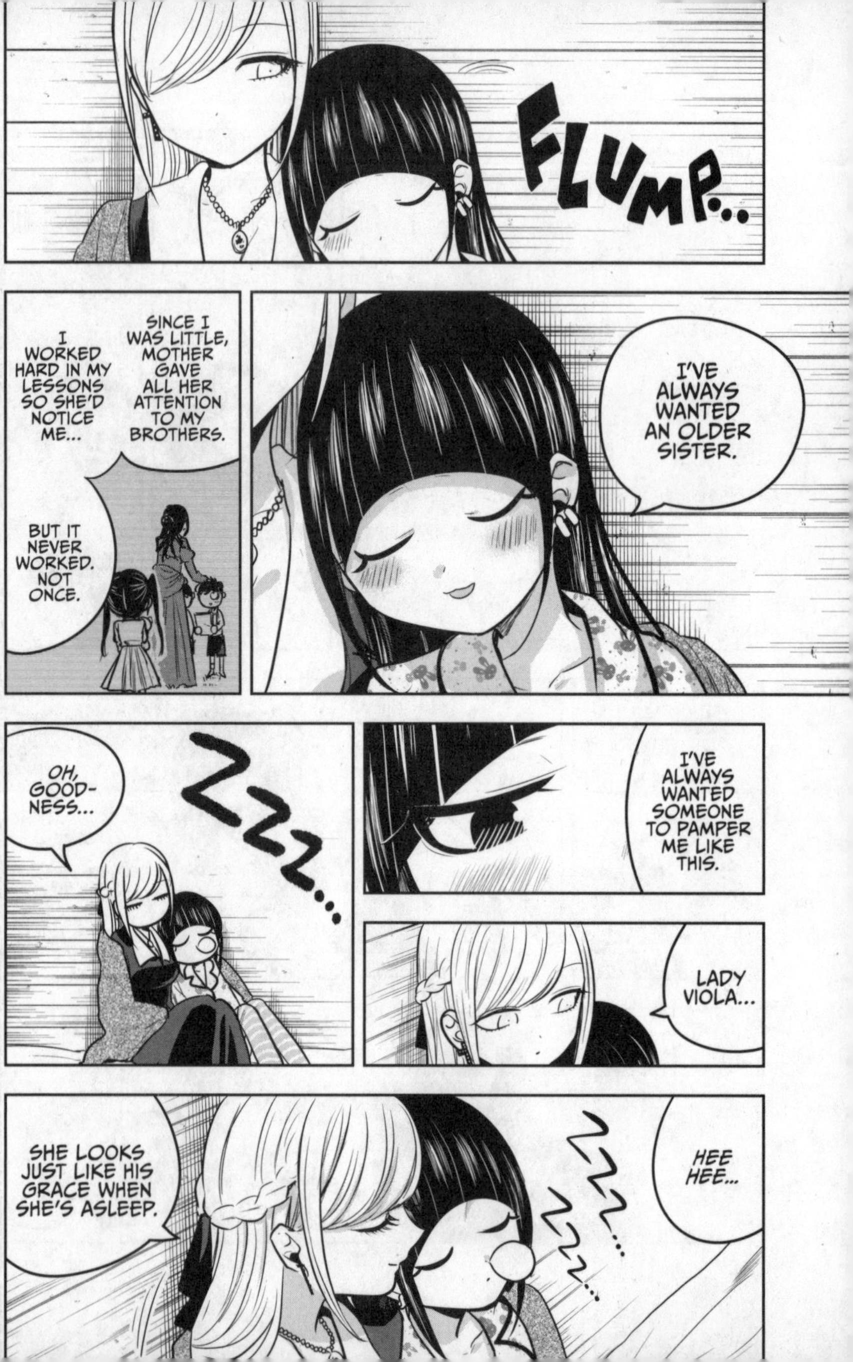
FLUMP...
I'VE ALWAYS WANTED AN OLDER SISTER.
SINCE I WAS LITTLE, MOTHER GAVE ALL HER ATTENTION TO MY BROTHERS.
I WORKED HARD IN MY LESSONS SO SHE'D NOTICE ME...
BUT IT NEVER WORKED. NOT ONCE.
I'VE ALWAYS WANTED SOMEONE TO PAMPER ME LIKE THIS.
LADY VIOLA...
ZZZ...
OH, GOODNESS...
HEE HEE...
ZZZ...
ZZZ...
SHE LOOKS JUST LIKE HIS GRACE WHEN SHE'S ASLEEP.

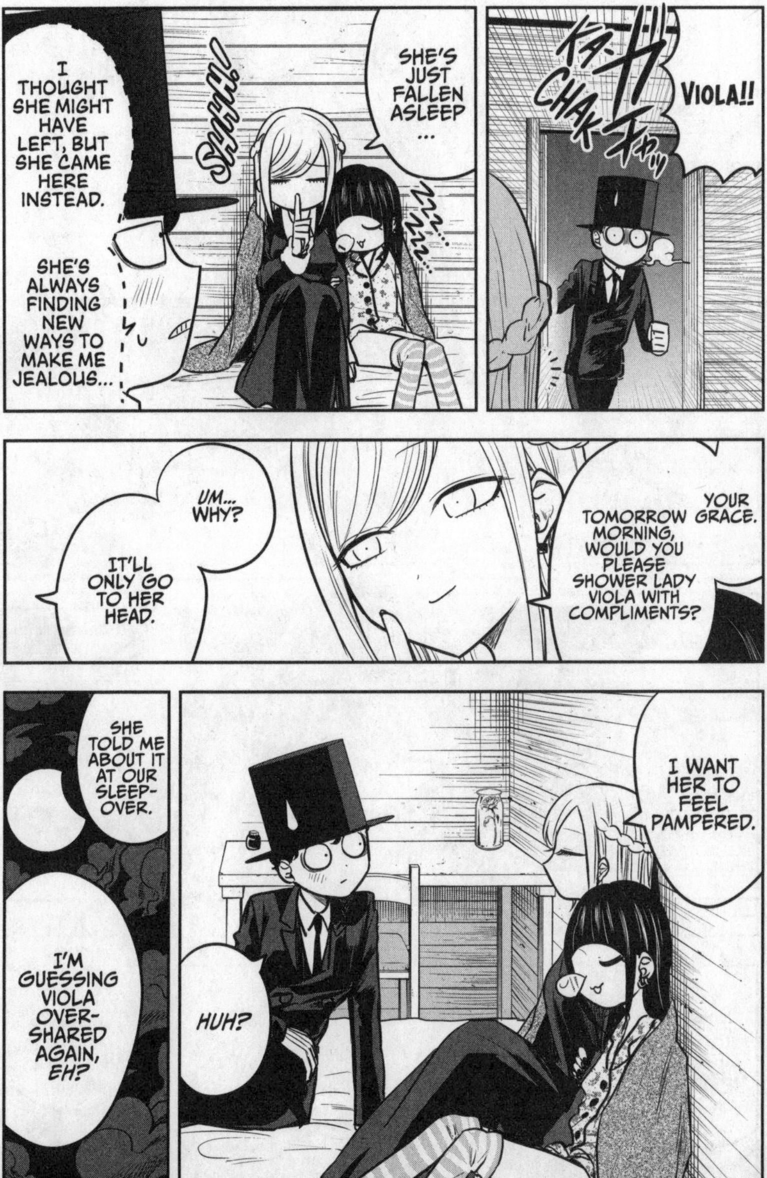
KA-CHAK
VIOLA!!
SHE'S JUST FALLEN ASLEEP ...
I THOUGHT SHE MIGHT HAVE LEFT, BUT SHE CAME HERE INSTEAD.
SHE'S ALWAYS FINDING NEW WAYS TO MAKE ME JEALOUS...
YOUR GRACE. TOMORROW MORNING, WOULD YOU PLEASE SHOWER LADY VIOLA WITH COMPLIMENTS?
UM... WHY?
IT'LL ONLY GO TO HER HEAD.
I WANT HER TO FEEL PAMPERED.
HUH?
SHE TOLD ME ABOUT IT AT OUR SLEEP-OVER.
I'M GUESSING VIOLA OVER-SHARED AGAIN, EH?

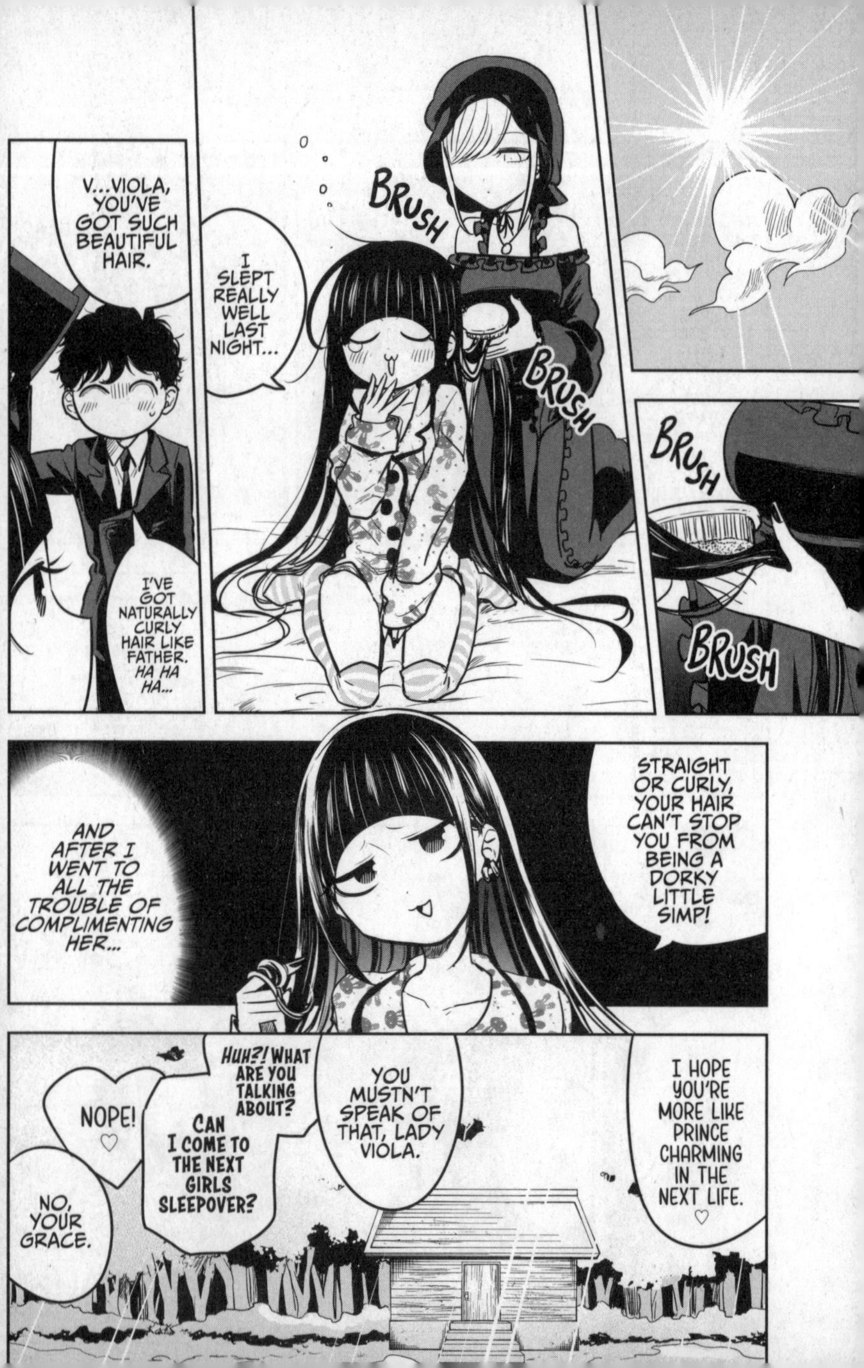
BRUSH
BRUSH
BRUSH
I SLEPT REALLY WELL LAST NIGHT...
BRUSH
V...VIOLA, YOU'VE GOT SUCH BEAUTIFUL HAIR.
I'VE GOT NATURALLY CURLY HAIR LIKE FATHER. HA HA HA...
STRAIGHT OR CURLY, YOUR HAIR CAN'T STOP YOU FROM BEING A DORKY LITTLE SIMP!
AND AFTER I WENT TO ALL THE TROUBLE OF COMPLIMENTING HER...
I HOPE YOU'RE MORE LIKE PRINCE CHARMING IN THE NEXT LIFE. ♡
YOU MUSTN'T SPEAK OF THAT, LADY VIOLA.
HUH?! WHAT ARE YOU TALKING ABOUT?
CAN I COME TO THE NEXT GIRLS SLEEPOVER?
NOPE! ♡
NO, YOUR GRACE.

THE DUKE OF DEATH AND HIS MAID

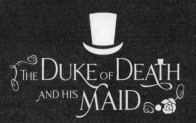

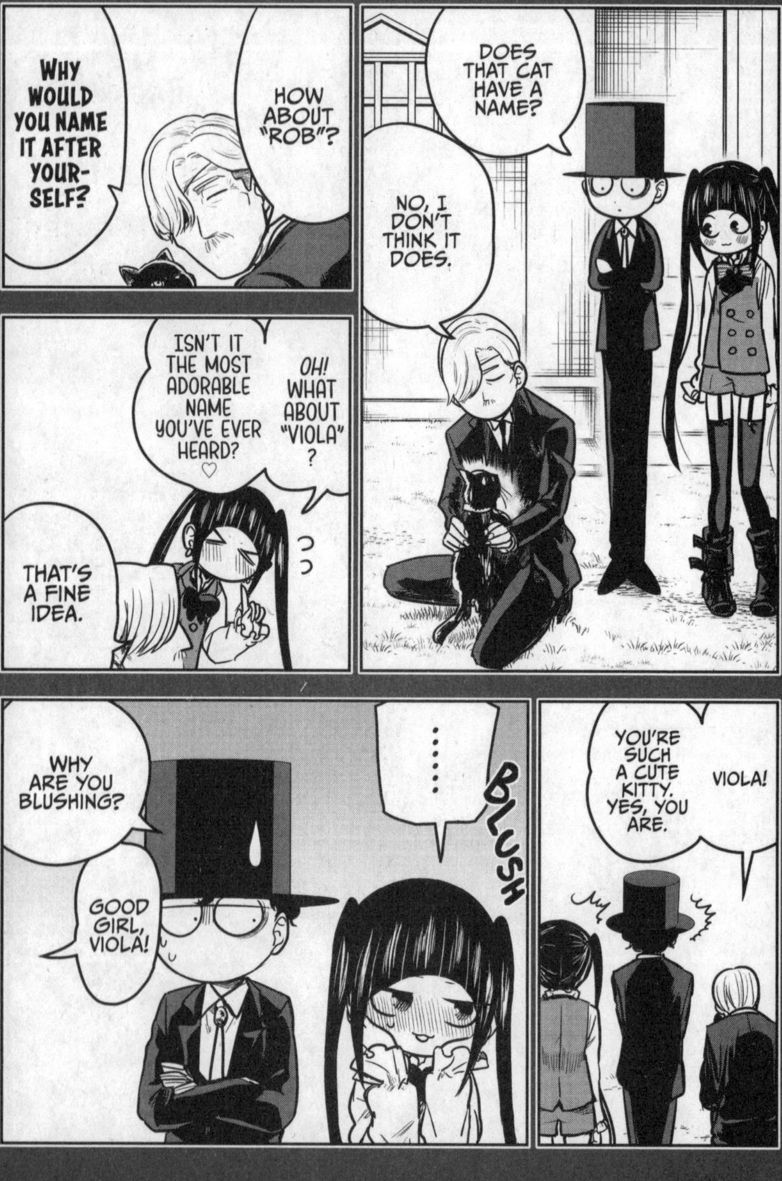
DOES THAT CAT HAVE A NAME?
NO, I DON'T THINK IT DOES.
HOW ABOUT "ROB"?
WHY WOULD YOU NAME IT AFTER YOUR-SELF?
OH! WHAT ABOUT "VIOLA"?
ISN'T IT THE MOST ADORABLE NAME YOU'VE EVER HEARD? ♡
THAT'S A FINE IDEA.
VIOLA!
YOU'RE SUCH A CUTE KITTY. YES, YOU ARE.
......
BLUSH
WHY ARE YOU BLUSHING?
GOOD GIRL, VIOLA!

Chapter 38: The Witches' Sabbath Pt. 1

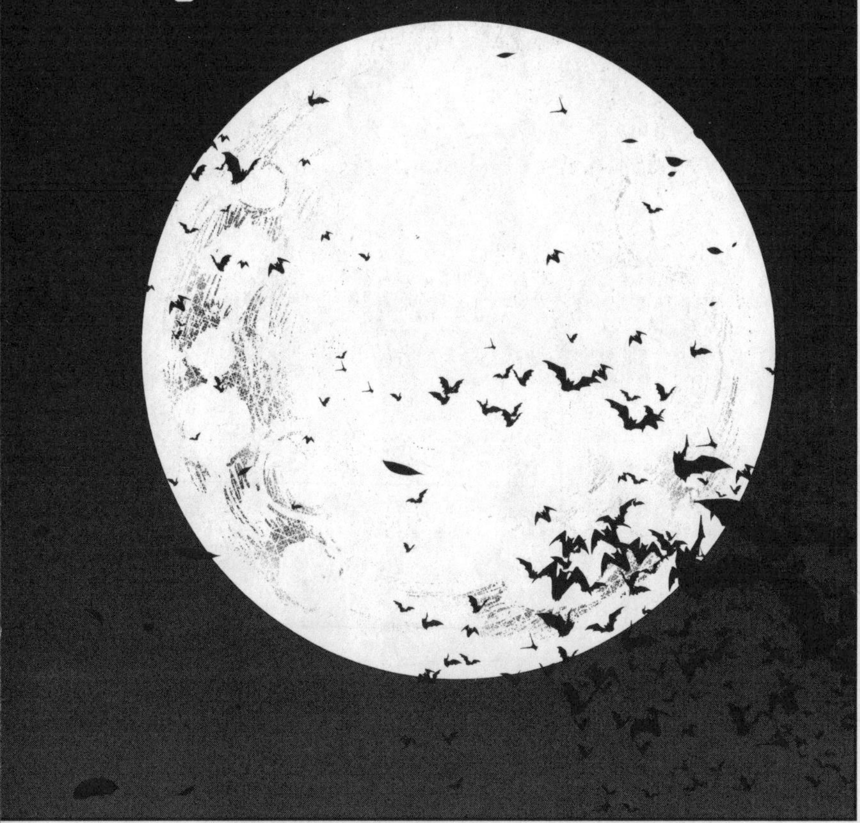

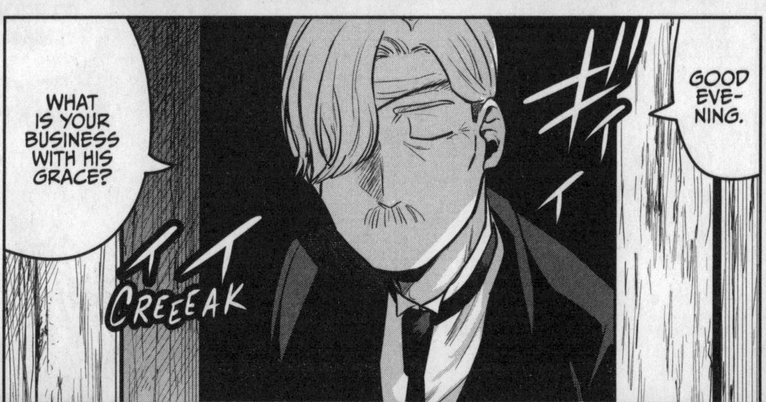
GOOD EVE-NING.
WHAT IS YOUR BUSINESS WITH HIS GRACE?
CREEEAK

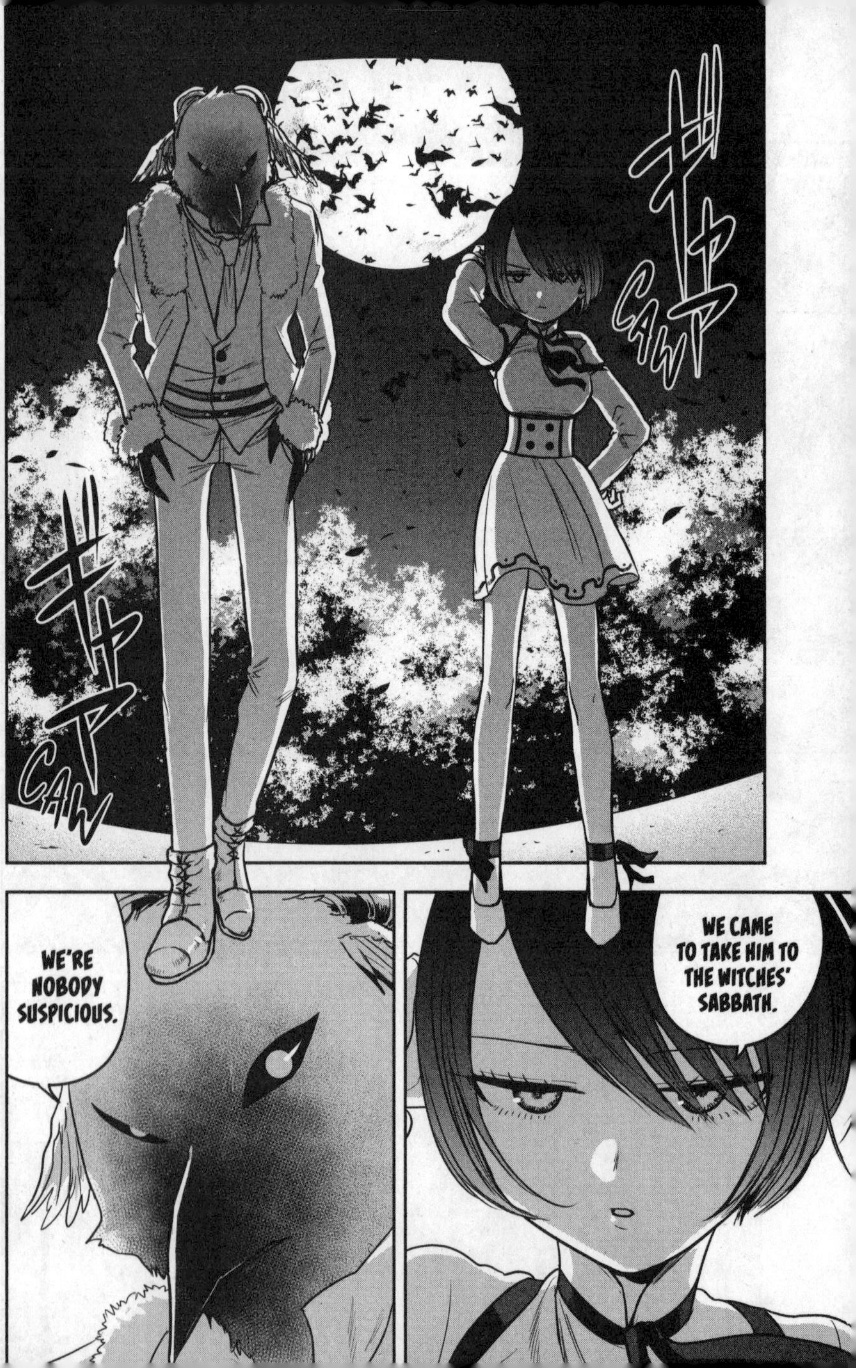
CAW
CAW
WE CAME TO TAKE HIM TO THE WITCHES' SABBATH.
WE'RE NOBODY SUSPICIOUS.

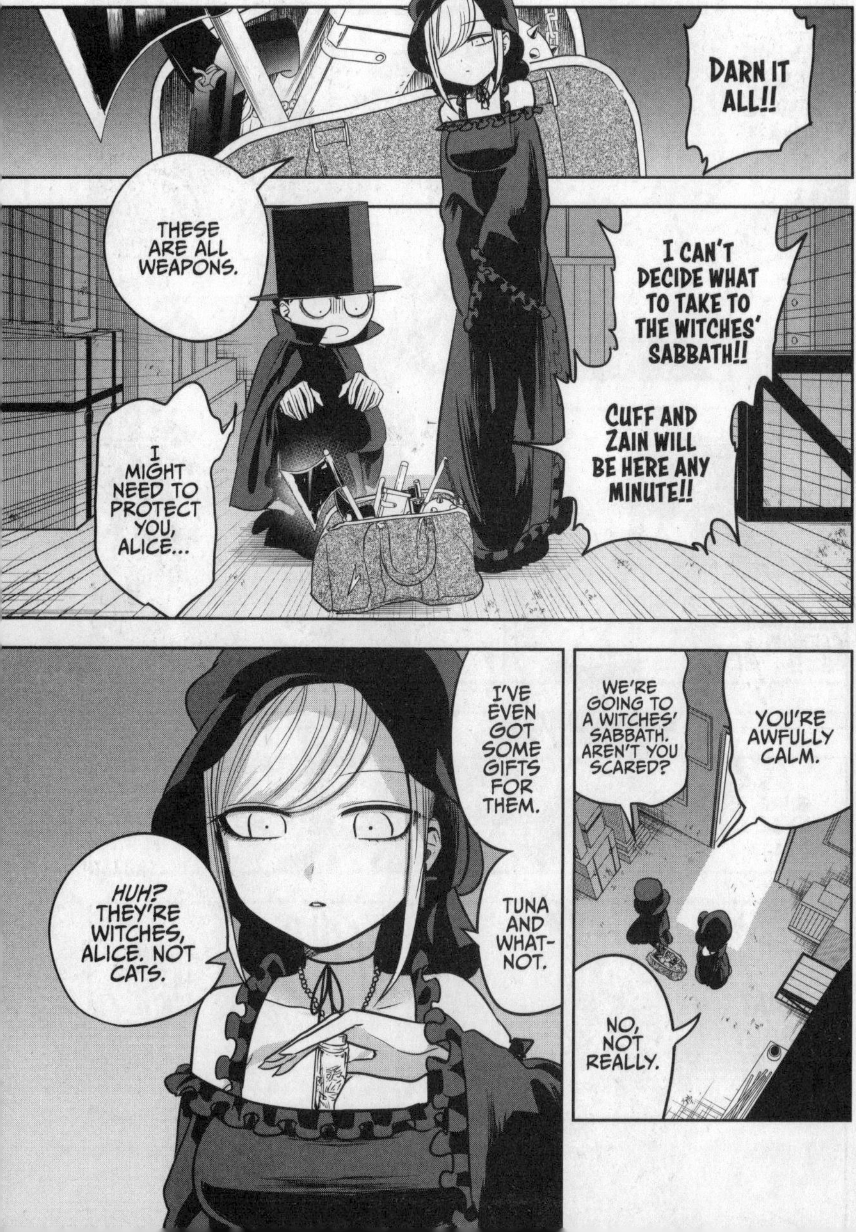
DARN IT ALL!!
I CAN'T DECIDE WHAT TO TAKE TO THE WITCHES' SABBATH!!
CUFF AND ZAIN WILL BE HERE ANY MINUTE!!
THESE ARE ALL WEAPONS.
I MIGHT NEED TO PROTECT YOU, ALICE...
YOU'RE AWFULLY CALM.
WE'RE GOING TO A WITCHES' SABBATH. AREN'T YOU SCARED?
NO, NOT REALLY.
I'VE EVEN GOT SOME GIFTS FOR THEM.
TUNA AND WHAT-NOT.
HUH? THEY'RE WITCHES, ALICE. NOT CATS.

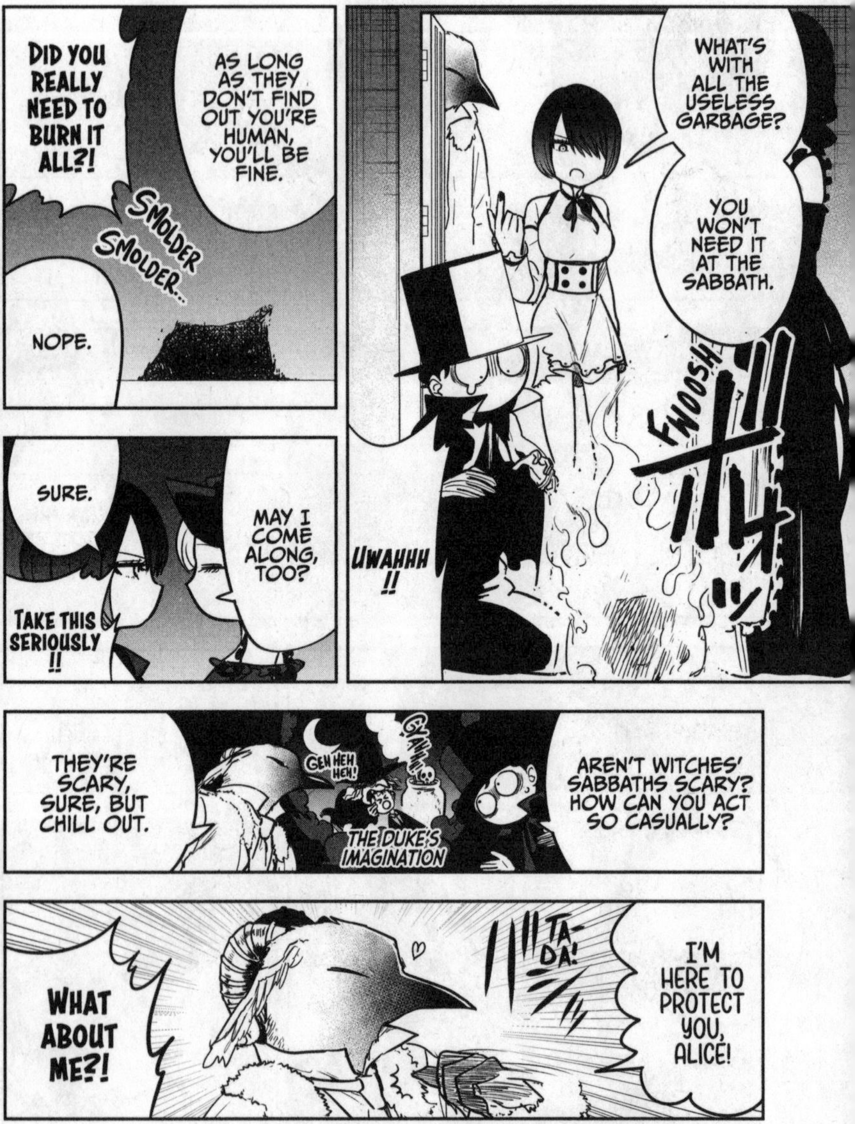
WHAT'S WITH ALL THE USELESS GARBAGE?
YOU WON'T NEED IT AT THE SABBATH.
FWOOSH
UWAHHH !!
AS LONG AS THEY DON'T FIND OUT YOU'RE HUMAN, YOU'LL BE FINE.
DID YOU REALLY NEED TO BURN IT ALL?!
SMOLDER SMOLDER...
NOPE.
MAY I COME ALONG, TOO?
SURE.
TAKE THIS SERIOUSLY !!
AREN'T WITCHES' SABBATHS SCARY? HOW CAN YOU ACT SO CASUALLY?
GEH HEH HEH!
THE DUKE'S IMAGINATION
THEY'RE SCARY, SURE, BUT CHILL OUT.
I'M HERE TO PROTECT YOU, ALICE!
TA-DA!
WHAT ABOUT ME?!

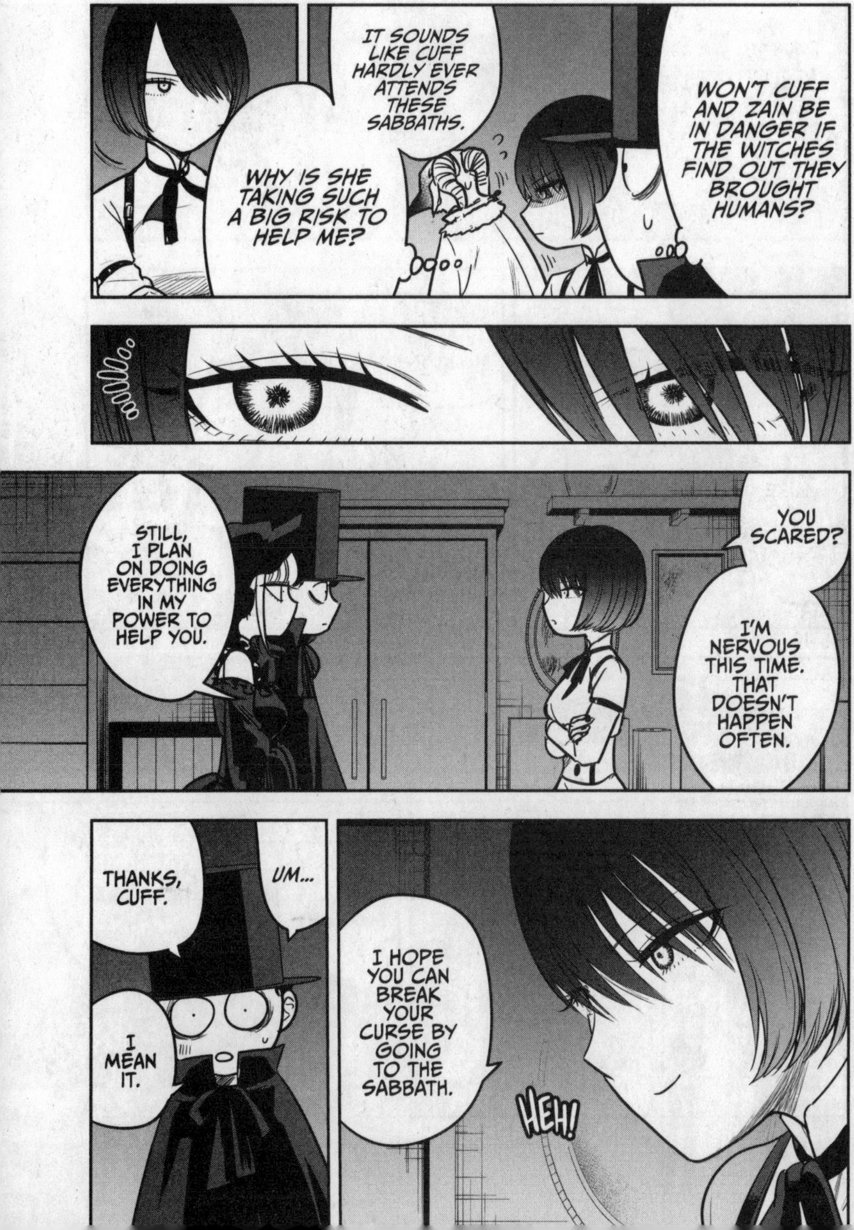
WON'T CUFF AND ZAIN BE IN DANGER IF THE WITCHES FIND OUT THEY BROUGHT HUMANS?
IT SOUNDS LIKE CUFF HARDLY EVER ATTENDS THESE SABBATHS.
WHY IS SHE TAKING SUCH A BIG RISK TO HELP ME?
YOU SCARED?
I'M NERVOUS THIS TIME. THAT DOESN'T HAPPEN OFTEN.
STILL, I PLAN ON DOING EVERYTHING IN MY POWER TO HELP YOU.
I HOPE YOU CAN BREAK YOUR CURSE BY GOING TO THE SABBATH.
HEH!
UM...
THANKS, CUFF.
I MEAN IT.

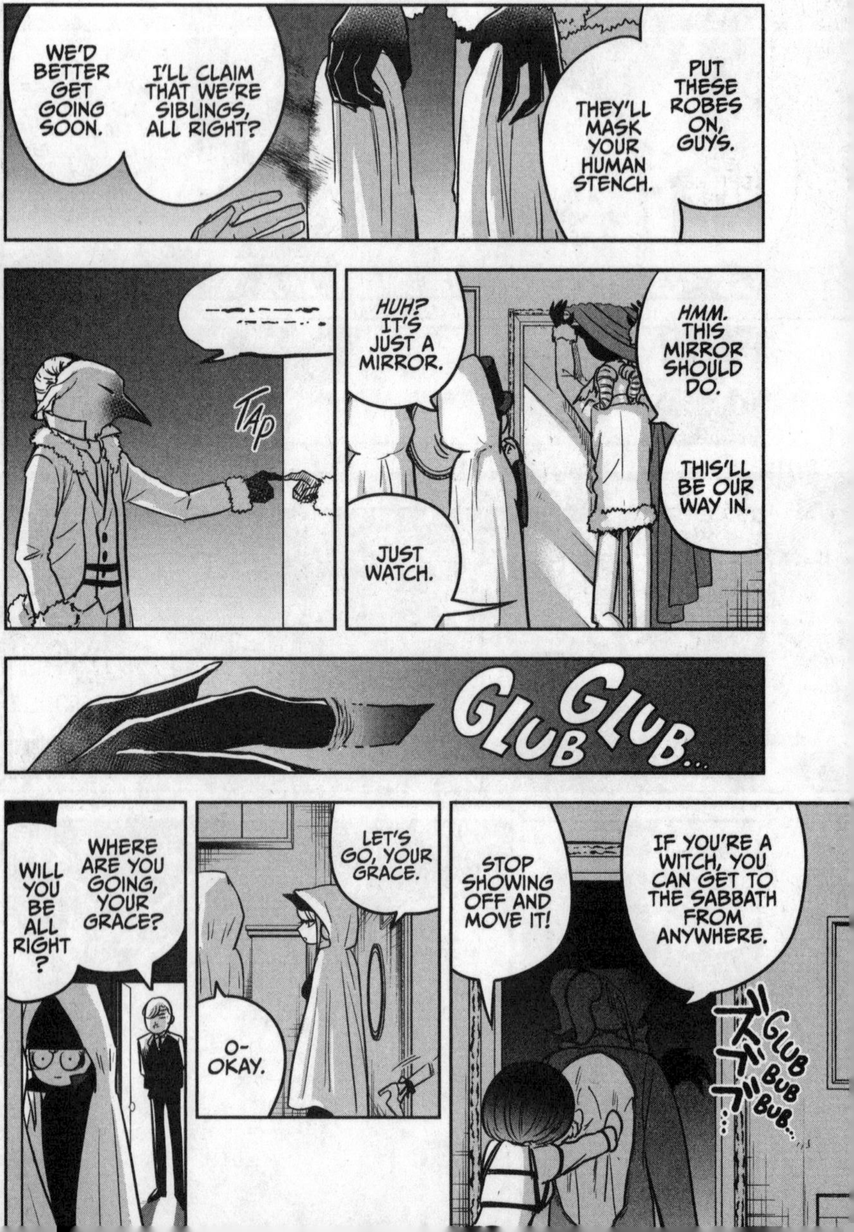

PUT THESE ROBES ON, GUYS.
THEY'LL MASK YOUR HUMAN STENCH.
I'LL CLAIM THAT WE'RE SIBLINGS, ALL RIGHT?
WE'D BETTER GET GOING SOON.
HMM. THIS MIRROR SHOULD DO.
THIS'LL BE OUR WAY IN.
HUH? IT'S JUST A MIRROR.
JUST WATCH.
TAP
GLUB GLUB...
IF YOU'RE A WITCH, YOU CAN GET TO THE SABBATH FROM ANYWHERE.
STOP SHOWING OFF AND MOVE IT!
GLUB BUB BUB...
LET'S GO, YOUR GRACE.
O-OKAY.
WHERE ARE YOU GOING, YOUR GRACE?
WILL YOU BE ALL RIGHT?

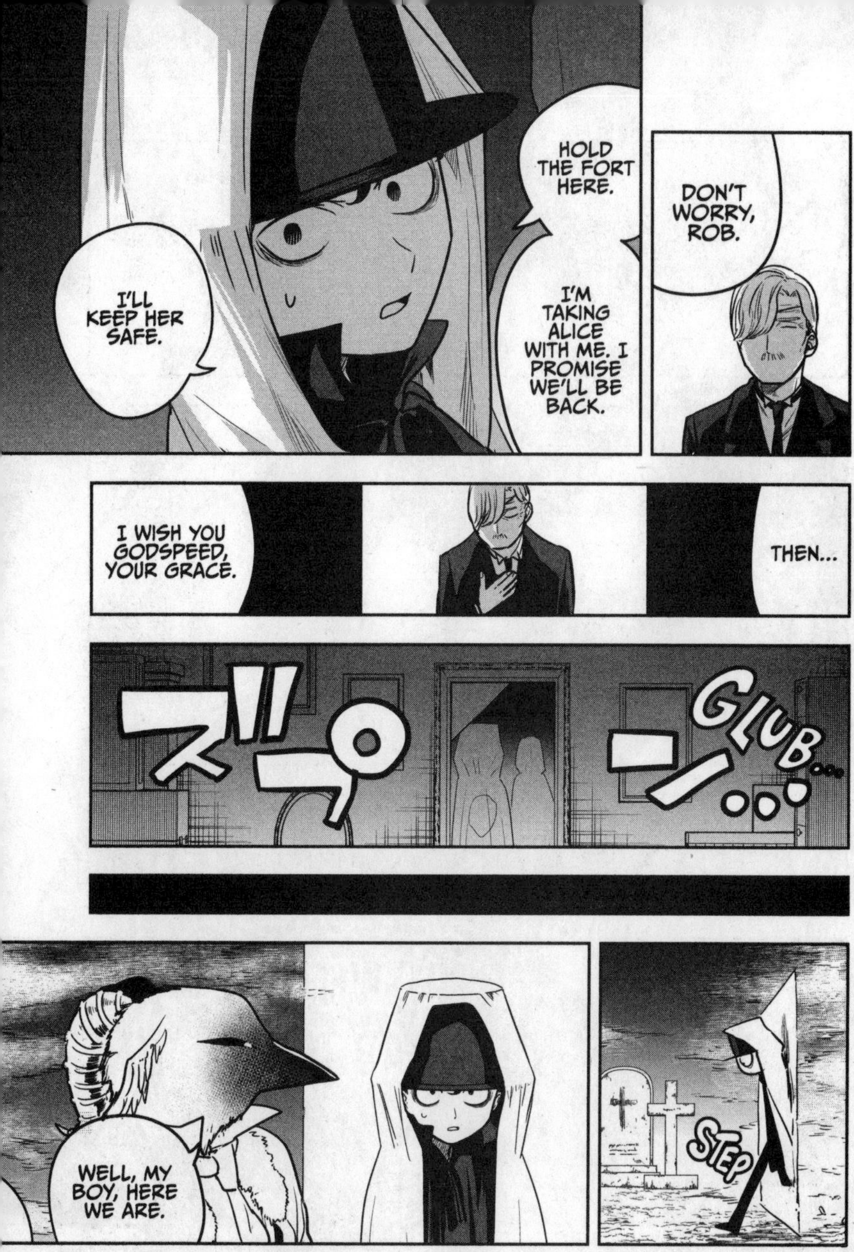
DON'T WORRY, ROB.
HOLD THE FORT HERE.
I'M TAKING ALICE WITH ME. I PROMISE WE'LL BE BACK.
I'LL KEEP HER SAFE.
THEN...
I WISH YOU GODSPEED, YOUR GRACE.
GLUB...
STEP
WELL, MY BOY, HERE WE ARE.

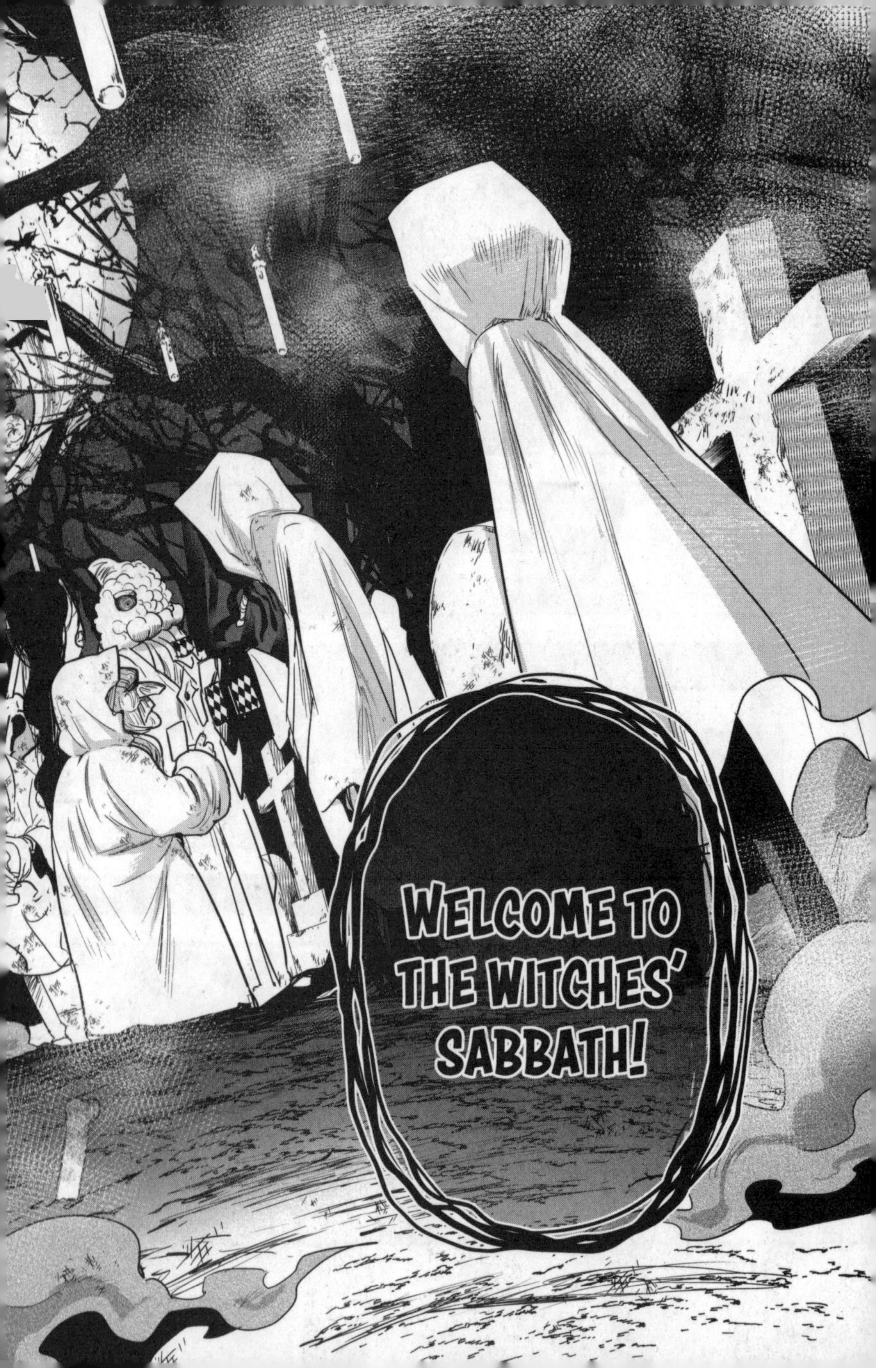
WELCOME TO THE WITCHES' SABBATH!

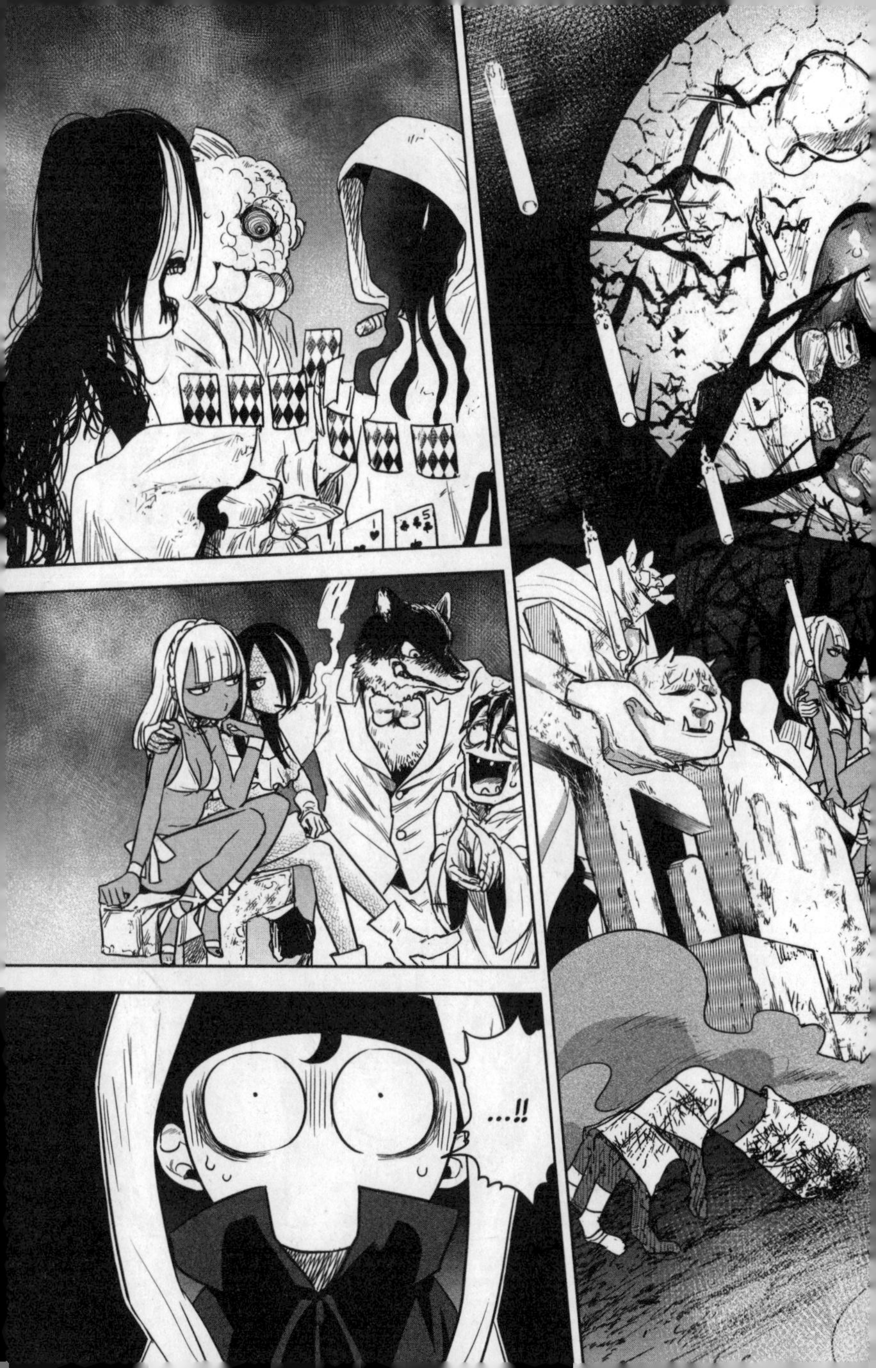
...!!

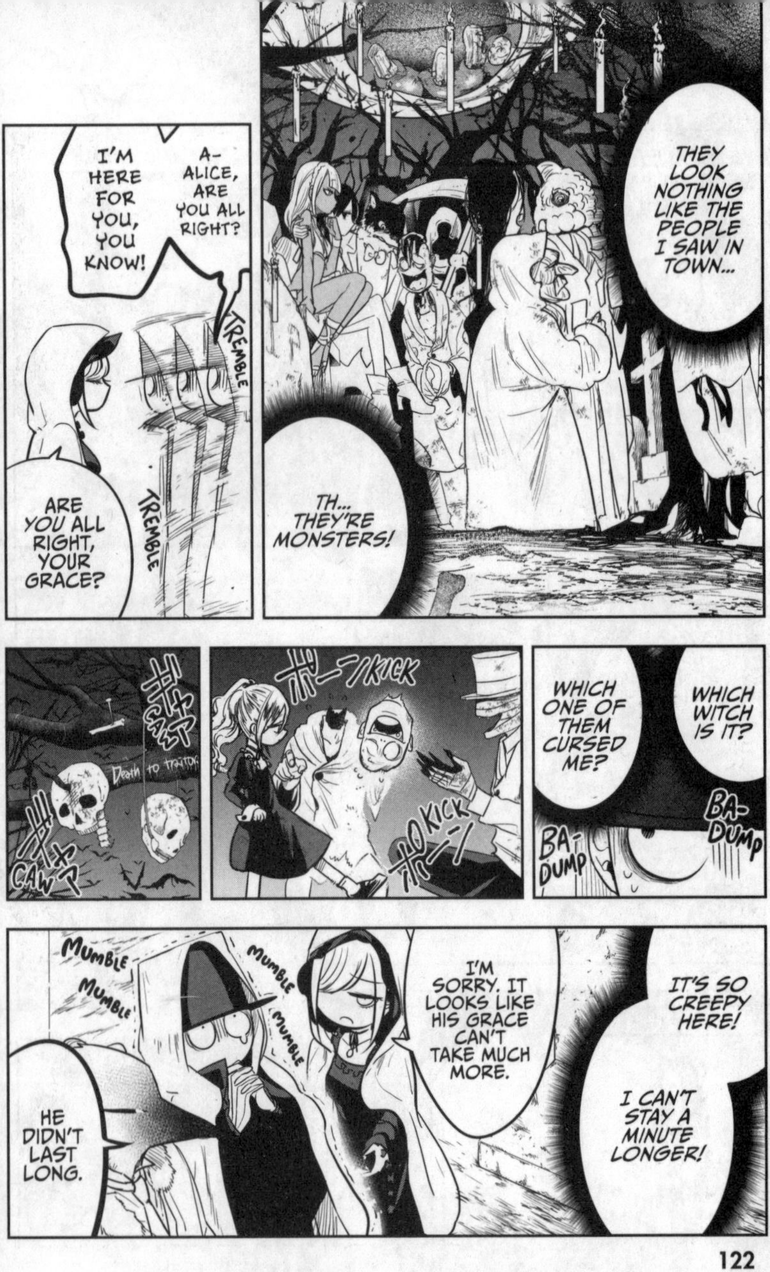
THEY LOOK NOTHING LIKE THE PEOPLE I SAW IN TOWN...
TH... THEY'RE MONSTERS!
A-ALICE, ARE YOU ALL RIGHT?
I'M HERE FOR YOU, YOU KNOW!
TREMBLE
TREMBLE
ARE YOU ALL RIGHT, YOUR GRACE?
WHICH WITCH IS IT?
WHICH ONE OF THEM CURSED ME?
BA-DUMP
BA-DUMP
ポーン/KICK
ポーン/KICK
ギャ CAW
Death to traitor
ギャ CAW
IT'S SO CREEPY HERE!
I CAN'T STAY A MINUTE LONGER!
I'M SORRY. IT LOOKS LIKE HIS GRACE CAN'T TAKE MUCH MORE.
MUMBLE
MUMBLE
MUMBLE
MUMBLE
HE DIDN'T LAST LONG.

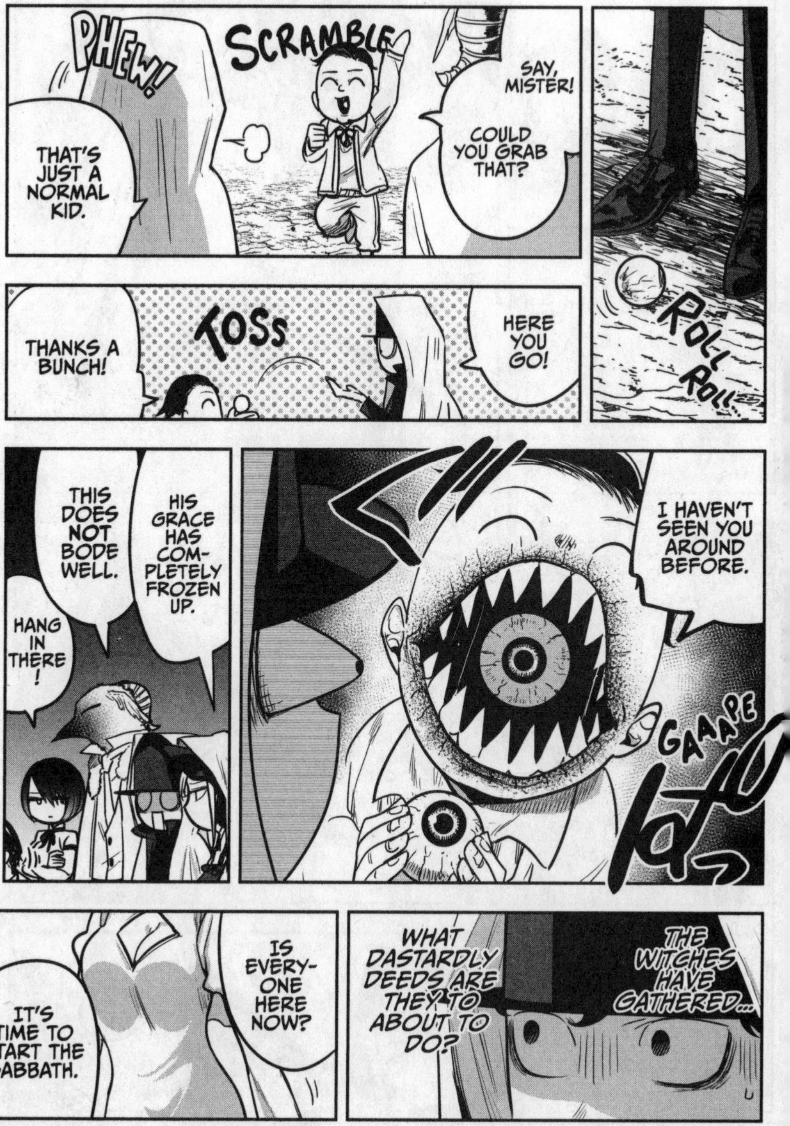
ROLL ROLL
SAY, MISTER!
COULD YOU GRAB THAT?
SCRAMBLE
PHEW!
THAT'S JUST A NORMAL KID.
HERE YOU GO!
TOSS
THANKS A BUNCH!
I HAVEN'T SEEN YOU AROUND BEFORE.
GAAAPE
HIS GRACE HAS COM-PLETELY FROZEN UP.
THIS DOES NOT BODE WELL.
HANG IN THERE!
THE WITCHES HAVE GATHERED...
WHAT DASTARDLY DEEDS ARE THEY TO ABOUT TO DO?
IS EVERY-ONE HERE NOW?
IT'S TIME TO START THE SABBATH.

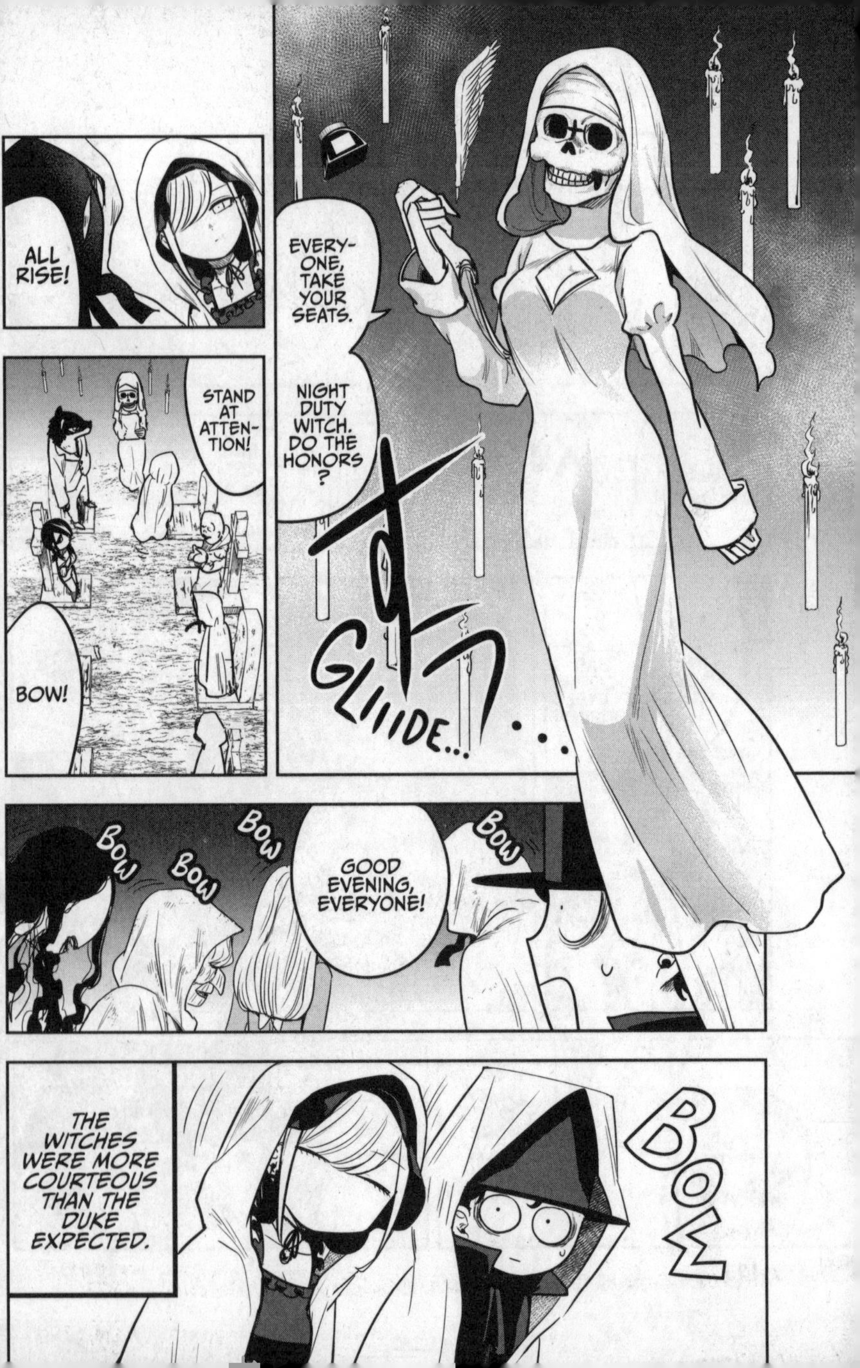
EVERY-ONE, TAKE YOUR SEATS.
NIGHT DUTY WITCH. DO THE HONORS?
GLIIIDE...
ALL RISE!
STAND AT ATTENTION!
BOW!
BOW
GOOD EVENING, EVERYONE!
BOW
BOW
BOW
BOW
THE WITCHES WERE MORE COURTEOUS THAN THE DUKE EXPECTED.

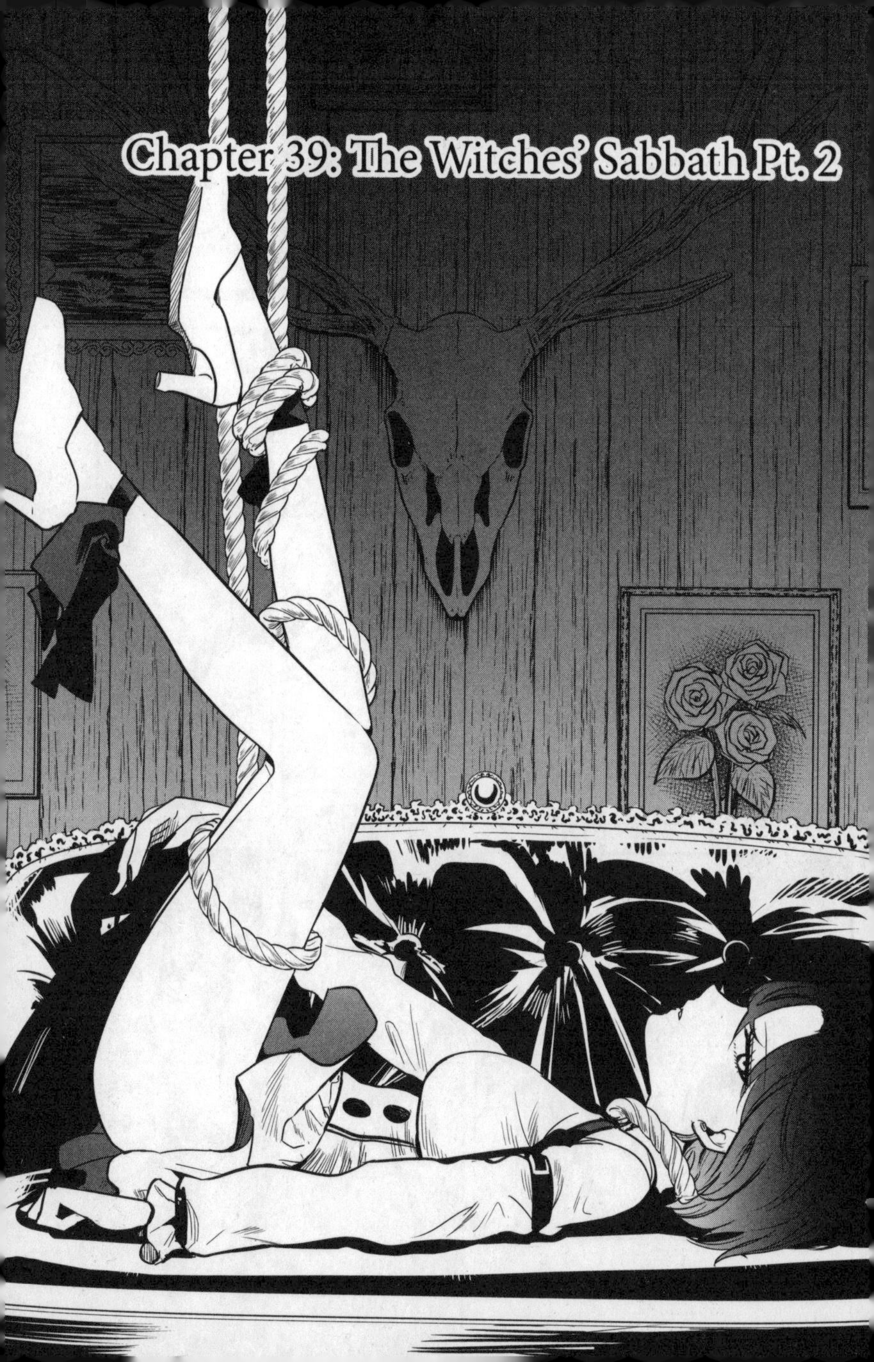
Chapter 39: The Witches' Sabbath Pt. 2

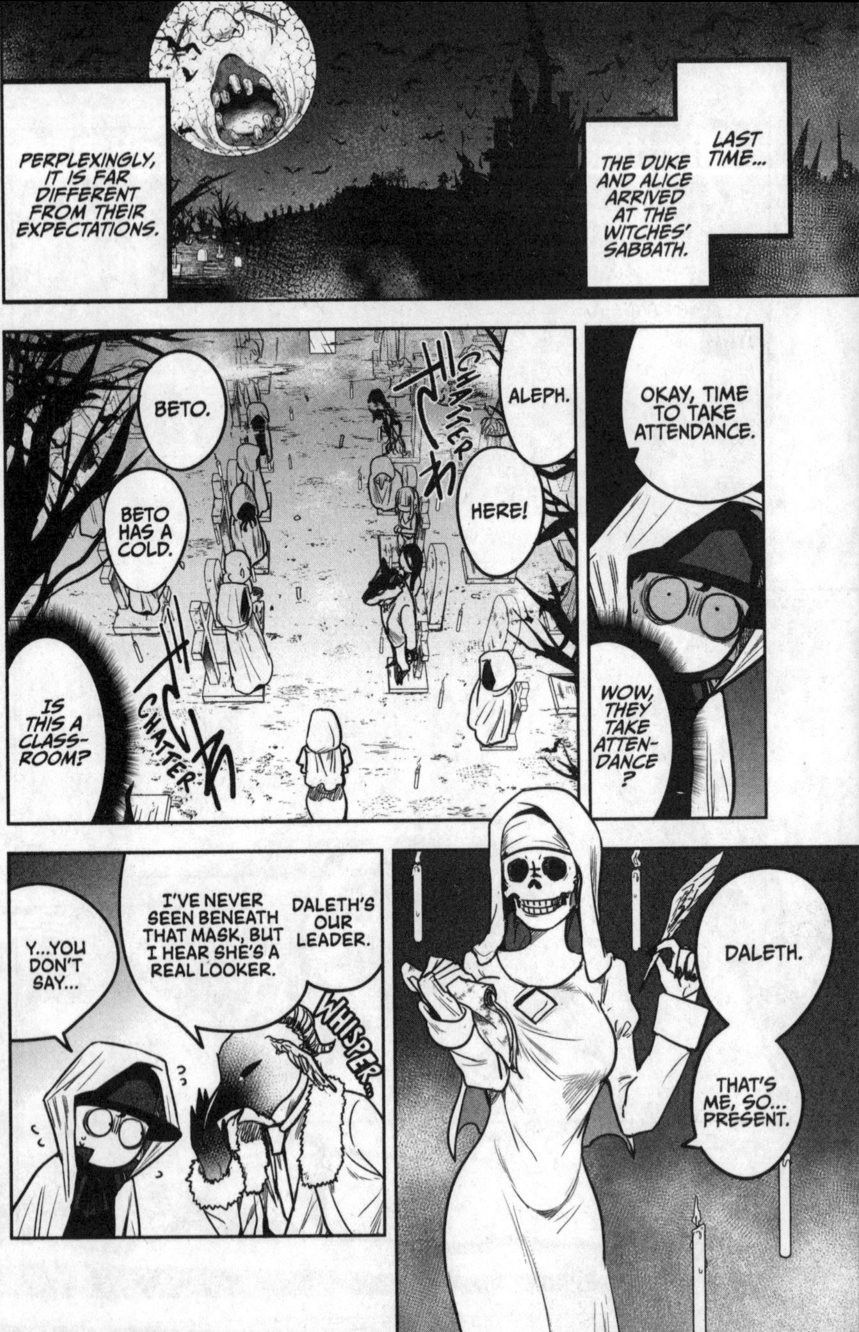
LAST TIME... THE DUKE AND ALICE ARRIVED AT THE WITCHES' SABBATH.
PERPLEXINGLY, IT IS FAR DIFFERENT FROM THEIR EXPECTATIONS.
OKAY, TIME TO TAKE ATTENDANCE.
WOW, THEY TAKE ATTENDANCE?
ALEPH.
HERE!
CHATTER
BETO.
BETO HAS A COLD.
CHATTER
IS THIS A CLASSROOM?
DALETH.
THAT'S ME, SO... PRESENT.
DALETH'S OUR LEADER.
I'VE NEVER SEEN BENEATH THAT MASK, BUT I HEAR SHE'S A REAL LOOKER.
WHISPER...
Y...YOU DON'T SAY...

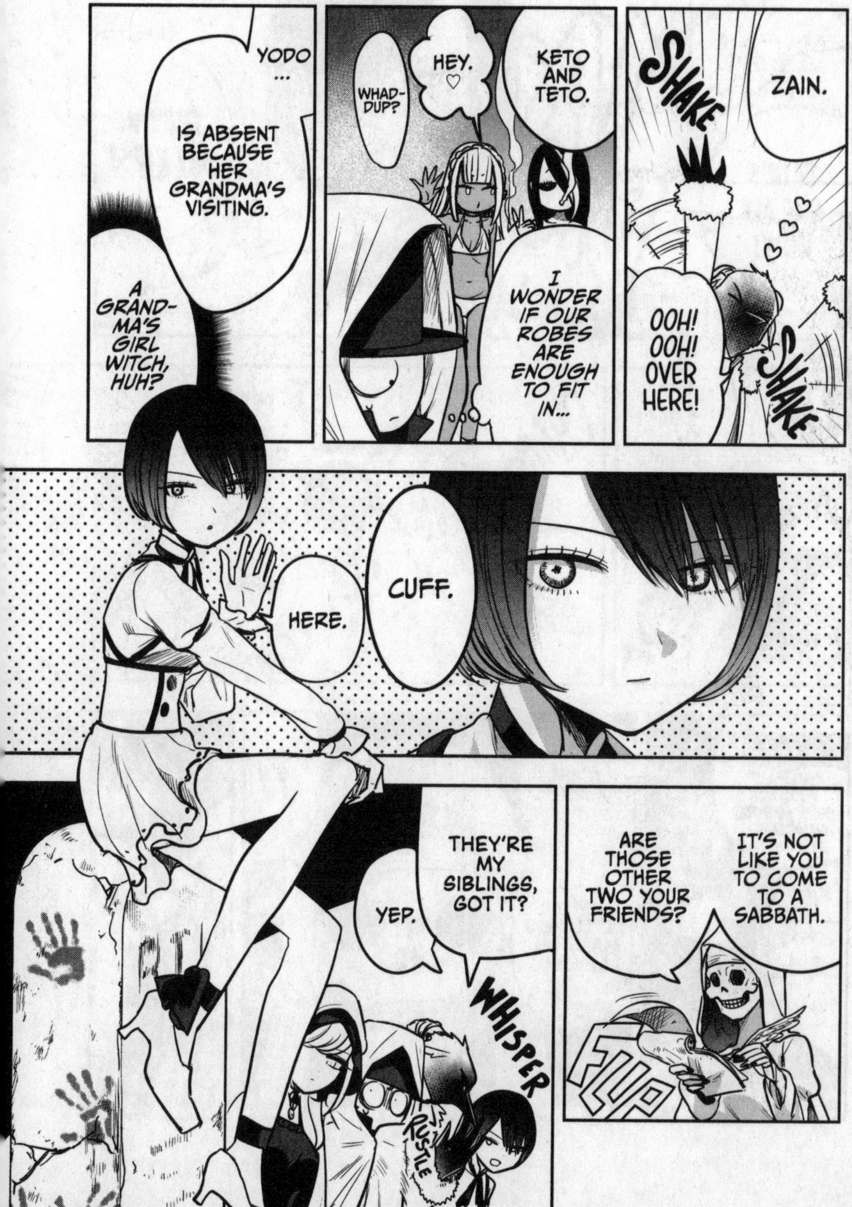
ZAIN.
SHAKE
SHAKE
OOH! OOH! OVER HERE!
KETO AND TETO.
HEY. ♡
WHAD-DUP?
I WONDER IF OUR ROBES ARE ENOUGH TO FIT IN...
YODO ... IS ABSENT BECAUSE HER GRANDMA'S VISITING.
A GRAND-MA'S GIRL WITCH, HUH?
CUFF.
HERE.
IT'S NOT LIKE YOU TO COME TO A SABBATH.
ARE THOSE OTHER TWO YOUR FRIENDS?
FLIP
THEY'RE MY SIBLINGS, GOT IT?
YEP.
WHISPER
RUSTLE

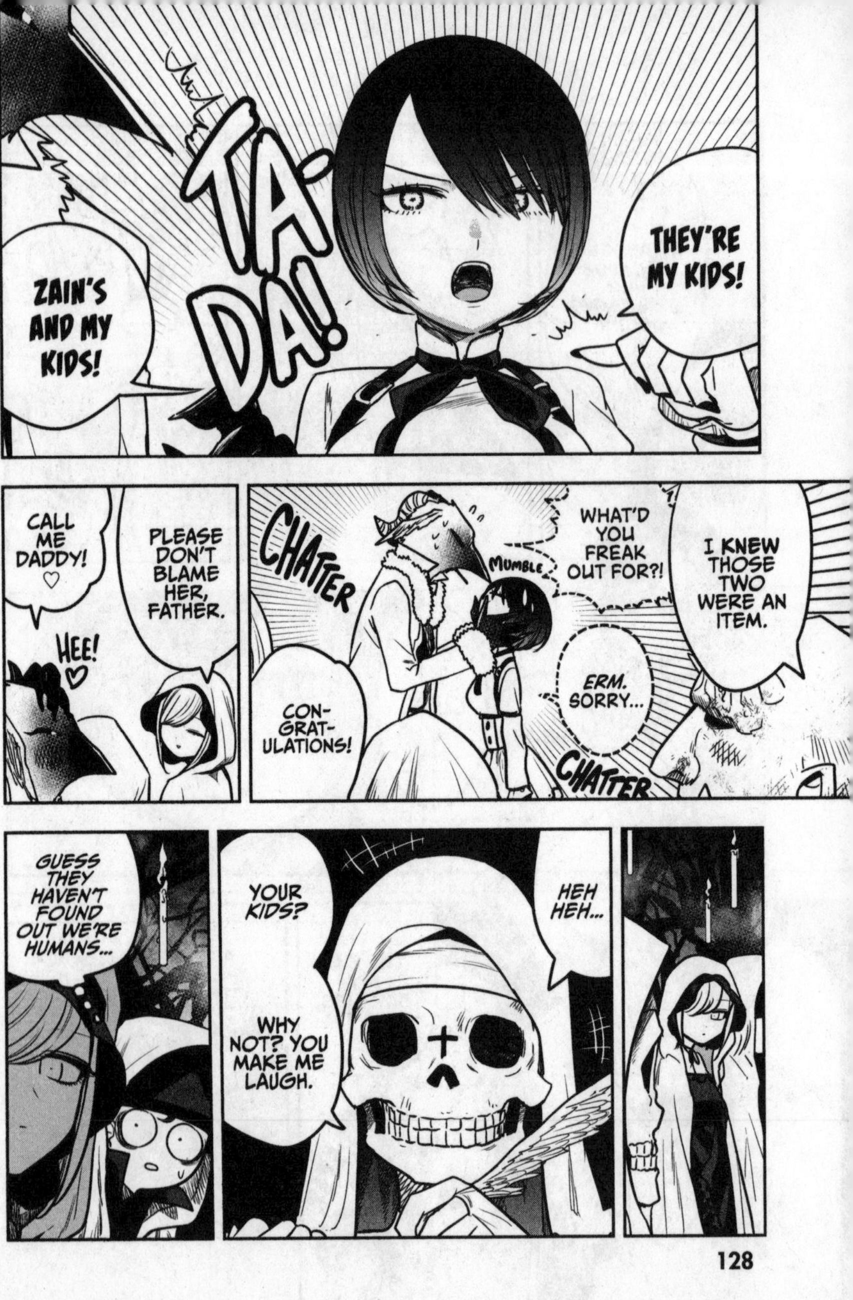
THEY'RE MY KIDS!
TA-DA!
ZAIN'S AND MY KIDS!
I KNEW THOSE TWO WERE AN ITEM.
WHAT'D YOU FREAK OUT FOR?!
ERM. SORRY...
MUMBLE
CHATTER
CON-GRAT-ULATIONS!
CHATTER
PLEASE DON'T BLAME HER, FATHER.
CALL ME DADDY! ♡
HEE! ♡
HEH HEH...
YOUR KIDS?
WHY NOT? YOU MAKE ME LAUGH.
GUESS THEY HAVEN'T FOUND OUT WE'RE HUMANS...

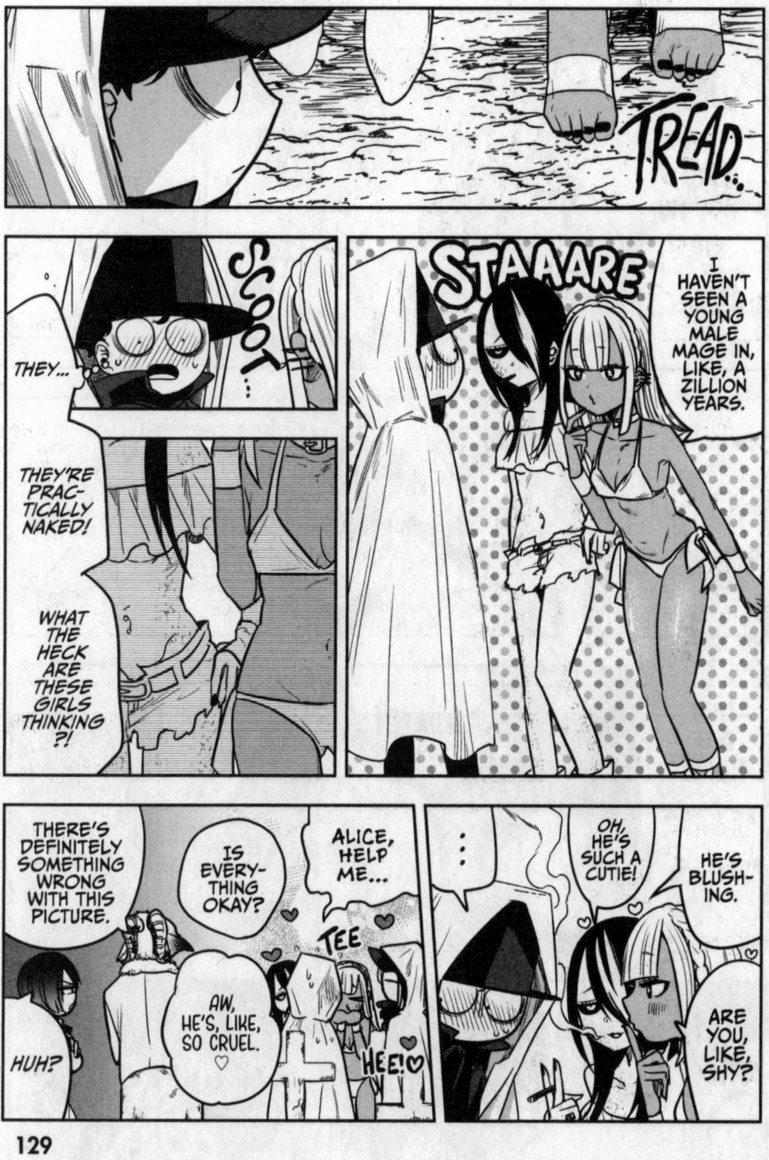
TREAD...
STAAARE
I HAVEN'T SEEN A YOUNG MALE MAGE IN, LIKE, A ZILLION YEARS.
SCOOT...
THEY...
THEY'RE PRAC-TICALLY NAKED!
WHAT THE HECK ARE THESE GIRLS THINKING?!
HE'S BLUSH-ING.
OH, HE'S SUCH A CUTIE!
...
ARE YOU, LIKE, SHY?
ALICE, HELP ME...
IS EVERY-THING OKAY?
THERE'S DEFINITELY SOMETHING WRONG WITH THIS PICTURE.
TEE
HEE!♡
AW, HE'S, LIKE, SO CRUEL. ♡
HUH?

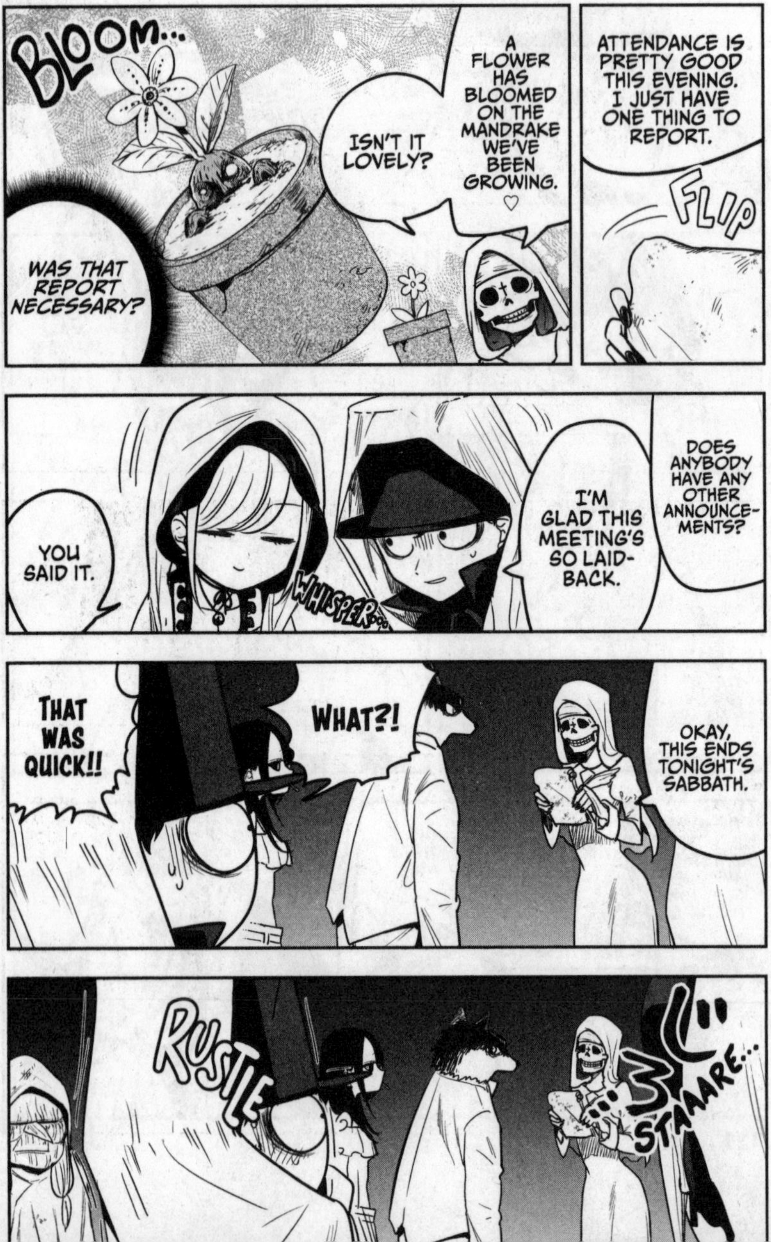
ATTENDANCE IS PRETTY GOOD THIS EVENING. I JUST HAVE ONE THING TO REPORT.
FLIP
A FLOWER HAS BLOOMED ON THE MANDRAKE WE'VE BEEN GROWING. ♡
ISN'T IT LOVELY?
BLOOM...
WAS THAT REPORT NECESSARY?
DOES ANYBODY HAVE ANY OTHER ANNOUNCE-MENTS?
I'M GLAD THIS MEETING'S SO LAID-BACK.
WHISPER
YOU SAID IT.
OKAY, THIS ENDS TONIGHT'S SABBATH.
WHAT?!
THAT WAS QUICK!!
STAAARE...
RUSTLE

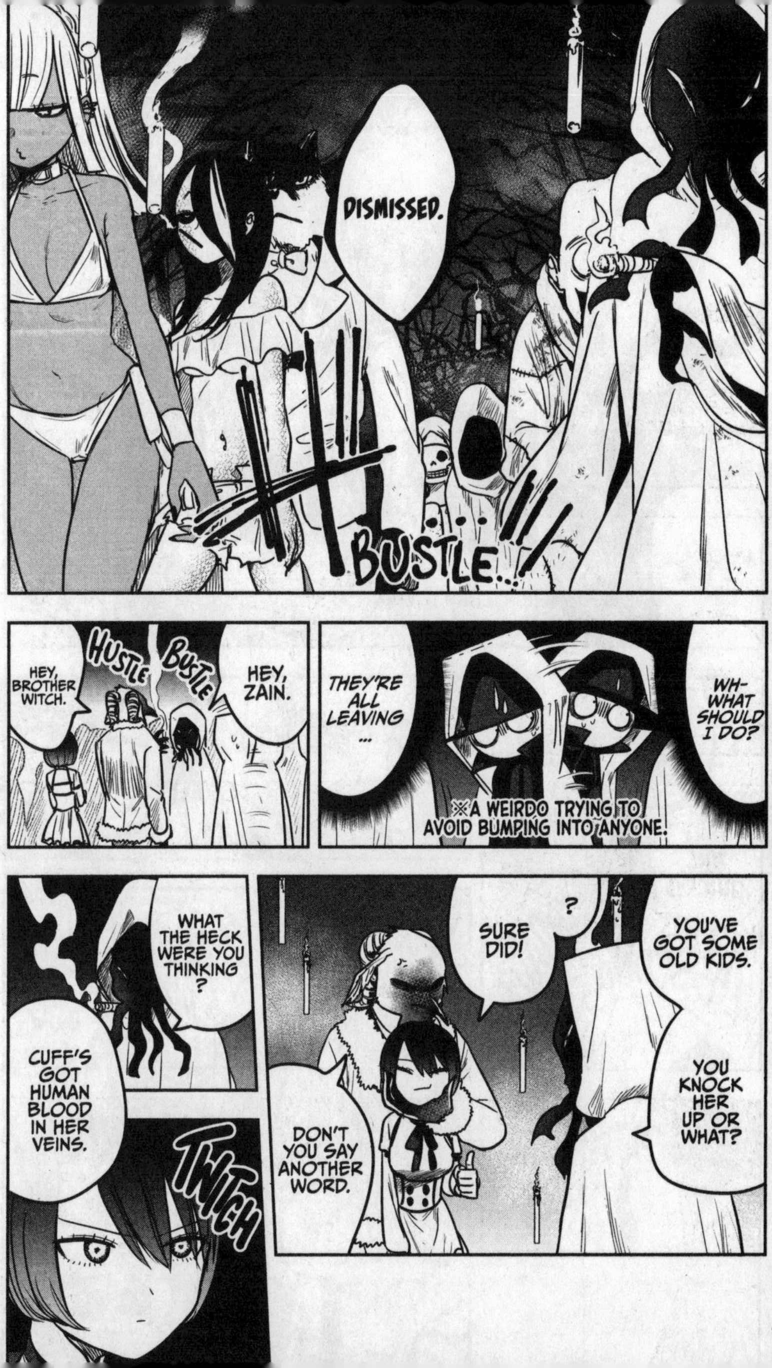
DISMISSED.
BUSTLE...
WH-WHAT SHOULD I DO?
THEY'RE ALL LEAVING ...
※A WEIRDO TRYING TO AVOID BUMPING INTO ANYONE.
HEY, ZAIN.
HUSTLE BUSTLE
HEY, BROTHER WITCH.
YOU'VE GOT SOME OLD KIDS.
?
SURE DID!
YOU KNOCK HER UP OR WHAT?
DON'T YOU SAY ANOTHER WORD.
WHAT THE HECK WERE YOU THINKING?
CUFF'S GOT HUMAN BLOOD IN HER VEINS.
TWITCH

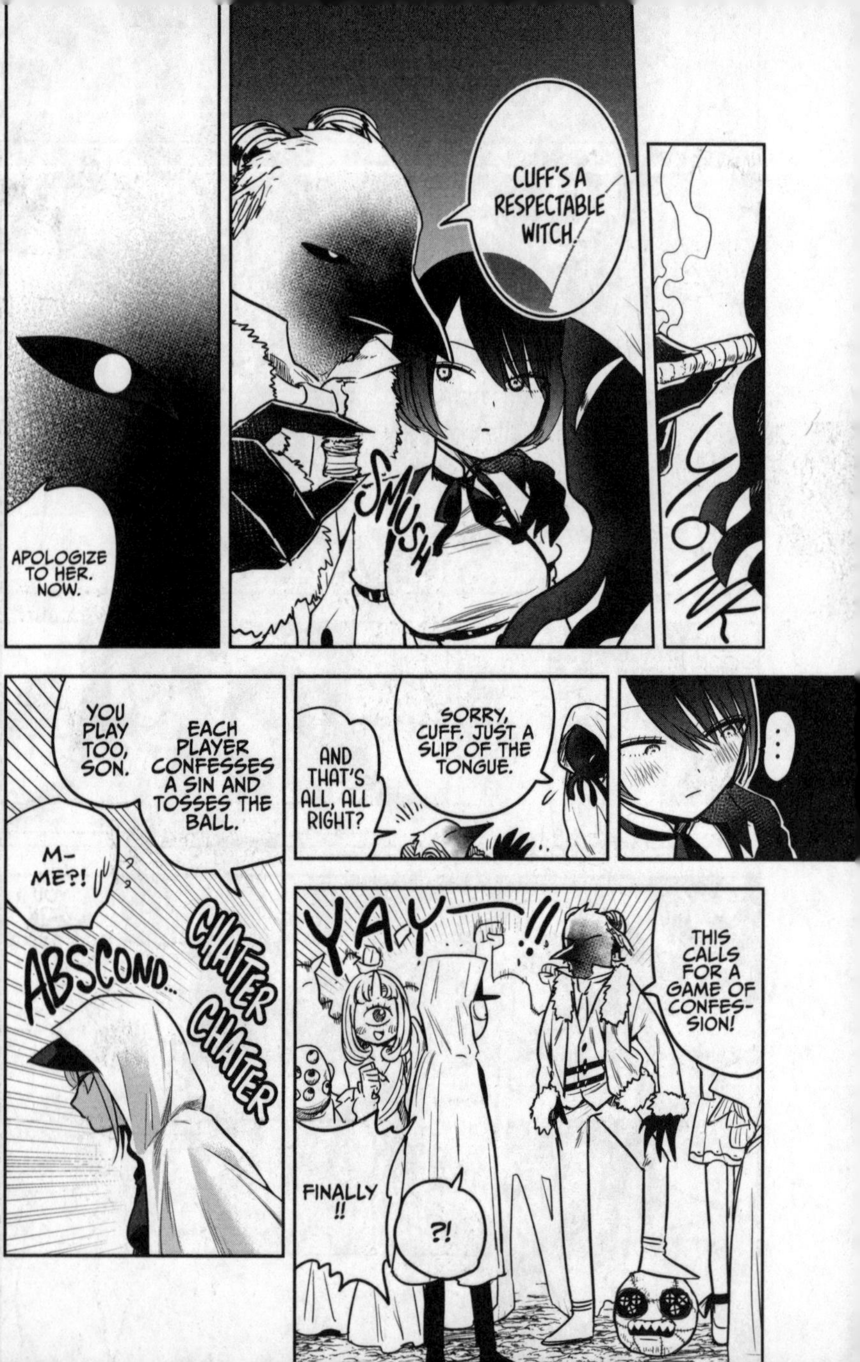
WHOINK
CUFF'S A RESPECTABLE WITCH.
SMUSH
APOLOGIZE TO HER. NOW.
...
SORRY, CUFF. JUST A SLIP OF THE TONGUE.
AND THAT'S ALL, ALL RIGHT?
THIS CALLS FOR A GAME OF CONFES-SION!
YAY—!!
FINALLY!!
?!
EACH PLAYER CONFESSES A SIN AND TOSSES THE BALL.
YOU PLAY TOO, SON.
M-ME?!
CHATTER CHATTER
ABSCOND...

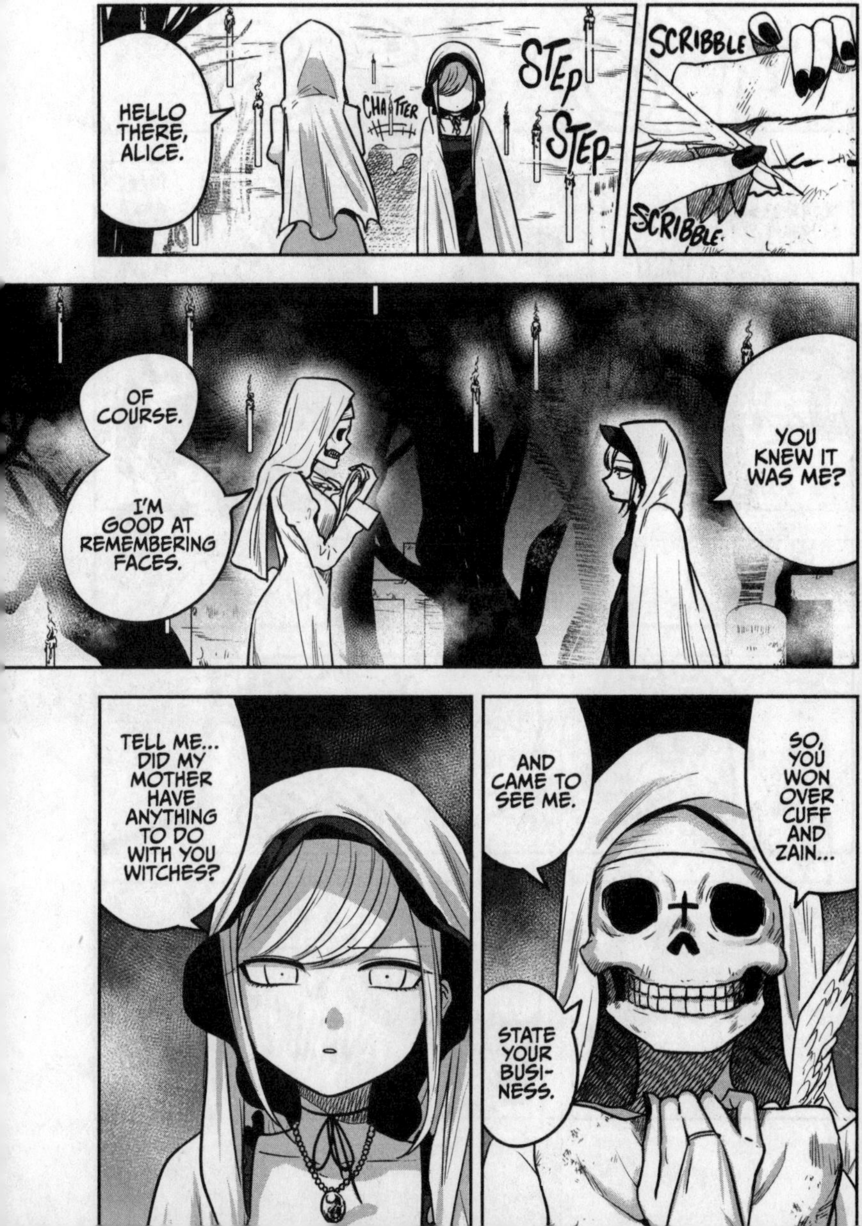
SCRIBBLE
SCRIBBLE
STEP
STEP
CHATTER
HELLO THERE, ALICE.
YOU KNEW IT WAS ME?
OF COURSE.
I'M GOOD AT REMEMBERING FACES.
SO, YOU WON OVER CUFF AND ZAIN...
AND CAME TO SEE ME.
STATE YOUR BUSI-NESS.
TELL ME... DID MY MOTHER HAVE ANYTHING TO DO WITH YOU WITCHES?

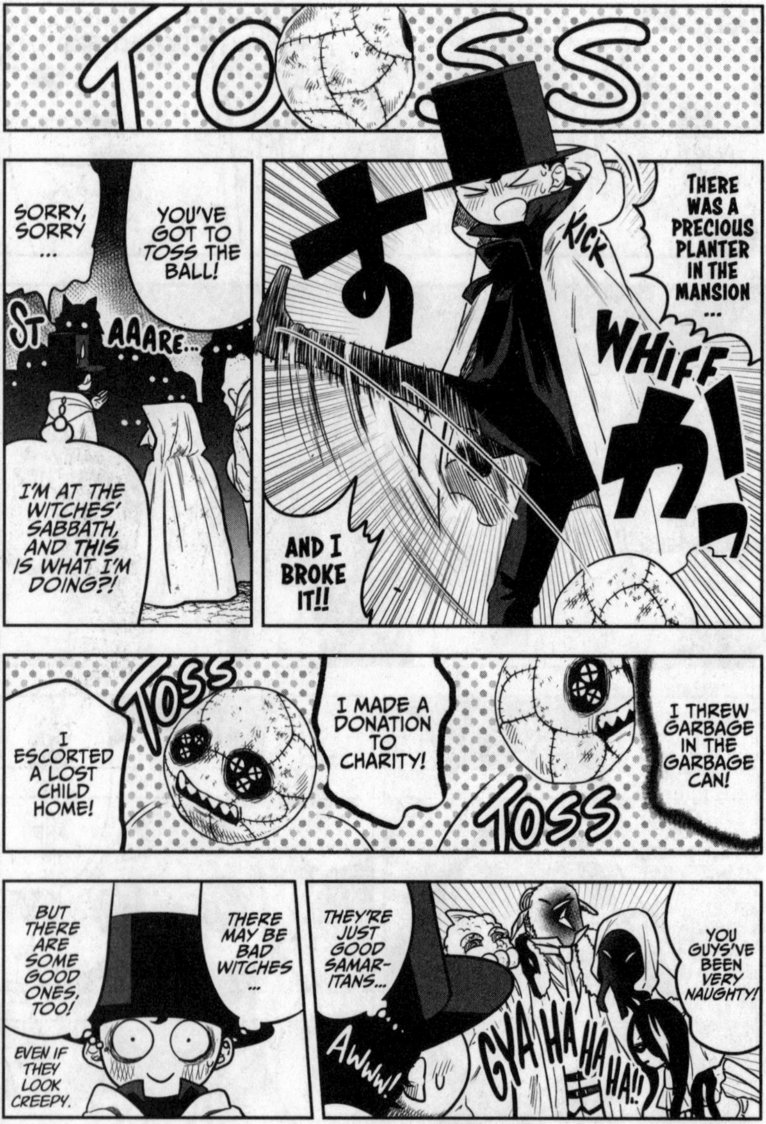
TOSS
THERE WAS A PRECIOUS PLANTER IN THE MANSION ...
KICK
WHIFF
AND I BROKE IT!!
YOU'VE GOT TO TOSS THE BALL!
SORRY, SORRY ...
ST AAAARE...
I'M AT THE WITCHES' SABBATH, AND THIS IS WHAT I'M DOING?!
I THREW GARBAGE IN THE GARBAGE CAN!
TOSS
I MADE A DONATION TO CHARITY!
TOSS
I ESCORTED A LOST CHILD HOME!
YOU GUYS'VE BEEN VERY NAUGHTY!
GYA HA HA HA HA!!
THEY'RE JUST GOOD SAMAR-ITANS...
AWWW!
THERE MAY BE BAD WITCHES ...
BUT THERE ARE SOME GOOD ONES, TOO!
EVEN IF THEY LOOK CREEPY.

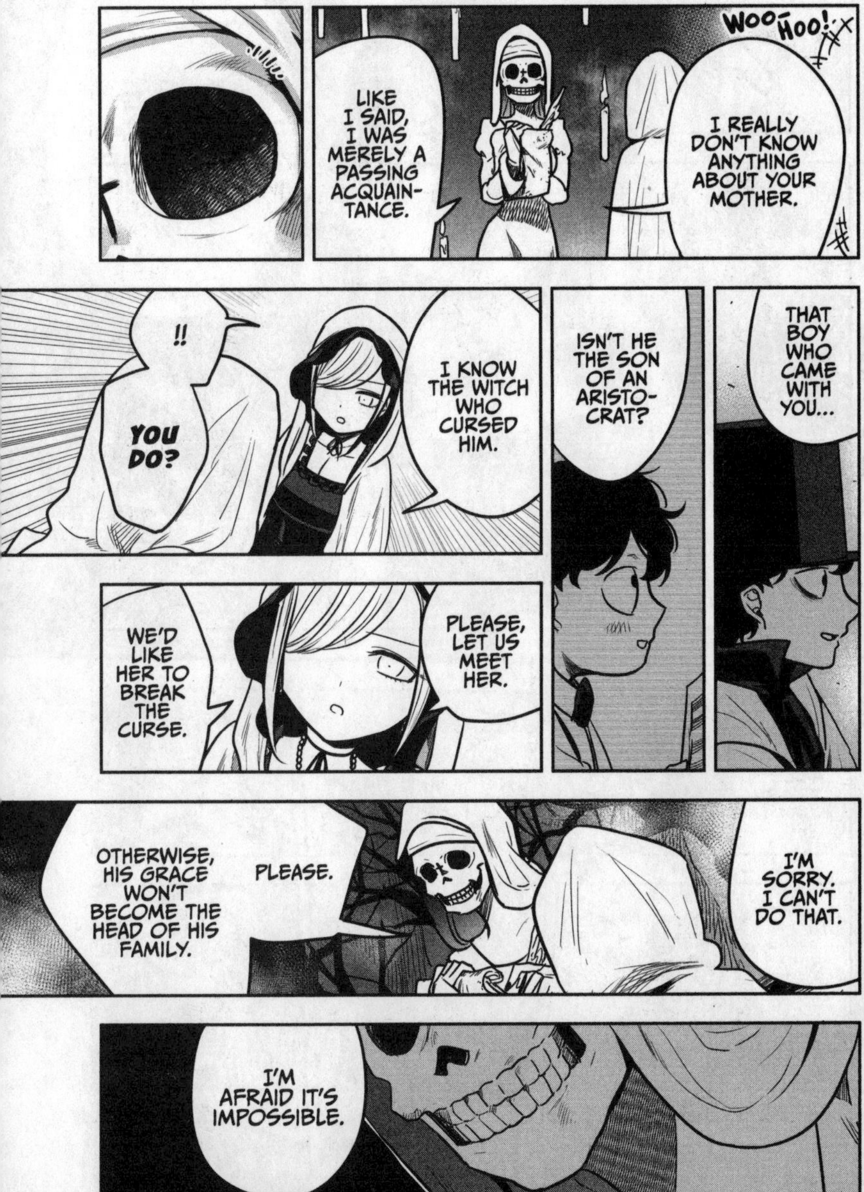

WOO-HOO!
I REALLY DON'T KNOW ANYTHING ABOUT YOUR MOTHER.
LIKE I SAID, I WAS MERELY A PASSING ACQUAINTANCE.
THAT BOY WHO CAME WITH YOU...
ISN'T HE THE SON OF AN ARISTOCRAT?
I KNOW THE WITCH WHO CURSED HIM.
!!
YOU DO?
PLEASE, LET US MEET HER.
WE'D LIKE HER TO BREAK THE CURSE.
I'M SORRY. I CAN'T DO THAT.
PLEASE.
OTHERWISE, HIS GRACE WON'T BECOME THE HEAD OF HIS FAMILY.
I'M AFRAID IT'S IMPOSSIBLE.

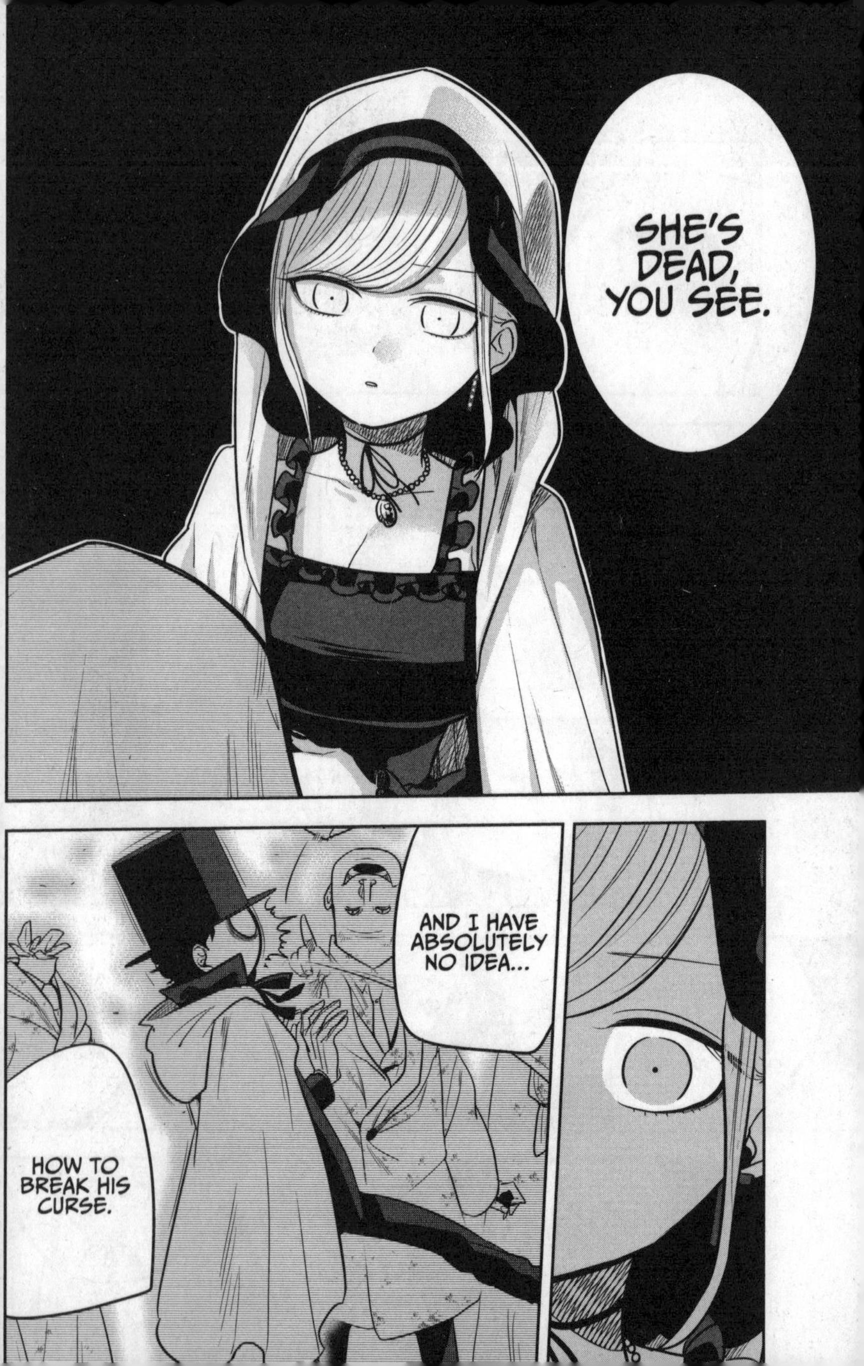
SHE'S DEAD, YOU SEE.
AND I HAVE ABSOLUTELY NO IDEA...
HOW TO BREAK HIS CURSE.

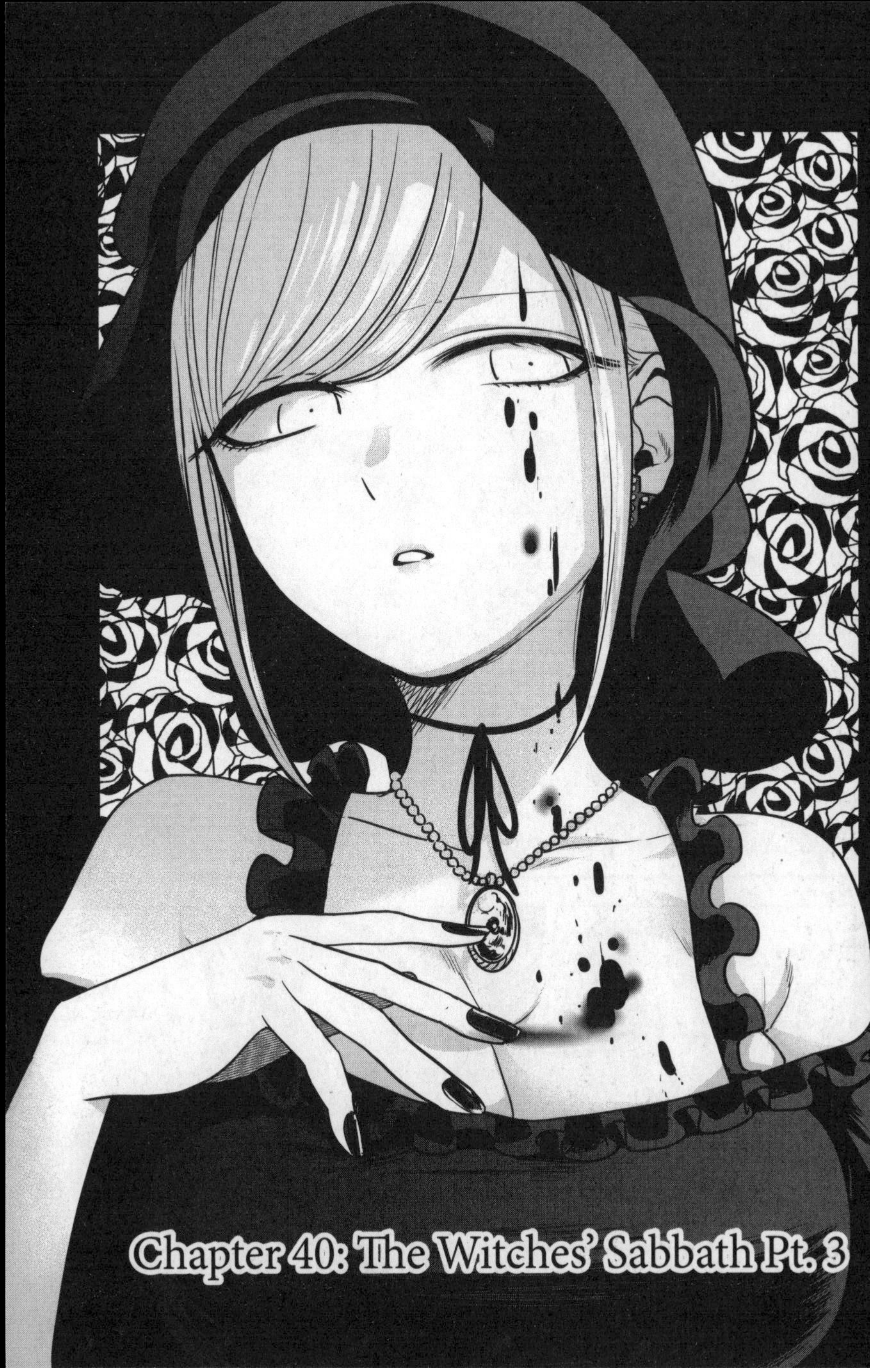

Chapter 40: The Witches' Sabbath Pt. 3

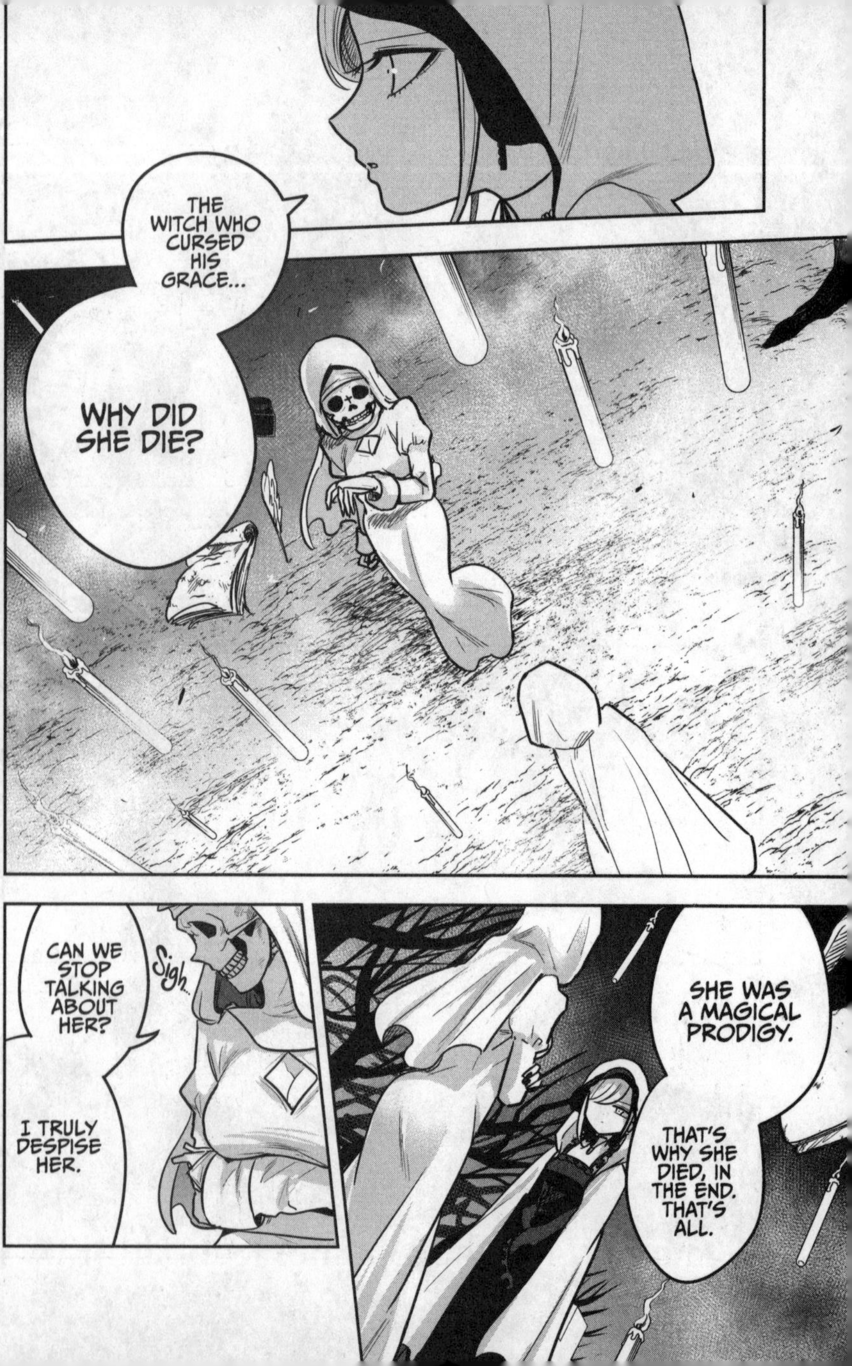
THE WITCH WHO CURSED HIS GRACE...
WHY DID SHE DIE?
SHE WAS A MAGICAL PRODIGY.
THAT'S WHY SHE DIED, IN THE END. THAT'S ALL.
Sigh...
CAN WE STOP TALKING ABOUT HER?
I TRULY DESPISE HER.

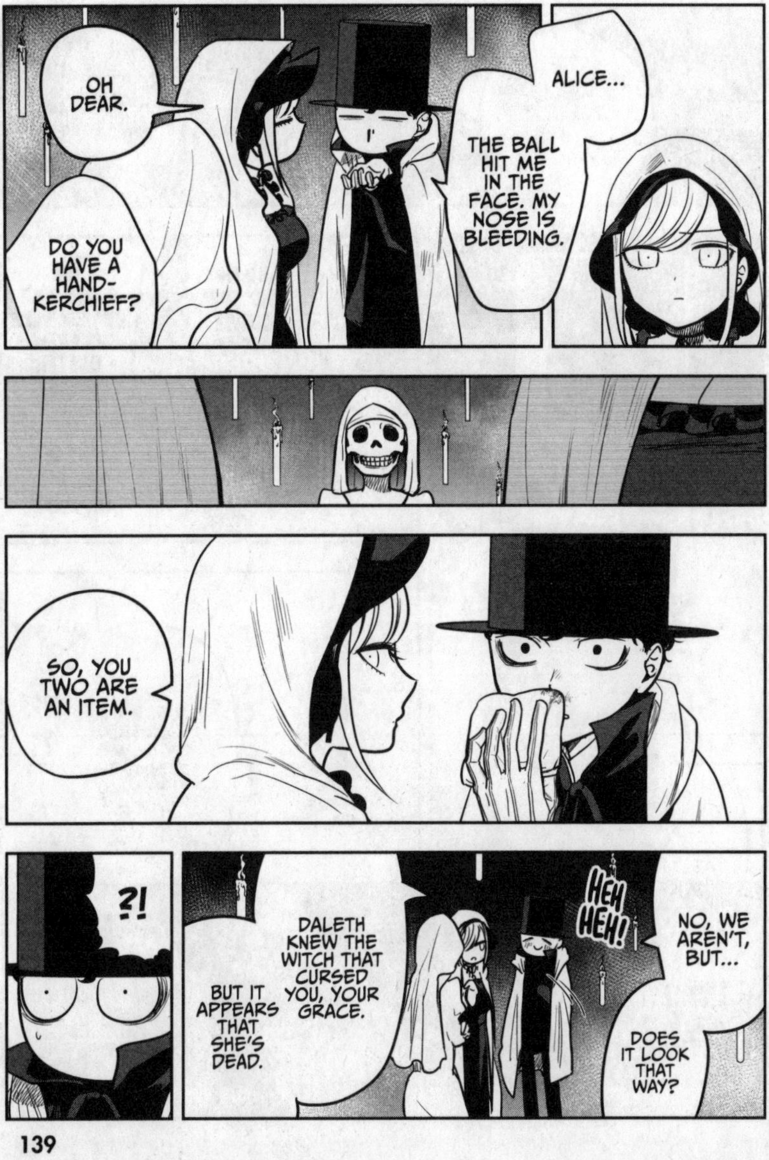
ALICE...
THE BALL HIT ME IN THE FACE. MY NOSE IS BLEEDING.
OH DEAR.
DO YOU HAVE A HAND-KERCHIEF?
SO, YOU TWO ARE AN ITEM.
NO, WE AREN'T, BUT...
HEH HEH!
DOES IT LOOK THAT WAY?
DALETH KNEW THE WITCH THAT CURSED YOU, YOUR GRACE.
BUT IT APPEARS THAT SHE'S DEAD.
?!

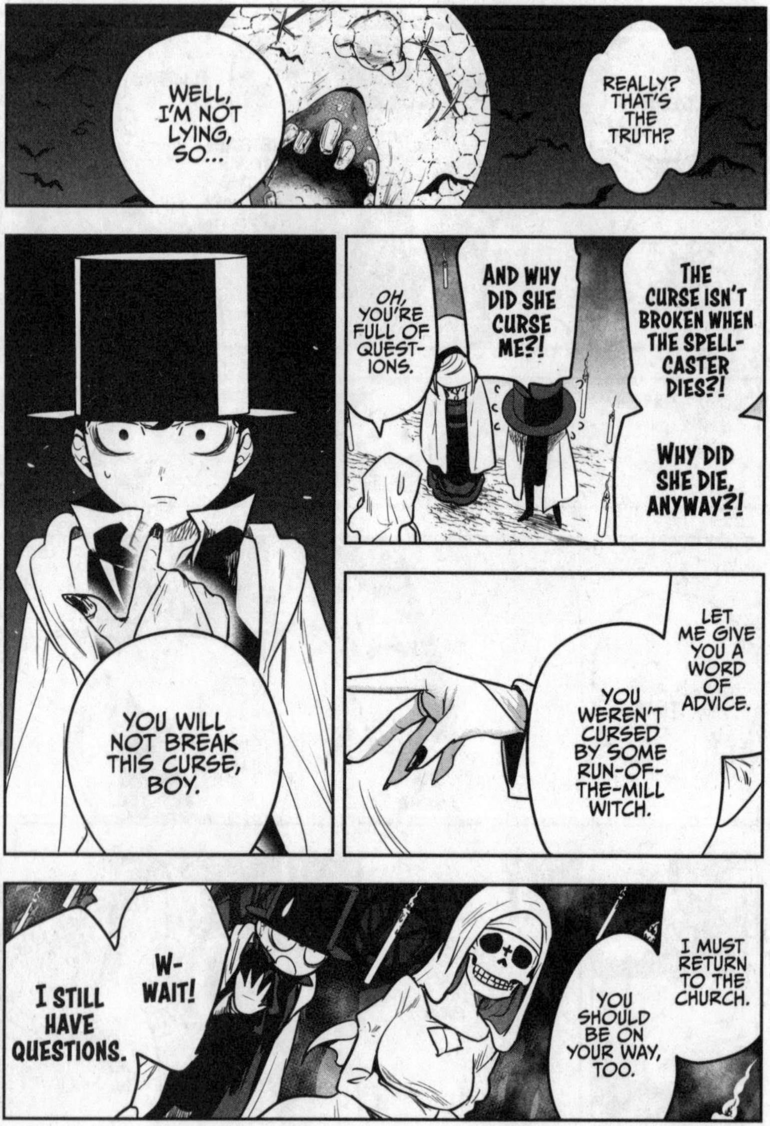
REALLY? THAT'S THE TRUTH?
WELL, I'M NOT LYING, SO...
THE CURSE ISN'T BROKEN WHEN THE SPELL-CASTER DIES?!
WHY DID SHE DIE, ANYWAY?!
AND WHY DID SHE CURSE ME?!
OH, YOU'RE FULL OF QUEST-IONS.
LET ME GIVE YOU A WORD OF ADVICE.
YOU WEREN'T CURSED BY SOME RUN-OF-THE-MILL WITCH.
YOU WILL NOT BREAK THIS CURSE, BOY.
I MUST RETURN TO THE CHURCH.
YOU SHOULD BE ON YOUR WAY, TOO.
W-WAIT!
I STILL HAVE QUESTIONS.

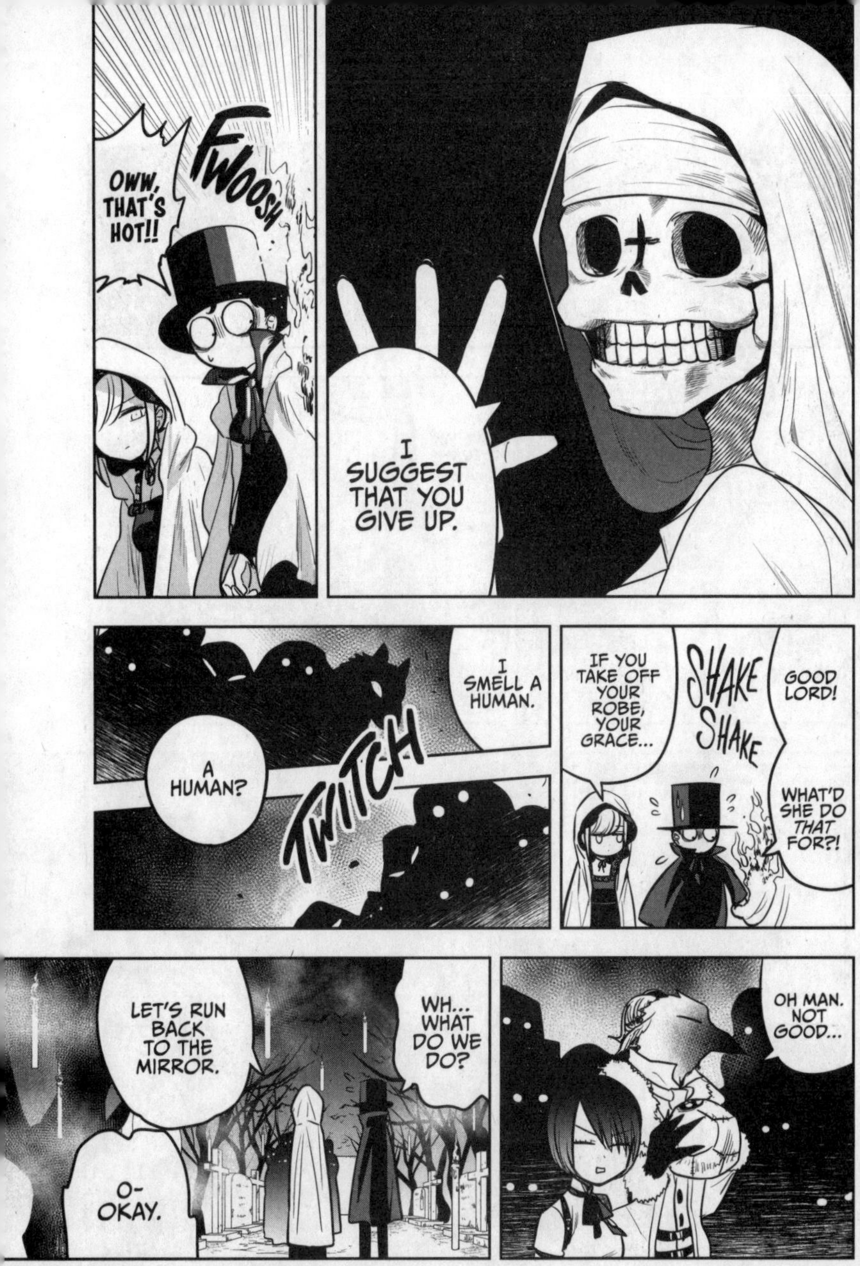
I SUGGEST THAT YOU GIVE UP.
FWOOSH
OWW, THAT'S HOT!!
GOOD LORD!
SHAKE SHAKE
WHAT'D SHE DO *THAT* FOR?!
IF YOU TAKE OFF YOUR ROBE, YOUR GRACE...
I SMELL A HUMAN.
TWITCH
A HUMAN?
OH MAN. NOT GOOD...
WH... WHAT DO WE DO?
LET'S RUN BACK TO THE MIRROR.
O-OKAY.

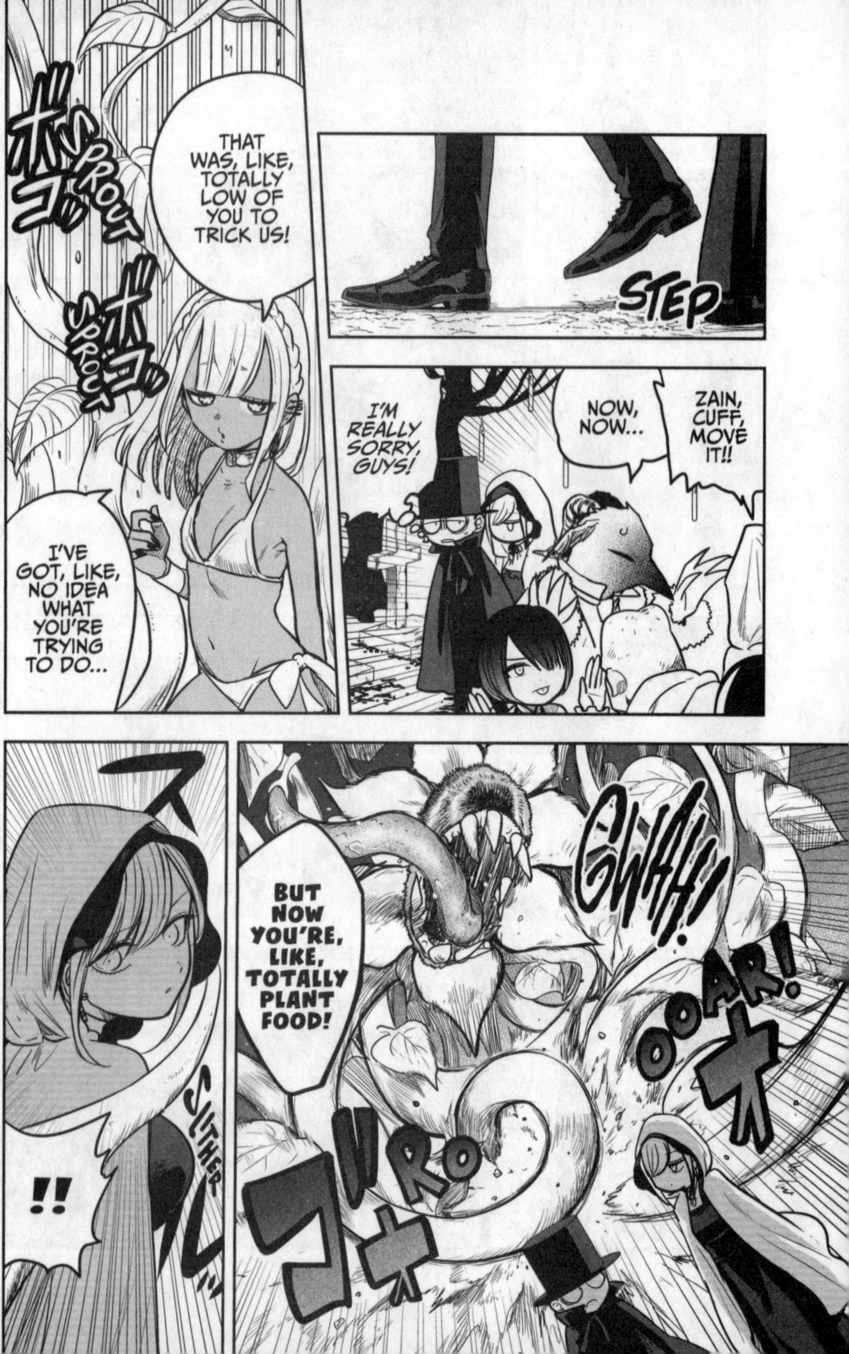
STEP
ZAIN, CUFF, MOVE IT!!
NOW, NOW...
I'M REALLY SORRY, GUYS!
SPROUT
SPROUT
THAT WAS, LIKE, TOTALLY LOW OF YOU TO TRICK US!
I'VE GOT, LIKE, NO IDEA WHAT YOU'RE TRYING TO DO...
GWAH!
OOAR!
BUT NOW YOU'RE, LIKE, TOTALLY PLANT FOOD!
VRO
SLITHER
!!

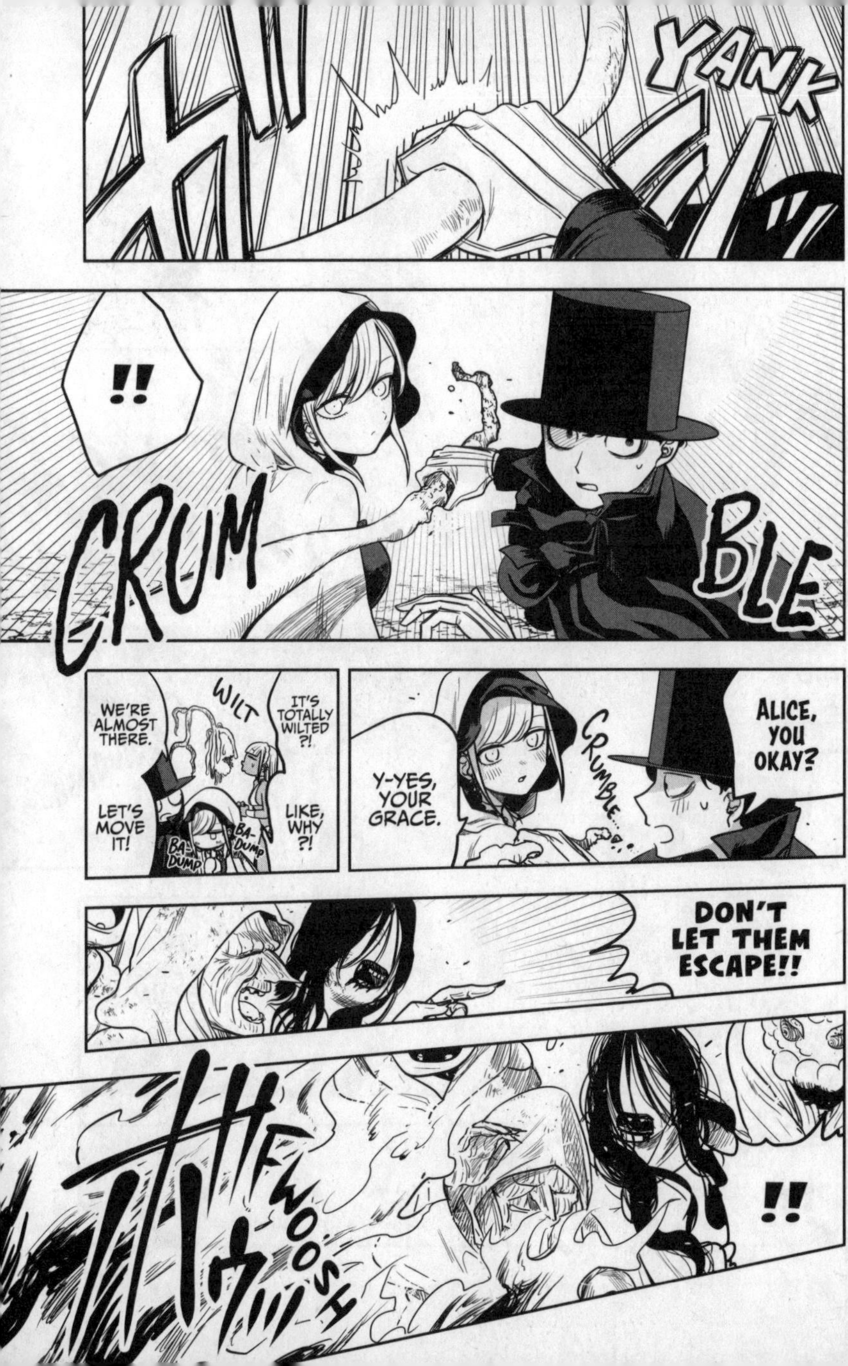
YANK
!!
CRUM BLE
ALICE, YOU OKAY?
CRUMBLE...
Y-YES, YOUR GRACE.
IT'S TOTALLY WILTED?!
WILT
WE'RE ALMOST THERE.
LIKE, WHY?!
BA-DUMP
BA-DUMP
LET'S MOVE IT!
DON'T LET THEM ESCAPE!!
!!
WOOSH

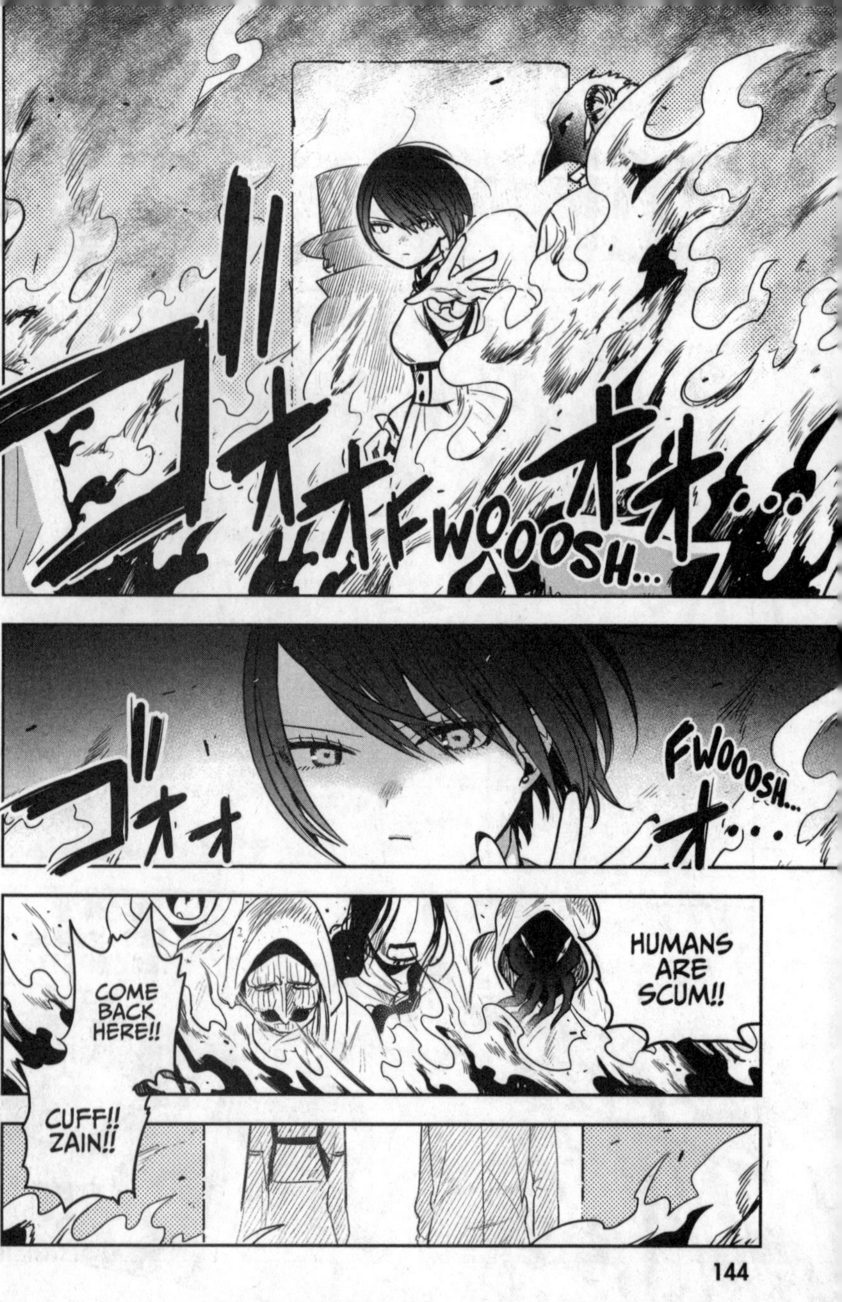
ゴオオ
FWOOOSH...
オオオ...
ゴオオ
FWOOOSH...
オ...
HUMANS ARE SCUM!!
COME BACK HERE!!
CUFF!! ZAIN!!

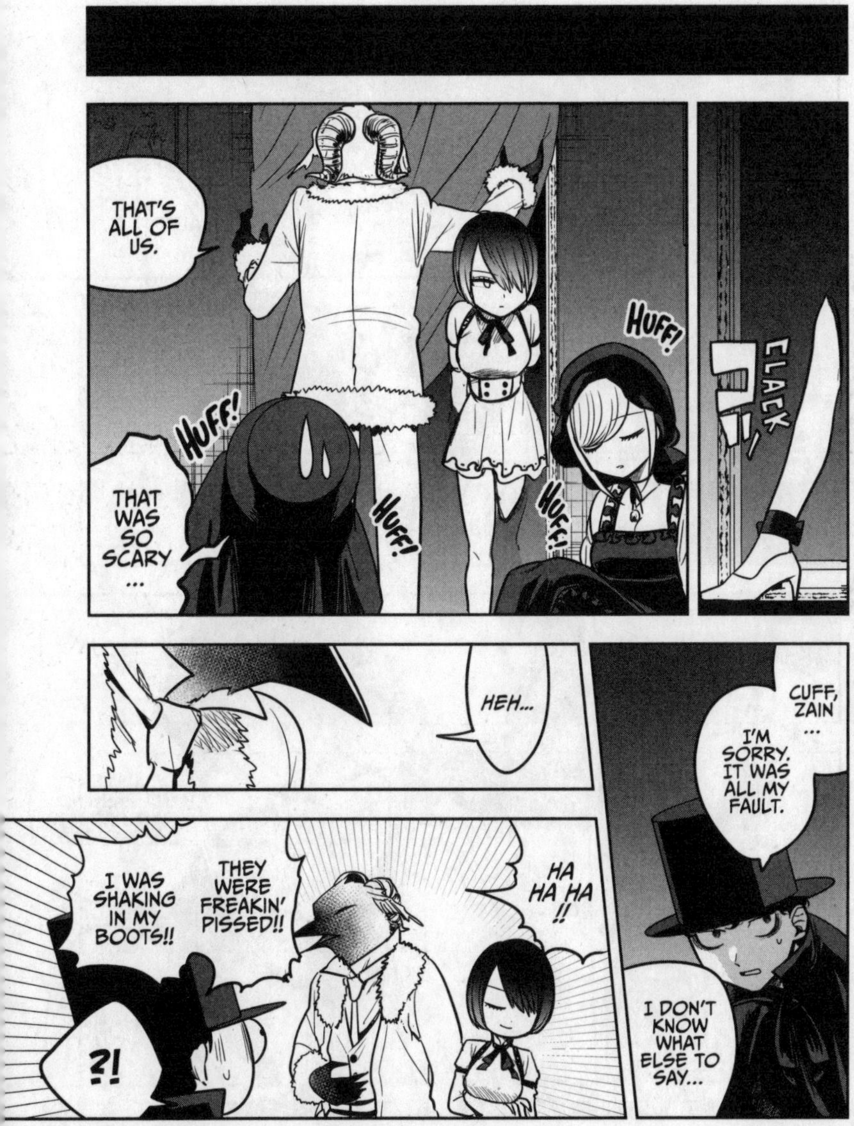
CLACK
HUFF!
THAT'S ALL OF US.
HUFF!
HUFF!
HUFF!
THAT WAS SO SCARY...
CUFF, ZAIN...
I'M SORRY. IT WAS ALL MY FAULT.
I DON'T KNOW WHAT ELSE TO SAY...
HEH...
HA HA HA!!
THEY WERE FREAKIN' PISSED!!
I WAS SHAKING IN MY BOOTS!!
?!

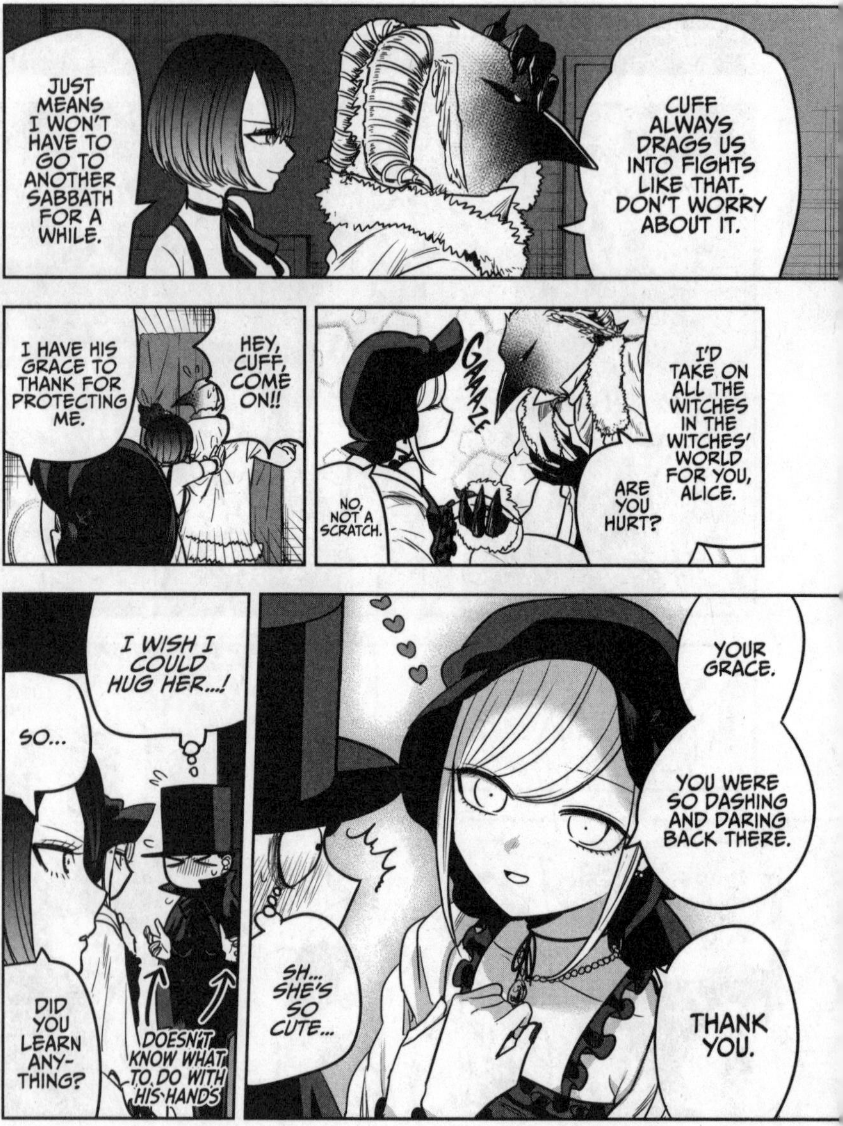
CUFF ALWAYS DRAGS US INTO FIGHTS LIKE THAT. DON'T WORRY ABOUT IT.
JUST MEANS I WON'T HAVE TO GO TO ANOTHER SABBATH FOR A WHILE.
I'D TAKE ON ALL THE WITCHES IN THE WITCHES' WORLD FOR YOU, ALICE.
ARE YOU HURT?
GAAAZE
NO, NOT A SCRATCH.
HEY, CUFF, COME ON!!
I HAVE HIS GRACE TO THANK FOR PROTECTING ME.
YOUR GRACE.
YOU WERE SO DASHING AND DARING BACK THERE.
THANK YOU.
SH... SHE'S SO CUTE...
I WISH I COULD HUG HER...!
SO...
DID YOU LEARN ANY-THING?
DOESN'T KNOW WHAT TO DO WITH HIS HANDS

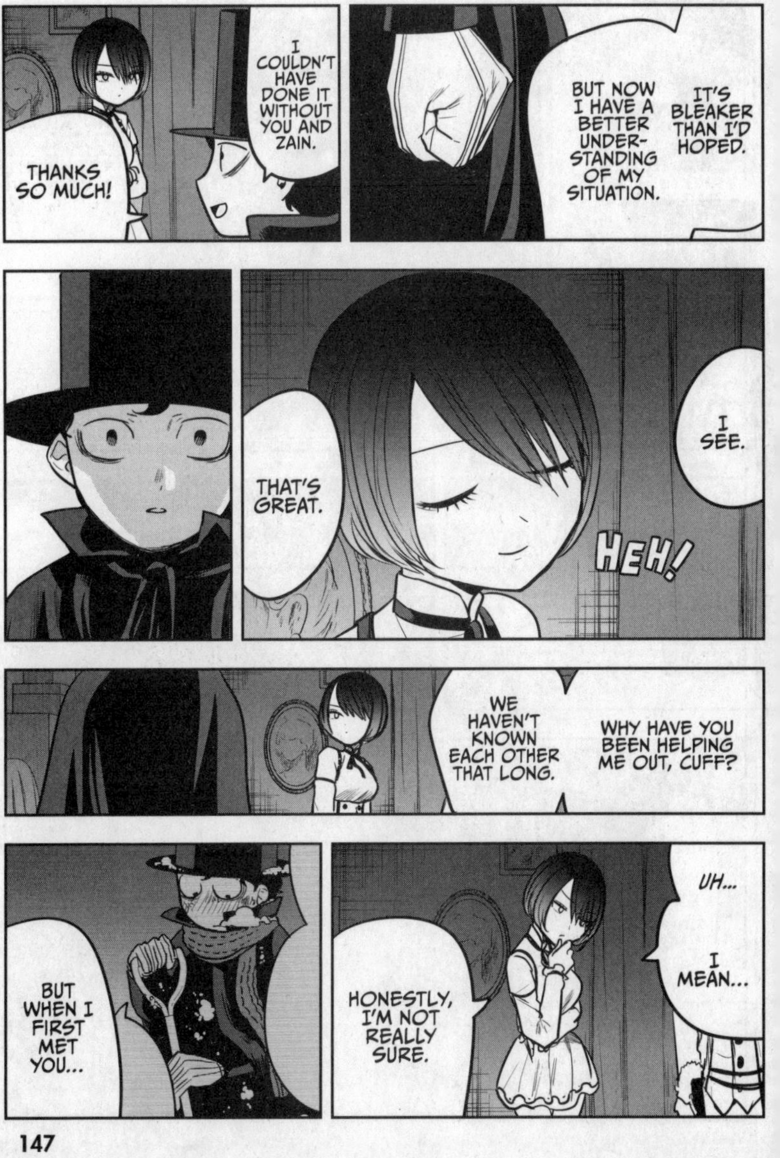
IT'S BLEAKER THAN I'D HOPED.
BUT NOW I HAVE A BETTER UNDER-STANDING OF MY SITUATION.
I COULDN'T HAVE DONE IT WITHOUT YOU AND ZAIN.
THANKS SO MUCH!
I SEE.
HEH!
THAT'S GREAT.
WHY HAVE YOU BEEN HELPING ME OUT, CUFF?
WE HAVEN'T KNOWN EACH OTHER THAT LONG.
UH...
I MEAN...
HONESTLY, I'M NOT REALLY SURE.
BUT WHEN I FIRST MET YOU...

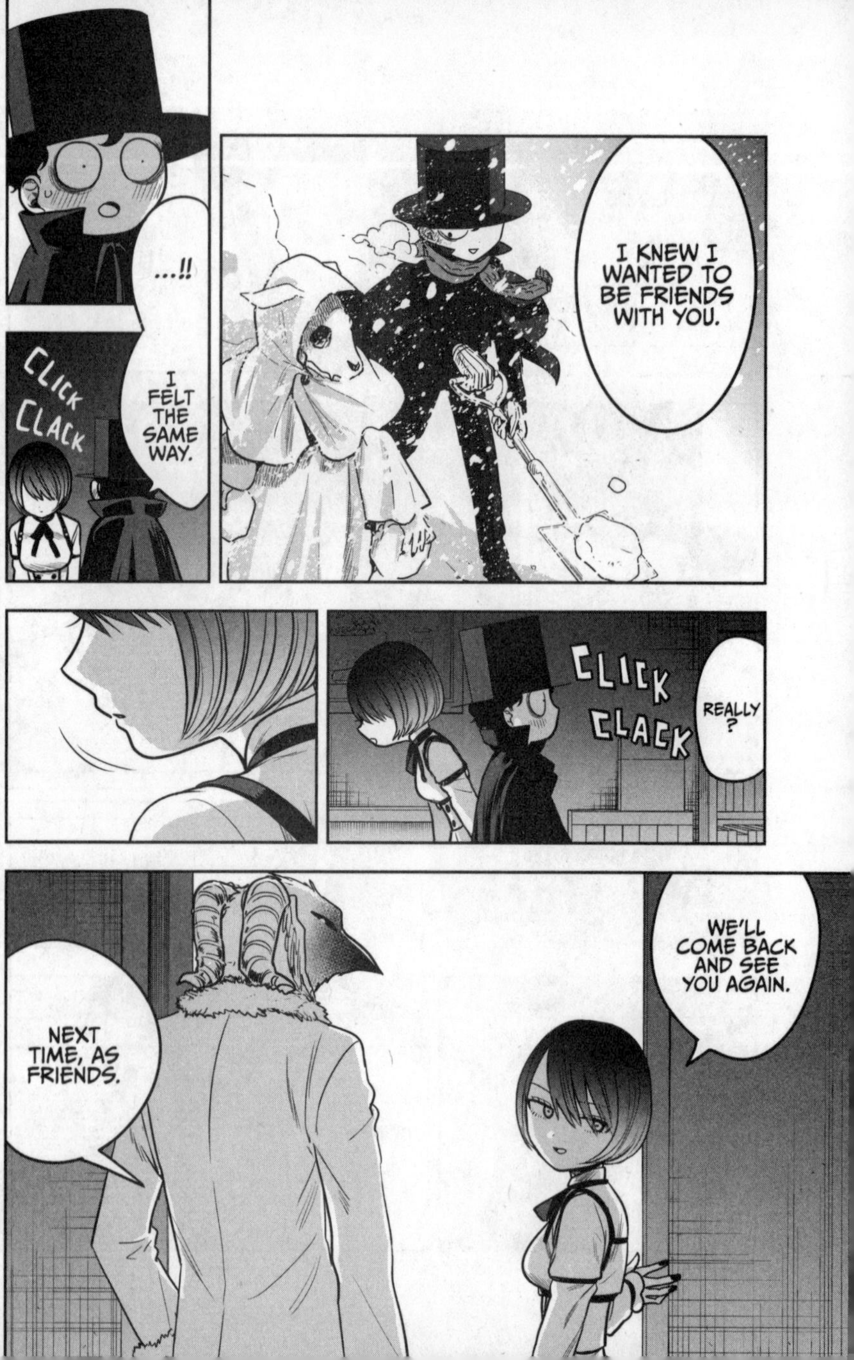
I KNEW I WANTED TO BE FRIENDS WITH YOU.
...!!
I FELT THE SAME WAY.
CLICK CLACK
REALLY?
CLICK CLACK
WE'LL COME BACK AND SEE YOU AGAIN.
NEXT TIME, AS FRIENDS.

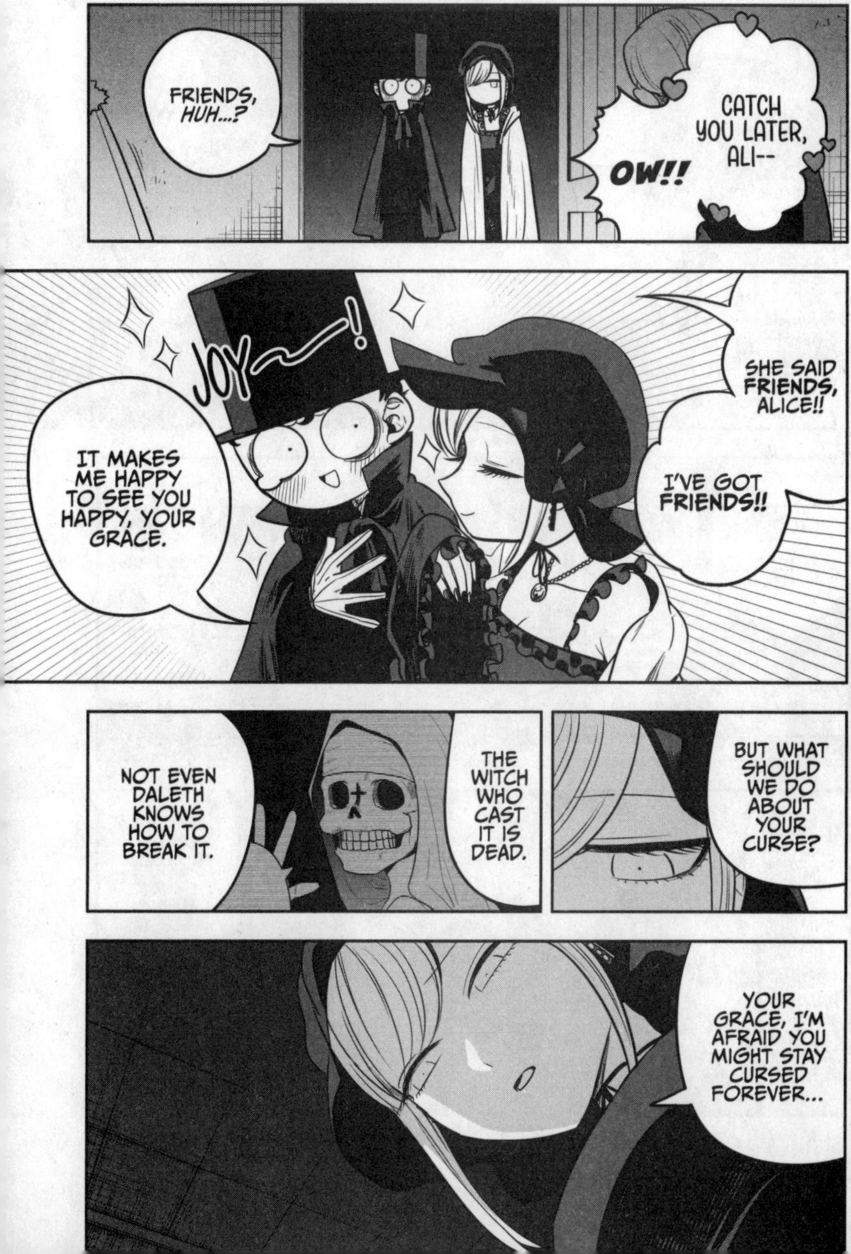
CATCH YOU LATER, ALI--
OW!!
FRIENDS, HUH...?
SHE SAID FRIENDS, ALICE!!
I'VE GOT FRIENDS!!
JOY~!
IT MAKES ME HAPPY TO SEE YOU HAPPY, YOUR GRACE.
BUT WHAT SHOULD WE DO ABOUT YOUR CURSE?
THE WITCH WHO CAST IT IS DEAD.
NOT EVEN DALETH KNOWS HOW TO BREAK IT.
YOUR GRACE, I'M AFRAID YOU MIGHT STAY CURSED FOREVER...

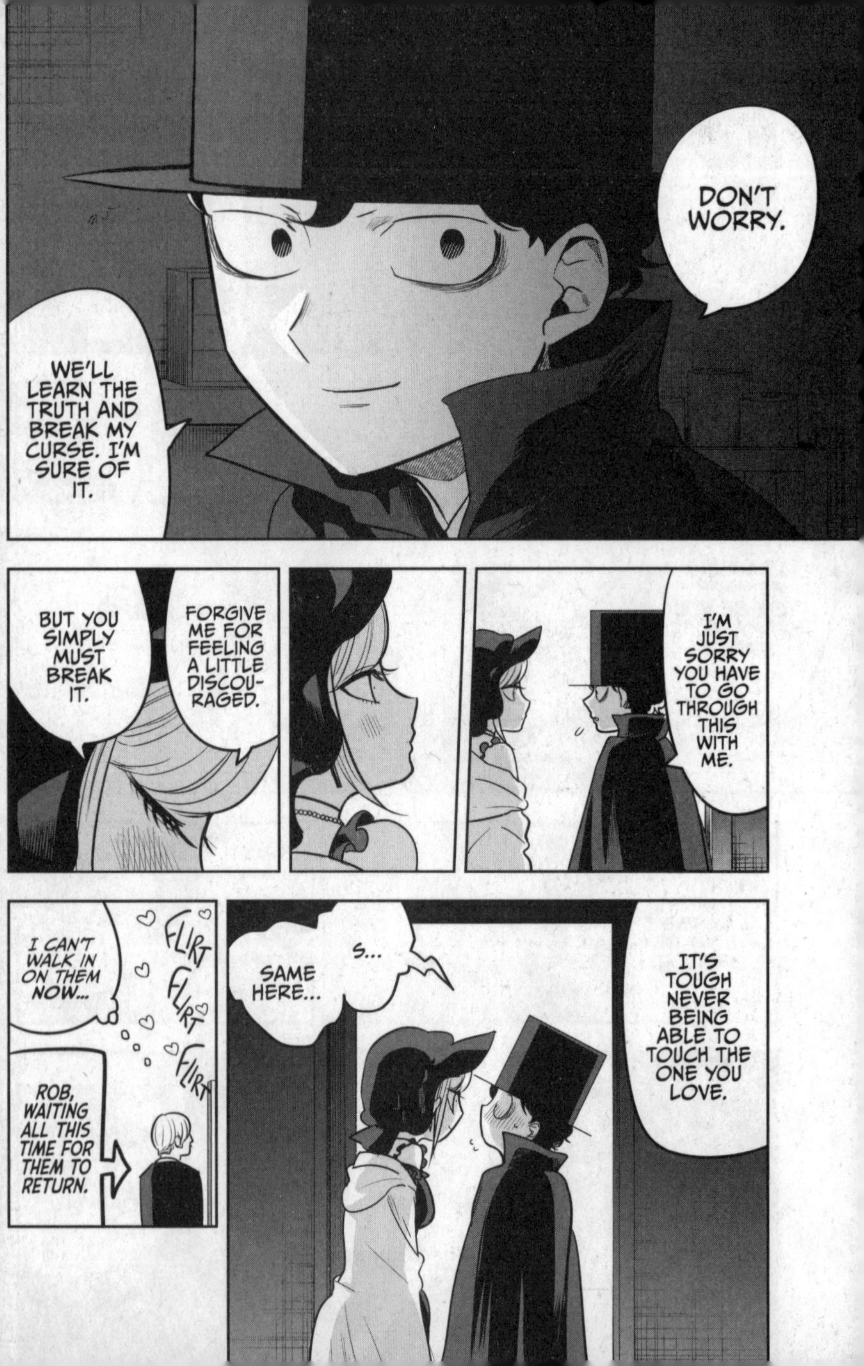
DON'T WORRY.
WE'LL LEARN THE TRUTH AND BREAK MY CURSE. I'M SURE OF IT.
I'M JUST SORRY YOU HAVE TO GO THROUGH THIS WITH ME.
FORGIVE ME FOR FEELING A LITTLE DISCOU-RAGED.
BUT YOU SIMPLY MUST BREAK IT.
IT'S TOUGH NEVER BEING ABLE TO TOUCH THE ONE YOU LOVE.
S...
SAME HERE...
I CAN'T WALK IN ON THEM NOW...
FLIRT FLIRT FLIRT FLIRT
ROB, WAITING ALL THIS TIME FOR THEM TO RETURN.

THE DUKE OF DEATH AND HIS MAID

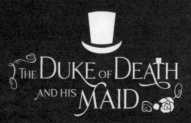

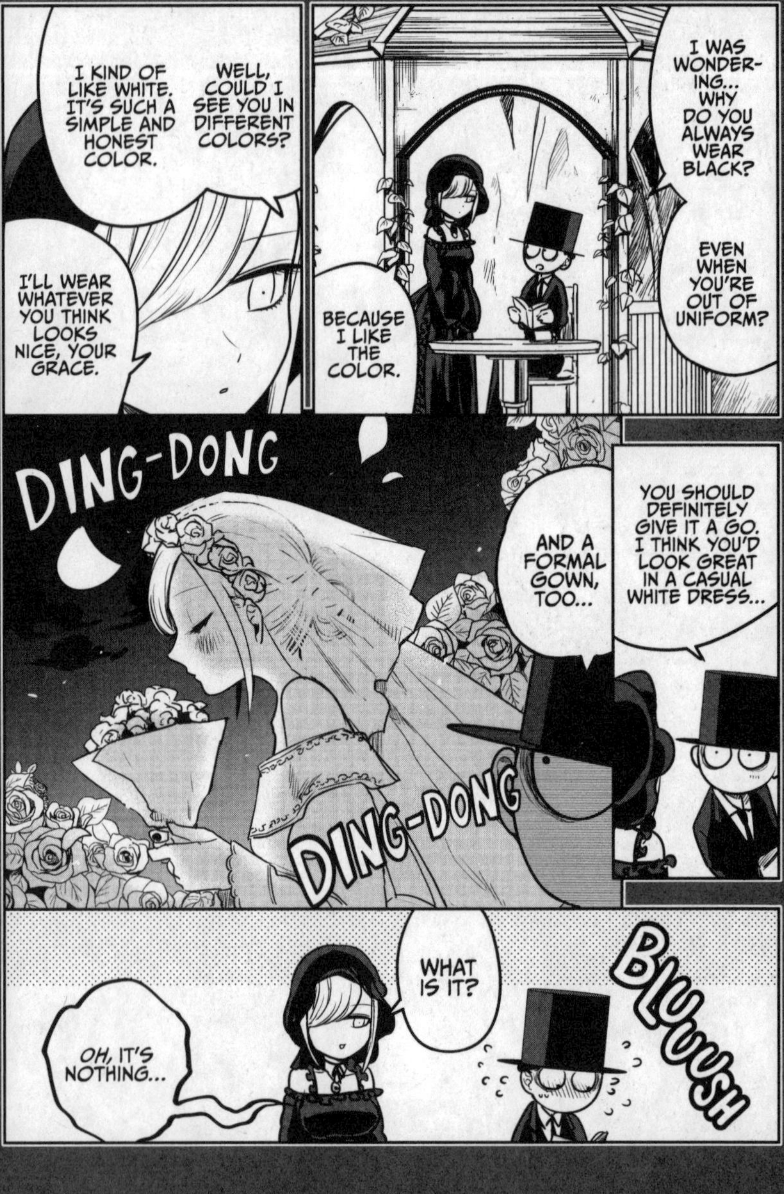
I WAS WONDERING... WHY DO YOU ALWAYS WEAR BLACK?
EVEN WHEN YOU'RE OUT OF UNIFORM?
BECAUSE I LIKE THE COLOR.
WELL, COULD I SEE YOU IN DIFFERENT COLORS?
I KIND OF LIKE WHITE. IT'S SUCH A SIMPLE AND HONEST COLOR.
I'LL WEAR WHATEVER YOU THINK LOOKS NICE, YOUR GRACE.
YOU SHOULD DEFINITELY GIVE IT A GO. I THINK YOU'D LOOK GREAT IN A CASUAL WHITE DRESS...
AND A FORMAL GOWN, TOO...
DING-DONG
DING-DONG
BLUUSH
WHAT IS IT?
OH, IT'S NOTHING...

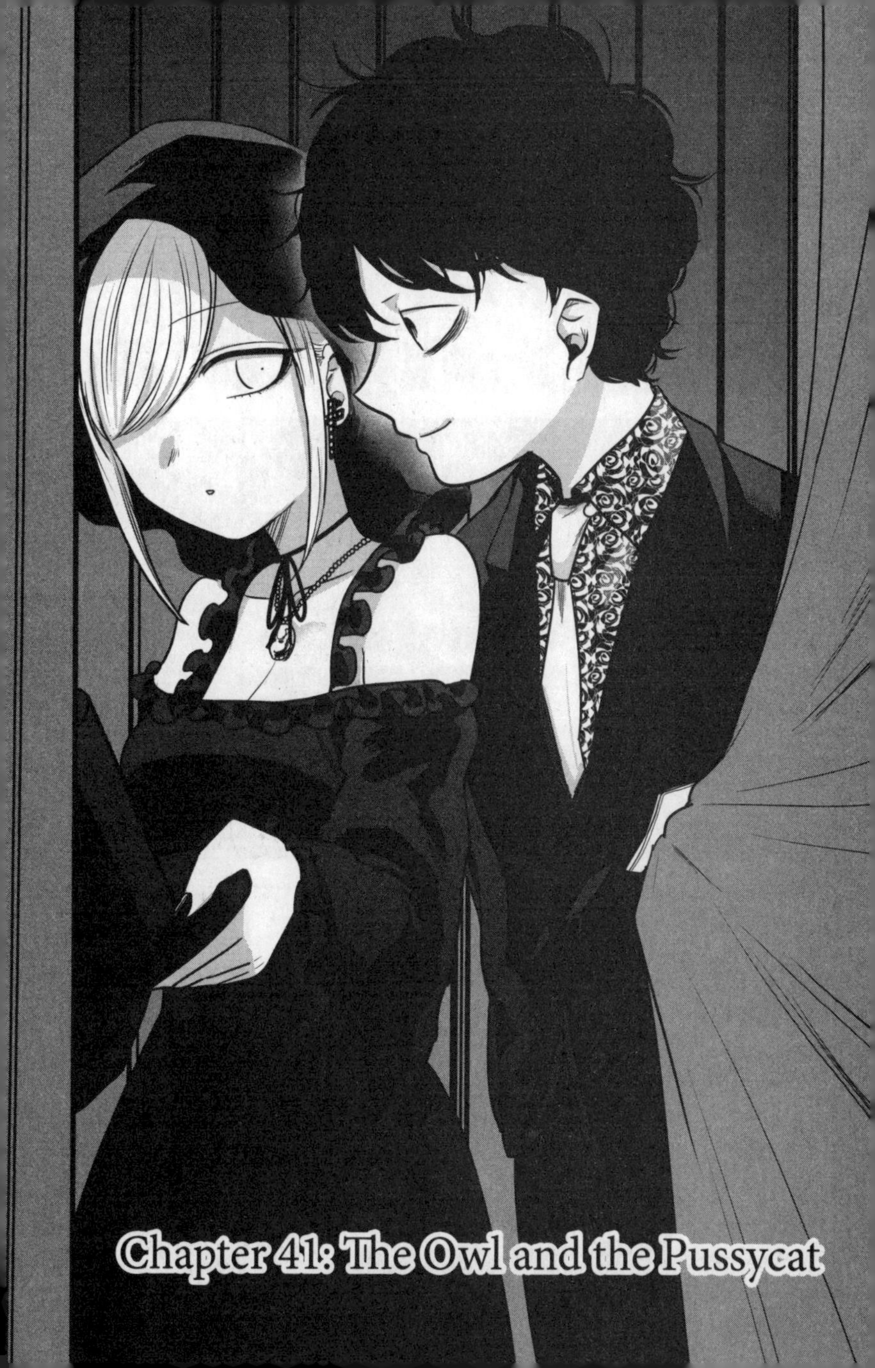
Chapter 41: The Owl and the Pussycat

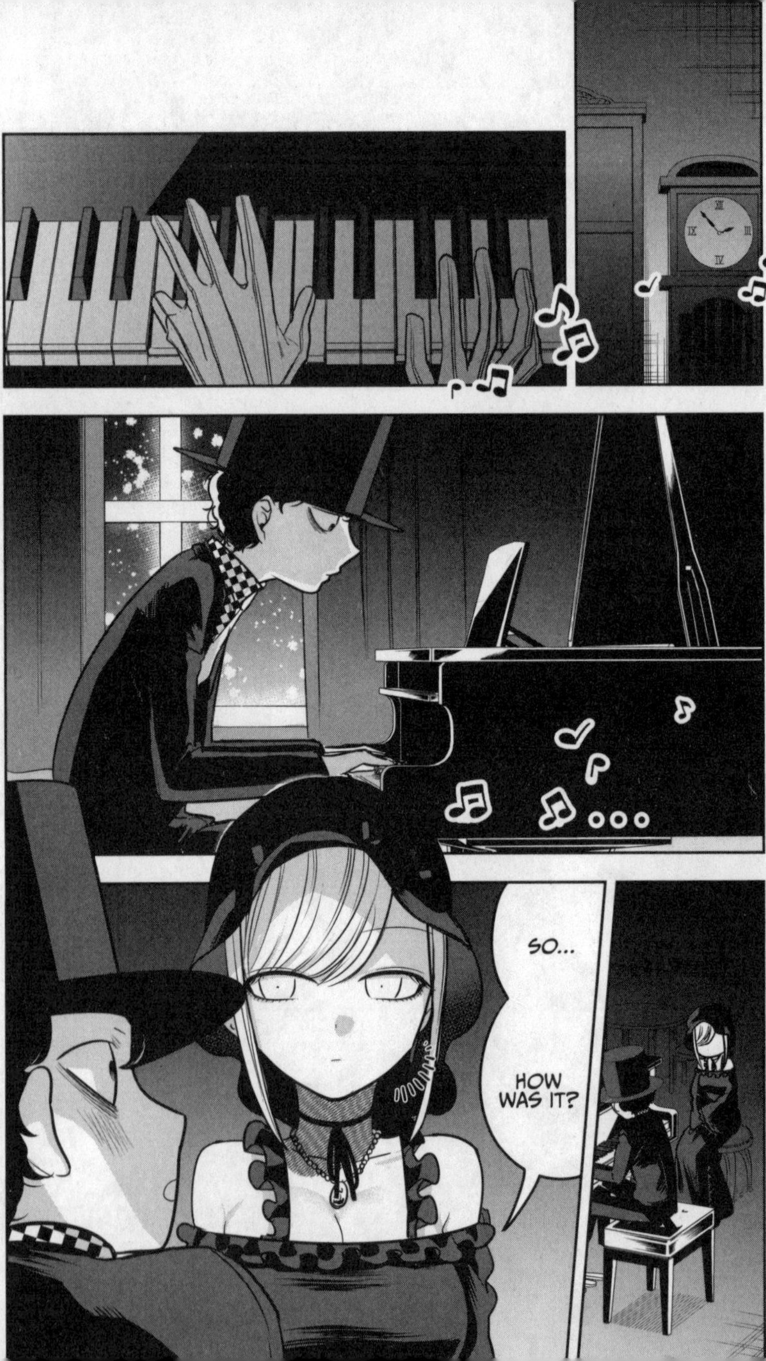
SO...
HOW WAS IT?

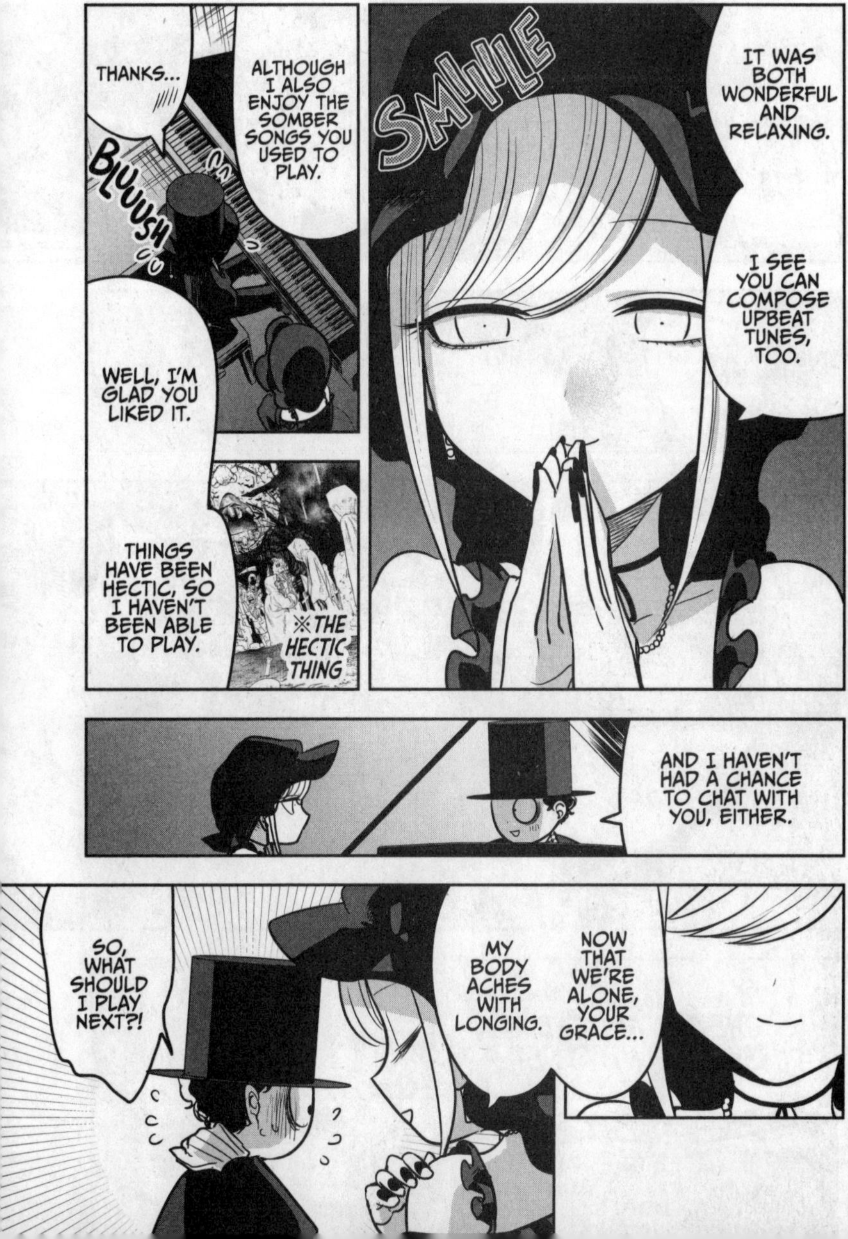
SMIIILE
IT WAS BOTH WONDERFUL AND RELAXING.
I SEE YOU CAN COMPOSE UPBEAT TUNES, TOO.
ALTHOUGH I ALSO ENJOY THE SOMBER SONGS YOU USED TO PLAY.
THANKS...
BLUUUSH
WELL, I'M GLAD YOU LIKED IT.
THINGS HAVE BEEN HECTIC, SO I HAVEN'T BEEN ABLE TO PLAY.
※THE HECTIC THING
AND I HAVEN'T HAD A CHANCE TO CHAT WITH YOU, EITHER.
NOW THAT WE'RE ALONE, YOUR GRACE...
MY BODY ACHES WITH LONGING.
SO, WHAT SHOULD I PLAY NEXT?!

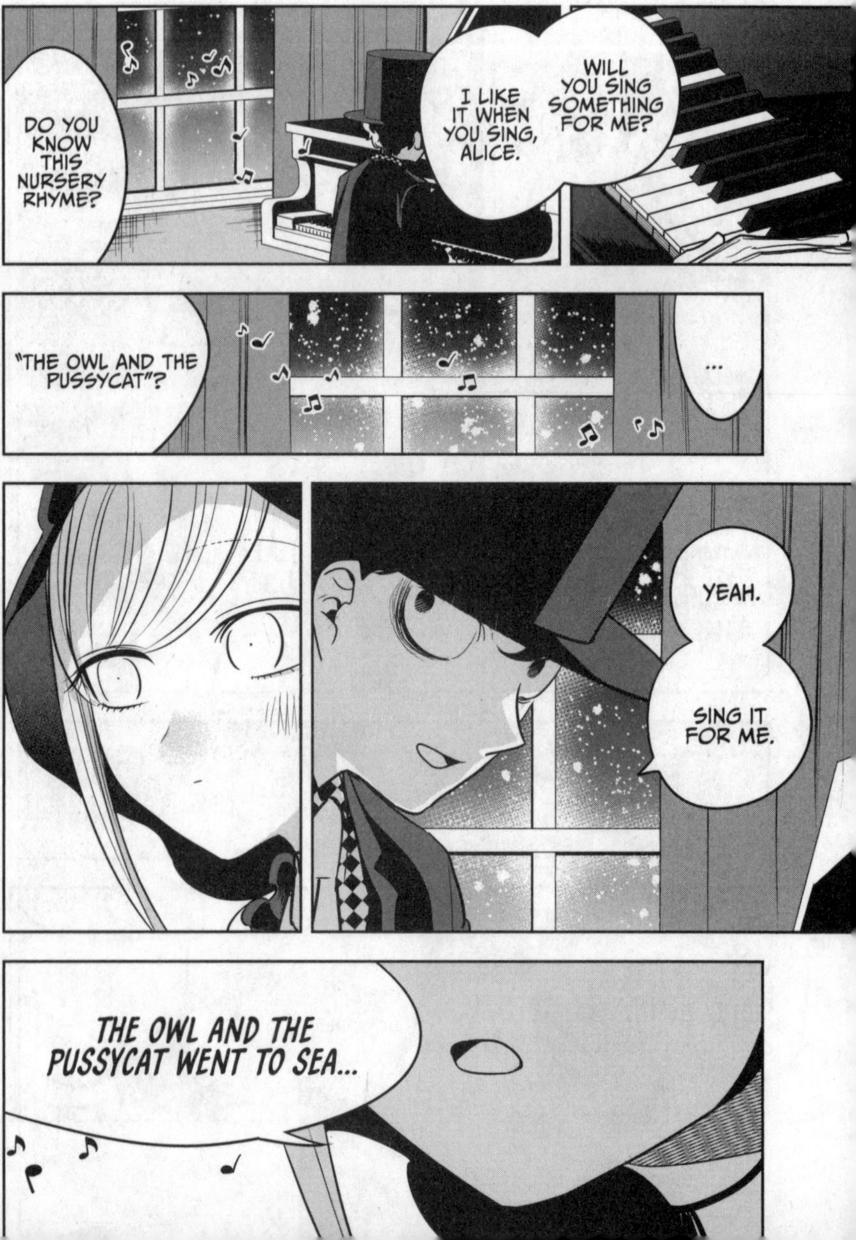
WILL YOU SING SOMETHING FOR ME?
I LIKE IT WHEN YOU SING, ALICE.
DO YOU KNOW THIS NURSERY RHYME?
...
"THE OWL AND THE PUSSYCAT"?
YEAH.
SING IT FOR ME.
THE OWL AND THE PUSSYCAT WENT TO SEA...

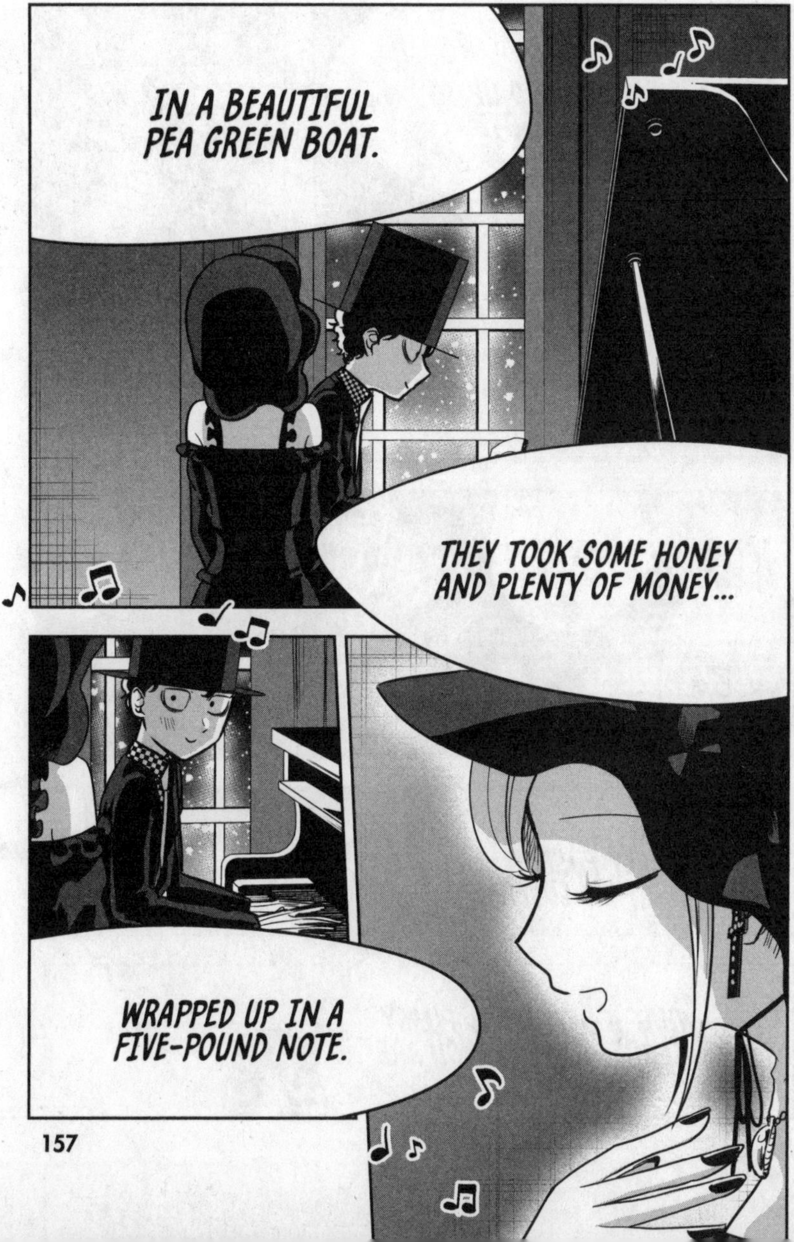
IN A BEAUTIFUL PEA GREEN BOAT.
THEY TOOK SOME HONEY AND PLENTY OF MONEY...
WRAPPED UP IN A FIVE-POUND NOTE.

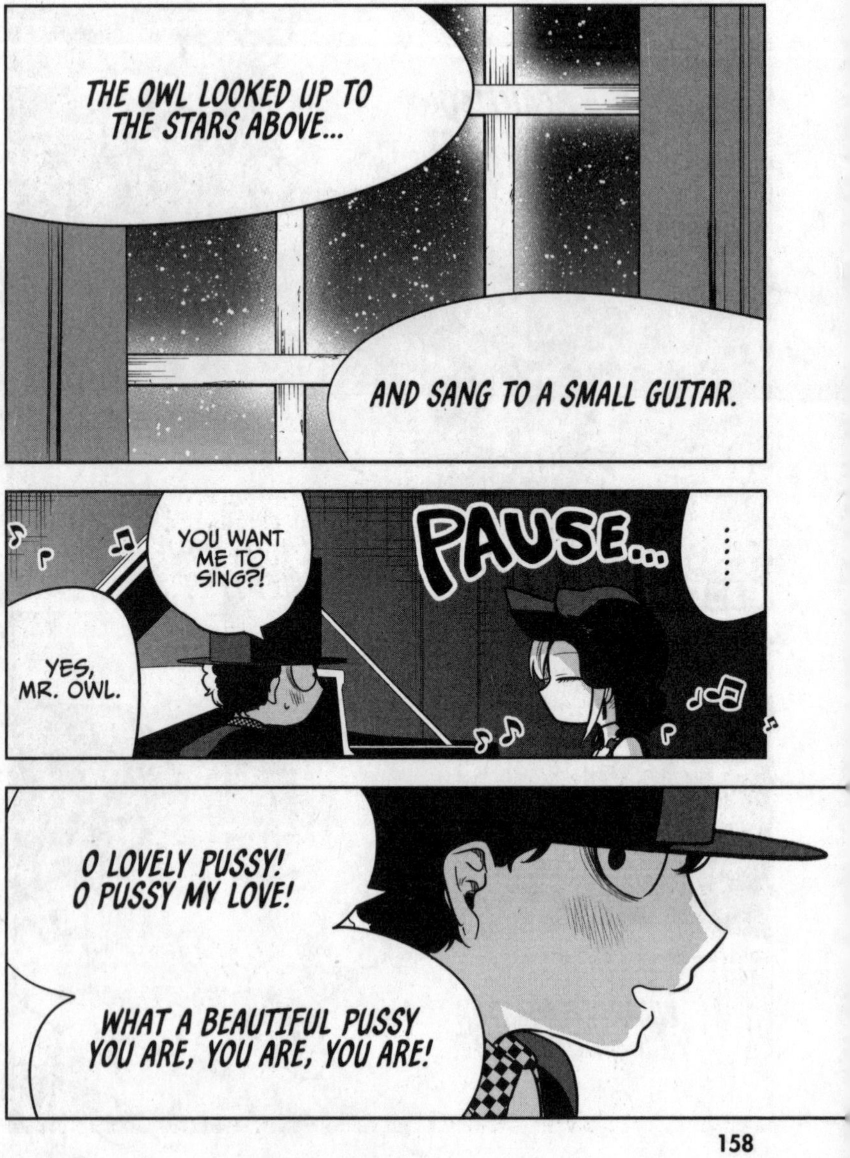

THE OWL LOOKED UP TO THE STARS ABOVE...
AND SANG TO A SMALL GUITAR.
......
PAUSE...
YOU WANT ME TO SING?!
YES, MR. OWL.
O LOVELY PUSSY! O PUSSY MY LOVE!
WHAT A BEAUTIFUL PUSSY YOU ARE, YOU ARE, YOU ARE!

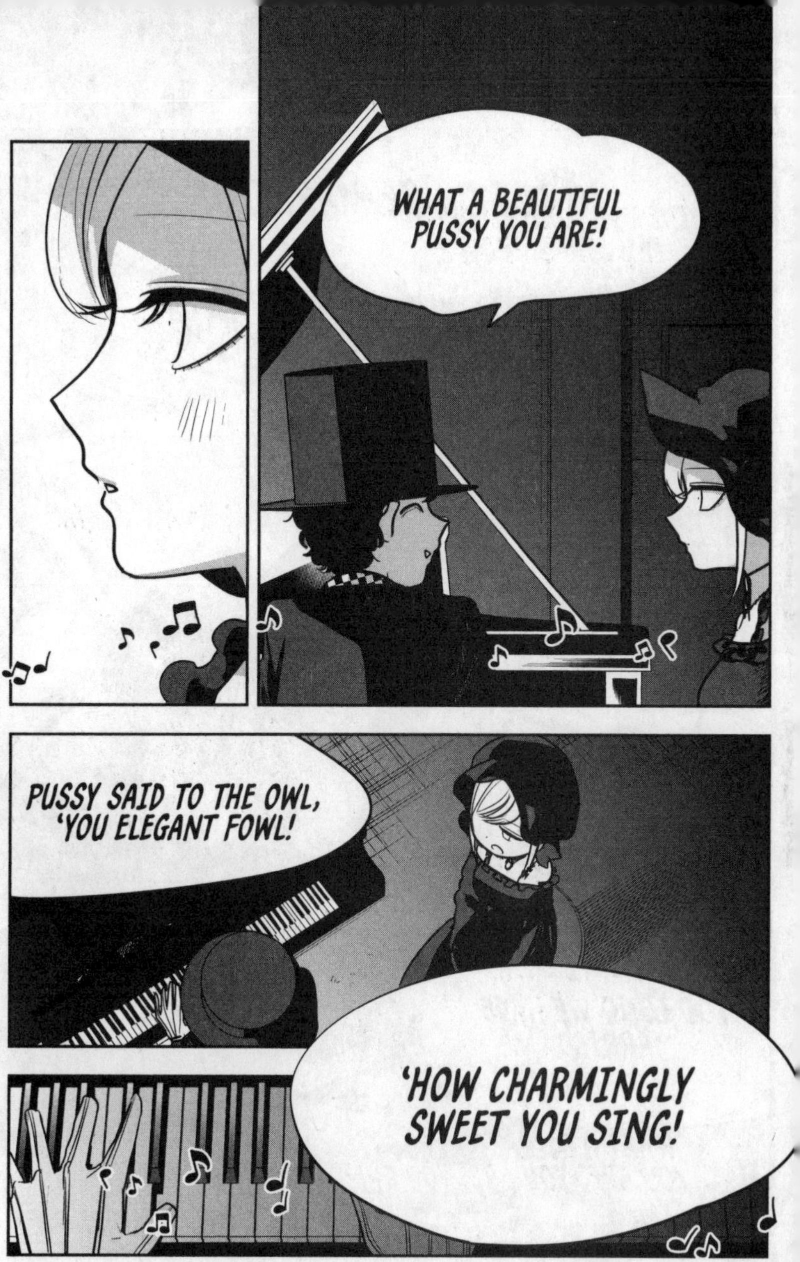
WHAT A BEAUTIFUL PUSSY YOU ARE!
PUSSY SAID TO THE OWL, 'YOU ELEGANT FOWL!
'HOW CHARMINGLY SWEET YOU SING!

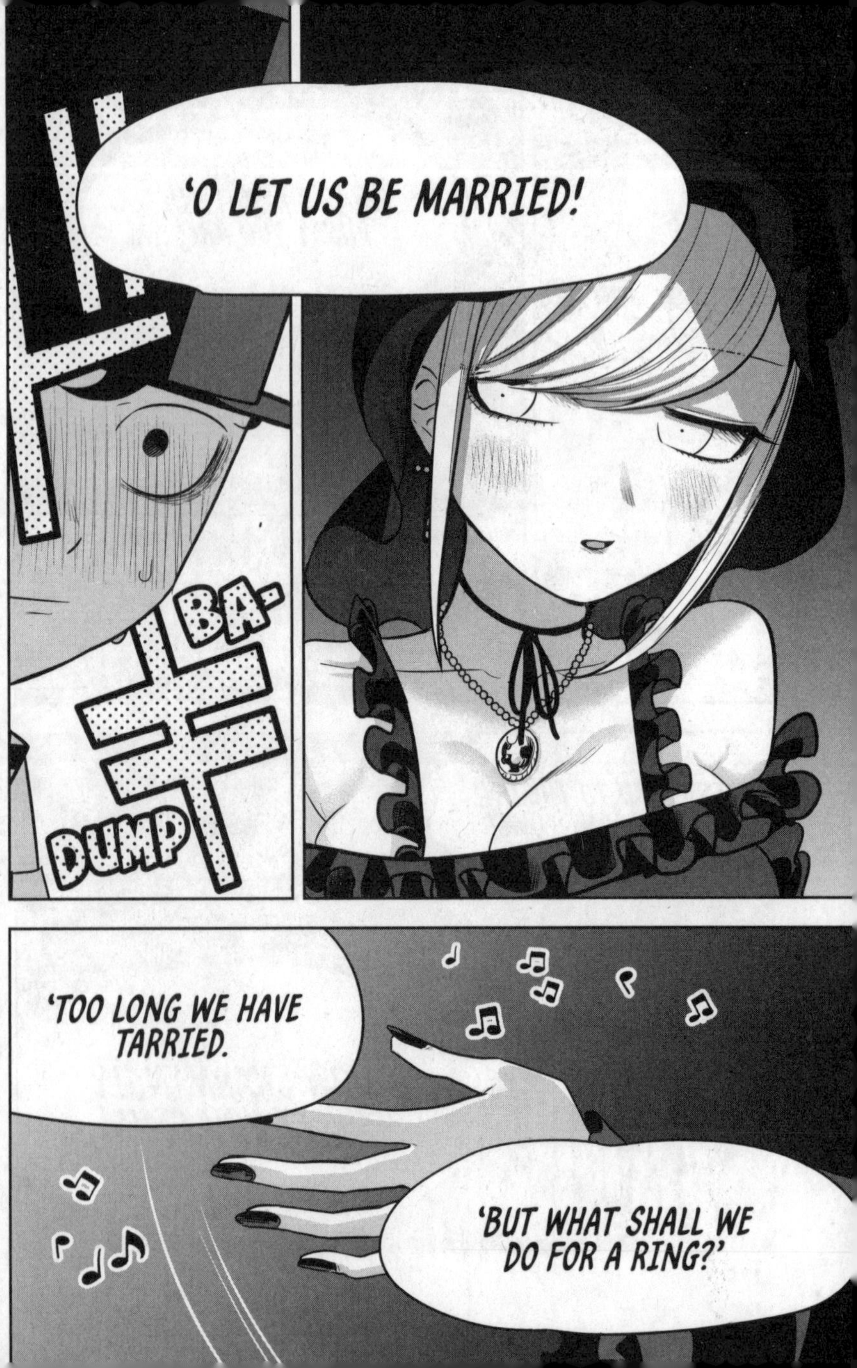
'O LET US BE MARRIED!
BA-DUMP
'TOO LONG WE HAVE TARRIED.
'BUT WHAT SHALL WE DO FOR A RING?'

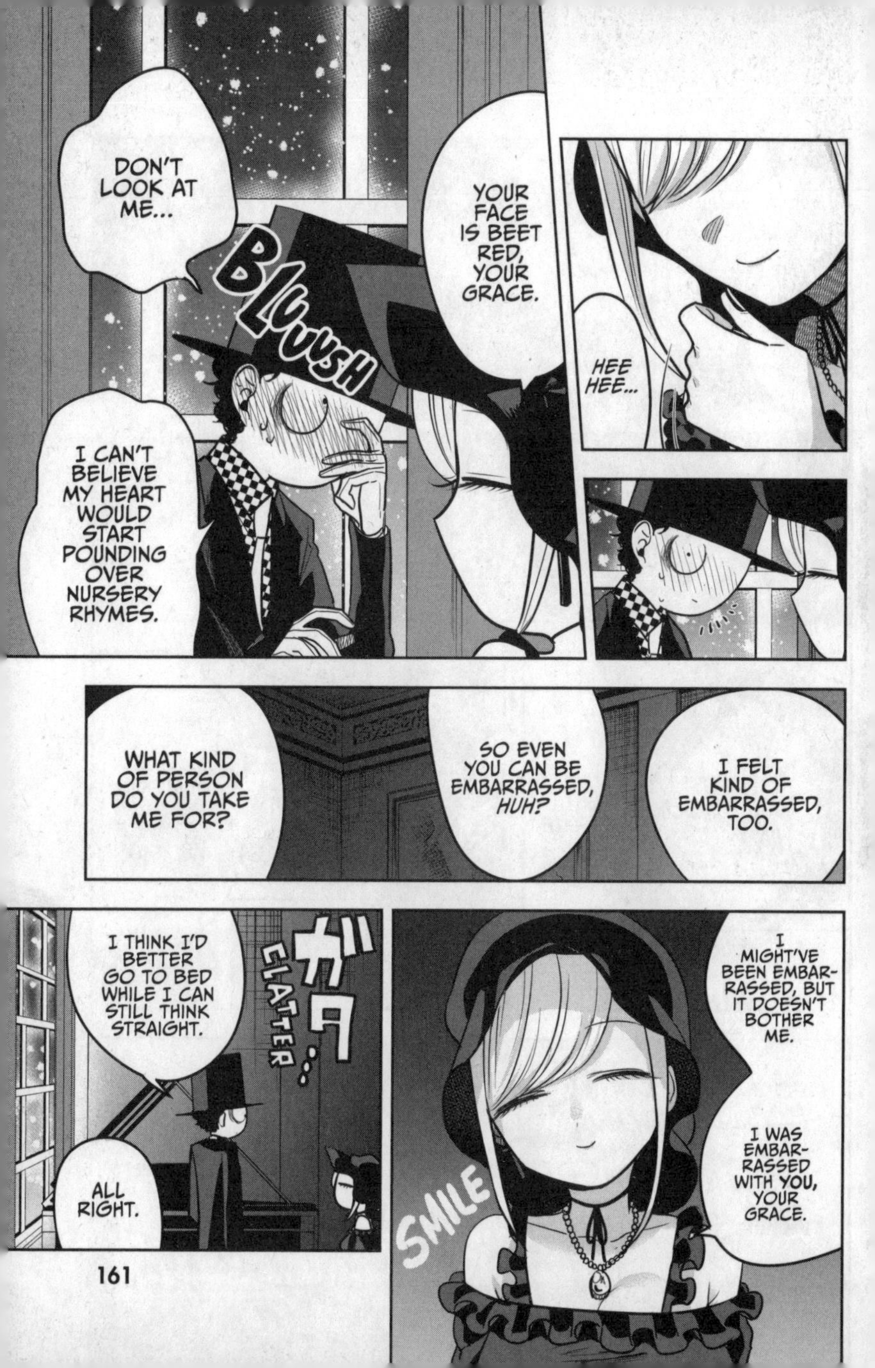

YOUR FACE IS BEET RED, YOUR GRACE.
HEE HEE...
DON'T LOOK AT ME...
BLUUUSH
I CAN'T BELIEVE MY HEART WOULD START POUNDING OVER NURSERY RHYMES.
I FELT KIND OF EMBARRASSED, TOO.
SO EVEN YOU CAN BE EMBARRASSED, *HUH?*
WHAT KIND OF PERSON DO YOU TAKE ME FOR?
I MIGHT'VE BEEN EMBARRASSED, BUT IT DOESN'T BOTHER ME.
I WAS EMBARRASSED WITH YOU, YOUR GRACE.
SMILE
ガタ
CLATTER
I THINK I'D BETTER GO TO BED WHILE I CAN STILL THINK STRAIGHT.
ALL RIGHT.

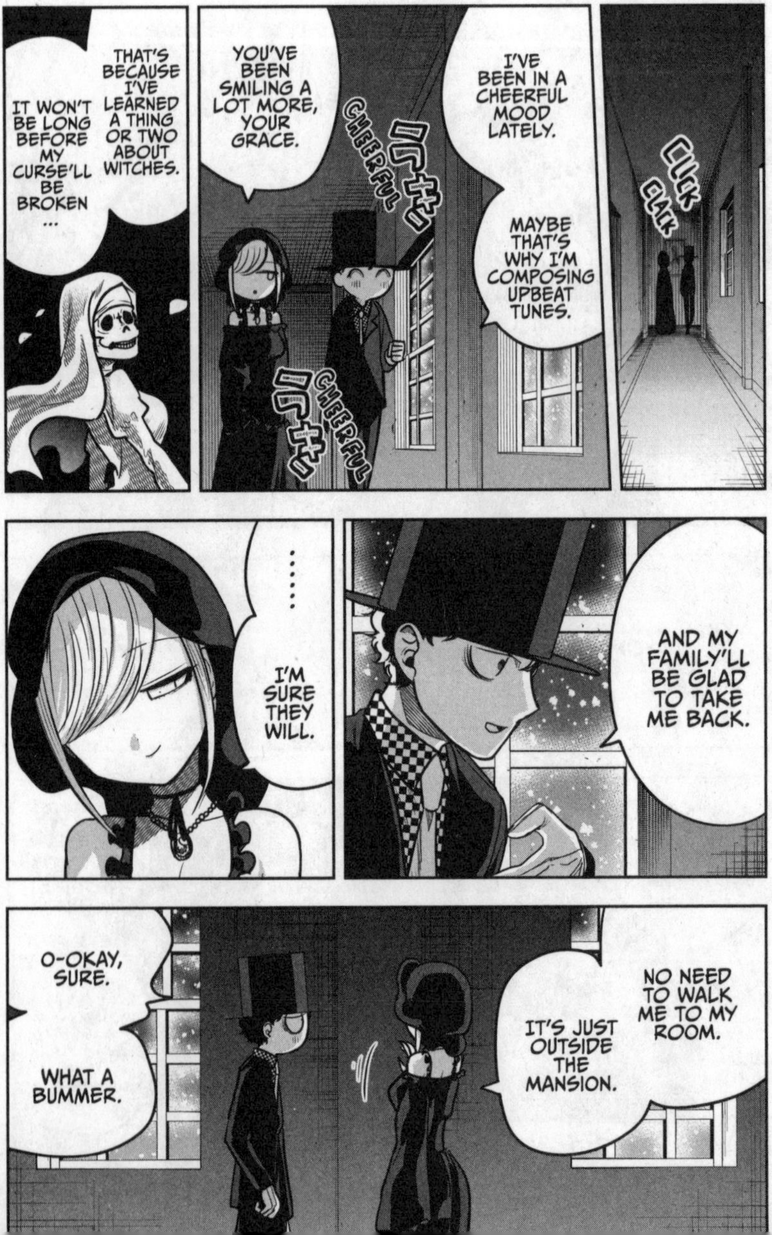
CLICK
CLACK
I'VE BEEN IN A CHEERFUL MOOD LATELY.
MAYBE THAT'S WHY I'M COMPOSING UPBEAT TUNES.
YOU'VE BEEN SMILING A LOT MORE, YOUR GRACE.
CHEERFUL
CHEERFUL
THAT'S BECAUSE I'VE LEARNED A THING OR TWO ABOUT WITCHES.
IT WON'T BE LONG BEFORE MY CURSE'LL BE BROKEN...
AND MY FAMILY'LL BE GLAD TO TAKE ME BACK.
......
I'M SURE THEY WILL.
NO NEED TO WALK ME TO MY ROOM.
IT'S JUST OUTSIDE THE MANSION.
O-OKAY, SURE.
WHAT A BUMMER.

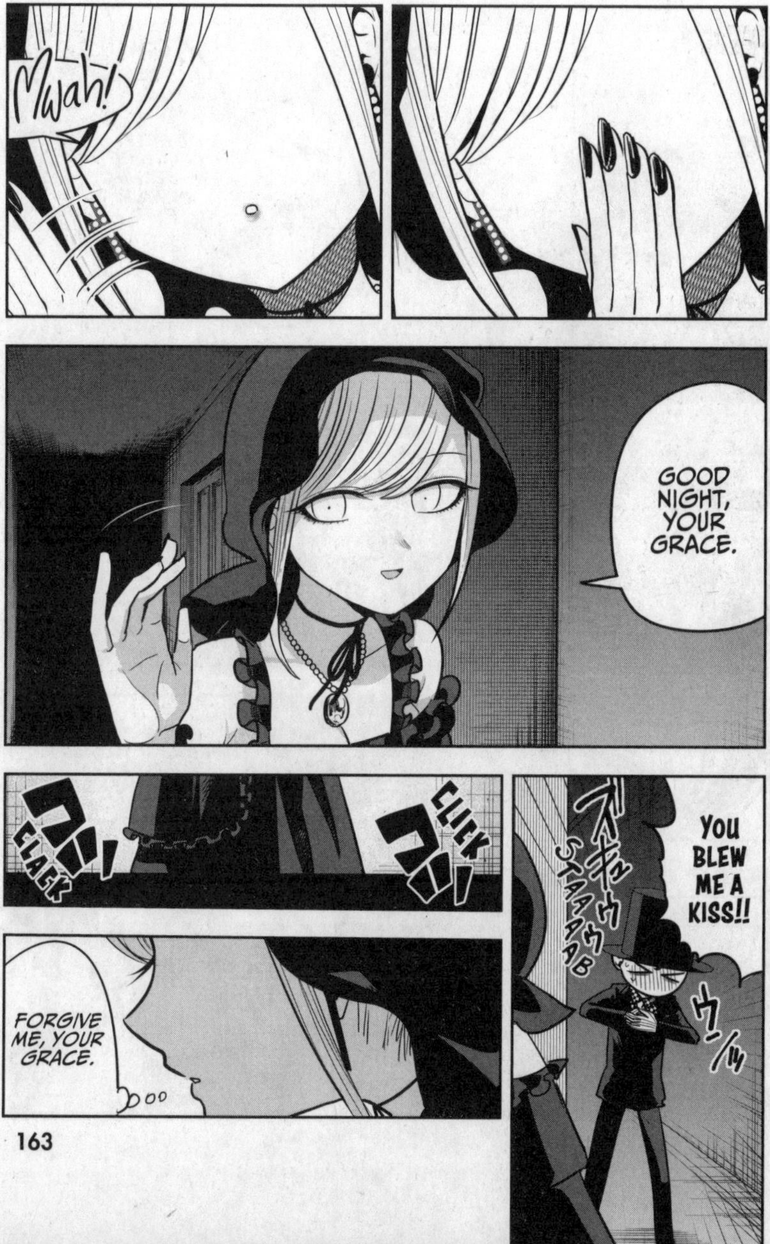
Mwah!
GOOD NIGHT, YOUR GRACE.
STAAAAB
YOU BLEW ME A KISS!!
CLICK
CLACK
FORGIVE ME, YOUR GRACE.

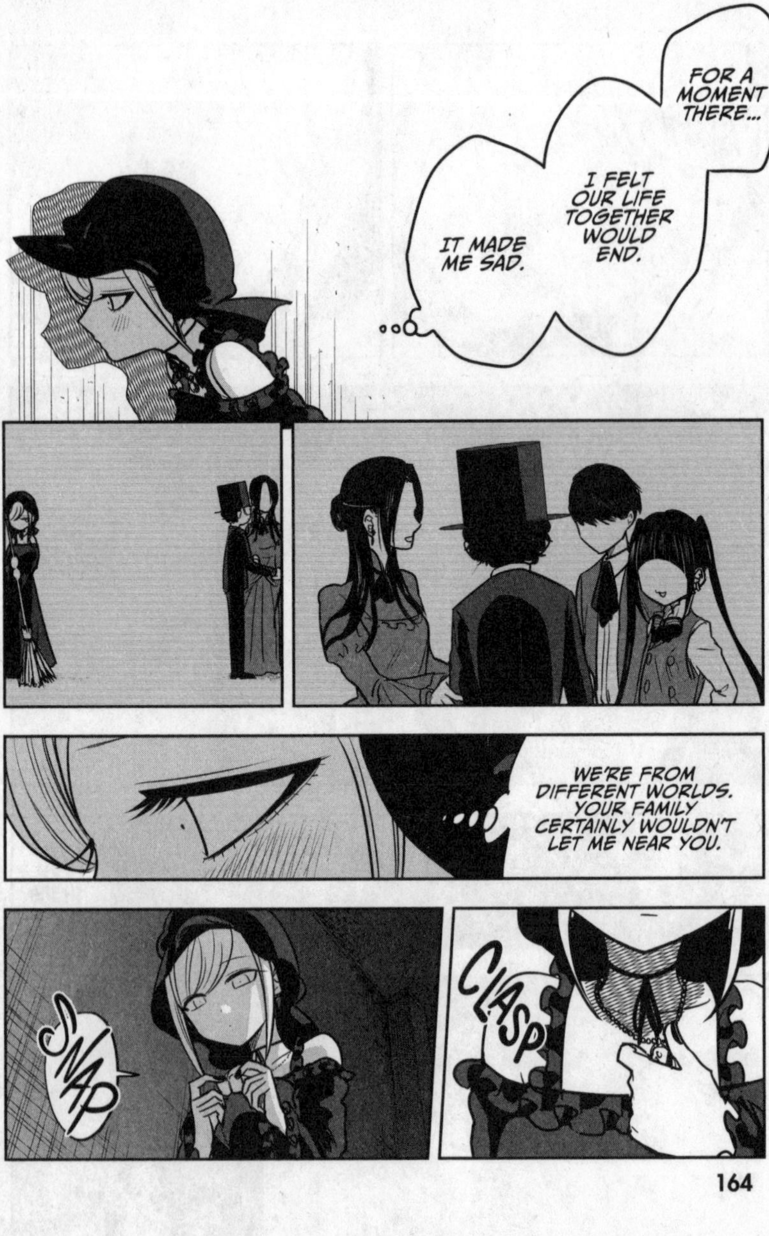
FOR A MOMENT THERE...
I FELT OUR LIFE TOGETHER WOULD END.
IT MADE ME SAD.
WE'RE FROM DIFFERENT WORLDS. YOUR FAMILY CERTAINLY WOULDN'T LET ME NEAR YOU.
CLASP
SNAP

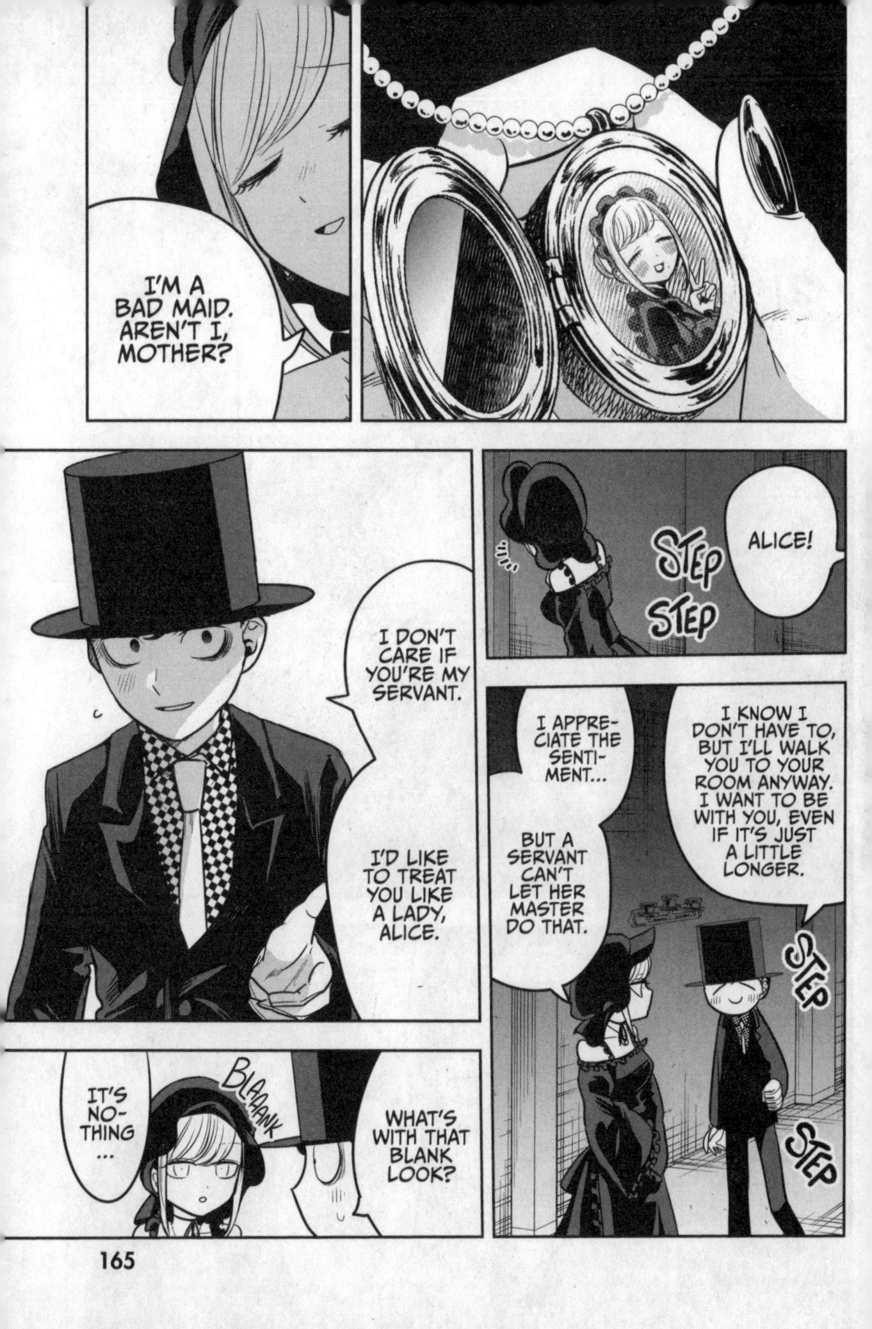
I'M A BAD MAID. AREN'T I, MOTHER?
ALICE!
STEP
STEP
I KNOW I DON'T HAVE TO, BUT I'LL WALK YOU TO YOUR ROOM ANYWAY. I WANT TO BE WITH YOU, EVEN IF IT'S JUST A LITTLE LONGER.
I APPRE-CIATE THE SENTI-MENT...
BUT A SERVANT CAN'T LET HER MASTER DO THAT.
STEP
STEP
I DON'T CARE IF YOU'RE MY SERVANT.
I'D LIKE TO TREAT YOU LIKE A LADY, ALICE.
WHAT'S WITH THAT BLANK LOOK?
BLAAANK
IT'S NO-THING ...

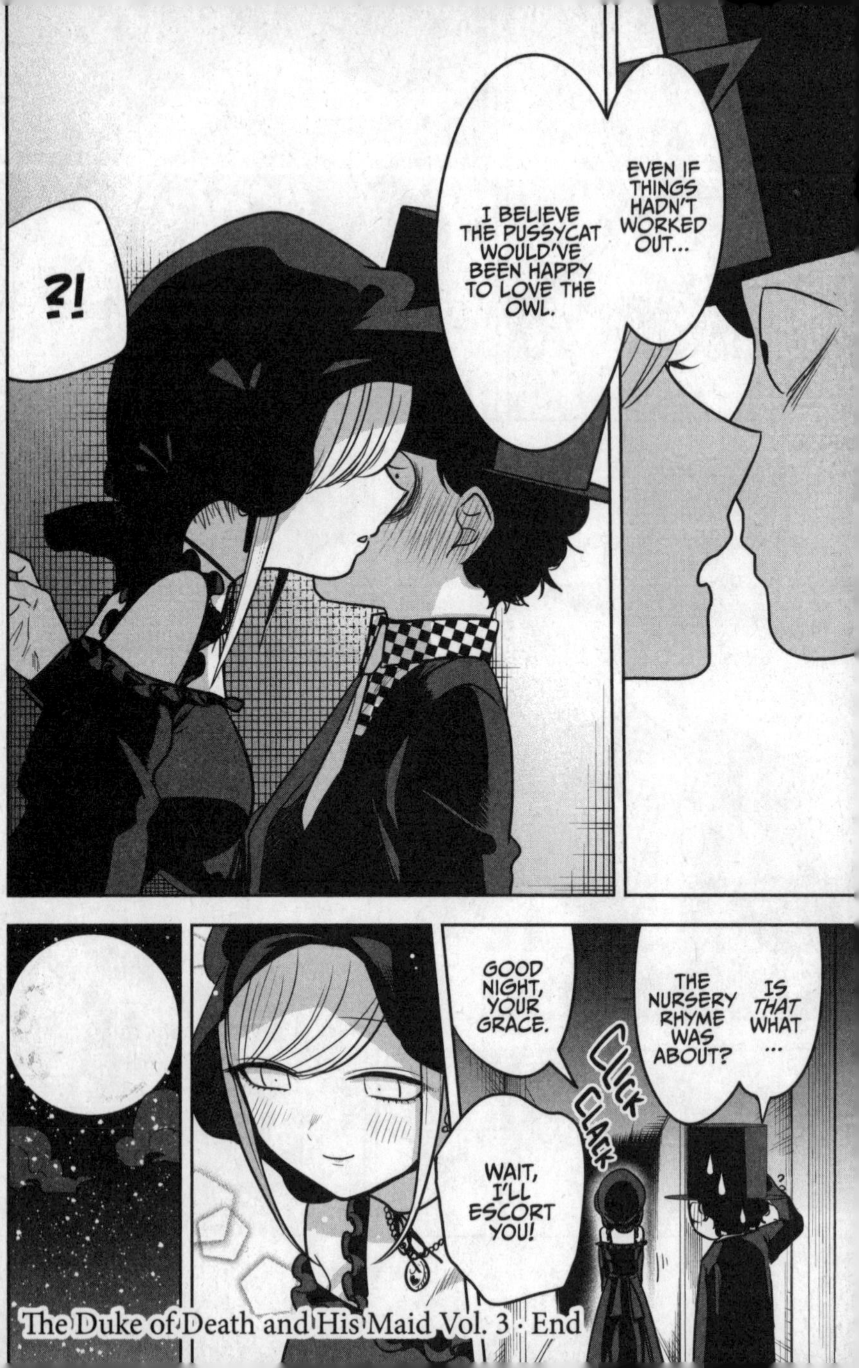
EVEN IF THINGS HADN'T WORKED OUT...
I BELIEVE THE PUSSYCAT WOULD'VE BEEN HAPPY TO LOVE THE OWL.
?!
IS *THAT* WHAT ...
THE NURSERY RHYME WAS ABOUT?
GOOD NIGHT, YOUR GRACE.
CLICK
CLACK
WAIT, I'LL ESCORT YOU!
The Duke of Death and His Maid Vol. 3 · End

THE DUKE OF DEATH AND HIS MAID

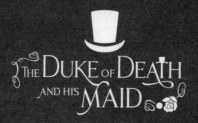

THE DUKE OF DEATH AND HIS MAID

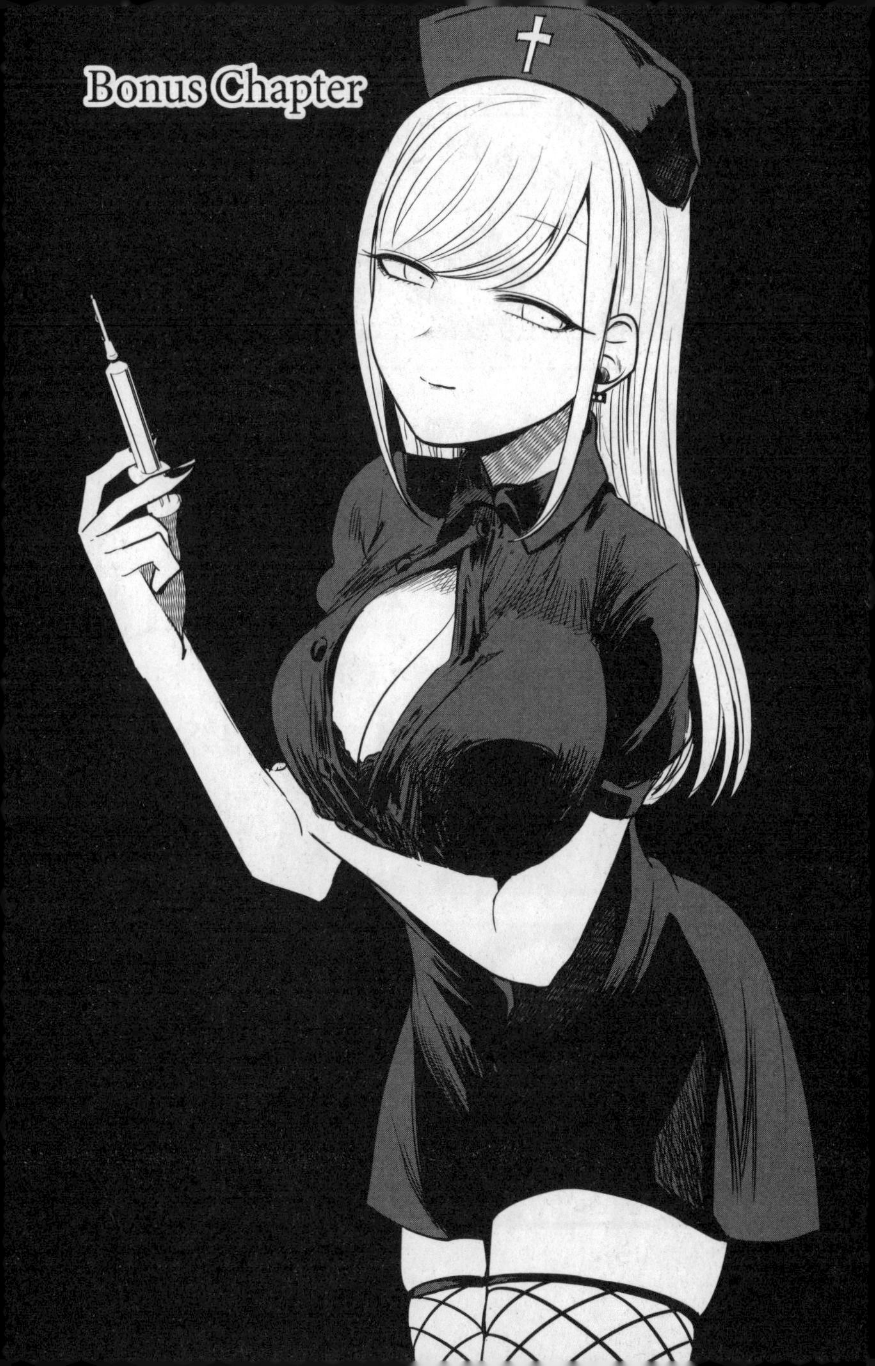
Bonus Chapter

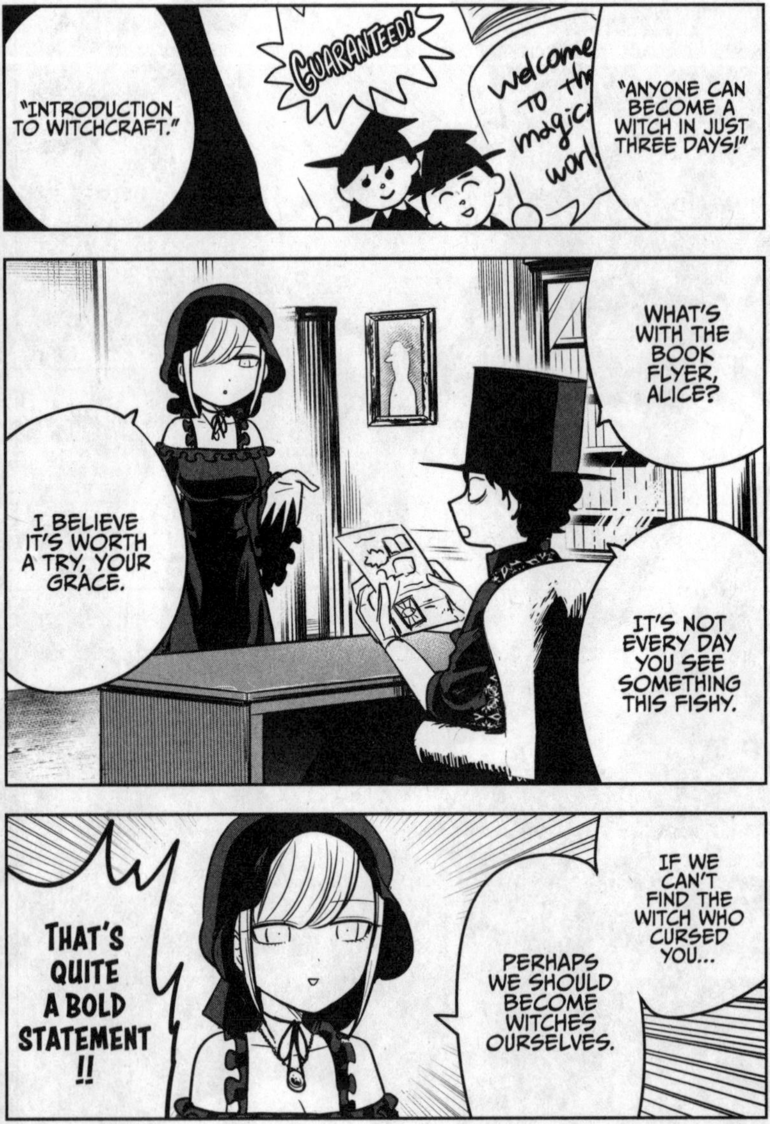
"ANYONE CAN BECOME A WITCH IN JUST THREE DAYS!"
GUARANTEED!
"INTRODUCTION TO WITCHCRAFT."
WHAT'S WITH THE BOOK FLYER, ALICE?
IT'S NOT EVERY DAY YOU SEE SOMETHING THIS FISHY.
I BELIEVE IT'S WORTH A TRY, YOUR GRACE.
IF WE CAN'T FIND THE WITCH WHO CURSED YOU...
PERHAPS WE SHOULD BECOME WITCHES OURSELVES.
THAT'S QUITE A BOLD STATEMENT !!

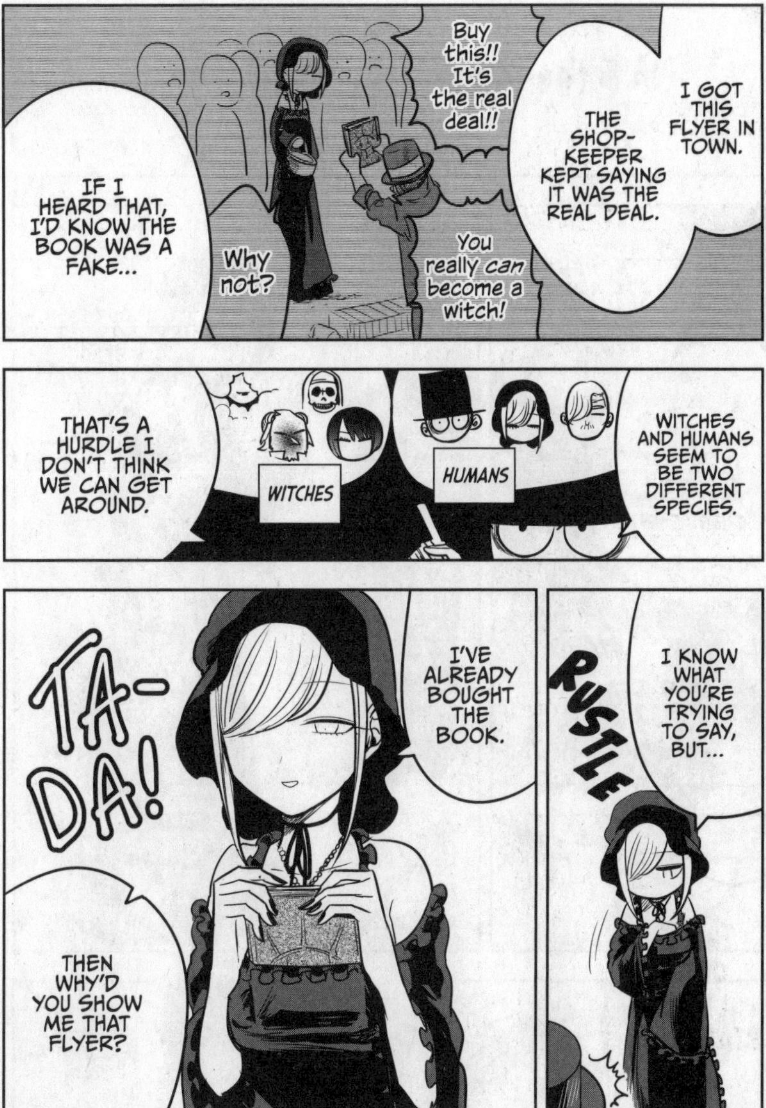
I GOT THIS FLYER IN TOWN.
THE SHOP-KEEPER KEPT SAYING IT WAS THE REAL DEAL.
Buy this!! It's the real deal!!
You really can become a witch!
Why not?
IF I HEARD THAT, I'D KNOW THE BOOK WAS A FAKE...
WITCHES AND HUMANS SEEM TO BE TWO DIFFERENT SPECIES.
HUMANS
WITCHES
THAT'S A HURDLE I DON'T THINK WE CAN GET AROUND.
I KNOW WHAT YOU'RE TRYING TO SAY, BUT...
RUSTLE
I'VE ALREADY BOUGHT THE BOOK.
TA-DA!
THEN WHY'D YOU SHOW ME THAT FLYER?

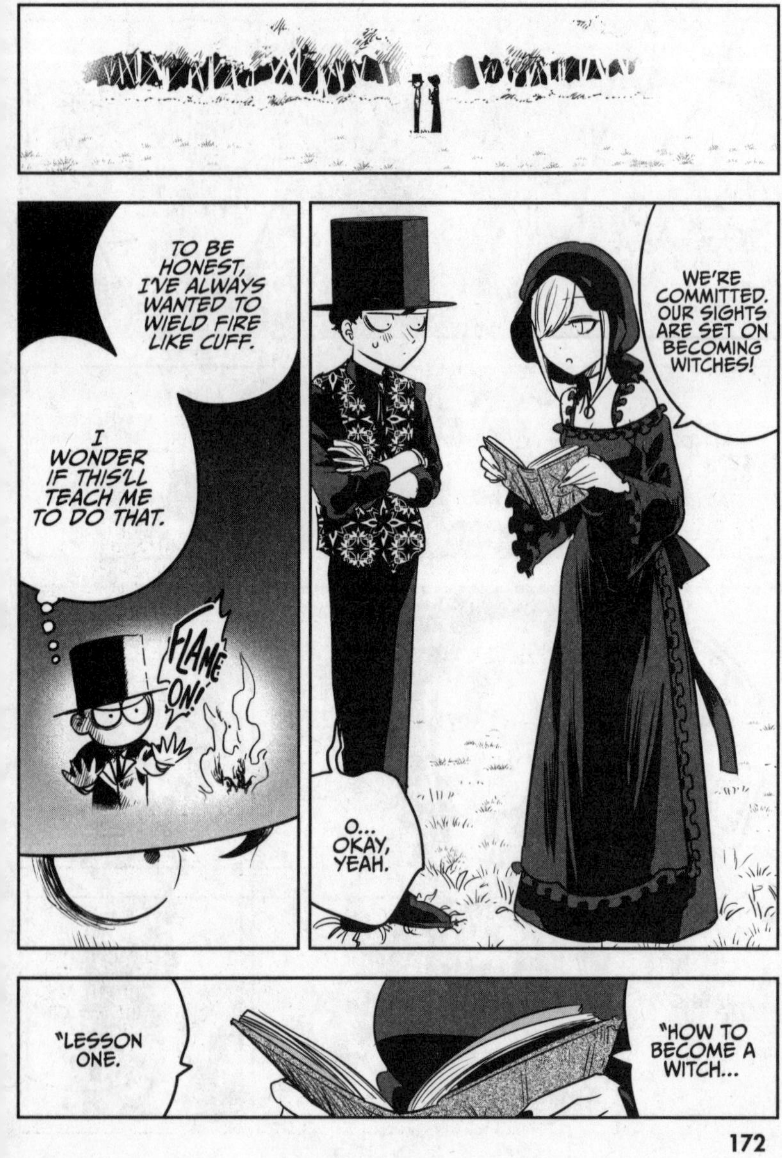
WE'RE COMMITTED. OUR SIGHTS ARE SET ON BECOMING WITCHES!
O... OKAY, YEAH.
TO BE HONEST, I'VE ALWAYS WANTED TO WIELD FIRE LIKE CUFF.
I WONDER IF THIS'LL TEACH ME TO DO THAT.
FLAME ON!
"HOW TO BECOME A WITCH...
"LESSON ONE.

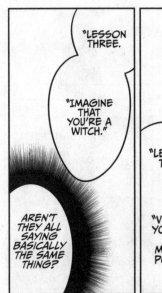

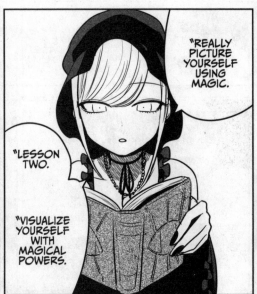

"REALLY PICTURE YOURSELF USING MAGIC.
"LESSON TWO.
"VISUALIZE YOURSELF WITH MAGICAL POWERS.
"LESSON THREE.
"IMAGINE THAT YOU'RE A WITCH."
AREN'T THEY ALL SAYING BASICALLY THE SAME THING?
PONDER
PONDER
PONDER
PONDER
IS SHE DOING IT RIGHT?
...
I MIGHT'VE FORGOTTEN TO PUT MY PANTIES ON TODAY.
GUESS NOT...
DROOP
HUH?!

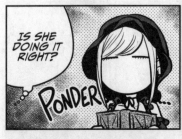

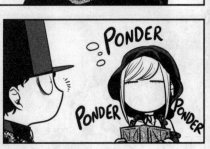

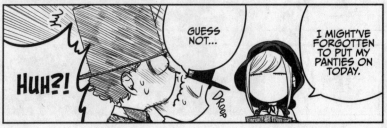

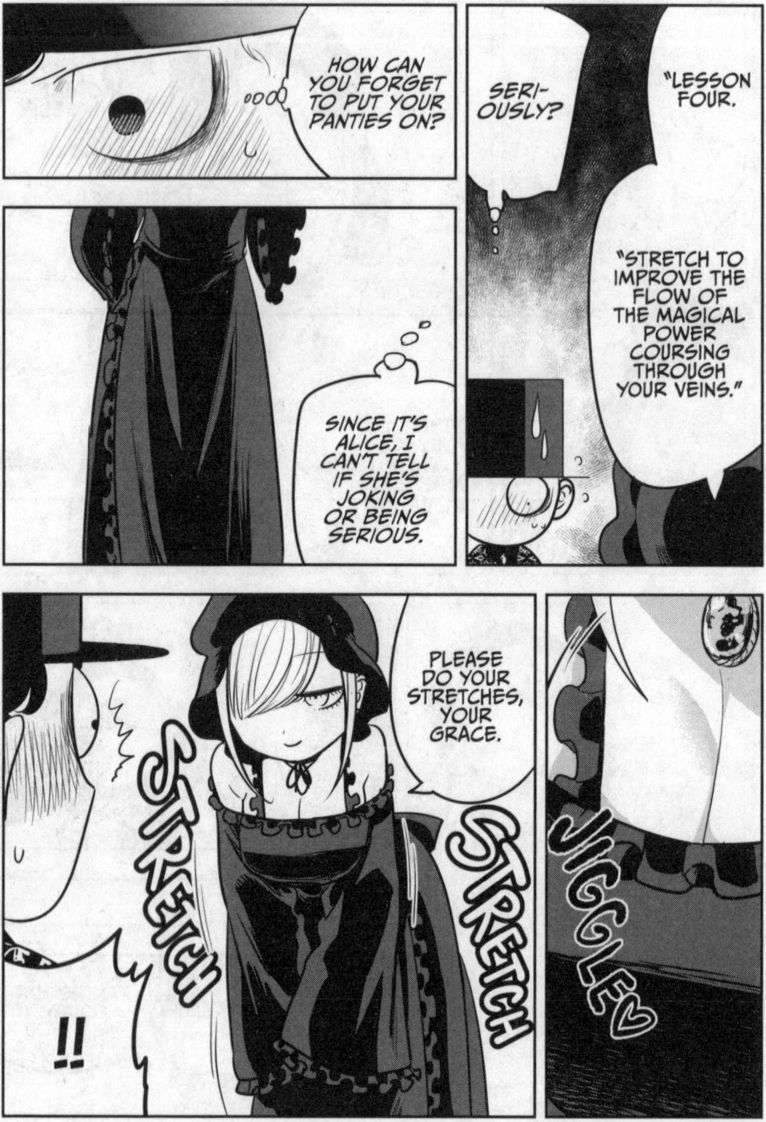
"LESSON FOUR.
SERI-OUSLY?
"STRETCH TO IMPROVE THE FLOW OF THE MAGICAL POWER COURSING THROUGH YOUR VEINS."
HOW CAN YOU FORGET TO PUT YOUR PANTIES ON?
SINCE IT'S ALICE, I CAN'T TELL IF SHE'S JOKING OR BEING SERIOUS.
JIGGLE♥
PLEASE DO YOUR STRETCHES, YOUR GRACE.
STRETCH
STRETCH
!!

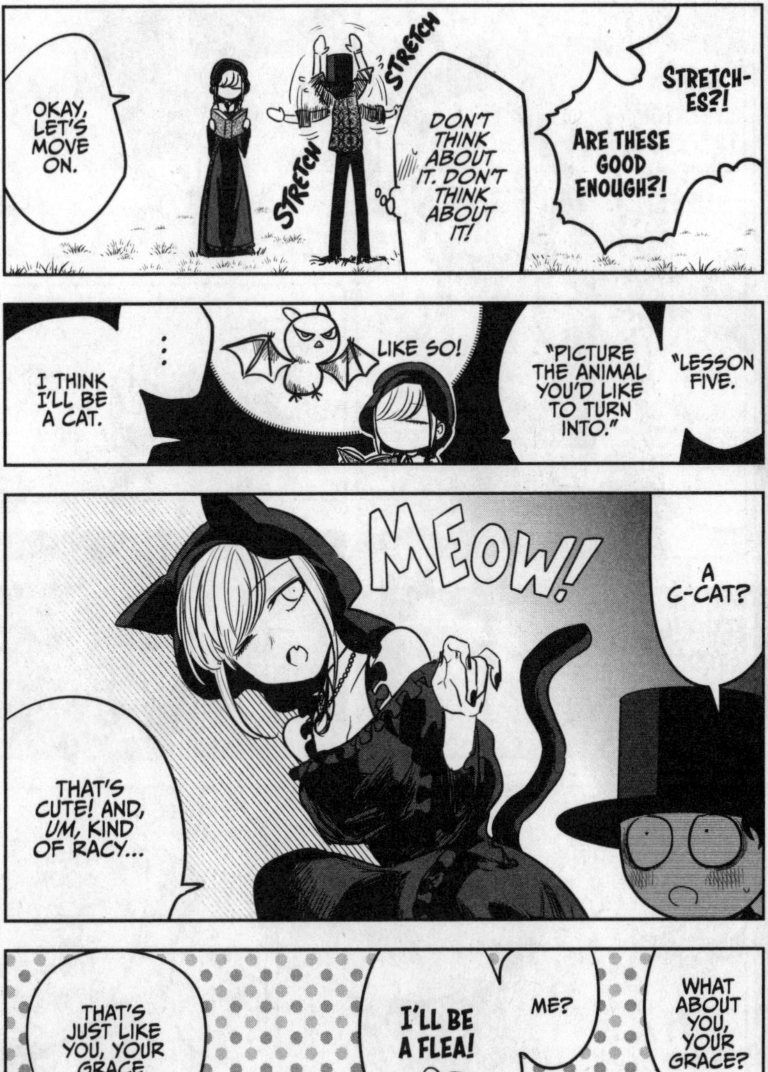
STRETCH-ES?!
ARE THESE GOOD ENOUGH?!
STRETCH
STRETCH
STRETCH
DON'T THINK ABOUT IT. DON'T THINK ABOUT IT!
OKAY, LET'S MOVE ON.
"LESSON FIVE.
"PICTURE THE ANIMAL YOU'D LIKE TO TURN INTO."
LIKE SO!
...
I THINK I'LL BE A CAT.
A C-CAT?
MEOW!
THAT'S CUTE! AND, UM, KIND OF RACY...
WHAT ABOUT YOU, YOUR GRACE?
ME?
I'LL BE A FLEA!
THAT'S JUST LIKE YOU, YOUR GRACE.

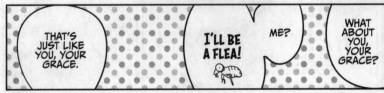

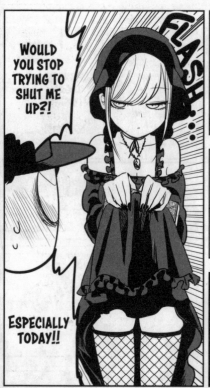

"LES-SON SIX."
......
ON SECOND THOUGHT, WE'D BETTER STOP.
WHAT?
BUT WE'VE MADE IT THIS FAR.
WHUMP
FLASH...
WOULD YOU STOP TRYING TO SHUT ME UP?!
ESPECIALLY TODAY!!
THAT BOOK REALLY WAS A FAKE, THEN.
FLIT...
YES, IT WAS.
"THIS BOOK IS COMPLETELY BOGUS! YOU THOUGHT IT WAS LEGIT? WELL, SORRY!"
SO THE AUTHOR HAD NO INTENTION TO APOLOGIZE ...

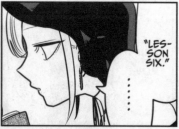

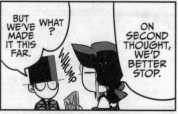

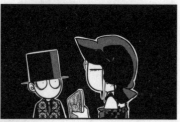

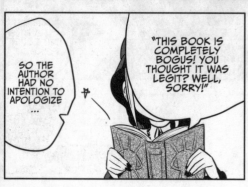

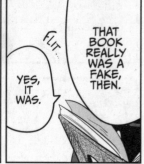

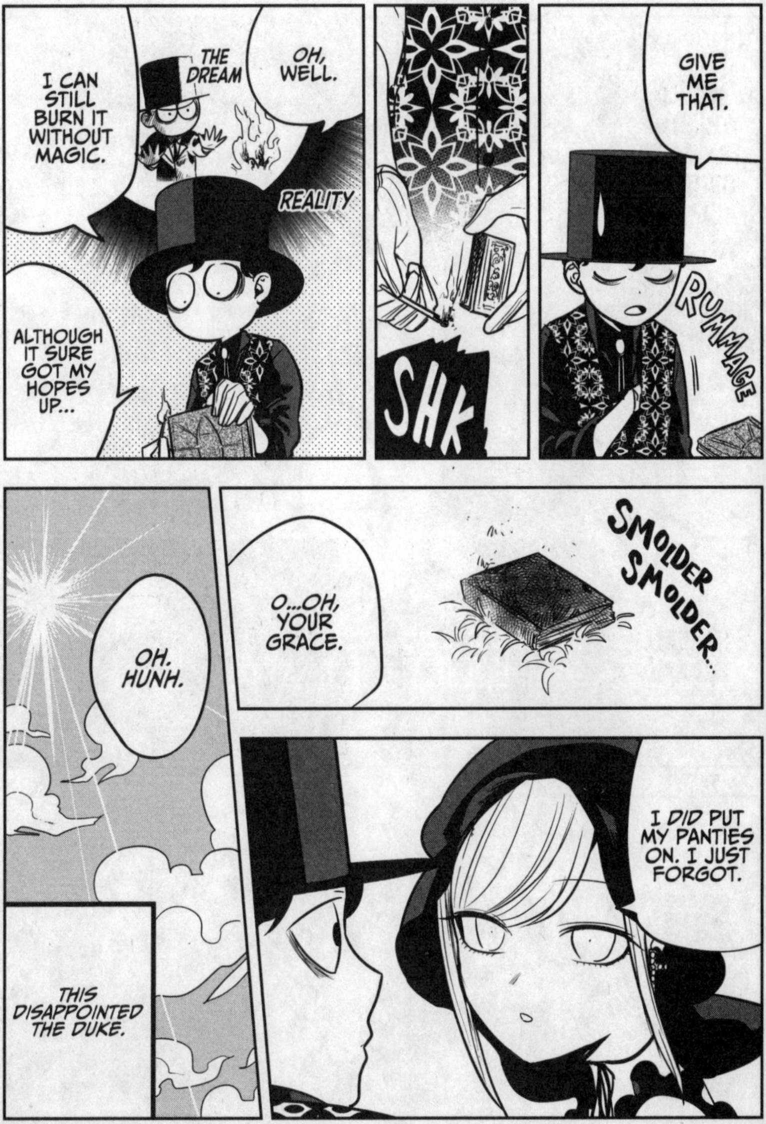
GIVE ME THAT.
RUMMAGE
SHK
OH, WELL.
THE DREAM
I CAN STILL BURN IT WITHOUT MAGIC.
REALITY
ALTHOUGH IT SURE GOT MY HOPES UP...
SMOLDER SMOLDER...
O...OH, YOUR GRACE.
I *DID* PUT MY PANTIES ON. I JUST FORGOT.
OH. HUNH.
THIS DISAPPOINTED THE DUKE.

End of Bonus Chapter

THE DUKE of DEATH
AND HIS MAID

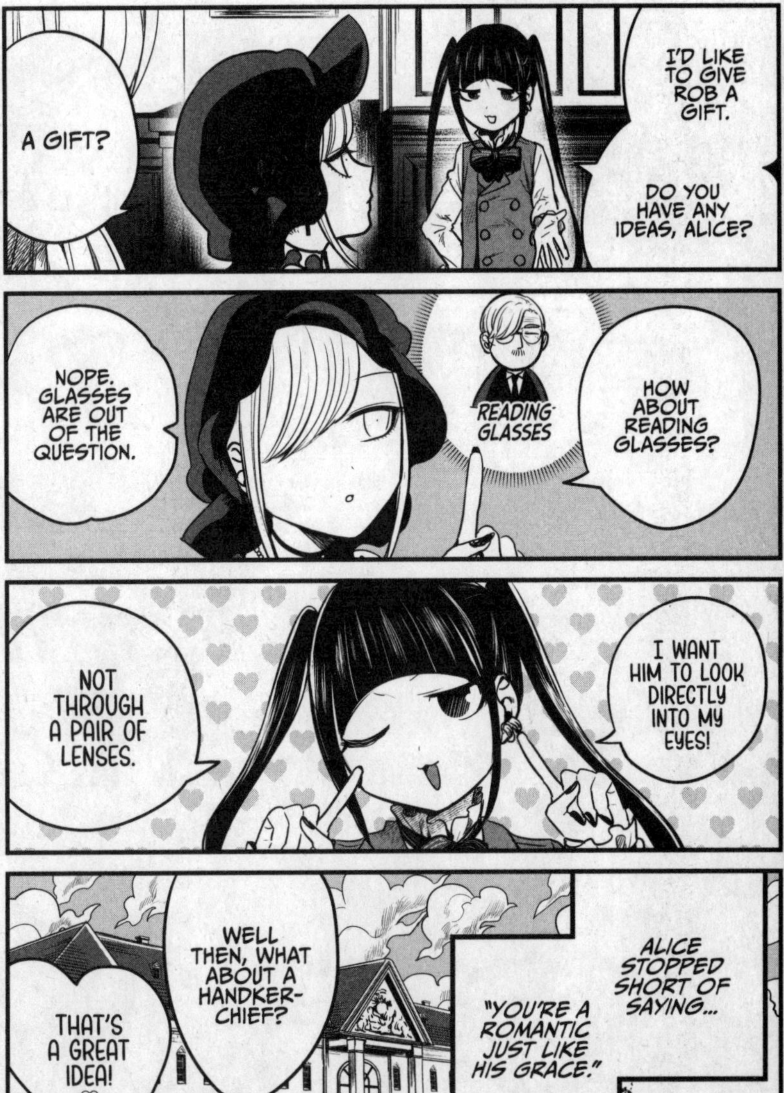
I'D LIKE TO GIVE ROB A GIFT.
DO YOU HAVE ANY IDEAS, ALICE?
A GIFT?
HOW ABOUT READING GLASSES?
READING GLASSES
NOPE. GLASSES ARE OUT OF THE QUESTION.
I WANT HIM TO LOOK DIRECTLY INTO MY EYES!
NOT THROUGH A PAIR OF LENSES.
ALICE STOPPED SHORT OF SAYING...
"YOU'RE A ROMANTIC JUST LIKE HIS GRACE."
WELL THEN, WHAT ABOUT A HANDKER-CHIEF?
THAT'S A GREAT IDEA! ♡

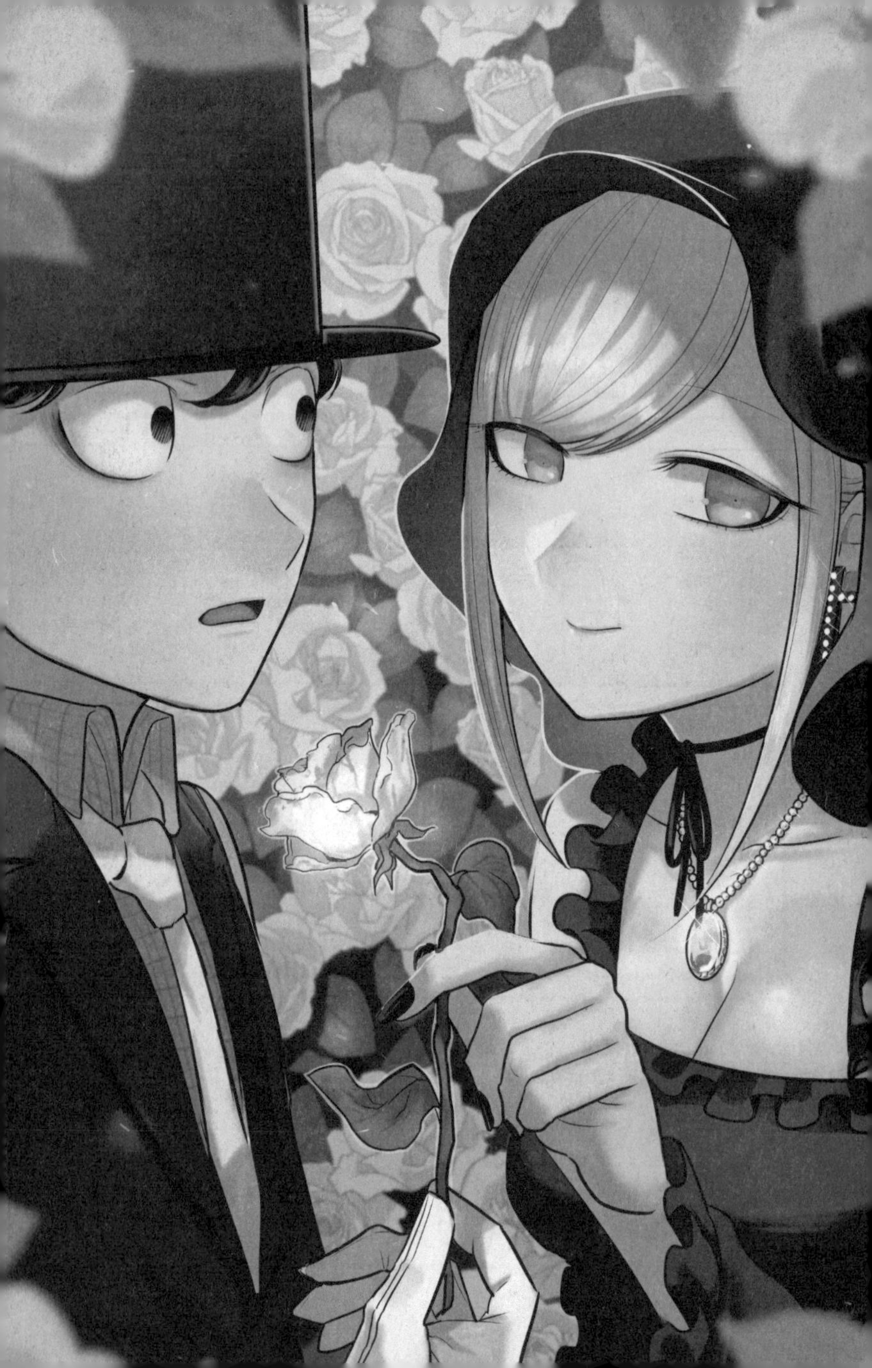

INOUE

I like the color black.
I buy black clothes, furniture,
and knickknacks. Since
they're all the same color,
I often lose stuff at home.
It's something to think about.

THE DUKE OF DEATH
AND HIS MAID

SEVEN SEAS ENTERTAINMENT PRESENTS

THE DUKE OF DEATH AND HIS MAID

story and art by INOUE — VOLUME 3

TRANSLATION
Josh Cole

ADAPTATION
Matthew Birkenhauer

LETTERING
Aila Nagamine

ORIGINAL COVER DESIGN
Yasuo Shimura (siesta)

COVER DESIGN
H. Qi

PROOFREADER
B. Lillian Martin

SENIOR COPY EDITOR
Dawn Davis

EDITOR
Abby Lehrke

PRODUCTION DESIGNER
Christina McKenzie

PRODUCTION MANAGER
Lissa Pattillo

PREPRESS TECHNICIAN
Melanie Ujimori

PRINT MANAGER
Rhiannon Rasmussen-Silverstein

EDITOR-IN-CHIEF
Julie Davis

ASSOCIATE PUBLISHER
Adam Arnold

PUBLISHER
Jason DeAngelis

SHINIGAMI BOCCHAN TO KURO MAID Vol. 3
by INOUE
© 2018 INOUE
All rights reserved.
Original Japanese edition published by SHOGAKUKAN.
English translation rights in the United States of America, Canada, the United
Kingdom, Ireland, Australia and New Zealand arranged with SHOGAKUKAN through
Tuttle-Mori Agency, Inc.

Seven Seas press and purchase enquiries can be sent to Marketing Manager Lianne
Sentar at press@gomanga.com. Information regarding the distribution and purchase of
digital editions is available from Digital Manager CK Russell at digital@gomanga.com.

Seven Seas and the Seven Seas logo are trademarks of
Seven Seas Entertainment. All rights reserved.

ISBN: 978-1-63858-724-8
Printed in Canada
First Printing: October 2022
10 9 8 7 6 5 4 3 2 1

READING DIRECTIONS

This book reads from *right to left*,
Japanese style. If this is your first time
reading manga, you start reading from
the top right panel on each page and
take it from there. If you get lost, just
follow the numbered diagram here.
It may seem backwards at first,
but you'll get the hang of it! Have fun!!

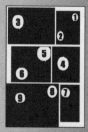

Follow us online: www.SevenSeasEntertainment.com

CONTENTS

INOUE PRESENTS

THE DUKE OF DEATH AND HIS MAID

3

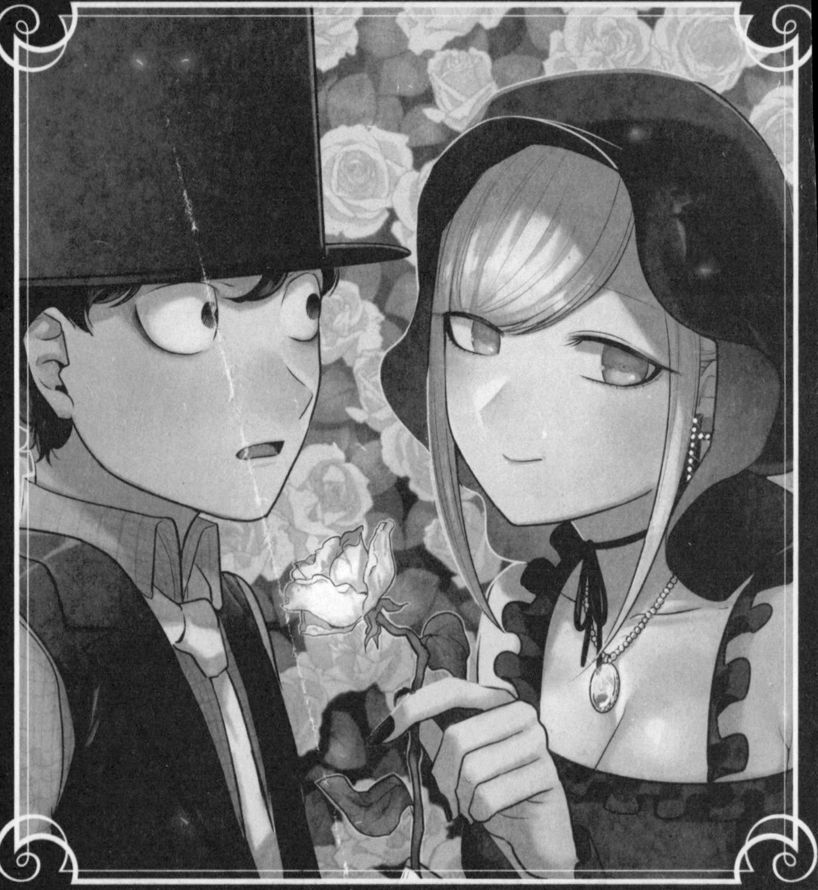